Vestry Minutes
of
St. Paul's Parish

Chowan County
North Carolina

-1701-1776-

Second Edition

Compiled By:
Ratmond Parker Fouts

Southern Historical Press, Inc.
Greenville, South Carolina

This volume was reproduced
from a personal copy located in
the Publishers private library

Please direct all correspondence and book orders to:
SOUTHERN HISTORICAL PRESS, Inc.
PO Box 1267
Greenville, SC   29602-1267

Copyright 1998 by: Raymond Parker Fouts
Copyright Transferred 2023 to:
               Southern Historical Press, Inc.
ISBN #978-1-63914-176-0
Printed in the United States of America

PREFACE

This verbatim transcription was made from North Carolina State Archives microfilm reel R.024.04001, *Chowan, St. Paul's Church, Edenton, N. C. Vestry Minutes 1701-1779*. The Vestry Minutes end 16 October 1776. The remainder of this film contains a few minutes of meetings of the Wardens of the Poor, not included here. This second edition is in a new format and typeface, with decedent, female given name and every name indices.

The written permission required for the duplication and release of these records, by the Archives, was graciously granted by the late Reverend Raymond W. Storie, Rector of St. Paul's Episcopal Church, Edenton, North Carolina, in 1982.

St. Paul's Parish adjoined the Upper Parish of Nansemond County, Virginia. After the NC/VA boundary was drawn in 1728, Chowan County acquired the former Nansemond County lands now lying in Gates County, North Carolina. The map on page 137 shows a number of the landmarks mentioned in the several orders for processioning of lands. It is *not* intended to depict the earliest boundaries of St. Paul's Parish. All the land west of Bennett's Creek, including Knotty Pine Chapel, was cut off to Hertford County, when it was formed in 1759. Knotty Pine Chapel was near Sarum, Constant's/Costen's was near Sunbury, and Farlee's was near Ballard's Bridge. Their approximate locations are indicated on the map by a representation of a chapel.

Writing in the margins of the original pages is printed in italics. Those in the original hand are printed before the appropriate entry, and annotations in a later hand follow that entry. Page numbers, in a modern hand, appearing at the bottom of right hand pages, are typed and underlined at the end of each original page. Each original page has been assigned a number, printed in boldface within parentheses. All the indices refer to the assigned numbers. Original page numbers are printed in italics, to the right of the assigned numbers. Some page numbers were not noted in the original and are out of sequence beginning with "236." The Vestry ordered that the "old Orders" be transcribed into a bound book at the meeting of 7 April 1729. Some Vestry meetings were not held at their appointed times. The Clerk of the Vestry omitted the minutes of 15 April 1745, and later recorded them in the middle of the minutes of 19 July 1745.

Lists of Vestrymen have been typed in paragraph form, instead of the original columnar form, to save space. All surnames are typed in bold uppercase. The left column was typed first. Numerous hands recorded these minutes. Some are very clear, and others present the usual challenges of reading and transcribing old records. The outer edges of some pages have crumbled away and others have faded badly, possibly from variations in ink quality. Some of the "look-alikes" are "ff=H;" "K=Gh;" "i=e;" "t=l" and "3=9." "T̶h̶o̶m̶a̶s̶" denotes a crossed-out word; ???? denotes crossed-out and illegible. "Mony" emphasizes verbatim spelling. "Chap__" denotes missing, or illegible, letters. All spellings of every name are indexed. All names in the Decedent Index, and Female Given Name Index, also appear under their surnames in the main index.

R. P. Fouts
30 April 1998

CONTENTS

Text..	1
Decedent Index................................	119
Female Given Name Index..................	121
Index..	123
Map...	137

VESTRY MINUTES OF ST. PAUL'S PARISH,

CHOWAN COUNTY, NORTH CAROLINA

1701-1776

Second Edition

(1) [Note: The right side of this page appears to have been trimmed.] *Anno Dom. 1701.}* Chown Prcinct Sc
In Obedience to an Act of Assembly made November the 1_ 1701 appointing a Vestry for this precinct Consisting of The Honoble Henderson **WALKER** Esqr. Coll. Thomas **POLLOCK** William **DUCKENFIELD** Esqr. Mr. Nickolas **CRISP** Mr. Edward **SMITHWICK** Mr. John **BLOUNT}** Mr James **LONG** Mr. Nathaniel **CHEVIN** Mr. William **BANBURY** Coll. William **WILKINSON** Capt. Thomas **LEUTON** Capt. Thomas **BLOUNT.}** *Vestry*

Who being all present at the House of Mr. Thomas **GILLAM** Dec. ye 15th, 1701. *Dec*

It being debated where a Church Should be built. Mr. Edward **SMITHWICK** undertakes to give one Acree of Land upon his old planta__ and to give a Conveyance for the Same to the Church-Wardens hereafter appointed for the Use and Service of the precinct to build a Church upon and for no other Use and to acknowledge the Same in open Cou__ *One Acre of Land p?__* [illegible] *for a Church by Mr Edd SMITHWICK*

The Choice of Church-Wardens *Ch Wardens*

It is appointed that Colln. William **WILKINSON** and Capt. Thomas **LEUTEN** shall be Church-Wardens for the following Year who Shall agree with a Workman for building a Church 25 feet long [Remainder of line is blank.] posts in the Ground [Remainder of line is blank.] and held to the Collar Beams and to find all Manner of Iron to? Vizt. Nails and Locks &c. with full power to contract and agree with Said Workman as to their Discretion shall Seem meet and convenient *Provision for building a Ch. of Wood 25 ft. long*

It is agreed that Nathaniel **CHEVIN** shall be Clerk of the Vestry and keep a Book of the proceedings of the Vestry for which he Shall be allow__ 10 Shillings per Day for every Day he attends upon the Vestry or Church Ward___ *Clerk {*

Ordered that the Church-Wardens aforesaid having agreed with _ Workman for the Building of a Church as aforesaid, Whatsoever Ch_ shall accruee for and towards the building of the aforeSaid Church or other Charge relating to the Same (altho' not here particularly mentione_ by the Said Church-Wardens be levied by the pole upon the Tythables of ___ precinct, the Church-Wardens first Endeavouring to raise the Said Mon__ Contribution, and in Case of Failure to raise it by the pole as aforeSaid to agree with a Collector or Collectors to receive the Same with power __ destrain in Case of Refusal. 4

(2) _om. Ordered? that the Church Warden [Remainder of line partially torn away and illegible.] vide a Reader and Shall agree with Him for his Service And that each Ve____ Man shall do his Endeavour to enquire for a Reader and give thereof an Account to the Church-Wardens if any presents. ___em. [Torn away.] *for a reader?*

Ordered that the Inhabitants of the So. West Shore build a Chappel of Ease on their Shore at the Charge of the precinct after the aforesaid Church be built and that they may there have a Reader at their own Cost and Charge and be excused from paying any thing to a Reader on the North Shore. __ *of __ on the ___ Shore.*

And that either the Honoble. Coll. Thomas **POLLOCK** or William **DUCKENFIELD** Esqr. agree with the said Reader.

Ordered that Twelve pence be levied on every Tythable in the precinct and that Eight pounds be paid out of it to Christ. **BUTTLER** towards the Supply and maintainance of Robert **WILLSON**. And that ffrancis **WELLS** Collect the lower part of the precinct as high as Mr. **CRISP**'s and William **EARLY** from thence Upwards On the West Shore by William **JONES**. On the South Shore by John **WALKER**, And Shall render an Account of the Same to the Church-Wardens, and the Said Churc_ Wardens shall pay out of it to Christopher **BUTTLER** Eight pounds and shall give Account of the Remainder to the Vestry. And the Constable of each District shall deliver the Copy of this Order to the respective Collector: And if any of the aforesaid Collectors Shall refuse the Same, the Constable or Constables of this District shall bring them before the Honoble Henderson**WALKER** Esqr &c or before the Honoble. Thomas **POLLOCK** Esqr. to answer their Contempt.

30 June 1702

(2) (Cont.) At a Vestry holden the 30th. of June 1702 at the House of Thomas **GILLAM**.
Present
Coll. William **WILKINSON** Capt. Thomas **LEUTEN** Capt. Thomas **BLOUNT** William **DUCKENFIELD** Esqr.}
Mr. Edward **SMITHWICK** Mr. Nicholas **CRISP** Mr. William **BANBURY**. Mr. James **LONG**.} Nathl. **CHEVIN** _702

In Obedience to a late Act of Assembly made in March last impowering the Vestry of each precinct to provide a Standard for Weights and? Measures And it being debated how the Said Weights and Measures shall be procured. ___ndard of ___ghts and _easures.

Agreed that the Church-Wardens shall Use their Utmost Endeavour by the first Convenience to Send for Weights and Measures as th_
Law?

(3) __no Dom. 1702.} Law directs, and agree with Some person for that purpose at as Cheap a? a [sic]Rate as possible, and also one fair and large Book of Common prayer [Torn] One Book of Homilies. _ook of____ n Prayers ___Homilies

Ordered that the Church-Wardens Shall agree with and pay the _____ or Collectors for Collecting the precinct Levies:
And then the Meeting broke up.

At a Vestry held at Thomas **GILLAM**'s October ye. 13th. 1702.
Present
The Honoble. Henderson **WALKER** president Coll. Wm. **WILKISON** Capt. Thomas **LEUTEN**} Church-Wardens
Mr. Nicholas **CRISP**.} Mr. John **BLOUNT** Capt. Thomas **BLOUNT** Mr. Edward **SMITHWICK** Mr. William **BANBURY**}

Whereas at the last Vestry it was ordered that there Should be __ Standard of Weights and Measures Sent for for the Use of the precinct in Obedience to the Act of Assembly, the Charge whereof with the Rest of the total? Charge being as followeth. Vizt.

	£	Shill	d?
To building the Chappel to Mr. John **PORTER**	25	0	0
To Richard **CURTON** Reader	7	10	0
To the Standard for the precin/c/t	10	10	0
To clearing an Acree of Ground and flooring the House to} Mr. **SMITHWICK**	2	10	0
To Nathaniel **CHEVIN** acting as Clerk	1	10	0
To the Joiner for Windows Table Forms and Benches	6	0	0
To Thomas **GILLAM** for Trouble of his House	1	10	0
To the poor of the precinct	8	0	0
To John **TYLER** for Attendance	0	1	0
To Sallery for Collecting at 10 pr. Ct.	6	8	0
The Total amounts to	70	19	0?

Chapel __ Reader
The List of Tythables in the precinct being taken is found to be 283 at the Sum [End of entry.]
Ordered that the Church-Wardens collect from each Tythable person in the precinct fiv_ _____ings And Col. William **WILKINSON** __ undertaker of __ Collection [Remainder of line torn away and illegible.] 5

(4) __no Dom 1702} Ordered that Coll. William **WILKINSON** do collect upon all and every __ Tythables within this precinct (a List whereof is delivered to him under the Ha__ of the Clerk of the Vestry) five Shillings pr. pole and for non payment there to make Distress according to Law and likewise to pay unto the Several persons aforementioned the Several Sums due to them and allotted by this Vestry and He together with the other Church-Wardens do provide and pay for the other things mentioned in the aforesaid Order and render an Account of the Same to this Vestry to be holden the last Tuesday in April next and finish all the Collection.

Let it be remembred that Coll. William **WILKINSON** on his own Behalf and Mr. Nicholas **CRISP** on Behalf of the Said **WILKISON** do oblige them Selves their Heirs &c. to this Vestry in the penal Sum of one hundred pounds Sterling to Collect the aforesaid Money and render a perfect Account of the Said Collection and payment at the Vestry the last Tuesday in April next at the House of Mr. Thomas **GILLAM**.

Ordered that a Warrant be directed for the Summoning of the Several Collectors hereafter named to appear at the next Meeting of the Vestry at the House of Mr. Thomas **GILLAM** the 15th. day of December next to give an Account of their Several Collections the two last Years And accor [sic] the whole Vestry does pray the Honoble. the president to direct his Warrant unto William **BUSH** ffrancis **PERROT** Capt. Thomas **BLOUNT** Nicholas **SYMMONS** And for the present Year last past ffrancis **WELLS** William **EARLY** William **JONES** and John **WALKER**.

Ordered that the Vestry meet to Morrow Morning to view the Chappel

14 October 1702

(4) (Cont.) October ye. 14th. 1702
The Vestry being met and having viewed the Chappel the Major part of the Vestry do declare their Dislike of the ceiling of the Chappel by Reason of the Boards being defaced. *The Vestry disapproved the ceiling on the Chapel*

    Ordered that Mr. Edward **SMITHWICK** and Mr. Nicholas **CRISP** on? Behalf of the Vestry do Choose one indifferent Man that is Skilled in building and Mr. John **PORTER** shall choose another who shall meet at the Chappel the Second Saturday in November to give their Judgment whether the Boards ___ fit for ceileing Such an House: And if these two persons chosen as aforesai_ cannot agree in their Opinions, then they Shall choose an Umpire and what Opinion he the Said Umpire Shall give Shall be a full and final Determ___tion of the Matter about the ceiling and Boards and the Agreement between the Church-Wardens and Mr. John **PORTER** shall be thence. [End of entry.]

(5) *1702}* At a Vestry holden at the House of Mrs. Sarah **GILLAM** ye __ Day of December 1702.
Present
Coll Wm. **WILKINSON** Capt. Thos: **LEUTON**} Church-Wardens Mr. Wm. **DUCKENFIELD** Mr. Edward **SMITHWICK** Mr Nicholas **CRISP**} Capt. Thomas **BLOUNT** Mr. William **BANBURY** Mr. Nathl. **CHEVIN** Mr. James **LONG**

    The Several Collectors being Summoned to render an Account of their Several Collections which being duly examined there is found to be Due to the Church-Wardens for the Use of the precinct these following Sums of Money

	£
In the Hands of Coll: Thomas **POLLOCK**	1 :13? _
In Christopher **BUTTLER**'s Hands	[illegible]
In William **EARLEY**'s Hands	3 1? __
In John **WALKER**'s Hands	1 :18 __
	£.6. ____

Coll. William **WILKISON** and Capt. Thomas **LEUTEN** having Served a Year in the Station of Church-Wardens and the Choice of New Church? ___ being debated

    Mr. William **DUCKENFIELD** and Mr. Edward **SMITHWICK** are ap_____ Church-Wardens for the ensuing Year.

    There being found the abovesaid Sums of Money due to the precinct and also the Reader being gone whereby the Publick Charge of the Precinct is ____ and abated:

    Therefore ordered that the Collector collect from every Tythable person __ the Precinct four Shillings Pr. Pole.

The Chappel being this Day viewed by all the Vestry here present and are Satisfyed therewith and do receive the House and Keys from Mr. John **PORTER** he? promising to provide So much Lime as will Wash the Ceiling of the Chappel and the Vestry to be at the Charge of a Workman to do the Same. *Chapel finished & received* 6

(6) *1703.}* April ye. 24th. 1703.
    At a Vestry holden at the House of Mrs. Sarah **GILLAM**.
Present
The honoble. Henderson **WALKER** Esqr. Mr. William **DUCKENFIELD** Mr. Edwad. **SMITHWICK**} Church-Wardens Coll. Wm. **WILKINSON** Capt. Thomas **LEUTEN**} Capt. Thomas **BLOUNT** Mr. Nicholas **CRISP** Mr. Wm. **BANBURY** Nathl. **CHEVIN**}

    The Church-Wardens &c. having agreed with Coll. Wm. **WILKINSON** for the Sending for a Standard of Weights and Measures for this precinct and he having received the Same from Boston comes and produces an Account of the Same from under the Hand of Mr. William **WELSTEAD** Mercht. of Boston as followeth Vizt

	£ Shll. d
5 ½ Ct's. one Qr. Ct. one shll. at 20 Sh per. Ct.	2:.17: 6
One Brass Yard 25 Shll. One Iron Do. at 2 shll	1: 7 0
Three Brass Weights. Vizt. 4 & 2 &c.	0: 14: 0
One pair of Brass Scales	0: 16: 0
One Wine Gallon Pewter Pot	0: 18: 0
One pottle and one Quart Do.	0:15: 0
One ½ Bushel and one Peck	0: 5: 0
Paid the the [sic] Town Sealer for Sealing the Weights &c_	0: 3: 8
Paid Porterage to the Vessel	0: 1: 0
First Cost. __	£7:17: 2.

Weights & measures.

    Ordered that Coll. William **WILKINSON** deliver to? Mr. Edward **SMITHWICK** the aforesaid Weights and Measures who is impowered to keep the Same by Act of Assembly &c. And that Mr. Edward **SMITHWICK** give a Recei__ for the Same.

24 April 1703

(6) (Cont.) Whereas Robert **WILSON** who was kept by William **BRETHELL** for the Space of 2 or 3 Months upon the Precinct Charge: and is dead and Coll. **WILKINSON** declaring that he has paid unto the Said **BRETHELL** for the Care and keeping of the Said **WILLSON** the Sum of Eight Pounds which was the full Consideration for one whole Year.

Ordered that William **BRETHELL** Shall reimburse Coll. William **WILKINSON** the aforesaid Eight pounds except So much as he Shall make appear to have disburst for his Burial and the time he keptHim.

It being debated for a Reader to be agreed with to read Divine Service.

It is agreed that the Church-Wardens shall make Choice of a Reader who shall remain until the next Vestry and if approved of by the Vestry *Reader*

(7) *1703* Shall remain and if not Shall be paid for his Time and discharged.

Information being made by Capt Thomas **BLOUNT** that Elinor **ADAMS** is? of Infirmity and Indigence is in great Danger of being lost for want of Assist____

The Same being taken into Consideration.

Ordered that Capt. Thomas **BLOUNT** treat with Docr. Godffrey **SPRUILL** in __ to her Cure and that Doctor Godffrey **SPRUIL** be paid for his physick and Car_ the Church-Wardens five pounds, and Capt. Thomas **BLOUNT** is requested by ___ Vestry to endeavour to oblige the Said Elenor to Serve the Doctor for the ___ of his House and nursing.

There being three Church Bibles intended for this Country one wh___ belongs to this precinct and the Same being Sent for to Williamsburgh by? William **JONES**. *Bible*

Ordered that the Church-Wardens pay one third of the Charge for fetching in the Said Bibles.

There being Want of Some Letters for the Stamping the Weights ___ Measures for the Standard And Capt. Thomas **BLOUNT** undertakes to ma__ a Small Letter C for Stamping the Styllyards and potts and Weights &c and? Larger C for the half Bushell and peck.

At a Vestry holden at the Chappell ye. 6th Day of October 1___

Present

the Honoble. Henderson **WALKER** Esqr. Mr. Wm. **DUCKENFIELD** Mr. Edward **SMITHWICK**} Church-Wardens Coll. Wm. **WILKINSON** Capt. Thos. **BLOUNT**} Capt Thomas **LEUTEN** Mr. John **BLOUNT** Mr. Nicholas **CRISP** Mr. Wm. **BANBURY** Nathl. **CHEVIN**.}

In pursuance of a former Order.

Ordered that the Church-Wardens shall immediately Account with William **BRETHELL** for eight pounds paid him by Coll. Wm. **WILKINSON** and if h_ Shall refuse to deliver and pay the Same, that they Commence an Action agt. Him for the Recovery thereof.

Ordered that the Church-Wardens shall with all possible Speed ___ the Windows of the Chappell finished and that Glass may be Sent for __ purchased here if possible. *7*

(8) __*03* At a Vestry met at the Chapel the 9th Day of March 1703/4.

Present

The Honoble. Henderson **WALKER** Esqr. Coll. Wm. **WILKINSON** Wm. **DUCKENFIELD** Esqr. Mr. Edward **SMITHWICK**} Mr. Nicholas **CRISP** Mr. John **BLOUNT** Mr. Wm. **BANBURY** Nathl. **CHEVIN**}

William **DUCKENFIELD** Esqr. and Mr. Edward **SMITHWICK** being appointed Church-Wardens for the Last Year and having Served a year the 15th. of December last, and they having failed of Calling the Vestry together at that time in Order to be discharged.

Ordered that they Serve another year in that Station.

Whereas Dr. John **BLAIR** presenting himself before the Vestry, as a Minister of the Gospel and having the Approbation of the D. Governour, he is received as a Minister of the Gospel and the Church-Wardens for and in Behalf of the Vestry do assume to pay to the Said Dr. John **BLAIR** 30 pounds (as the Law provides) pr. Annum. The Year to begin the first of this Instant March. *Dr. John BLAIR chosen Minister Salary 30 pounds*

The Choice of a Reader and Clerk of the Church being debated and Daniel **LEIGH** presenting himself for that Office

It's agreed that Daniel **LEIGH** Serve in that Station and that he keep the Keys of the Church and keep the Church clean, and keep the Woods fired at the time of the Year round the Chappel also to provide Water for the baptizing of Children, and to attend the Chappel every Lords Day, when the Minister is here to officiate as a Clerk, and when the Minister is absent to read divine Service and a Sermon &c. to keep the Vestry Journal and to attend the Vestry at their Meetings. He promising to the Vestry to lead a Sober and exemplary Life in his Station his Year to begin this Day. *Daniel LEIGH chosen Reader & Clerk. His duties described*

Whereas his Excellency ffrancis **NICHOLSON** Esqr., his Majtys. Lieutenant and Governour of the Colony of Virginia hath been pleased to contribute the pious and Charitable Gift of ten pounds Sterling for the Use of the Church in this our precinct

9 March 1703/4

(8) (Cont.) and parish of St. Paul's and for a perpetual Memorial of his pious and Charitable Gift it is

Ordered that the ten Pounds in pieces of Eight wg. 17 p. wt. shall be Sent to Boston to purchase a Chalice for the Use of the Church with this Motto Ex Dono ffrancis **NICHOLSON** Esqr. her Majesty's Lieutenant Govr. of her Majesty's Colony and Dominion of Virginia. *Chalice Ordered*

Ordered that the Church-Wardens do Speedily agree with a Workman to make Pulpit and Pew for the Reader with Desks fitting for the Same and in as decent a Manner as may be and what they shall agree for the Vestry do oblige themselves to See paid And that they put a former Order in Execution for the Getting the Windows put up, and to get Glass and have it put up forthwith. *Pulpit and Reading Pew.*   Ordered

(9) *1:_____ {1703}* [Top line on this page is missing. Right margin is ragged.] the Vestry Coll. Wm. **WILKINSON** having accepted of the Ballance in his hands? ___ the Insolvents.

The Publick Charge is as followeth. Vizt.   £ Sh___

	£	Sh
To Doctr. **SPRUIL** for Curing [blank] **ADAMS**	5:	0___
To Luke **MEAZLE**'s Services	0:	9___
To Coll. **WILKINSON** a Barrel of Tarr	0:	10__
To Danl. **LEIGH** for tarring the Chapell and fetching the Tarr	1:	0___
To Nathl. **CHEVIN** Clk.	2:	10___
To Sallery for collecting at .15 Pr. Ct.	1:	10___
	£11:	9?

Ordered that the Collector collect of every Tythable in the p_____ the Sum of One Shilling and Eight Pence with power to destrain in Cas___ Refusal to be collected by the Church-Wardens or their Deputies and the _____ Church-Wardens do undertake for the faithfull Collection and true accountin___ the Same in the Sum of fifty pounds Sterling to be levied upon their goo_____ Chattells in Case of Default.

At a Vestry held at the Chappel the 26th of May 17__
Present
Coll. Wm. **WILKINSON** Wm. **DUCKENFIELD** Esqr. Mr. Edward **SMITHWICK** Mr. Nicholas **CRISP**} Mr. Nathl. **CHEVIN** Mr. John **BLOUNT** Mr. Wm. **BANBURY** Capt. Thomas **LUTEN**.}

Ordered that Mr. John **ARDERN** Serve as Vestry Man __ the Room of the Honoble. Henderson **WALKER** deceed.

Ordered that three pound be paid Richard **BOOTH** towards the Maintainance of an Orphan Child left destitute pr. Stephen **PRESTON**.

The Revd. John **BLAIR** Serving as Minister of the Gospel out of hi_ Charitable Gift hath given what Sallery is due to him to the poor for which the Gentlemen of the Vestry return him thanks. *Rev. Jno. BLAIR gives his Salary to the poor.* 8

(10) __ *no Dom _704}* A [sic] a Vestry mett at the Chappel ye 9th. Day of Sept 1705: -
Present
Coll. Thomas **POLLOCK** John **ARDERN** Esqr. Wm. **DUCKENFIELD** Esqr. Capt. Thomas **LUTEN** Mr. John **BLOUNT**} Mr. Nich____ [torn] **CRISP** Mr. Wm. _____RY [torn] Mr. Nathl. _____IN [torn] Mr. Edward **SMITHWICK**}

Mr. Henry **GERRARD** presenting himself to the Vestry as a Minister of the Gospel and he having the Honoble Deputy Govr.'s Approbation is received by the Vestry into this precinct and the Said Mr. Henry **GERRARD** declaring that by Reason of the great Distance betwixt this precinct and and [sic] pequimins and the Dirtyness of the Roads he is not able to Serve in the two precincts, and therefore is willing to attend in this precinct wholy and decline his Intentions of Serving in Pequimons. *Rev. Henry GERRARD chosen minister.*

And the Church-Wardens for and in Behalf of the Vestry do undertake to pay to the aforesaid Mr. Henry **GERRARD** thirty pounds Pr. Annum at [sic] the Law directs besides these Voluntary Subscriptions hereafter mentioned to which the Several Persons have Subscribed Vizt.

	£ s d?		£ s d
Coll. Thomas **POLLOCK**	4 :0 : 0 }Mr. Wm. **BANBURY**		0 : 8 : 0
Wm. **DUCKENFIELD** Esqr.	4 :0 : 0 }Mr. Nathl. **CHEVIN**		1 :0 : 0
John **ARDERN** Esqr.	3 :0 : 0 }John **WHEATLY**		0 :10 : 0
Mr. Edwd. **MOSELEY**	5 :0 : 0 }Richd. **ROSE**		0 :10 : 0
Capt. Thomas **LUTEN**	1 :0 : 0 }John **LINNINGTON**		0 :15 : 0
Mr. Nicholas **CRISP**	1 :5 : 0 }Capt. David **HENDERSON**		0 :10 : 0
Mr. Edward **SMITHWICK**	1 :0 : 0 }Henry **BONNER**		0 :10 : 0
Mr. John **BLOUNT**	1 :0 : 0 }		
			£25 : 8 : 0

9 September 1705

(10) (Cont.) It is agreed that a third part of the thirty Pounds be levied and raised in the Precinct in December next.
And the Vestry agrees to meet the 15th. of December next.

(11) *1705}* At a Vestry meet at the Chappel Decembr. ye. 16. 1705.
Present
Coll. William **WILKINSON** John **ARDERN** Esqr. Wm. **DUCKENFIELD** Esqr. Mr. John **BLOUNT** Mr. Edward **SMITHWICK**} Capt. Thomas **LEUTEN** Mr. Nichl: **CRISP** Mr. Wm. **BANBURY** Mr. Nathl. **CHEVIN**}

Ordered and agreed that Coll. Thomas **POLLOCK** and Mr. John **BLOUNT** Shall be Church Wardens for the ensuing Year.

And there being not a full Vestry it's agreed that the Vestry meet the Second Day of January next.

At a Vestry met at the Chappel ye. 3d. Day of Jany. 1705
Present
Coll. Wm. **WILKINSON** Capt. Thomas **LUTEN** John **ARDERN** Esqr. Wm. **DUCKENFIELD** Esqr. Capt. Thomas **BLOUNT**} Mr. John **BLOUNT** Mr. James **LONG** Mr. Edward **SMITHWICK** Mr. Nathl. **CHEVIN** Mr. Wm. **BANBURY**.

It being debated whether the Publick Account shall be examined Coll **POLLOCK** being absent, who is appointed one of the Church Wardens, before the Church-Wardens who have Served the Last Year cannot render in? their Account, because one of them is absent as aforesaid and So the Accou__ cannot be made up.

Also debated the Payment of John **DICKS** for Work about the pulp__ the Said Work not being, finished, whether he Shall be paid before the Work be done, He alledging that he could not finish it for Want of Nails & Boards. *And he brings an Rect. for his Work Six pounds.* [Original hand.]

Ordered that John **DICKS** be paid one pound Seventeen Shillings Nine Pence besides what he has been paid and that he finish the Work then Account with the Vestry.

Whereas several Scandalous Reports has been Spread abroad in th__ Government of the Reverend Mr. Henry **GERRARD** of Several Deauched pr____tions which (if true) tends highly to the Dishonour of Allmighty God a__ the Scandal of the Church. *Scandalous reports of Rev. H. GERRARD.* 9

(12) _705. It is debated whether he Sho___ be continued.

Ordered that he continue in this Precinct as a Minister till the first of May next in which time it is expected by the Vestry that he Use his Utmost Endeavours to clear himself of these black Calumnies laid to his Charge or else he may expect a Dismission.

It's agreed that if Coll. Thomas **POLLOCK** refuse to Serve as a Church-Warden he paying the Fine shall be excused and Nathaniel **CHEVIN** Shall Serve in his Stead with Mr. John **BLOUNT** as aforesaid.

It is agreed by the Vestry, Mr. **GERRARD** agreeing thereto, that Mr. **GERRARD** Shall once in two Months be fetch over to the South Shore by a Canoe and two Hands from thence to begin the first Monday in February, and So the first Monday in the Month every two Months, which Men shall be paid by the Publick.

Ordered that Richard **BOOTH** be paid three pounds towards the Maintainance of an Orphan Child left destitute by Stephen **BESTON**.

Ordered that the Collector of each District in this precinct Collect of every Tythable in their and either of their Districts two Shillings and Six Pence with power in Case of Refusal and the Church-Wardens do undertake for the faithfull Collection and accounting for the Same in the Sum of fifty Pounds Sterling to be levied upon their Goods and Chattels in Case of Refusal.

Memorandum December ye. 15th 1707.

Then the Church-Wardens John **BLOUNT** Esqr. and Nathl. **CHEVIN** having legally Summoned the Vestry and none appearing. Since Mr. William **BANBURY** and the aforesaid Church-Wardens having before encouraged Mr. James **BEASELEY** to attend this Vestry in Order to be established a Reader and he appearing in order thereunto, and there being no Vestry, he is willing to Officiate in the Station of a Reader of Divine Service untill a Vestry Shall meet and approve off and agree with him. *1707. James BEASLEY Reader.*

(13) *Anno Dom 1708}* At a Vestry at the Chapell the 18th. Day of April 1708
Present
Wm. **DUCKENFIELD** Esqr. John **ARDERN** Esqr. Capt. Thomas **LUTEN** Mr. Nichl. **CRISP**} John **BLOUNT** Esqr. Mr. Edward **SMITHWICK** Mr. Wm. **BANBURY** Mr. Nathl. **CHEVIN**}

Mr. Nathl. **CHEVIN** being now removing out of this precinct and it? being debated who shall Serve instead of him.

Agreed that Thomas **GARRET** Esqr. shall Succeed in the Room and Stead of Nathl. **CHEVIN**.

Also it being debated who Shall Succeed in the Room and Place of Capt. Thomas **BLOUNT** deceed.

18 April 1708

(13) (Cont.) Resolved that Edward **MOSELEY** Esqr. shall Succeed, in the Vestry in the Place of Capt. Thomas **BLOUNT**

It is also voted who Shall Succeed as a Vestry Man in the Place of William **WILKINSON**.

It is agreed that Wm. **CHARLTON** Esqr. shall Succeed as a Vestry man in the place and Stead of Coll. Wm. **WILKINSON**.

And accordingly Thomas **GARRET** and Wm. **CHARLTON** Esqrs. took their places in the Vestry.

Richard **BOOTH** having had an Allowance of three pounds pr? Annum for maintaining an Orphan Child of Stephen **BESSONS** comes here and Assumes to keep and maintain the Child without any further Charge.

This Day William **DUCKENFIELD** Esqr. and Mr. Edward **SMITHWICK** made up their Accounts in the time of their being Church-Wardens And upon adjusting their Accounts it appears that there is due to? Mr. **DUCKENFIELD** from the Vestry

	£ s d
the Sum of	4 : 5 : 0
And Mr. **SMITHWICK** stands indebted to the Vestry	1 : 2 : 6

Ordered that Mr. **SMITHWICK** pay the Same to Wm. **DUCKENFIELD** Esqr. and then and there will be due to him

	£ s d
from the Vestry	3 : 2 : 6

John **BLOUNT** Esqr. and Nathl. **CHEVIN** this Day producing their Acco____ of the publick Accounts. Upon adjusting

	£ s d
the Accounts there appears __ be due to the publick the Sum of	6 : 6 : 8

Ordered that Mr. **CRISP** be paid for the Use of his Canoe ten? Shillings and Six pence Pr. Nathl. **CHEVIN**.

So the Account Stands thus.

John **BLOUNT** and Nathl. **CHEVIN** Church-Wardens Stands }	£ s d	
Debtors to the publick for the years 1706 & 1707. -- -- }	6 : 6 : 8?	10

(14) *Dom* By Mr. **CRISP** — 0 : 2 : 4?
1708.} By Mr. **MOSELEY** — 1 : 2 : 6
By Mr. **DUCKENFIELD** — 3 : 2 : 6
£4 : 7 : 6

Ordered that Phillis **DICKS** Widow of John **DICKS** be paid by the Publick the Sum of two Pounds besides what he hath been allowed and paid by the publick for his Work on the Chapel.

On the petition of William **WALSTON** Shewing that Elenor **KIRKHAM** was accommodated at the petitioner's Eighteen Days being Sick and impotent and there died and was buried at the petitioner's Charge having no Estate prays Allowance &c.

And he prsenting No account.

Ordered that he appear at the next Vestry and present his Account.

On Petition of Madam Mary **BLOUNT** for accomodating a poor indigent Man named Thomas **WRIGHT** at her House in his Sickness one Week, whereof he died and was buried at her Charge, prays Allowance.

Ordered that She be paid by the publick forty Shillings.

Ordered that the Honoble. Coll. Thomas **POLLOCK** and John **ARDERN** Esqr. Shall be Church-Wardens for the Year ensuing.

Ordered that Mr. Nicholas **CRISP** agree with [blank] to officiate as a Reader in the Chapel for nine pound pr. Annum to execute in that Office and also as Clerk of the Vestry, And Mr. Nich. **CRISP** doth promise to give Notice to the Inhabitants of the Time when he shall begin upon that Employment.

(15) __*no Dom 1708}* At a Vestry met at the Chappel on Wednesday the 9th Day? of May 1708.
Present
William **DUCKENFIELD** Esqr. Edward **MOSELEY** Esqr. Capt. Thomas **LUTEN** Mr. John **BLOUNT**} Mr. William **BANBURY** Mr. Wm. **CHARLTON**} Mr. John **ARDERN**.} Church Wardens

In Observance to a late Act of Assembly intitled an Act for electing Vestrys, the Said Act being first read, the Vestry made Choice of the Reverend Mr. William **GORDON** (the Honoble. Presidents Approbation being Signified, to officiate in this precinct as a Minister of the Gospel.

It having this Day been Signified to the Vestry that the Honoble. Thom__ **POLLOCK** declines the Office of a Church-Warden. *Rev Wm. GORDON Chosen Minister*

Ordered that Mr. Nicholas **CRISP** officiate in his Room and that the Honoble. Coll. Thomas **POLLOCK** pay his Fine As appointed by the Act.

Mr. William **WALSTON** having this Day brought in his Account for the Interment of Ealinor **KIRCKUM** [sic] and demanding thirty Shillings for his Trouble and Charge therein, being thought a Reasonable Demand is therefore allowed the Same to

9 May 1708

(15) (Cont.) be paid by the publick.

It is ordered that a full Vestry pay their Attendance at the Chapel on Tuesday the 11th. of this Month for the further Settling of Matters relating to the Church.

At a Vestry Met at the Chappel on Tuesday the 11th Day of May 1708
Present
William **DUCKENFIELD** Esqr. Edward **MOSELEY** Esqr. Mr. Edward **SMITHWICK** Capt. Thomas **LUTEN** Mr. John **BLOUNT**} Mr. Nicholas **CRISP** Mr. William **BANBURY** Mr. Thomas **GARRET** John **ARDERN** Esqr.} 11

(16) _nno Dom 1708.}_ Mr. Nicholas **CRISP** being present and refusing to perform ___ Office of a Church-Warden.

Ordered that he pay his Fine pursuant to the Act and that Mr. Thomas **GARRET** be Church-Warden in his Room.

It having this Day been debated (for the better Encouragement of a Minister for this precinct only) which is the most proper Place to Purchase for a Glebe, it's unanimously agreed upon that the plantation now belonging to Mr. ffrederick **JONES** whereon the Church now Stands is the fittest Place can be thought on for that Use the Tract of Land in Quantity containing five hundred Acres. *Glebe*

It is therefore the humble Request of the Vestry that Edward **MOSELEY** Esqr. (having now Business into Virginia) will please to treat with Mr. Frederick **JONES** concerning the purchase of the Said Land and agree with him for the Same provided he exceed not an Hundred pounds in Country Commodities.

Ordered that the Church-Wardens endeavour to have the Pulpit finished with all possible Speed as likewise the Desk and what other things belong to it, As likewise to have the Church Floor laid with Brick, but upon further Debate of the Matter, it's agreed upon that the ffloor Shall be laid with Plank as being the Cheapest and Most expeditious way of having it done. *Pulpit. Floor*

There appearing upon the Adjousting of Mr. John **BLOUNT**'s and Mr. Nathaniel **CHEVIN**'s Accounts to the Vestry on the Eighteenth of April last, Mr. **CHEVIN** remains Debtor to the publick - £ 1: s 19: d 2

Ordered that the Said £ 1: s 19: d 2 be paid to Mrs. Mary **BLOUNT** in part of forty Shillings due to her by a former Order.

Ordered that the Vestry Meet at the Chapell the following Day to our next precinct Court.

(17) *(17) 1708* At a Meeting at the Chapell of Edward **MOSELEY** Esqr. Capt. Thomas **LEUTEN** and Mr. John **BLOUNT** on Wednesday ye. 7th. of July 1708.

As likewise of John **ARDERN** the Rest of the Vestry not appearing.

Ordered that a full Vestry make their Appearance at the Chapell on Sabbath Day next being the 11th. of this Instant.

Memorandum The Vestry having been legally Summoned to make their Appearance at the Chapell on Sunday the Eleventh of July 1708 but none appearing except Edward **MOSELEY** Esqr. Mr. Edward **SMITHWICK** Mr. Nicholas **CRISP** John **ARDERN** and William **BANBURY** there being no Majority no Bussiness could be accomplisht.

Ordered that a full Vestry make their Appearance at the Chapell on Sunday ye 25th of July 1708.

At a Meeting of the Vestry holden at the Chapell on Sunday the 25th. of July 1708.
Present
Edward **MOSELEY** Esqr. William **DUCKENFIELD** Esqr. Capt. Thomas **LUTON** Mr. Nicholas **CRISP**} Mr. Edward **SMITHWICK** Mr. William **BANBURY** Mr. William **CHARLTON** John **ARDERN** Esqr.

Whereas the Reverend Mr. William **GORDON** is Speedily designed for England hath therefore recommended unto this precinct for a Reader Mr: Charles **GRIFFIN** of whom he renders a good Character the said Mr. **GRIFFIN** being likewise made known to Some Gentlemen of the Vestry. *Rev Wm GORDON going to England*

It's unanimously approved of to accept of the Said Mr. **GRIFFIN** for our Reader in Mr. **GORDON**'s Absence and to allow for his Officiating as such and performing the Office of a Clerk to the Vestry twenty poun_ pr. Annum to be paid by the Publick. *Mr. Charles GRIFFIN is Chosen Reader.* 12

(18) _18) Anno Dom 1708._ Whereas it hath been taken into our mature Consideration the many and great Inconveniences which attend the Chappel which is already built both in Respect of it's ill Scituation Smallness and rough and unfit Workmanship.

We therefore to Shew our true Zeal for the Glory of God and propogating So good a Work do unanimously agree that a Church of forty Feet long and twenty four wide fourteen Feet from Tenant to Tenant for Hight, the remaining part of the Work to be proportionable, the Roof to be first Plankt and then Shingled with good Cypress Shingles and the whole to be ceiled with Plank and floored with Plank for the Speedy accomplishment of which Said Work, it's the Earnest Request of the Present Members of the Vestry that Edward **MOSELEY** Esqr. and Capt Thomas **LEUTEN** will undertake to See the Same performed, they living convenient, and to agree with Workmen at as easy Rates as may be. It being well and Substantially performed. *New Church pro-*

25 July 1708

(18) (Cont.) *posed.*

There appearing to this Board that Eight pounds are due to the Reverend Mr. William **GORDON** for Officiating as a Minister in this precinct.

Ordered that the Said Eight pounds be paid to the Revd. Mr. **GORDON** or his Order by the publick.

At a Vestry held at the Chapell on Thursday the 27th of Febry. 1708/9.

Present

John **ARDERN** Esqr. Mr. John **BLOUNT** Capt. Thomas **LUTEN** Capt. Nichl. **CRISP** Capt. James **LONG**} Mr. Thomas **GARRET** Mr. Edwd. **SMITHWICK** Mr. Wm. **BANBURY** Mr. Wm. **CHARLETON** Mr. Edward **MOSELEY**}

(19) *(19) _nno Dom 1708* Thomas **GARRET** and John **ARDERN** being this Day dismist from the Office of Church-Wardens adjuted their Accounts with the Vestry which Stands as followeth Vizt.

Publick - - - - -	Dr				Cr:	
	£ s, d				£ s d	
Widow **DICKS** Claim	-	-	2: 0: 0	Pr. Currituck and } Pasquotanck Fines}	1:10: 0	
Pr. Wm. **WALSTON**	-	-	1:10: 0	Pr. Ballance of }		
By Mrs. **BLOUNT**	-	-	2: 0: 0	Widow **DICKS**'s Account}	1:19: 2	
By John **ARDERN** Sterling	-	-	0: 5: 0	By 500 feet of Inch Board }		
Pr. Mr. **GORDON**	-	-	8: 0: 0	by Mr. **SMITHWICK** towards} laying the Floor - - - - - - - }	2:10: 0	
Pr. a late Demand of} Mr. **GORDON** - - }			1: 0: 0			
Pr. Mr. **GORDON**s Expences} about the Books - - - - - }			0:15: 0			
Pr. Richd. **BOOTH**	-	-	3: 0: 0			

But if the Payment of the Said three Pounds be found a Mistake, It's to be refunded back. £ s d

Pr. Mr. **GRIFFIN** - - - - - - - - - 20:0:0?

Ordered that the Collector of this Precinct do collect from each Tythable the Sum of two Shillings and Nine Pence which rise? Sufficient to pay the publick Debts here mentioned and will advance the Sum of twelve Pounds towards the beautifying of the Chapell over and above the Charge the Charge of the Collection.

Ordered that Mr. Edward **SMITHWICK** do with all reasonable expedition deliver the Standard now in his Custody into the Care of Mr. Nicholas **CRISP** he living more convenient to the Precinct.

Ordered that Mr. John **LINNINGT0N** be constituted Clerk of the Vestry and be allowed for each Days Attendance five Shillings for each Days Attendance to be paid by the publick.

Ordered that the Way and Method of beautifying the Church be left to the Descretion of the Church Wardens for the Year ensuing Viz_ enlarging repairing &c. *Beautifying Church*

Ordered that Edward **MOSELEY** Esqr. and Majr. **LUTEN** be appointed Church-Wardens for the Year ensuing and have taken their Places accordingly. 13

(20) (_0) *Anno Dom 1708.* The Proceedings of the Vestry for the Precinct of Chowa_ in the County of Albemarle in the Province of North Carolina met at the Honoble. Coll. **HYDE**'s then President.

Present. The Honoble. Edwd. **HYDE** Esqr. Prsdt. The Honoble. Thomas **POLLOCK** Esqr. William **DUCKENFIELD** Esqr. The Honoble. Thos. **PETERSON** Esqr. Mr. Thomas **LUTEN.**} Mr. Edward **SMITHWICK** Mr. Jno. **BIRD** Mr. Thomas **LEE** Mr. John **WALKER**}

Ordered Imprimis.

That there be allowed and raised in the Said Precinct of Chowan forty five Pounds and paid by the hereafter named and appointed Church-Wardens to the Revd. Mr. **URMSTON** for having Officiated in this precinct from the Time of his first Coming into this Governmt. till the 25th. Instant in the Commodities appointed by the Vestry Act. *Rev. Mr. URMSTON.*

Ordered that the Honoble. Thomas **PETERSON** Esqr. and Mr. Thomas **LEE** be and are hereby chosen and appointed Church-Wardens for the year ensuing the Date hereof and that they levy raise and Collect all Sums appointed to be raised for the Use of the Parish and that they be allowed for their So doing after the Rate of 20 be? pr. Ct.

That the Ten Pounds Sterling given by Coll. **NICHOLSON** and now in the Hands of Mr. Edward **MOSELEY** be demanded and received by the aforesaid Church-Wardens. *Chalice money taken back*

That for want of the Act of Assembly for regulating of Vestries Establishing the Church and Making Provision for Ministers, and the Vestry Book with the Late Church-Wardens Accounts. Another Vestry be held at the Honoble. the prsidts. the first Day of Janry. next ensuing and that the late Church Wardens be warned to attend there and then to give up their accounts.

Edwd. **HYDE** Thos. **POLLOCK** Thos. **PETERSON** Thos. **LEUTON**} Edward **SMITHWICK** John **BIRD** Thomas **LEE**

(20) (Cont.) John **WALKER**.}

(21) *(21) Anno Dom 1711.* Chowan Precinct

At a Vestry held at the Honoble. the prsident's the 1st Day of Janry 1711/12.
Present.
The Honoble, the president The Honoble Thos **POLLOCK** Esqr. The Honoble. Thos. **PETERSON** Esqr. Wm. **DUCKENFIELD** Esqr. Mr. Edwd. **SMITHWICK**} Mr. Jno. **BIRD** Mr. Thos. **LEE** Mr. Jno. **WALKER**.

Ordered then that the Honoble the prsident be humbly requested to issue his Warrant to the Several Constables of this prcinct to take a List of the Tythables within their Charge and bring in the Same or make Return of the Same to the Honoble. the president within the Space of one Month after the Date hereof.

Ordered that the Honoble. Thomas **PETERSON** Esqr. together with Mr. Thomas **LUTEN** be desired to take Mr. **MOSELEY**'s Account of late Office of Church Warden for this Precinct.

Ordered that the Reverend Mr. **URMSTON** be allowed for officiating in this prcinct the year following commencing from th_ twenty fifth of December last past at the Several Times and Places hereafter mentioned, Seventy Pounds to be levied and paid as the Act of Assembly for establishing the Church and making Provision for Ministers doth appoint and direct dated March ye. 12th. 1706? Vizt. One Sunday on the South Shore the two next Sundays on the Western Shores alternately, Provided always that he officiate the fourth Sunday on the other Side opposite to that where he officiated the two foregoing Sundays, and that he provide a passage at his own Cost and Charge. *Rev. Mr. URMSTON provided for --his Stations*
Jno. **URMSTON** Missr. Edward **HYDE** Tho. **PETERSON**} Tho. **LEE**} Church Wardens William **DUCKENFIELD**} Thomas **POLLOCK** John **BIRD** John **WALKER** Edward **SMITHWICK**.} 14

(22) _2) *Anno Dom 1711.* At a Vestry held at the Honoble. the Presidents Febry. ye 6th. 1711/12

Whereas there is no Constable appointed for the lower District of the North Shore from Edward **STANDING**s lower down the Precinct the Church Wardens or either of them are hereby impowered to hire a fit Person to take a List of the Tythables within the Said District and after having received all the Several Lists of all the Districts within this precinct to assess and collect or cause to be Collected the aforesaid Sum of forty five Pounds and the Additional Charge for collecting the Same to be raised equally Pr. Pole.

Item that whereas the Honoble. Thomas **PETERSON** Esqr. and Mr. Thomas **LUTEN** have not been able to take and receive Mr. **MOSELEY**'s the late Church Warden's Account of his Said Office according to the Order of the last Vestry, It is hereby ordered that they demand and take and lay the Same before the next Vestry.
Thos. **PETERSON** Church-Warden John **BIRD** Samuel **PATCHET** Leonard **LOFTEN**? William **DUCKENFIELD** Thos. **LUTEN**} Edward **HYDE** Thos. **POLLOCK** John **URMSTON** Missry. Thos. **LEE** Church Warden John **WALKER**.}

At a Vestry held at the Honoble. Thomas **POLLOCK**'s Esqr. President at his House on the West Shore in the precinct of Chowan in the Province of North Carolina Febry ye 6th. 1712/13.

It was then ordered that in pursuance of an Act of Assembly dated March ye. 12th. 1710. and likewise by an Order of Vestry met at the House of the Honoble. Edward **HYDE** Esqr. President dated December ye 18th. 1711. appointing the Collection of forty five Pounds with

(23) *(23) Anno. 1712* with the Charge of Collecting the Said Sum to be paid to the Revere_ Mr. John **URMSTON** Missionary.

These are therefore to impower You John **HARDY** to collect and receive of every Tythable Person in the precinct of Chowan twenty pence in the Staple Commodities of the Country and to lodge the Same in places convenient upon the Water giving the Said Mr. **URMSTON** Notice and order to receive it, and for the So doing You shall receive fifteen Pr. Cent out of the Said Collection. Given under our Hands this 6th. day of Febry. 1712/__

Ordered upon Complaint of Mr. Thomas **LEE** that Mr. Edwd. **MOSELEY** had bought of him the Said Thomas **LEE** fourteen hundred fee_ of Plank on Pretence of laying a Floor and repairing the Church on the North Shore in this Precinct and now refused to pay for the Same and therefore upon Application made 'twas then to be entred in the Vestry Book that We the Vestrymen for the Said Precinct are of Opinion that Said Mr. **MOSELEY** is indebted and obliged to pay for the Same and ___ the parish, there appearing no order of Vestry for the purchase of the Said Plank, neither hath it been applyed as pretended but is wasted or destroyed and rendred Useless.

That Mr. Edward **MOSELEY** refund the three pounds received of Vestry on Account of Richard **BOOTH** to the Church-Wardens for this Year the Same appearing not due to the Said Richard **BOOTH**.

That Mr. John **BIRD** and Mr. Samuel **PATCHET** be and are hereby chosen and appointed to be Church Wardens of this Precinct for the Year ensuing.

Ordered that Thomas **WEST** be Clerk of the Vestry and be allowed as formerly.

6 February 1712/13

(23) (Cont.) Ordered that the Church-Wardens for the Year ensuing demand of the Executor of Mr. Robert TENDALL deceed twelve pounds which the Said Robert TENDALL collected for the Use of this precinct and in Case of Refusal to Sue him for the Same.

That the Bible now in the Custody of Mr. Nicholas CRISP be delivered to Majr. Thos. LUTEN, he obliging himself to See it forthcome the Gift of the Honoble. Society de propoganda &c. by the Reverend Mr. URMSTON. *Bible presented by the "Socy. for propagating the Gospel."*

That the Bible now in the Custody of Mr. Thomas LEE be delivered to the Vestry when demanded. 15

(24) *4) Anno Dom 1712* That the Standard of Weights and Measures is committed into the Custody of Mr. Thomas PETERSON and that he demand and receive the Same wherever they be and that the Said Mr. Thomas PETERSON give an Account thereof to the next Vestry.

That Capt. Robert WEST and Capt. David HENDERSON be and are hereby chosen Vestrymen in the Room of the Honoble. Edward HYDE Esqr. our late Govr. and Mr. John WALKER deceed.

That Mr. Thomas PETERSON and Mr. Thomas LEE do Sue Mr. Edward MOSELEY pursuant to a former Order of Vestry for the Money in his Hands, which was given for the purchase of Church Plate.

Thomas PETERSON Thomas LEE William DUCKENFIELD John BIRD} Thomas POLLOCK Thomas LEUTEN Leonard LOFTIN.}

1713. At a Vestry met at the Church on the North Shore of the Sound in Chowan prcinct March ye. 2nd. 1713/4 [sic]
Present
The honoble Thoms. POLLOCK Esqr. Prsedt. William DUCKENFIELD Esqr. Thomas PETERSON Thomas LUTEN} Thomas LEE Leonard LOFTIN Samuel PATCHET.

And They having taken into Consideration the Letters from the Honoble Society by the Honoble. Coll. NICHOLSON together with one from his Honor. the following Answers to the Said Letters were ordered.

To Honoble. Society de propoganda &c.

We whose Names are here underwritten Vestrymen and Church-Wardens of the Precinct of Chowan in the County of Albemarle   in

(25) (25) *Anno Dom. 1713.* in the Province of North Carolina, do for our Selves and on Behalf of the Rest of the Inhabitants of this Said Precinct in a most Gratefull Manner Return our hearty Thanks to the Honoble. Society &c for their great Care of our Soul's Health in Sending over Missionaries to preach the Word of God and Administer the Holy Sacraments among Us. We and the whole English America ought to bless and praise the Allmighty for having put it into the Hearts of So many Honorable and Great Persons to think of their Poor Country Folks who_ Lot it hath been to come into these Heathen Countries, Where We are in Danger of becoming like the Indians themselves, without a God in the World. We? of this Precinct with the Rest of the Govermt. in Particular have been for Some time happy in the Pious Endeavours of divers of the Clergy Missrs. and others who have Set up the Worship of God according to the Church of England by Law established amongst Us, but by the Poverty of the Country, Unsetledness and Opposition of Sectaries, We never Yet were able to make due provision for those of that holy Order, which hath We fear been the Occasion of their Short Stay with Us: None of them ever abode So long here as the Reverend Mr. URMSTON hath done, Yet have not been So happy in him neither as he? would have desired, by reason that for the most part there hath been no? other Minister in these Parts Since his Arrival; and Seeing the Confusion and Distractions of this Unhappy Colony were So great, the Opposers of the holy Church so numerous and their Endeavours to Subvert the Same indefatigable?, he hath made the other Precincts Sharers with Us in his Ministry. His great Pains and unwearied Dilligence to keep together those of our Church hath had good Success and will undoubtedly be very acceptable to the Society. It were to be wished he had met with due Encouragement proportionable to the great Feteagues and hardships, which he hath Undergone, but fear he hath failed thereof. We of this precinct allowed him according to our first Act of Assembly in Favour of the Church of England (which was not obtained without hard Strugling) 30 £? pr. Annum for the first Year and half hoping the other Precincts where he officiated would have done the like, We cannot Say we have full filled our Promise As for the two Years last past he hath been prevailed with, and indeed Necessitated, not being able to travel any longer about the Country, to confine himself to this precinct, where his Residence hath constantly been. We have a large Parish many poor Inhabitants and those Seated at a great Distance from each other, Passages very Uncertain by Reason of a broad River which runs through the Heart of the Parish near 100 Miles in length and in many places broad, and but one Sorry Church on the North Shore of the Sound never finished, no Ornaments belonging to a Church nor wherewith to buy any except the Bounty of the Honoble. Coll. NICHOLSON Vizt. 10 Pounds part of the 30 £ given by him, when Govr. of Virginia to three Parishes   *of An interesting letter of the Vestry to the "Society for propagating the Gospel."* 16

2 March 1713/14

(26) *(26)* of this County, which is not Yet expended for want of an Addition according to the Intention of the Donor. Parsonage House and Glebe we have none nor a School: the first Library of great Value Sent Us by the Direction of the Reverend Dr. **BRAY**, thro' an Unhappy Inscription on the Back of the Books or Title Page Vizt. Belonging to the parish of St. Thomas of pamptico, in the then rising but now miserable County of Bath, falsly Supposed to be the Seat of the Governmt. was lodged there and by that means rendred Usless to the Clergy, for whose Service it was chiefly intended, and in what Condition We know not, We fear the worst by Reason of the late War. The Library Sent in by Mr. **GORDON** was all left with Mr. **WALLACE** late Minister of Keketan in Virginia, Save **WILBY**'s Annotations on the New Testament 2 Vol. Fol. and **PEARSON** on the Creed, which We have, the Said Mr. **WALLACE** upon Our Application refused to deliver the Books without an Order from the Society or Mr. **GORDON**. There were missing Collection of Cannons, **BEVERIDGE** on the Catechism, **BENNET** agt. the Quakers, **LUCAS** of Happiness 2 Vol. 800 **EACHARD**s Ecclesiastical History fol. and now the Said Mr. **WALLACE** is dead, we fear the like ill Fate may attend the rest: those Charity Books to the Value of 5 £? the generous Gift likewise of the Society have been Since Mr. **GORDON**'s Departure disposed off as was intended. What relates to the other Parishes within this Government, we presume will be laid before the Society by their respective Vestries, their Necessity We believe to be great, but being under the like unhappy Circumstances beg leave only to Supplicate for our Selves, and to pray the Honoble. Society to continue or rather add to the Salary of Mr. **URMSTON** to the End he may be enabled to Stay with Us, and that they will out of their great Charity concurr with our Honest but weak Endeavours to establish a Church, Ministry and a School, with the allowance of 10 or 15 £ Pr. Annum to a Person whom We shall make Choice of to teach our Children in this prcinct and we shall be bound ever to pray that God Allmighty may encrease their Store and Strengthen their Hands in the carrying on the great Work they have So piously Undertaken and may meet with happy Success in that their Glorious Design.

So prays Sirs,
Your most obliged poor Countrymen
of the Vestry aforesaid.

(27) *(27)* To the Honoble. Coll. **NICHOLSON**.
Honoured Sr.
The Reverend Mr. **URMSTON** having acquainted Us with your ____ good Intentions towards this poor Country, particularly Us of this Parish, and the Continuance of Your Generosity to Usward. We humbly pray your Acceptance of Our unfeigned thanks for all your Favours, Hoping We have complied with the Orders of the Holy Society in the enclosed: We humbly beg your Honr. would be? pleased to concurr with our Request to the Society and promote the Intere__ of a poor Country which You seem to wish so well. Your Presence here is very much desired, all honest Men and Friends of the Church are big in ___? Expectation of the great Influence your good Endeavours may have over Us all, to confirm and make all the Members of our Church adhere more? Zealously to the Interest thereof, Silence the Gainsayers and reduce the _____ of our late Confusions to a due Obedience to all lawfull Authority in _____ and State. These with all unfeigned and humble Respects are for _____
Honod. Sr.
Your &c. *Letter to Coll. NICHOLSON Gov*

Upon Complaint from Mr. **URMSTON** that the Sherriff _____ had failed in the Collection of forty five Pounds ordered to be paid to the Said Mr. **URMSTON** December ye. 10th. Anno 1711.

Ordered that the Said John **HARDY** do give an Account to the Church Wardens, who ordered him to Collect the Same of all he hath? received and paid on that Account on or before the last of this Month?

Ordered that the Present Church Wardens pay James **BEA**____ for a Desk in the Church as Soon as it can be raised.

Ordered that Doctr. **SPRUILL** be paid for the Cure of Ebeno? **ALDRIDGE** his Claim of twelve Pounds by the present Church Wardens as Soon as money can be raised.

Ordered that Mr. **MOSELEY** be allowed forty Shillings for the ___ of the Said Eben: **ALDRIDGE** for four Months by the present Church Wardens as Soon as Money can be raised.

That Mr. Edward **MOSELEY**'s Request for an Allowance towards his Loss in the Plank bought for the Use of the Church be referred to the Consideration of the Next Vestry.

Thos. **LEE** Leonard **LOFTIN** Thos. **PETERSON** Thos. **POLLOCK** Wm. **DUCKENFIELD** Thos **LUTEN** 17

(28) *28)* _nno Dom 1714./15 At a Vestry met at the Church on the North Shore of the Sound in Chowan Janry. ye. 3d. 1714/5.
It was then Ordered.
Imprimis that in the Place of Mr. Thos. **PETERSON** deceed the Honble: Charles **EDEN** Esqr. Govr. &c. be and is hereby chosen Vestry Man and in the Abscence of Mr. Thos. **LEE** Coll. Edward **MOSELEY** hereby is Chosen Vestry man.

Item upon Mr. David **HENDERSON**'s declaring himself a Dissenter from the Church and that it is Contrary to his Conscience to act as a Vestry man He the Said David **HENDERSON** is hereby dismissed from being a Vestry man &? in his Place Mr.

3 January 1714/15

(28) (Cont.) John HARDY be and is hereby chosen a Vestryman

Item that at the Request of Mr. Edward SMITHWICK to be dismissed by Reason of his Age and Infirmity, He be and is hereby dismist from being a Vestryman and in his Place Capt. Henry BONNER be and is hereby Chosen one of the Vestry.

Item that Mr. HARDY do attend and lay before the next Vestry his Account of the Collection made by him for the Use of the Parish by Order of Mr. Thos. PETERSON deceed and Mr. Thos. LEE the then Church Wardens.

Item that Coll. MOSELEY be allowed and paid by the present Church Wardens three Pounds for and in Consideration of the Loss Sustained in Plank, which he Provided for the Use of the Church.

Item it is resolved by the Vestry now Present that the next Assembly be petitioned by Coll. MOSELEY on behalf of the Vestry to divide this Parish and make two Parishes of it. *Division of the Parish*

Item ordered that Capt. Nich. CRISP be desired to demand of the Widow PETERSON and all others who have any Part or Parcel of the Weights and Scales and Measures belonging to the Standard for the Use of this Parish and keep the Same.

Item that the Church Wardens pay to Thomas LUTEN Junr. Ten Shillings for the Writing two Letters.

Ordered that the Church Wardens do Collect or Cause to be collected the Sum of two Shillings and Six Pence of every Tythable Person in this Precinct.

And that after that the Comissioners for Receiving the other Debts of the Precinct are paid, the Remainder be paid to the Revd. Mr. Jno. URMSTON in Part of the one hundred and ten Pounds which is due to him for Officiating 'till last New Years Day.

(29) (29) Ordered that Capt. Thomas WEST Robert WEST and Mr. Leonard LOFTIN be Church Wardens 'till next New Years Day. Thomas LEUTEN Jno. BLOUNT Robt. WEST Edwd. MOSELEY Henry BONNER Jno. PATCHET Samll. PATCHET Edwd. SMITHWICK Wm. DUCKENFIELD

Chowan Sc   At a Vestry held at the Chappel on the North Shore the 4th of May 1717
Present

The Honoble Charles EDEN Esqr. Govr. &c. Edward MOSELEY Nichl. CRISP Thomas LUTEN John JORDAN Henry BONNER Samll PATCHET} of the Vestry.

Who qualified themselves according to an Act of Assembly in the Behalf made and provided.

Mr. James BEASLEY is received into the Vestry in the Room of Mr. James FARLOW who refuseth to Qualify himself as a Vestry Man.

Coll Edward MOSELEY and Mr. James BEASLEY are Chosen Church Wardens.

It is agreed by this Vestry that So Soon as the Accts. of the former Collectors are made up, that the Vestry will then proceed to pay the pro___tionable Part of Such Sums of Money As were due from the parish of the Precinct of Chowan to the time of the Division of that Parish into the Eastern Parish and the South West Parish. And that Mr. HARDY and the other Collectors be desired to lay before this Vestry the Accounts of their Severall Collections between this Time and the first Sunday in the Next Month.

Ordered that the Church Wardens do receive of Each Tythable Person in this Parish the Sum of five Shillings Pr. Pole being for the Parish Taxes due last New years Day. Out of which Sum they are ordered to pay to the Revd. Mr. John URMSTON Missionary the Sum of fifty Pounds for his Officiating in this parish 'till last New Years Day. 18

(30) __0) _nno Dom 1717.} The honoble. the Govr. moving that the Reverd. Mr. John URMSTON Missionary Should be inducted.

The Vestry did not allow thereof.

But it is ordered that the Said John URMSTON be paid the Sum of fifty Pounds on or before the first of Janry next.

Provided the Said Mr. URMSTON does give his Attendance and officiate every third Sunday at Some Convenient Place near the Indian town and the remaining Sundays at the Chappell.

It is also ordered that each Tythable Person in the Parish do bring to the Church Wardens or either of them the Sum of five Shillings on or before the first of Janury. next being the Tax for the Present Year.

At a Vestry held at the Chappel the 15th Day of Septembr. 1717.
Present
Nicholas CRISP James BEASLEY Thos. LUTEN} Samll. PATCHET Henry BONNER.}

Capt. Frederick JONES and Mr. John BLOUNT qualifyed themselves as Vestry-men.
Ordered that the Vestry meet this Day Fennight.

At a Vestry held at the Chappel the 22d. Day of September 1717.
Mr. James FARLOW qualified himself as a Vestry-man by taking and Subscribing the Several Oaths by law appointed and is taken into the Vestry in the Room of the Honoble. the Govr. who is removed to Bath County.

22 September 1717

(30) (Cont.) Mr. John URMSTON having failed to receive the parish Tax due from Such of the Inhabitants as live near the Indian Town which he had Undertaken to do at Such Times as he was appointed to preach there.

It is ordered that the Church Wardens do cause the Collection to be compleated with all Expedition imaginable and Payment to be made the Said John URMSTON according to Order.

(31) _31) Anno Dom 1717_ This Day Edward MOSELEY one of the Church Wardens laid before the Vestry a Letter from the Society for Propogation of the Gospell in forreign Parts da___ June the 11th. 1716 which the Said Edward MOSELEY declared he had received open from John URMSTON.

It is ordered that the Church Wardens with Such other of the Vestry as can conveniently meet together do prepare an Answer thereto and that in the doing thereof they have regard to the Several Orders passed in the Vestry of Chowan And that the honoble. Society be informed of the State of Reglig Religion in these Parts.

James BEASELEY Nichl. CRISP Fred: JONES E MOSELEY Jno. FARLOW.

Chowan Sc   At a Vestry held at the House of the Honoble. ffred: JONES Esqr. the 16th Day of August 1719.
Present

The honoble. ffred: JONES Esqr. Edwd. MOSELEY James.} James BEASELEY} Church Wardens} Nichl. CRISP John JORDAN James ffARLOW.

Mr. Thomas GARRET Senr. is quallified as a Member of the Vestry by taking and Subscribing the Several Oaths by Law appointed.

Ordered that Thomas GARRET Junr. be appointed a Member of the Vestry in the Room of Mr. Thomas BRAY. The Said Thomas GARRET took and Subscribed the Several Oaths by Law appointed for his Qualification.

Robert HICKS Collector of the two five Shilling Pole Taxes due the first Day of Janry 1717 made Up his Accounts of the Same which are here incerted and it appearing that there is due to the Parish the Sum of Eighty Nine Pounds Excepting Such Insolvents as shall be returned by the Said HICKS.

It is ordered that the Said HICKS accounting for the Said Eighty Nine Pounds be referred 'till the Reverend Mr. John URMSTON can attend.

	£ shs d		£ shs d
Commissions for receiving 101 --	3: 0: 0	By 189 Tyth: 1716/7 -- --	47: 5:0
Paid Thomas LUTEN his Claim --	0: 10: 0	By 215 Tyth: 1717/8 -- --	53:15:0
Mr. BEASLEY for a reading Desk -	0: 10: 0		101
Mr. MOSELEY for }	2: 0: 0		12
allowed by a former Vestry}			89
Mr. MOSELEY for Loss of Plank	3: 0: 0 19		

(32) _32) Anno Dom 1719}_   £ s d
Edward WOOD for looking after Mary GENT and burying her -- --   3:0:0

Edward MOSELEY and James BEASLEY Church Wardens having made up their Accounts and desiring to be discharged of their Office.

It is ordered that Mr. Nicholas CRISP and Mr. John JORDAN be Church-Wardens in their Room And that they do collect five Shillings Parish Tax due last Janury.

It is further ordered that for the Ease of the Church Wardens in their Collections the Parish be divided into two Districts by Rockahock Creek and that Branch of it that runs by tottering Bridge.

Ordered that Robt. HICKS be allowed forty Shillings for his Attending as Clerk to the Vestry and that it be paid out of the Eighty Nine Pounds.

Ordered that the Vestry meet at the Church this Day fortnight and that the Revd. Mr. John URMSTON be desired to attend there.

Chowan Sc.   At a Vestry held at the Chappel the 20th Day of August 1719.
Present.

Nicholas CRISP Jno. JORDAN} Church Wardens The honoble. ffred. JONES Esqr. Coll. Edward MOSELEY Majr. Thomas LEUTEN John BLOUNT} Thomas GARRET Senr. James ffARLOW Thomas GARRET Junr. Capt. Henry BONNER James BEAZLEY}

John SIVERS having maintained Elizabeth MUNS for Eight Months past and has engaged to maintain her 'till new Years Day next.

Ordered that he be allowed and paid the Sum of Six Pounds. It is further ordered that the Church Wardens do take Care to

20 August 1719

(32) (Cont.) provide for the Said Elizabeth MUNS necessary Apparel.

This Vestry viewing the Church Wardens Certificate of the Collection of the 20d? Pole Tax upon the Precinct of Chowan for Paying the Sum of 45 Pounds in the Year 1711. do find that of that Sum of 45 Pounds the Mon__ raised amounts to but £22:10s:0d whereby there Remains unpaid to the Said Doctr. URMSTON the Sum of £12:10s:0d. It is therefore agreed by this Vestry

(33) *(33) Anno Dom 1719.* that they will cause the proportionable Part of the Same to be paid by t__ Parish when the Rateable Part of the hundred and ten Pounds is levied by bo__ Parishes as the Same Stands due to the Said Doctr. URMSTON by a former Order Dated the 3d. Day of Janury. 1714/15.

It appearing to the Vestry that the Ballance in the late Church Wa_dens Hands amounts to no more than the Sum of £979.

It is ordered that the Same be paid to the Revd. Mr. John URMSTON Minister in full of what is due to him from this Parish to the first of Janry 172_/_ with which he is content. And in Regard that the Said Minister hath not officiated in the Parts near the Indian Town according to the former Order of the Vestry.

It is agreed that the Said Minister be paid the Sum of? Eighty Pounds for the Two Years to be compleat and ended Next New Years Day, the Minister being content therewith and Promising that for the Remainder of the time 'till New Years Day, he will Officiate every third Sunday at Some convenient Place near the Indian Town.

It is ordered that the Church Wardens do agree with Some proper Person to build a Chappel at the most convenient Place for the persons? People of the upper Parts of the Parish and that the Charge thereof be de_____ out of the Monies that Shall be collected for the last Year and this prese__ Year So as the whole Charge of building the Said Chappel do not exceed thirty? Pounds out of the two Years Collections. *Order to build a Chapel.*

Mr. Paul PHILLIPS having Served as a Reader near the _____ Town from the first of June 'till this Present and offering to officiate ____ New years Day coming

It is ordered that he be paid for the Same after the Rate of Sixteen? Pounds Pr. Annum.

It is ordered that the Church Wardens do with all Convenient Speed after the first Day of Janury. next Levy and collect the Sum of five Shillings Pr. Pole upon all the Taxables in this Parish to defray the Charges of this Present Year. 20

(34) __4) No. Et. Parish of Chowan Sc. __. D._720

At a Vestry held at the Chappel the 18th Day of April 1720.

Present

Nicholas Crisp John JORDAN} Church Wardens The honoble. ffred JONES Esqr. Majr. Thos LUTEN Capt. Henry BONNER} Capt. Samll. PATCHET Mr. James FARLOW Mr. Thos. GARRET Senr. Mr. Thos. GARRET Junr.}

Ordered that Mr. Thomas ROUNDTREE be a Vestry Man in the Room of Mr. James BEASELEY deceed.

Ordered that the Clerk of the Vestry do keep a fair Book and Enter the Lists of Tythables yearly.

Ordered that Mr. John JORDAN do place Elisabeth MUNS with Such a Person as he Shall think proper and that She be allowed and paid as formerly Six Pounds Pr. Annum.

Ordered that Mr. Paul PHILLIPS be continued Reader at the Indian Town upon the Same Allowance as he was formerly paid.

No. Et. Parish of Chowan Sc.

At a Vestry held at the Chappel the 10th Day of December 1720.

Present

Nicholas Crisp John JORDAN} Church Wardens ffred JONES Esqr Capt. Henry BONNER} Capt. Samll. PATCHET Mr. James ffARLOW Thomas GARRET Junr.}

Thomas ROUNTREE took and Subscribed the Several Oaths for his Qualification as a member of this Vestry.

Mr. John JORDAN Church Warden for the Upper District from Tottering Bridge and Upwards made up his Accounts Vizt.   Cr

	£ s d	Pr. Contra	£ s d
John JORDAN Dr. 211 Tythables at 5 shll. each is -- --	52:15:0	Paid Paul PHILLIPS for reading } at the Indian Town from 1st of June} to the 1st. of Janry. last -- -- -- }	9: 6: 8
	54: 2:11		
Due to Mr. JORDAN -- --	1: 7:11		

(35) *(35)*   A. D. 1720

And is Dr. for 6 Tythables 2 years		Paid Edwd. WOOD for keeping} Mary GENT -- -- -- }	£ s d 3: 0: 0
		Paid John SIVERS for keeping }	

10 December 1720

(35) (Cont.)

Elizabeth **MUNS** }	6: 0: 0
To Building the Chappel --	30: 0: 0
Comissns. at 3 Pr. Cent --	1:11: 0
Cloths to Elisabeth **MUNS**	4: 5: 3
	54: 2:11

Robert **HICKS** Collector of the Parish Dues in the lower Part of the North Shore of Chowan made up his Accounts for 228 Tythables at 5 Shillings each £55:s5:d0- and paid the Same to the Revd. Doctr. **URMSTON**

Ordered that the Sum of £24:s15:d0 be paid to the Revd. Doctr. **URMSTON** out of the ensuing Years Collection.

Ordered that Mr. **JORDAN** be paid the Ballance of the Account out of his Delinquents.

Ordered that Capt. Henry **BONNER** and Mr. James **FARLOW** be appointed Church Wardens for this year.

Ordered that Thomas **MATTHEWS** be paid the Sum of 15? pounds for keeping &c. Elisa. **HARRIS**

Ordered that the Church Wardens Sue William **BRANCH** for? the Money paid by this Vestry for keeping Elisa. **HARRIS** She being wounded at the Said **BRANCH**es House and in his Service.

Ordered that Thomas **YATES** be allowed £3:s10:d0 and Thomas **MUNS** £2:s10:d0 for maintaining Elisa. **MUNS** And that the Church Hardens do further provide for her as they See Necessary.

Ordered that Mathew **BRYAN** be allowed 50 sh? for maintaini__ Wm **JONES**.

Ordered that the Sum of 40£ be paid to the Revd. Doctr. **URMSTON** for this Present Year.

Ordered that the Church Wardens do levy and Collect the Sum of five Shillings on every Tythable Person in this Paris_ on or before the first of Janury. next being the Levy due for this Present Year. 21

(36) _36? No. Et. Parish of Chowan *A D 1722*

At a Vestry held at the Chappel the 7th Day of May 1722.
Present
Capt. Henry **BONNER** James **ffARLOW**} Church Wardens Coll. Edward **MOSELEY** Majr. Thos. **LUTEN** Mr. Jno. **BLOUNT**} Mr. Thos. **GARRET** Senr. Mr. Thos. **GARRET** Junr. Capt. Samll. **PATCHET** Mr. Jno **JORDAN**}

Ordered that Christopher **GALE** Esqr. be appointed a Member of the Vestry in the Room of ffrederick **JONES** Esqr. dececd.

There appearing to be due to the Revd. Mr. Jno. **URMSTON** the Sum of one hundred thirty Eight Pounds five Shillings for the time he has officiated in this Parish including the one half of the Money that was due to the Said Mr. **URMSTON** before the Division of the precinct into two Parishes.

Ordered that the Church Wardens for the Year 1720 do upon making up their Accounts for the Same Year pay the Ballance in their Hands towards paying that Sum due to the Said Mr. **URMSTON**.

It is also further Ordered that the Said Church Wardens do Collect of each Tythable in the parish the Sum of 7s/6d Pr. Pole for the Year 1721. And pay the Ballance of the Said Collection or Payment to the Said Mr. **URMSTON** as Part of the Money due to him And that what Shall appear to remain unpaid of the aforesaid £138:s5:d0 to the Said Mr. **URMSTON** when the two Payments are made shall be raised and Collected out of the Parish Tax to be Collected for this Present Year.

Ordered that for the more Speedy and easy Payment of the aforesaid 7/6 Tax the Church Wardens or Such as shall be appointed by them do collect the Same by going from house to House in Regard that timely and convenient Notice can't well be given to the Inhabitants to bring in their Taxes and that there is no List of Tythables taken, for which They be allowed on their Accounts ten pr. Cent.

Ordered that a Vestry be appointed at the Chappel on Sunday next the 13th. of this Inst.

(37) *(37)* At a Vestry held at Edenton for the No. Et. Parish of Chowan the 9th. Day of March 1722/3. *A. D. 1722/3* [Three illegible words.]
Present
Coll. Edward **MOSELEY** Mr. Jno. **BLOUNT** Majr. Thos. **LEUTEN** Capt. Nichl. **CRISP**} Capt. Samll **PATCHET** Mr. Thos. **GARRET** Senr. Mr. Thos. **GARRET** Junr. Mr. Jno. **JORDAN**

Capt. Henry **BONNER** Church Warden for the Lower District made up the Accounts of his Collections as followeth Vizt.

Dr.	£ s d	Cr	£ s d
To 139 Tythables at 5 shill. }		Paid **MATTHEWS** for keeping}	
for the Year 1720 deducting }	31. 5. 6	Elisabeth **HARRIS** -- -- }	15: 0 0
10 pr. Cent. for Commissions}		To Matthew **BRYAN** for burying}	
To 173 Tythables at 7s/6d }		&c. Wm. **JONES** }	2:10: 0
for the year 1721 deducting}	58:17: 6	To Thos. **YATES** for Widow}	

9 March 1722/3

(37) (Cont.) Commissions}

To ffines Nt. Proceeds	17:02: 0	**MUNS** -- }	3:17: 6
	107: 5: 0	To Henry **BONNER** for clearing}	
	29 : 1:10	Church Lotts &c -- --	3: :
Ballance due -- --	78: 3: 2	To Henry **BONNER** for burying}	
		Thomas **ffAVOUR** }	2
			26:17:
		Paid Clerks fees for }	
		Prosecuting the Suit}	
		agt. **BRANCH** }	2: 4: 1?
			29:10:10?

Which was all paid to Mr. **MOSELEY** in Part of the Money due to the Revd. Doctr. **URMSTON** Pursuant to a former Order of the Vestry.

Mr. James **FARLOW** Church Warden for the Upper District his Accounts are thus Stated Vizt.

Dr.

	£ s d		£ s d
To 135 Tythables at 5 shillings}		Paid Paul **PHILLIPS** for 2}	
for the Year 1720 Nt. proceeds}	30: 7:6	Years Reading -- -- -- }	32:0:0
To 114 Tythables at 7/6 for the}	38:10:0	To Thomas **MUNS** for main- }	
Year 1721 -- -- -- --		taining of the Widow **MUNS** }	
To Fines -- -- -- --	1: 2:6	and Cloathing her excepting }	13:8:
	70: 0:0	the last 9 Months when discharged}	
	49: 0:6		
Ball. Due is -- -- -- --	20:19:6 22		

(38)

	To **COPELAND** for clearing round} £ s d	A. D. 1723
	the Chappel and one Years keeping it} 1:10:0	
	clean -- -- -- -- }	
	To John **CHAMPION** in Part for the}	
	Chappel Floor -- -- -- -- -- } 1:10:0	
	To Mr. **JORDAN** -- -- -- -- 0 12:6	
	49: 0:6	

Which Said Ballance of £20:s19:d6 is also paid to Mr. **MOSELEY** in Part of the Money due to Mr. **URMSTON** So that there Remains now due to the Said Doctr **URMSTON** -- -- -- -- -- £29 s2:d4.

There appearing to be less Tythables in Mr. **FARLOW**s List of Tythables for the Last Year than is in the first Years List.
Ordered that he do account for the Tythables uncollected in the last Years List.
There appearing to be due to Dr. Godfry **SPRUIL** the Sum of 12£ for his Cure of an Indigent Person.
Ordered that the Sum of 4 Pounds be paid by this Parish which is their Proportionable Part thereof.
There appearing to be due from the Parish these Sums following

Vizt.   £ s d
To Doctor **URMSTON** -- -- -- -- -- --   29: 2: 4
To Doctor **NEWNAM** -- -- -- -- -- --   10: 0: 0
To Mr. **JORDAN** for Paul **PHILIPS** -- --   4: 0: 0
To Godfrey **SPRUIL** -- -- -- -- -- --   4: 0: 0
To Thomas **MUNS** -- -- -- -- -- -- --   4:10: 0
To Robert **HICKS** -- -- -- -- -- -- --   4:17: 6
                                         56: 9:10

Ordered that Mr. John **BLOUNT** and Mr. Thos. **GARRET** Junr. be appointed Church Wardens and that they Levy and collect the Sum of three Shillings from every Tythable Person in this Parish for this Present year which ends the 25th of this Instant March.

Ordered that a Meeting of the Vestry be appointed on the first Day of May next.

(39) *(39)* At a Vestry held at Edenton the first Day of May 1723. *Edenton first mentioned*
Present. Thomas **NEWNAM** Missr: Thos. **GARRET** Church Warden Coll. Chrr. **GALE** Coll. Edward **MOSELEY**} Majr. Thomas **LUTEN** Capt. Henry **BONNER** Mr. James **FARLOW** Mr. Thomas **ROUNTREE** *A. D. 1723*.

1 May 1723

(39) *(Cont.)* The honoble: Christopher **GALE** Esqr. paid to this Vestry forty Shillings the Fines of John **CHARLTON** and William **CHARLTON** Junr.

Also fifty Shillings for the Lapse of Lotts in Edenton deducting 5 pr. Ct. commissions makes the Sum Total -- -£4:s5:d6

Capt. Henry **BONNER** paid in 10 shillings for the Fines of David **AMBROSS** and William **SADLER**. Also accounted for five Pounds Edward **HOWCOTT**s Fine four Pounds of which was paid to John **ffARLOW** [or **HARLOW**] towards the Maintainance of Sarah **SIMPSON**s Bastard Child. The Sum in the whole deducting Commissions at 5 Pr. Cent was -- £1?:s5:d0

Robt. **HICKS** Collector of the Parish Dues made up his Accounts for 370 Tythables at 3 shillings Pr. pole deducting Commissions at 15 Pr. Ct. made the Sum of £46:3:6. which together with £5:s10:d0 paid in by Coll. **GALE** and Capt. **BONNER** made the whole to be £51:s14:d0 in the Hands of the S___ Robt. **HICKS**. Which the Said Robert is ordered to pay According to the Orders of the last Vestry.

Ordered that the Reverend Mr. **NEWNAM** Missionary be paid the Sum of ten Pounds out of the next Years Collection to make good the Sum of twenty Pounds which was promised by the Vestry for his Officiating part of the last Year in this Parish. *Rev. Mr. NEWNAM.*

Ordered that the Sum of Sixty Pounds shall be paid to the Revd. Mr. **NEWNAM** out of the next Years Collections in Consideration that the Said Mr. **NEWNAM** officiate in this Parish for one whole Year to Commence from this Day, That is to Say, twenty Sundays in the next? Year at Edenton and ten Sundays in the Same Year at the Chappel neer the Indian Town the other Sundays in the Year being allowed the Said Missionary for his Attendance on other Parts of the Governm___ *{Division of Ministers time.*

Ordered that Mr. **ROUNTREE** be paid the Sum of five Pounds for his Reading at the Chappel near the Indian Town. 23

(40) *(40)* Mr. James **FARLOW** by Reason of Age and Infirmity praying to be discharged from his Attendance as a Vestry Man. *A. D. 1723.*

Ordered that he be discharged.

Ordered that Adam **COCKBURN** Esqr. be appointed a Member of the Vestry in the Room of Mr. James **FARLOW**, who was present and took and Subscribed the Declaration according to Law.

Ordered that William **COPELAND** be paid the Sum of twenty Shillings out of the next Years Collection for this last Years looking after the Chappel at the Indian Town.

At a Vestry held at Edenton the 18th. Day of Novbr. 1723
Present

Thomas **GARRET** Junr. Church Warden The honoble. Coll. Christr. **GALE** Coll. Edward **MOSELEY** Majr. Thomas **LUTEN** Capt. Nichl **CRISP**} Capt. Henry **BONNER** Capt. Samll. **PATCHET** Mr. Thomas **ROUNTREE** Adam **COCKBURN** Esqr.}

Mr. Thomas **GARRET** Senr. by Reason of Age and Infirmity Prays to be discharged from any further Attendance as a Vestry man.

Ordered that he be discharged and that Mr. William **BADHAM** be appointed a Member of the Vestry in the Room of Mr. Thomas **GARRET** who took and Subscribed the Oaths and Declaration by Law appointed for his Qualification

Coll. Christopher **GALE** paid into the Vestry the Sum of £3:s18:d6 which he received for Fines and Sales of Lotts.

The Reverend Mr. **NEWNAM** Missionary having officiated but one half of the Year and being departed this Life, the Vestry in Consideration of the Said Mr. **NEWNAM**'s Pious and good Behaviour during the Time of his Mission among Us and also being willing to contribute towards the Accommodation of his Widows intended Voiage to great Britain. *Rev. Mr. NEWNAM dies.*

It is Ordered that the whole Years Sallary be paid to his Widow notwithstanding his Decease. *His Widow receiving his years Salary.*

Ordered that a Letter be prepared to be Sent to the Society for propagating the Gospel in fforreign Parts humbly requesting to Send another Missionary to this Province.

(41) *(41)* Edenton in North Carolina. Novembr. ye. 18th. 1723.
Sr:

This brings You the Melancholy News of your worthy Missionary Mr. **NEWNAM**'s Death on whose Character and prudent Deportment We should think it our Duty to be herein very particular did not the Resolves of this Days Vestry (a Copy whereof is herein inclosed) Sufficiently Shew our Concern for so great a Loss; which occasions Us again to be Petitioners to Your honourable Board, that You would Still continue Your Favours towards Us by filling that Vacancy with Some Person of equall Meritt and unblameable Conversation, a thing to be wished for rather than expected. We heartily recommend his Widow to your Consideration of her Slender Circumstances occasioned by the Endeavours he was making to Settle himself amongst Us (the Circumstances of our parish not admitting Us to do more than what We have done) So not Doubting but the Same Charitable Disposition which has hitherto occasioned Your particular Notice of Us will _____ that Religious Worship within this Province may wholy _____ to your benign Influence. We have now not one Clergy Man with _____ Province, tho' it consists of Eleven Parishes

18 November 1723

(41) (Cont.) which unhappy State ___ humbly Submitted to the Consideration of the Honoble. Society by

Your most obliged and ___ obedt. humble Servants? *Second Letter to the "Society for propagating the Gospel"*

At a Vestry held at Edenton ye. 11th. Day of June 1724.
Present
Mr. Thos. **GARRET** Church Warden Capt. Nichl. **CRISP** Majr. Thos. **LUTEN** Capt. Henry **BONNER**} Capt. Samll. **PATCHET** Mr. John **JORDAN** Mr. Thos. **ROUNTREE** Mr. Adam **COCKBURN**.}

Ordered that Mr. John **BLOUNT** and Mr. Thomas **GARRET** Church Wardens do levy and collect the Sum of five Shillings from every Tythable Person in this Parish for the [sic] 1723. <u>24</u>

(42) The Choice of a Reader being debated and Mr. Robert **ROUTE** presenting himself for that Office. *A. D. 1724*

It is agreed that the Said Mr. Robert **ROUTE** do Serve in that Office And that he be allowed the Sum of fifteen Pounds Pr. Annum his Year to begin from the first of this Instant. *Mr. Robert ROUTE Reader.*

Ordered that there be a Meeting of the Vestry on the last of September next.

At a Vestry held at Edenton the 31st Day of November 1724.
Present
Thos. **GARRET** Jno. **BLOUNT**} Church Wardens Coll. Edward **MOSELEY** Majr. Thos. **LUTEN**} Majr. Henry **BONNER** Mr. Adam **COCKBURN** Capt. Samll. **PATCHET** Mr. Wm. **BADHAM**}

Ordered that the Church Wardens do collect the Sum of 5 shll. from every Tythable Person in this Parish for the Year 1724.

Ordered that Mr. Robert **JEFFRYS** be paid the Sum of fifteen Pounds Pr. Annum for his Officiating as a Reader at Edenton to commence from the first of July last. *Mr. Robt. JEFFRYS Reader.}*

Ordered that Mr. Thomas **ROUNTREE** be paid the Sum of ten Pounds Pr. Annum for his Officiating as a Reader at the Chappel at the Indian Town to commence from the last Year he was allowed five Pounds. *Mr. Thomas ROUNTREE Reader}*

Ordered that the Widow **COPELAND** be paid the Sum of 20 shillings Pr. Annum for keeping Clean the Chappel and Ground belonging to it at the Indian Town.

Ordered that the Church Wardens desire the Commissioners for building the Court House &c. to draw out of the Hands of the Lds. Proprs. Receiver General the Sum of two hundred Pounds Sterling and also the Sum of two hundred Pounds out of the Hands of the Publick Treasurer the Same being appropriated for the building a Church at Edenton, And that the Commissioners be desired to proceed on the Same Building. *Appropriations for building a Ct. House & Church}*

(43) (43) Pursuant to the Act of Assembly entitled an Act for Settling the Titles and Boundaries of Lands. The Vestry proceed to lay out this parish into Six Cantons or Districts as followeth: Vizt. *A. D. 1724*

The first being the Easternmost part of the parish from **DRUMMOND**s Point to that Part of Queen Ann's Creek whereon **HOSKINS**'s Bridge Stands inclusive for which Wm. **STUART** and Wm. **HAUGHTON** are appointed Processioners. *Parish boundaries defined.*

The Second District from that Branch of the Creek to the other Branch whereon the Long Bridge commonly called **LUTEN**'s Bridge inclusive for which Thomas **LUTEN** Jnr. and John **CHARLTON** are appointed Processioners

The third District from the last mentioned Creek to Indian Town Creek whereon **BALLARD**s Bridge Stands inclusive for which ffrancis **BRANCH** and William **HOLSEY** are appointed Processioners.

The fourth District from the Said Indian Creek [sic] to Catharine Creek all the Lands inclusive for which John **PARKER** and John **JORDAN** Junr. are appointed Processioners.

The fifth District from Catharine Creek to **BENNET**s Creek all the? Lands inclusive for which Aaron **BLANCHARD** and Richd. **MINSHEW** are appointed Processioners.

The 6th. all the Lands to the Northward of **BENNET**s Creek _____ John **COLLINS** and Jacob **OADHAM** are appointed Processioners.

Ordered that the Vestry be appointed to meet the third ___ in April next.

At a Vestry held at Edenton the 18th Day of Aug? 1725.
Present Thomas **GARRET** Church Warden Coll. Christopher **GALE** Coll. Edward **MOSELEY** Majr. Thomas **LEUTEN**} Capt. Nichl. **CRISP** Capt. Samll. **PAGET** Majr. Henry **BONNER** Mr. Wm. **BADHAM**}

The Honoble. Sr. Richard **EVERARD** Barrt. is appointed a Member of this Vestry who was accordingly qualified. <u>25</u>

(44) (44) Also the Reverend Doctr. John **BLACKNAL** who is received Minister Resident was Accordingly qualified. *Rev. Dr.*

18 Aug? 1725

(44) (Cont.) *John BLACKNAL Minister. A. D. 1725*

The honoble. Christopher **GALE** Esqr. paid in £3:s15:d0 he received for Fines.

Ordered that Majr. Thomas **LEUTEN** and Mr. Wm **BADHAM** be appointed Church Wardens in the Room of the former Church Wardens and that they Settle and receive the Accounts from the late Church Wardens.

This Vestry being acquainted that the Society expects that the Sum of fifty Pounds Sterling or the Value thereof Should be raised by the three Parishes wherein the Reverend Mr. **BLACKNAL** Shall officiate.

It is ordered that he be paid for his Officiating in this Parish the Ballance of the Church Wardens Accounts after the contingent Charges of the parish are deducted.

At a Vestry held at Edenton ye. 18th. Day of Janury. 1725/6

Prsent.
Majr. Thos. **LUTEN** Mr. Wm. **BADHAM**} Ch: Wardens Sr. Richd: **EVERARD** Bart. Christr. **GALE** Esqr. Edwd. **MOSELEY** Esqr.} Majr. Henry **BONNER** Capt. Nichl. **CRISP** Thos. **ROUNTREE** The Revd. Jno. **BLACKNAL** Missr.

Coll. Christopher **GALE** paid in the Sum of three Pounds which he received for Fines and the Sale of Lotts in Edenton.

Majr. Henry **BONNER** paid in the Sum of Seven Pounds which he received for Fines.

Information being made to the Vestry that there is Several Sums of Money in the Hands of Majr. John **WORLEY**.

(45) *(45)* Ordered that he do Account with the Church Wardens for Such Moneys as are due to this Parish before the Division of the Parish.

Information being made to the Vestry that there is Several Sums of Money in the Hands of Mr. William **CHARLETON** and Thos. **MATTHEWS** due to this Parish.

Ordered that they do Account with the Church Wardens for the Same.

Ordered that the Sum of five Shillings be levied and collected from every Tythable Person in this Parish for the Year 1725.

Capt. Nicholas **CHRISP** having paid the Sum of five Pounds to Mr. **BAILEY** for this Parish.

Ordered that the Same be paid him by the Vestry.

At a Vestry held at Edenton for the _____ Parish of Chowan the 10th. of July 1726. *A. D. 1726*

Prsent. Majr. Thos **LUTEN** Mr. Wm. **BADHAM**} Ch: Wardens The honoble. Sr. Richd: **EVERARD** Bart. Coll Christr. **GALE**} Coll. Edwd. **MOSELEY** Capt. Nichl. **CRISP** Capt. Samll. **PATCHET** Majr. Henry **BONNER**.

Mr. Wm. **LITTLE** is appointed a Vestry Man in the Room of Mr. John **BLOUNT** deceed who took and Subscribed the Oaths and Test by Law appointed for his Qualification.

There being a Vacancy of a Reader and Mr. Samuel **WARNER** offering himself.

Ordered that he be appointed to read at Edenton and that he be allowed the Sum of Sixteen Pounds Pr. Annum. *Mr. Samuel WARNER Reader.}*

Ordered that there be a Meeting of the Vestry on the Secand Sunday in August Next and that the Collector of the Parish Tax make up his Accounts and lay the Same before the Vestry. 26

(46) *(46)* At a Vestry held at Edenton the 5th Day of Janury. 1726. *A. D. 1726*

Present Wm. **BADHAM** Church Warden The honoble. Sir Richd **EVERARD** Bart. Coll. Edward **MOSELEY** Coll. Christr. **GALE**} Capt. Nichl **CRISP** Majr. Henry **BONNER** Mr. Wm. **LITTLE**

It being reported that Mr. **ROUNTREE** who is a Member of this Vestry is turned Anabaptist.

Ordered that the Clerk of the Vestry make Enquiry and report thereof to the next Vestry and that Mr. **ROUNTREE** be then desired to give his Attendance.

Ordered that the Sum of 2/6 be levied and collected from every Tythable Person in this Parish being the Parish Tax for the Year 1726.

May the J D? [sic]
At a Vestry held at Edenton the 23d Day of July 1727.
Present Majr. Thos. **LUTEN** Mr. Wm. **BADHAM**} C. Wardens The honoble. Sir Richd. **EVERARD** Bart. Coll. Christr. **GALE**} Majr. Henry **BONNER** Mr. Wm. **LITTLE** Mr. Thos. **GARRET**.

Thomas **HOBBS** an Indigent Person and an Inhabitant of this Parish praying to be relieved by this Vestry for his Maintainance.

Ordered that the Church Wardens enquire into the Circumstance of his Sons and report to the next Vestry if they are able to maintain him and that in the meantime the Said Thomas **HOBBS** be allowed by the Vestry fifteen Shillings Pr. Month for Maintainance to be paid by the Church Wardens.

23 July 1727

(47) *(47)* Upon the Petition of Wm. WESTON praying to be allowed for mai_taining one Francis PORIGREEN who lay Sick five Months who was delivered of two Children and then dyed with her Children. *A. D. 1727.*

Ordered that he be allowed and paid five Pounds for the Same and Trouble of Burial.

Ordered that Mr. Thomas ROUNTREE be allowed and paid Sixty? Pounds Pr. Annum for the Time he has read and Shall continue to Officiate in the Office of a Reader at the Chappel at the Indian [sic]

Ordered that Mr. Samll. WARNER be paid the Sum _____teen Pounds for Officiating in the Office of a Reader at Edenton the last Year and that he be continued in the Said Office.

Ordered that Mr. Edmond GALE be appointed a Member of this Vestry in the Room of Mr. Nichl. CRISP deceased who was _____dingly qualifyed.

Mr. Thomas ROUNTREE moving to the Vestry by Coll. _____ and Mr. GARRET to be excused from being a Member of this Vest__

Ordered that he be excused and that Jno LOVICK__ appointed a Member of the Vestry in his Room.

At a Vestry held at Edenton the 20__ ____ of ffebry. 1727/8.
Present Majr. Thos. LUTEN Mr. Wm. BADHAM} C. Wardens The honoble. Sir Richd. EVERARD Bart.} Coll. Chrr. GALE Coll. Edwd. MOSELEY Mr. Edmd. GALE.

Jno. LOVICK Esqr. qualifyed himself a Member of this Vestry

Coll. Christr. GALE paid to the Church Wardens forty five Sh__ arising by the Sale of 5 Lotts in Edenton Commiss. deduct 27

(48) *(48)* The Honoble. Sr. Richard EVERARD Barrt. and Coll. Edward MOSELEY are appointed Church Wardens in the Room of Majr. LUTEN and Mr. BADHAM

Coll. Edward MOSELEY made a Present to the Parish of a Silver Chalice and Plate with his Own Name Engraven thereon. *A. D. 1728 A Silver Chalice & Plate presented to the parish.*

Ordered that the Former Church Wardens make up their Accts. in Easter Week next

At a Vestry held at Edenton the 22d Day of April 1728.
Present Mr. William BADHAM-Church-Warden.
The Honoble. Sr. Richd EVERARD Bart. Coll. Edward MOSELEY Coll. Christr. GALE Jno. LOVICK Esqr.} Wm. LITTLE Esqr. Majr. Henry BONNER Capt. Samll. PAGET}

Mr. Wm. BADHAM Church Warden delivered his Accounts and there is a Ballance due to the Parish of £2:s10:d0 which is allowed him for the Maintainance and Care of Mary JOHNSON.

Robt. HICKS delivered his Accounts of the Collections of the Parish Tax and there appeared in Ballance due to the Parish £14 s18:d6. which is ordered to be Paid to Mr. WARNER towards his Sallary from July last.

Ordered that if the Inspectors of the Parish Accts. desire to See the Accounts of the Parish that the Clerk of the Vestry lay the Same before them and Suffer them to take Copys thereof in his Presence if required.

Mr. BADHAM late Church Warden delivered the Chalice and Plate to the Honoble. the Govr. now one of the Church Wardens.

The former Church Wardens having made up their Accounts are discharged The Honoble. the Govr. and Coll. Edward MOSELEY now Church Wardens enter upon their Office.

(49) *(49)* Mr. John JORDAN praying to be excused from attending as a Member of this Vestry by Reason of Age and Infirmity. *A. D. 1728.*

Ordered that he be excused and that Mr. Thomas LEUTEN Junr. be a Member of the Vestry in his Room.

Dr. the the [sic] No. East Parish of Chowan in No. Carolina to William BADHAM Church-Warden.

		£ Shll d
1725	For Doctor's Fees for attending Alexander GOREHAM -- -- --	1: 0: 0
Sept. 12th	For Expences and Funeral Charges on the Said GOREHAM -- --	5: 0:0
Decbr. 24th	Paid for Sweeping and adorning the Church -- -- -- -- -- --	0: 5:0
	For Bread and Wine for the Sacrament -- -- -- -- -- -- --	1: 0: 0
	For Bread and Wine for the Sacrament the Easter following -- --	1: 0: 0
1726	Pd to Elijah HEWS for Making Benches -- -- -- -- -- --	1: 0: 0
Decbr. 24th.	Pd for Sweeping and adorning the Church -- -- -- -- -- -- --	0: 5:0
1727 June ye 10th.	For Bills pd. to Abraham HOBBS for Relief -- -- -- --	1: 0: 0
Sept. 28th	To Wm. PEARCE for keeping the Said HOBBS from the 20th. of July last	2: 5:0
Octobr. 12th.	To Do for keeping the Said HOBBS from the Said Day to the 22d of April 1728}	6: 5:0?

22 April 1728

(49) (Cont.) Decbr.the 24th. ffor Sweeping and Adorning the Church			0: 5:0
To Mary **TANNER** for cleaning the Same Sundry Times			0:10:0
To an Abatement by the Vestry of Wm. **SADLER** it being allowed} to his Widow }			0:10:0
Ballance due to the Parish and is allowed to the Said **BADHAM**} for maintainance and Care of Mary **JOHNSON** and Indigent } Person in the Said Parish }			2:15?:0
	Except Errors ye. 22d. April 1728		£23: 0: 0
	Pr. William **BADHAM** Church Warden.		

1725	Pr. Contra.		Cr.	£ s d
Sept. ye. 13th.	By a Fine Received from Jno. **NORCOMB** for fighting	F		0:10:0
	By Do. from Bat **SCOTT** for fighting and being drunk	i		0:15:0
Octbr. the 18th.	By Do. of Wm. **DAY** for Sabbath-breaking	n		0:10:0
Janry 25th.	By Do. of Geo. **ALLEN** for beating Mr? **MARSTON**	e		0:10:0
March ye. 22d.	By Do. of Mrs. **RUSTON** for her Maid's Fornication	s		2:10:0
1726	By Do. of Luke **WHITE** the 9th. Instant for Fornication			2:10:0 28

(50) *(50)*		£ s d
April ye. 6th.	By Do of Mr. Everard **BOWDEN** and **CITTERN** for fighting	1:10:0
May ye. 5th.	By Do. of Wm. **SADLER** and peter **YOUNG** for fighting	1: 0:0
Do. 9th.	By Do. of Peter **OSBURN** for Beating Jane **TAYLOR**	0:10:0
Do. 14th.	By Do. of Catharine **DENEVAN** for beating little Judith	0:10:0
Do. 26th.	By Do. of Bat **SCOTT** for beating Thos. **BETTERLY**	0:10:0
Janury. 6th	By Do. Luke **WHITE** for Fornication	2:10:0
March ye. 11th.	By Do. of Bat. **SCOTT** for beating Cath. **DENEVAN**	0:10:0
1727		
May ye. 29th.	By Do. of Judith **SLADE** for ffornication	2:10:0
June ye. 24th.	By Do. of Mr. **EVERARD** for Beating Mrs. **LLOYD**	0:10:0
Do. ye. 27th.	By Do. of Jno. **SYMONS** for Fornication	2:10:0
Novbr. ye. 1st.	By Do. of Mr. **JONES** and Michael **RYAN** for fighting	1: 0:0
	By Coll. **GALE** receed 45 sh. for Sale of Lotts in Edenton	2: 5:0
	(Fines. See above)	£23: 0:0

1725	Dr. the No Et Parish of Chowan Prcinct to Robt **HICKS** Collector of the Parish Levy.	£ s d
	To the Commissions for the Collecting £157.s5:d11	22: 2:6
	Paid Majr. **BONNER**	4: 0:0
	Paid Mr. **ROUNTREE**	5: 0:0
	Paid Thos. **MUNNS**	10: 2:0
	ffor Copys of the Laws for the Processioners	1:10:0
	Over paid to the Parish by Mistake last Year	7:10:0
	Attending the Vestrys	3: 0:0
	Paid Mr. **SPRUIL**	4: 0:0
	Paid the Widow **COPELAND**	2: 0:0
	Paid Jno. **CHAMPION**	15: 0:0
	Paid Mr. **NEWNAM**	70: 0:0
	Paid Mr. **JEFFRYS** Reader	16: 5:0
		£160: 9:6

1726}			
	Pr. Contra	Cr	
By the Collection of 590 Tythables at 5s. each including} the Years 1723 & 1724 }			147:10:0
By receed of Coll **GALE** for Fines and Sale of Lots in Edenton}			3:15:0

22 April 1728

(51) *(51)*

	£ s d
By Receed of Majr. BONNER -- -- -- -- -- -- -- -- -- -- -- -- -- -- -- --	7: 0:0
By Receed of Coll. GALE -- -- -- -- --Witness -- -- -- -- -- -- -- --	3: 0:0
	£161: 5:0
	160: 9:6
Ballance due to the Parish	£...:15:6
Except Errors Pr. Robt. HICKS Collr.	

{1726} Dr. the No. Et. Parish of Chowan Prcinct to Robt. HICKS Collector of the Parish Levys.

	£ s d
Paid Mr. BLACKNALL -- -- -- -- -- -- -- -- -- -- -- -- -- -- --	54:10:0
Paid Do. by Majr. BONNER -- -- -- -- -- -- -- -- -- -- -- -- --	1: 0:0
Paid Do. by Edward STANDING -- -- -- -- -- -- -- -- -- -- -- --	0:10:0
Paid Do. by Mr. ROUNTREE -- -- -- -- -- -- -- -- -- -- -- --	0:10:0
Paid Mr. CRISP -- -- -- -- -- -- -- -- -- -- -- -- -- -- -- --	0: 5:0
Paid Mr. ROUNTREE for Reading -- -- -- -- -- -- -- -- -- --	5?:10:0
Pd. Widow COPELAND -- -- -- -- -- -- -- -- -- -- -- -- --	2:10:0
Pd. Reading at Indian Town Chappel 3 Months -- -- -- -- -- --	4: 0:0
Attending and Summoning Vestrys -- -- -- -- -- -- -- -- -- --	3: 0:0
To Commissions of £97:s15:d0 -- -- -- -- -- -- -- -- -- --	4:10:2
	£87:15:9?

Pr. Contra	Cr
By Ballance of My last Accts. as above -- -- -- -- -- -- -- -- -- --	15:6
By the Collection of 391 Tythables at 5 Shill. Each for the } Year 1725 -- -- -- -- -- -- -- -- -- -- -- -- -- -- --}	97:15:0
	£98:10:6
	87:15:9
Ballance due to the Parish	£10:14:9
Except Errors Pr. Robt. HICKS Collr. 29	

(52) *(52)* 1726} Dr. the No. E. Parish of Chowan to Robt. HICKS Collector

	£ s d
To Commissions of £49.s12:d6 -- -- -- -- -- -- -- -- -- --	7: 9:0
Pd. Mr. WARNER for Reading to July last -- -- -- -- -- -- --	16: 0:0
Pd. Mr. ROUNTREE for Reading to this 22d. of April 1728 -- --	16: 0:0
Pd. Wm. WESTON -- -- -- -- -- -- -- -- -- -- -- -- -- --	5: 0:0
Pd. the Widow COPELAND -- -- -- -- -- -- -- -- -- -- --	1: 0:0
	£45: 9:0

Pr. Contra	Cr
By Ballance of last Accounts -- -- -- -- -- -- -- -- -- --	10:14:9
By 397 Tythables at 2/6 each for the Year 1726 -- -- -- -- -- --	49:12:6
	£60: 7:3
	45: 9:0
	£14:18:3
Except Errors this 22d. Day of April 1728.	
Pr. Robt. HICKS Collectr.	

At a Meeting of the Vestry for the No. Et. Parish of Chowan at Edenton the 23d. of Febry. 1728/9
Present E MOSELEY Church Warden Jno. LOVICK Esqr. Coll. Chrr. GALE Edmond GALE Esqr.} Wm. LITTLE Majr. Henry BONNER Capt. Samuel PATCHET}

Ordered that the Sum of twelve Pounds be paid unto Coll. Edwd. MOSELEY for Moneys by him Expended for the Parish Service Vizt.

Five Pounds to the Revd. Mr. FOUNTAIN *Rev Mr. FOUNTAIN-*
Five Pounds to the Revd. Mr. MARSDEN " " *MARSDEN-*

23 February 1728/29

(52) (Cont.) for their Officiating at Edenton and forty Shillings Pd. to the Revd. Mr. **MARSDEN**s Clerk who attended him.

(53) *53* Also Sixteen Pounds to Mr. **WARNER** Reader for the Present Year ending the 17th. of July next 'till which Time he is to officiate for it. *A. D. 1728.*

Also to Mr. Wm. **WILLIAMS** £6:s17:d6 for Expences and attendance on Margaret **SCOTT** during her Sickness And for Coffin and ffuneral Charges.

Also to the Reader of the Upper Chappel as usual.

Ordered that there be a Parish Tax of 2/6 on Every Tythable Person in the Parish to be Collected by the Person that Collects the Publick Tax, if he will undertake it, at a Rate not exceeding 10 Pr. Ct., and if the Collector of the Publick Tax will not undertake the Collection, then the Church-Wardens are to agree with Such Person as they Shall think proper for which Collection Security is to be given to the Church Wardens.

And that Edmond **GALE** Esqr. and Mr. Thos. **LUTEN** be Church Wardens for the next ensuing Year.

Ordered that the Reader at Edenton be Clerk of the Vestry
Ordered that all Moneys Fines &c be brought to the Vestry at? Easter next.
Then the Vestry adjourned untill Easter Monday Next.

E. **MOSELY** Church Warden Chrr. **GALE** Jno. **LOVICK** Wm. **LITTLE** Edmond **GALE** Henry **BONNER** Samuel **PATCHET** 30

(54) *(54)* At a Meeting of a Vestry for the No. Et. Parish of Chowan at Edenton the 7th. of April 1729. *A. D. 1729*
Present Edmd. **GALE** Esqr, Ch-Warden Majr. Henry **BONNER** Capt. Thos. **LUTEN** Ch-Warden Christr. **GALE** Esqr.} Jno. **LOVICK** Esqr. Wm. **LITTLE** Esqr. Mr. Wm. **BADHAM**.

Mr. Thomas **LEUTEN** Junr. having been formerly chosen a Vestryman this Day appeared and qualifyed himself according to Law and took his Place in the Vestry accordingly.

Edmond **GALE** Esqr. and Mr. Thomas **LUTEN** Junr having been named for Church-Wardens by the last Vestry are now elected and Chosen Church-Wardens for this Parish for the Year ensuing.

Ordered that another Vestry meet on Whitson Monday next and that the Clerk of the Vestry give Notice of the Said Meeting to the late Church-Wardens that they may prepare to make up their Accounts to the Said Vestry and that in the mean while the Honoble. the Govr. be desired to deliver up the Chalice and Plate to the Clerk of the Vestry to be delivered to either of the Prsent Church-Wardens. *Church Plate*

It is ordered that the Present Church Wardens make Enquiry for the Standards for Weights and Measures that belong to the Parish and make Report thereof to the next Vestry.

And that the Clerk Search the old Orders of the Vestry to See what Standards were bought for the Use of the Parish, and return an Account thereof to the Next Vestry.

Mr. **HICKS** the former Clerk being ordered to transcribe the old Orders of the Vestry into a Bound Book and he failing therein It is ordered that the Present Clerk do the Same.

Edmond **GALE** Thos. **LUTEN** Junr.} Ch-Wardens Christr. **GALE** Jno. **LOVICK** Wm. **LITTLE** Henry **BONNER** Wm. **BADHAM**

(55) *55)* At a Meeting of a Vestry for the No. East Parish of Chowan at Edenton the 2d. Day of Novbr. 1729. *A. D. 1729.*
Present Edmond. **GALE** Esqr. Mr. Thos. **LEUTEN** Junr.} Ch-Wardens Jno **LOVICK** Esqr. Chrr. **GALE** Esqr. Mr. Wm. **LITTLE** Mr. Wm. **BADHAM**.

Ordered that the Child be returned to Charles **WILKINS** that was left by Him at Mr. Thos. **LUTEN**'s, and that the Said Charles appear the next Vestry.

Ordered that there be a Meeting of the Vestry the Sunday next ensuing.

Chowan Sc

At a Meeting of the Vestry for the No. East Parish of Chowan at Edenton the 9th Day of Nov__ 1729.
Present Edmd. **GALE** Capt. Thos. **LUTEN** } Church-Wardens Jno **LOVICK** Esqr. Coll. Christr. **GALE**} Mr. Wm. **BADHAM** Majr. Henry **BONNER** Wm. **LITTLE** Esqr.

Ordered that there be a Parish Tax of Two Shillings & Six Pence on every Tythable Person in the Parish to be collected by the Church Wardens with the Arrears due last Year.

Ordered that Charles **WILKINS** be paid for Expences and Funer__ Charges on the Account of Ann **PETER** - £.9:5:0. 31

(56) Ordered that Edmond **GALE** Esqr receive from Charles **WILKINS** all the Cloaths and other things belonging to Ann

9 November 1729

(56) (Cont.) PETER deceed, he giving Bond to indemnifie the Parish of? the Said Ann PETER's Child and that he also receive Six Pounds more Advance. *56*

Majr. Henry BONNER paid into the Church Wardens Hand Six Pounds which he received from Mr. Wm. CHARLTON Senr. for Fines the Said Wm. CHARLTON had formerly received.

And the Tax Money was then Paid to Edmond GALE Esqr. being the Six Pounds allowed on Account of his taking the Child aforementioned.

Edmond GALE Thos. LUTEN Junr. Jno. LOVICK Christr. GALE Wm. LITTLE Wm. BADHAM Henry BONNER

At a Meeting of the Vestry for the No. East Parish of Chowan Easter Munday 1731. *A. D. 1731*
Present Edmd. GALE Esqr. Mr. Thos. LUTEN} Church Wardens John LOVICK Esqr. Ed MOSELEY Esqr. Major Hen: BONNER Mr. Richd. PARKER Wm. LITTLE

Ordered that the tax this year be So Much pr Poll as with the Last years order will make in the Whole two Shillings & Six pence pr Ann: for the last y the Present year.

Order'd that Mr. WARNER be paid twenty five Shillings the Balance of Acts. due to him & that the Sd Acct. be enter'd in the Vestry book

Order'd that the Parish Accts be made up as Soon as may be & when ye Same are ready to be laid before the Vestry, that the Clerk of the Vestry doe Sum ons [sic] the Vestry to Meet.

Order'd that John CHAMPION be paid for Singling [sic] the Chappel.

Ed. MOSELEY Jno. LOVICK Emd. GALE Thos. LUTEN Hen: BONNER Richd. PARKER Wm. LITTLE

(57) [First line appears torn and illegible.] Parish of Chowan held at Edenton July the ___ 1731 *57 A. D. 1731.*
Present Edmd. GALE Esqr. Mr. Thos. LUTEN} Church Wardens John LOVICK Esqr. Ed MOSELEY Esqr. William LITTLE Esqr. Henry BONNER Esqr. Capt. Samuel PAGGETH [sic], Major Thos LOWICK, & Mr. Wilm. HINTON.

Edmund GALE Esqr. & Mr. Thos. LUTEN former Church Wardens made up their Accts. of what money they had Received & Pay'd which Accts. are as here followeth-Which are Ordered to be entered at So? in the Parish Book; the ballance Due to the Parish being 10 Shill. 6 pence.

Ordered that John ARLINE be continued & Paid for Mending ye. Chapel?

The following List of Weights & Measures belonging to the parish ___ given in by the Late Clark &c? Said to have been Lodged in the hands of Nicholas CRISP deceas'd viz. &c as pr: list

5½ Ct. one Qrtt? Do: one 14 One brass Yard One Iron Do: 3 brass Weights vizt. 4lb: & 2lb. &c. One Pair of brass Scales One Wine Gallon pewter One Pottle & one Quart Do: One half Bushell. One Peck.

Ordered that the Church Wardens do demand & Receive the Said Standard weights & Measures of the Executors of Nicholas CRISP.

Mr. LUTEN Church-Warden is allowed a Demand on the Parish 10 Shillings & 6 pence; which is Allowed & ballences ye Acct. of ___ Said former Church Wardens *32*

(58) [First line missing.] *58*
Dr	To Sundry payments made pr Order viz: to Mr. LUTEN}		
	Church Warden-- -- -- -- -- -- -- -- -- -- -- }		39:15:0
	To Mr. GALEs Acct Church Warden}		
	[illegible] To Mr. JEFFRYES -- --}	12:00:0	
	To himself-- -- -- -- -- -- -- --	25:00:0	
	To Ditto -- -- -- -- -- -- -- --	2:00:0	
	To Ditto-- -- -- -- -- -- -- --	18:10:0	
	To Ditto-- -- -- -- -- -- -- --	20:10:0	
		78 00:0	78:00:0
	To William BRANCH pr Order -- -- -- -- -- -- -- --		1:10:
	To pd. to Mr. CLAXTON pr Order-- -- -- -- -- -- --		1:00:
	To Mr. WARNER &c -- -- -- -- -- -- -- -- -- --		1:05:
	To Ditto -- -- -- -- -- -- -- -- -- -- -- --		3:02
	To Mr. Thos. ROUNTREE-- -- -- -- -- -- -- --		5:09:
	To Mr. WARNER the Collections he Received -- -- -- --		10:00:
	To Coll: MOSELEY pd.-- -- -- -- -- -- -- --		3:05:
	To Commiss. on 170:12:6 at 15 pr Ct.-- -- -- -- --		25:12:
	To Ballance Due to Church Wardens -- -- -- -- --		168:18:

July 1731

(58) (Cont.)
To Commissn. on Mr. **PORTER**s Levyes & Mr. **VEAL**s -- --   0:17
                                                               169:15
                                                                 6:11
                                                               170:07

        Cr.
By Levyes received for the year 1728 being 661}
Tythables at 2s. 6d. -- -- -- -- -- -- } -- --   82:
By Levyes for the year 1729 being 704 at 2s & 6}
pr head -- -- -- -- -- -- -- -- -- --} -- --   88:
By Mr. **PORTER**'s Levyes -- -- -- -- -- -- -- -- -- -- -- --   03:
By Mr. **VEAL**s Ditto -- -- -- -- -- -- -- -- -- -- -- --   02?
                                                              178?

00072. _72 [Written vertically near bottom of page.]

(59) The Vestry of the North ____ Parish of Chowan *A. D. 1731*
To Edmund **GALE** Esqr. & Mr. Thos. **LUTEN**. Church Wardens
Dr.
To Commission allowed of Edwd.? **HAUCOT** for Collecting}
£176:7:6 -- -- -- -- -- -- -- -- -- -- -- -- } --   25:12:
To money paid to Mr. Thos **ROUNDTREE**. pr Ed. **HAUCOT** -- --   05:__:
To Mr. **WARNER** in Mr. **HAUCOT**s Acct. -- -- -- -- -- --   10:00:
To Ditto -- -- -- -- -- -- -- -- -- -- -- -- --   03:02:?
To Ditto -- -- -- -- -- -- -- -- -- -- -- -- --   01:00:
To Collonel **MOSELEY** pr Ditto -- -- -- -- -- -- -- --   03:__:
To More Commissions allowed alowed [sic] Mr. **HAUCOT** -- -- --   00:10?
To Ditto's Acct. pd. Mr. **CLAXTON** 20S. & Wm. **BRANCH** 30S.   02:10
To **JEFFRYES** for keeping the Butcher -- -- -- -- -- -- --   12:00
To Mary **STONE** 2£:5s.:0d: Judith **SLADE** 20s. -- -- -- --   03:05:
To Mr. Wm. **ARKILL** for Boarding Rachel **DOLDRIGE** -- -- --   12:1_
To Wm **BRANCH** 20S. pr Thos **LUTEN**? 20S. Ditto pr Ed. **GALE**   _:0
To Rachell **DOLDRIGE**   01:_
To John **PARKER** ___ burying? _ta_am **HOBBY**   06:04?
To Mr. **WILLIAMS** for Marget **LEE** -- -- -- -- -- -- --   06:17?
To John **FLENCER**? for Rachel **DOLDRIGDE** -- -- -- --   05:15?
To boarding John **WILLIAMS** -- -- -- -- -- -- -- --   01:15?
To lining & Making up Breeches for Ditto -- -- -- -- -- --   00:__
To Carrying him to Tarripin hill -- -- -- -- -- -- -- --   00:__
To the Revd. Mr. **MARSDEN** for a Sarmen -- -- -- -- --   05:00 *Rev Mr. MARSDEN*
To the Revd. Mr. **ROBINSON** for a Sarmen -- -- -- --   05:00 *Rev. "ROBINSON*
To the Butcher-Sundries -- -- -- -- -- -- -- -- -- --   01:11?
To Mr. **JEFFRYES** More for John **WILLIAMS** -- -- -- -- --   02:13
To Charles **WILKINS** pr Order -- -- -- -- -- -- -- --   09:05
To Bills paid Mr. **WARNER** -- -- -- -- -- -- -- --   25:15
To John **WILLIAMS** 5S -- -- -- -- -- -- -- -- -- --   00:05
To Linnen & Shirt Made for Ditto -- -- -- -- -- -- --   01:07?
To Ditto Britches & Making -- -- -- -- -- -- -- --   00:15
To 3½ yards Dowless for Ditto -- -- -- -- -- -- -- --   01:09
To the Revd. Mr. **JONES** for a Sermon -- -- -- -- --   05:00 *Rev Mr. JONES*
To Collonel **MOSLEY** wt. he Advanced for the Parish -- -- --   08:15
To ballance Due to the Parish -- -- -- -- -- -- -- --   00:10
                                                         187:04 33

(60) By the Collections for the Years 1728 & 1729} *A. D. 1731*   s d
pr Mr. Ed **HAUCOT** vizt. 176£. 7s: 6d -- }   75:7:6

July 1731

(60) (Cont.)

By Judith SLADE fine	1: 5:0
By Mary JONES fine	1: 5:0
By William CULLs? fine	2:10:0
By Rebecca HILL?	1: 5:0
By bills of Christor. GALE Esqr for Lots Sold	2:17:6
By Anne HILL a fine	1: 5:0
By Mr. WILLIAMS a fine	0:10:0
	127:04:0

Made up July 3d. 1731

Mr. Thos. LORVICK & Mr. Richard PARKER having been Chosen Church-Wardens to Succeed Mr. GALE & Mr. LUTEN when they made up their Accts, which they having now done the Said Church-Wardens for the year Coming are now Confirmed, & for the future to Act and on Settling Accts. of ye. Parish it Appears that the Parish Levy of 2s. & 5d. for the Year 1730 is Unpay'd, & also for the present Year the Levy of 2s. & 6d to be Collected next Season by law Appointed for Collections; but there being Money Due to Mr. SAGG for his Reading it is Order'd that the Church Wardens Impower Mr. SAGG to Collect in the Neighbourhood So much of the Year 1730 Due as will pay him, & give in the Rect; And Mr. ROUNTREEs Acct. is Referred till ye Collections Come to be made, & then what Shall Appear Due to him to be paid.

Order'd that Mr. ROUNTREE Read One Sunday at the Chappell and another about Mr. Abraham HILLs till further Order: -- And his Acct. is Settled & that their is Due to him 42£: 11s. 0d. for being Reader till Aprill ye. 22d. 1731. And that the Church Wardens Impower him to Collect in his Neighbourhood So much for the Year 1730 as to pay him.

Edmund GALE Thos. LUTEN} Church Wardens John LORVICK Wm. LITTLE Hen: BONNER Thos LORVICK Samll. PAGGETH Ed: MOSELEY Wm HINTON

(61) Att a meeting of the Vestry for the North East Parish of Chowan on Easter Munday 1732. The following Persons were voted and allowed to be of the Vestry viz. Christopher GALE Esqr. Edward MOSELEY Esqr. Edmund GALE Esqr. William LITTLE Esqr. Henry BONNER Esqr. Mr Thos LUTEN} Capt. Samuel PAGGITH Thos. LOVICK Esqr. Mr. William HINTON Mr. Isaac HUNTER George MARTIN Esqr. Mr. John PERRY Senr.} A. D. 1732

Easter Monday 1732 Present of the Vestry

Edward MOSELEY Edmund GALE William LITTLE Henry BONNER Thomas LUTEN Thomas LOVICK Samuel PAGGITH George MARTIN

The following Persons were Chosen Church wardens for the year Ensuing

George MARTIN Esqr. Mr. William HINTON} Church Wardens

It was agreed that a Parish tax be lay'd on all the tythables of this Parish of five Shillings pr Tythable to be Levyed for this Current year to be paid to the Church wardens for the Use of the Parish.

The Revd. Mr. GRANVILE having performed Divine Service in this Parish begining one forth night [sic] before Easter Sunday and the Vestry being willing to encourage him to Continue as well as that he be pay'd for the time past *Rev Mr. GRANVILLE*

It is Ordered that he be paid from the Sd Time he begun for One Year the aforesd. Sum to be raised by the Parish Tax now lay'd excepting Sixteen pounds pr Annum to be allowed to Mr. ROUNTREE for Continuing as Reader and the same to Mr. SAGG to Continue Reader and what other accidental Charges Shall arise in ye. Parish. And that the Said Mr. GRANVILE be Allowed pro rato for the time he Officiates, if he Serves less then a Year. And that he Officiate two Sundays out of five in the upper Parts of the Parish. viz. one at the Chappell & 34

(62) ___ Sunday in ye. five at or near Abraham HILLs and the Remaining Sun___ at Edenton; And the Church wardens Shall get what Subscriptions? [Approximately 10 words illegible.] for the encouraging him to stay amongst us

Ordered that the late? Church wardens make up their Accounts ____ the Present Church wardens as Soon as they Can to be laid before the next Vestry.

At a Vestry held at Edenton for the North East Parish of Chowan in the year 1733 March 26th

Present George MARTYN Mr. HINTON} Church Wardens William LITTLE Esqr. Edmd. GALE Esqr. Henry BONNER Esqr. Thomas LOVICK Esqr.} Mr. Thomas LUTEN Capt. Samuel PADGET Mr. John PERRY Mr. Isaac HUNTER}

Mr. Thomas LOVICK former Church Warden now produced his Accot. which are ordered to be Entered by the Clerk & the Ballance of his Accot. was £29..6..10.½. and the Accot. being Examoned it appeared that Mr. ROUNDTREE has been paid as

26 March 1733

(62) (Cont.) Reader till April 1732 & Mr. SAGG till Febry. 1732 and that Mr. ROUNDTREE collected of the Parish dues above BALLARDs bridge £105..7..0? and Mr. SAGG below BALLARDs Bridge in the whole the Sum of £59..9..0.. The Ballance is ordered to be paid to the Succeeding Church Wardens & accordingly was paid down £29..2..6 to George MARTYN Esqr Church Warden.

    Mrs. WILLIAMS Exx. to William WILLIAMS of Edenton deceasd. of Eight Pounds five Shillings due from the Parish for keeping Abraham PERKINS & the same is allowed & Ordered to be paid by the Church Wardens.

    Mr. HINTON Church Wardens accot

                                          Dr

(63) 63 Dr.

Parish to Mr HINTON		Cr.	
To money paid Vizt.		by money recd. by Sundry	
To cleaning the Chappel }		Collections	
5 Year & Eight Months }	£ 5..17..6	Tythables above BALLARDs	
for burying Anthony }		bridge	497
MACKEIL }	3..--..--	Insolvts.	33
Table for the Parish	1..10..--		464 at 5/ £116..--..--
Plank for the Chapple	3..--..--		
for burying F? GULLIVER	6.. 7..6		
To John CHAMPION for }			
burying a man }	5..--..--		
To Coms. on 116 at 15- }			
pr. Cent. }	17..18..--		
	42.. 2..--		
Due to Ball.	73..18..--		
	116..--..--		
John FREEMAN for }			
reading 6 Months }	73..18..--		
till Lady day 1733 }	- 8..--..--		
Due-	65..18..--		

According [sic] the Sum of £65..18..--. was paid to the Vestry and put into the Hands of Capt. MARTYN and the ____ pounds due to Mr. ROUNDTREE for the former Six months of this last Year he officiated, he is to be paid out of the Levys due in 1730 which he undertook to collect.

    John FREEMAN is continued Reader for the upper parts of ye Parish for the year Ensuing on the same terms Mr. ROUNDTREE officiated.

    The Vestry Ordd. a Levy of to be raised in the Parish the year Ensuing Year of five Shillings Pr. Pole. 35

(64) 64 [This page was written, in two columns, at 90° to the normal orientation.]

Dr. Thomas LOVICK   to the North East Parish of Chowan Precinct   Cr [Left column]

For fines arising & becoming due to the said parish & were delivered into his hands by Joseph JENOURE? Esqr.	-5 -- --
For Ditto Recd. of Mr. Thomas JONES and Mr. Samuel SWANN for fighting in Edenton	-1 -- -- Fine
For Do. recd. of W JONES for fighting as aforesd.	-1 -- -- Do
For Do. recd from J. VANPELT for prophane swearing	- 15 -- Do.
For Parish Levys Collected by Mr. SAGG as by his List appears	56 1 6
For Parish Levys Collected by Mr. ROUNDTREE as by his col? Lists ap will appear	105 .7 --
For more parish Levys recd. by Mr. SAGG as by his Accot. appears	3 7 6
	172 11 --

By Cash paid for boarding of John WILLIAMS } [Right column]
from ye 20th Augt 1731 till the 12th of April 1732 }

26 March 1733

(64) (Cont.) being 7 Months & 22 days at 30/ pr. Month} 11 12 6
by Do paid for 7 yds. Of Osinbrigs to make him two}
shirts also pd. for making & thread -- -- -- -- -- } .. 3 -- --
Ap 10. 1732-by ditto. paid Thomas **ROUNDTREE**}
pursuant to two Orders of Vestry as by Rect. will }
appear -- -- -- -- - -- -- -- -- } 58 11 --
pd. to Apl. 10 ___ By ditto paid to Mr. **SAGG** as by his
Accot. appears 45 -- --
By Coms. for Collecting of 161..8..6. at 15 pr Cent 2?4 4 6
Ballance due to the sd. parish -- -- -- -- -- -- 29 6 10
By Coms for receiving & Collecting ye £3..7..6 -- 1̶0̶ 10 1
                                                  172 11 --

    Except Errors March ye 14th. 1732
      pr. Thos. **LOVICK**

(65) 65 At a Vestry [overwritten] Meeting of the Vestry for Chowan parish held at Edenton March 25 1734. *A. D. 1734*
Present George **MARTYN** Willm. **HINTON**} C Wardens Edwd. **MOSELEY** Henry **BONNER**} {Saml **PADGET** Thomas **LUTEN** Jno **PERRY** Isaac **HUNTER**}

  By the Accot. exhibited by Mr. **MARTYN**, it appear [sic] that he hath accounted for 318 Tithables & by Mr. **HINTON**s Accot he hath collected 464 Tithables for the year 1732. both which Collections together with the Sum of £29..2..6 recd. from the former Church Warden Mr. Thomas **LOVICK**? appear to have been paid away as by the Accots now ———? exhibited more fully appear.

  Ordered that the Minutes of the Late Vestry held March the 26, 1733 together with several Accots. above specified be Enterd in the Vestry Book And that for the future the? Proceedings & orders of Vestry as well as Accots. of the Church Wardens & Collectors be Entered in the Vestry Book as soon as may be.

  Ordered that Mr. William **MACKY** be paid the Sum of five? pounds for the Burial of Francis **FLETCHER**.

  Ordered that Mr. Edwd. **HOWCOT** be paid the Sum of Five pounds for sundry Expences concerning his care & Maintainance & other Charges about Christian **NEWTON**.

  Moseley **VAIL** is appointed Clerk of the Vestry.

  Geo **MARTYN** Wm. **HINTON** T **LUTEN** Sam **PATCHET** J **PERRY** E **MOSELEY** Henry **BONNER** Isaac **HUNTER** 36

(66) [This page was written, in two columns, at 90° to the normal orientation.]
The No. East Parish of Chowan [Left column]
1732
Septr.	To pd. Jno **BALLARD** for boarding of Jno **WILLIAMS**	£. 4 10 --
	To pd. the Wido. **WILLIAMS** by ye Vestry's order	8 .5 --
Apl.	To pd. Doctor **BLACKHAL** for sallavating Eliz. **POWERS**	25 -- --
	To pd. Mr. **SAGG** for Attendance - - - - - - - -	-1 -- --
	To pd. for 11 yd. Ozenbrigs for Francis **JONES** -- --	-4 .2 .6
	To pd. for washing Doctr. **BOYD**s Surpice	-- 10 -- *Surplice*
May	To pd Robt. **KINGHAM** for boarding Eliz **POWERS**	28 -8 --
	To pd. Mary **STACY** for boarding Eliz **POWERS**	20 .5 --
	To pd. Doctr **GRANVILE** ½ the Nt. Levy for last Year	52 17 --
	To pd. Robt. **KINGHAM** for Christian **NEWTON**	. 7 10 --
	To pd. Doctr **BOYD** for Preaching - - - - - - - -	5 -- -- *Rev. Dr. BOYD*
1733 --	To pd. Doctr. **BLACKHAL** in part for Christian **NEWTON**	10 -- --
	To pd. Jno **ROBINSON** part of his Accot. for F. **JONES**	.5 14 6
		173 -7 --

Per Contra   Cr [Right column]
  By fines recd for fighting in Town   £ .1 -- --
  By Do. Recd. from Colo. **BONNER** & Mr. **BADHAM**   .3 15 --
  By Do. - - from Colo. **BONNER** -- -- + -- --   .1 5 --
  By Do. -- -- from **VANPELT** -- -- -- -- --   -3 15 --

25 March 1734

(66) (Cont.)

By Do -- -- from Mr. BADHAM for Mr. GALE	-- 10 --
By 2 levys from Doctr. BLACKHAL -- -- --	-- 10 --
By Bills reced of Mr Thomas LOVICK-- -- --	29 2 6
By Do of Mr HINTON -- -- - -- -- --	65 10 --
By Do of Robt. KINGHAM the last year Levys	67 11 6
	173 7 --

        Errors Excepted
            Geo: **MARTIN** Mar. 25th. 1734

(67) *67* April the 15th. 1734, being Easter Monday *A. D. 1734*

    The Vestry & Parishioners having met proceeded to choose a New Vestry agreeable to Law & by pole chose Edward **MOSELEY** Henry **BONNER** Thomas **LUTEN** Jno. **MONTGOMERY** George **ALLEYN** Samuel **PADGET** Wm. **HINTON** John **PERRY** Isaac **HUNTER** Jno. **SUMNER** Thomas **WALTON** Senr. & William **LUTEN** to Serve as Vestrymen for the Ensuing year and Chose? Parishioners Edmd. **PORTER** Henry **BAKER**} Inspectors the Same day

    Present Henry **BONNER** Thos **LUTEN** Saml **PADGET** Jno **MONGOMERY**} Wm. **HINTON** Isaac **HUNTER** Wm. **LUTEN** Geo **ALLEYN** and choose George **ALLEYN** & Isaac **HUNTER**} Church Wardens for the Ensueing year.

    Ordered That the late Church Wardens do appear before the Vestry on the last Satturday in May next And accot. for the Parish money by them Collected? the last year past.

    I do declare that I do beleive there is not any transubstantiation in the Sacrament of the Lords Supper or in the Elements of Bread and Wine at or after the consecration thereof by any person whatsoever *N. B. Declaration against Transubtantiation signed by the Vestry.*

    Samll. **PAGETT** Geo. **ALLEYN** William **HINTON** Jno. **MONTGOMERY** Henry **BONNER** Thos. **LUTEN** Wm. **LUTEN** Isaac **HUNTER** 37

(68) *68* At a Vestry held at the Court house in Edenton the 25th. of May Anno Dom 1734. *A. D. 1734*

    Present George **ALLEYN** Isaac **HUNTOR**.. Ch: Wardens John **MONTGOMERY** Esqr Colo. Henry **BONNER** Capt. Saml. **PADGET** Mr. Thos. **LUTEN**} Mr. William **LUTEN** Mr. Thomas **WALTON**

    Ordered That John **PARKER** be paid the Sum of Twenty five pounds out of the Arrears now due & of the present year for his keeping & looking after Francis **JONES**.

    Ordered That John **ROBINSON** be paid the Sum of Twenty one pounds Tenn Shillings & Six pence ball of his Accots. for Entertaining Francis **JONES**

    Ordered That Mr. James **TROTTER** be paid the Sum of Eight pounds for sundry Charges in burying David **SMITH**.

    Ordered That Thomas **ROUNDTREE** be paid the Sum of Seven pounds fifteen Shillings for maintaining of Francis **JONES** & that his Charge for reading be postponed till the next meeting.

    Upon Information of Capt. Saml. **PADGET** that the Chalice & plate is in the hands of Colo. Christopher **GALE** Ordered That it be Deld. to the Clerk.

    Ordered That there be a parish Tax of Five Shills. for Every Tithable person in the parish to be collected by the Church Wardens.

    Ordered That Colo. Henry **BONNER** and Mr. William **LUTEN** be impowered to receive the Taxes due for the Last Year and all Arrears and Accot. for the Same at their Meeting in July

    Ordered That the Vestry meet on the Third Thursday in July next

    Geo **ALLEYN** Isaac **HUNTOR** John **MONTGOMERY** Henry **BONNER** Saml. **PADGET** Thos. **WALTON** William **LUTEN**

(69) *69* At a Vestry held at Edenton for the N East parish of Chowan the 19th. day of July 1734.

    Present Doctr George **ALLEYN** Mr. Isaac **HUNTOR** C: Wardens

    Colo. Edward **MOSELEY** Mr. John **MONTGOMERY** Colo. Henry **BONNER**} Mr. Thomas **LUTEN** Mr. Thomas **WALTON** Mr. William **LUTEN** Mr. William **HINTON** Mr. Saml **PADGET**

    Pursuant to the Order of the Last Vestry Colo. Henry **BONNER**, produced an Accot. of his Rect. of ~~July~~ 137. Tithables for the year 1733. Also he delivered into the Vestry a List of such Tithables who have not paid.

    Mr. William **LUTEN** who produced his Accot of the Rect of 189 Tithables for the year 1733.

    The aforegoing Lists of Colo. Henry **BONNER** & Mr. Wm. **LUTEN** being for the Lower part of the parish from **BALLARD**s Bridge.

    Mr. William **HINTON** who was to Accot. for the upper part of the parish from **BALLARD**s Bridge, not being ready to

19 July 1734

(69) (Cont.) produce his Accots. by reason Mr. Richd. **KENSHY**? who was his Collector has failed to appear It is Ordered That Mr. **HINTON** do cause his Accots. to be laid before the Vestry with all convenient Speed.

Colo. **BONNER** & Mr. **LUTEN** with their Accots. delivered into the Church Wardens the Sum of £51.5.6 being the Bal due from them.

Ordered That their Accots. be Entered in the Vestry Book.

Ordered That Moseley **VAIL** as Clk be paid the Sum of Five pounds for his Entring in the Vestry Book the former proceedings and for his Attendance as Clerk including this day.

Ordered 38

(70) 70) Ordered that the Church Warden [sic] be allowed on their Accot 45/ pr Month for the Care of Elisabeth **POWERS** *A. D. 1734*

Ordered That a Vestry be held the third Thursday in Octr next. — Geo **ALLEYN** Isaac **HUNTER**} C Wardens
E **MOSELEY** J **MONTGOMERY** Henry **BONNER** Thos. **LUTEN** Thos. **WESTON** Willm. **HINTON**

At a Vestry held the 17th. day of October Anno Dom 1734 at the Court House in Edenton *Vestry meet at the Court House* Present } Colo Edwd. **MOSELEY** Colo. Henry **BONNER** Mr S. **PADGET** Mr. Thos **LUTEN** Mr. Thos. **WALTON** Mr. Isaac **HUNTOR** Mr. John **PERRY** Mr Thos. **LUTEN** Mr. W **LUTEN**}

Mr. **HINTON** not attending this Vestry according to Ordr. of the last Vestry Ordered That he attend & make up his accounts the next Vestry.

It is agreed that Mr. Isaac **HUNTOR** be reader for the upper part of the parish & that he be paid for the time he officiates.
E **MOSELEY** J **PERRY** Saml **PADGET** T **WALTON** T **LUTEN** Henry **BONNER** Wm **LUTEN** Isaac **HUNTOR**

(71) *71)*
Colo. **BONNER**. W. **LUTON** 137} Tithables at 5/. £81..10..--

Commissions: 15 pr Cent -- --	£12..4..6
pd to James **TROTTER** -- --	8..-..-
to Henry **BONNER** for -- --	3..-..-
to Ed. **MOSELEY** for Do}	5..-..-
to Geo **ALLEYN** Do}	2..-..-
pd. in at the Table to Dr. G **ALLEY** [sic] Ch W	51..5..6
	£81..10..0 39

(72) 72) At a Meeting of the Vestry for Chowan Parish at Edenton March the 29 1735. *A. D. 1735*
Present, Isaac **HUNTER** Ch Warden
E **MOSELEY**, Jno **MONTGOMERY**, Henry **BONNER** Saml. **PADGET** Thos **LUTEN** & Wm. **LUTEN**.

Doctr George **ALLEYN**, one of the Church Wardens being dead, and the time of Collecting the Parish dues being near Mr. William **LUTEN** is appointed Church Warden to continue till Esther [sic] Monday in the year 1736. Isaac **HUNTER**
E. **MOSELEY** Saml. **PAGET** Henry **BONNER** Thos **LUTEN** J **MONTGOMERY** W **LUTEN**.

At a meeting of the Vestry for Chowan parish the 3d day of May Anno Dom. 1735.
Present. Mr. Isaac **HUNTER** Mr. William **LUTEN** Ch Wardens
{Colo. Henry **BONNER** Mr. Sam. **PADGETT** Mr. Thomas **WALTON** Mr. William **HINTON** Mr J. **PERRY** Mr. Thos **LUTEN**}

Ordered That Mr. John **CHAMPEN** be paid the Sum of Fifteen pounds for his finding Nails & Shingling the Indian Town Chappel formerly.

Mr. John **RICHARDS** Exr. of the Estate of Doctr. George **ALLEYN** late Church Warden not being ready to make up the said **ALLEYN**s acco. now, it is ordered that he attend the next Vestry & make it up.

Ordered That Mrs. **BUTLER** be paid the Sum of Six pounds fifteen Shillings for Three months board of Elizabeth **POWERS**. Mr.

(73) 73) Mr William **HINTON** former Church Warden now produced his account and there appeared to be due to the parish the sum of Twenty Eight pounds Seventeen Shils & three pence Ordered that he pay the said Sum to Mr. **HUNTOR** Chu [overwritten] Present Church Warden

Ordered That Mr. Charles **WESTBEESE** be paid the Sum of Thirty Shillings for part of the Expences in burying Mary **REED**.

3 May 1735

(73) (Cont.) Ordered That John **PARKER** be paid the Sum of Twenty Seven pounds five Shillings for the Board and maintainance of Francis **JONES**.

Ordered That Hannah **WALTON** be paid the Sum of Eighteen pounds Tenn Shillings for maintainance of Will **WESTON**.

Ordered That Robert **KINGHAM** be paid the Sum of Three pou___ Seven Shillings & Six pence for the board of Eliza. **POWERS**.

Ordered That Mr. James **POTTER** be paid the Sum of Three pou___ for maken [sic] a Coffen to bury a man that dyed on the parish.

Ordered That there be a parish tax of Five Shillings __ on the Tithables of Five Shillings [sic.]

Ordered That Mr. William **LUTEN** & Mr. Isaac **HUNTOR** make up their Accounts the next Vestry.

Ordered That Moseley **VAIL** be paid the Sum of Five pounds for acting as Clerk.

Henry **BONNER** Thos **WALTON** Will: **HINTON** Thos **LUTEN** Saml **PADGET** Jno **PERRY** Isaac **HUNTOR** Will **LUTEN**

By order Moseley **VAIL** Clk 40

(74) 74)
Dr. William **HINTON** Church Warden to the No East parish   Cr

1733	To 497. Tithables at 5/ p. Tithable	124 . 5 0	Comissions at 5 pr. Cent -- --	.18 12 9
F	To Mary **BRODY**s fine for a Molatto Bastard	. . 3 - -	pd. John **ARLINE**	..1 10
i	To Eliz: **REED**s fine for Two? -- -- Do.	. . 6 - -	pd. John **ROBINSON** for keeping Frans.	.21 10 0
n	To Olive **MORGAN**s fine for Fornication	. . 1.5 -	**JONES**	
e	To Eliz **JINN**s? fine for -- -- Do.	. . 1.5 -	pd. Jno **FREEMAN** for reading	.16 - -
s	To Eliz **DANIELS** fine for -- -- Do.	. . 1.5 -	pd John **CHAMPEN**	..3 - -
	To Josiah **BRODY**s fine for -- -- Do.	. . 1.5 -	pd. Jno **WHITE** by order of John. **PARKER**	..4 10 -
		138.5 0	pd. Jno **CHAMPEN** by order of Jno.	
		109.7 9	**PARKER**	.20 10 --
	The Ballance due to the parish is	£28 17_	pd. E: **HOWCOTT** for Expence on Ch:	
			NEWTON	..5 -- --
			pd. Thos **ROUNDTREE** for Expences on	
			Frans **JONES**	18 15 --
				109 -7 9

(75) 75) April the 26th day 1736 Being Easter Monday. *A. D. 1736*

The Vestrey and parishnors having mett proceeded to Chuse a new Vestrey agreeable To Law and by pole Chose William **SMITH** Esqr. John **MONTGOMERY** Esqr. Robt **FFORSTER** Esqr J **HODGSON** Esqr Henry **BONNER** Thos **LUTEN** Edmund **GALE** Abraham **BLACKALL** Jos **ANDERSON** Henry **BAKER** John **SUMNER** Samll. **PADGETT**. Duely quallifyed themselves as Vestrey men by taking the Othses? By law directed.

And Chosed Abram: **BLACKALL** & Henry **BAKER**} Church Wardens for The Ensuing Year.

And then the Vestrey by plurality of Votes Chose Henry **BONNER** Junr. Clerk of the vestrey who was duely quallifyed by Taking the publick Oaths by law directed.

Itt is Ordered by the Vestrey that the Sd Henry **BONNER** have And receive the Sum of Thirty pounds Curret: Money pr annum As a Salary for his Service as Clerk of the Vestrey.

And the Church Wardens of this parish are Authori_ed And directed to pay the Sd Sum of Thirty pounds pr annum to the Sd. Henry Out of the parish Levies which Shall by them be Collected from The Inhabitants of this parish.

Itt is Ordered that a Vestrey be held at Edenton this day fortnight and the late Church Wardens do make up their accounts & lay them before the Vestrey on that day.

The Church wardens are directed to pay Twenty Shillings each? for the Support of [blank] **THOMPSON** till the Next meeting of the Vestrey.

Itt is Ordred that the Clerk of the Vestrey give Notice? to Henry **BAKER** & John **SUMNER** Gent. that they are Chosen Vestrey Men of this parish and that it is Expected by the Vestrey that they appear at Edenton this day fortnight and quallifie them Selves for that Office and the Sd **BAKER** quallify & accept of the Office of Church Warden.

Abraham **BLACKALL** C Warden 41

(76) Chowan A [sic] Att a Vestry held for the No East Parish of Chowan Prcinct att Edenton the tenth day of May 1736. *A. D. 1736*

Present - Mr: Abraham **BLACKALL** Ch Warden

10 May 1736

(76) (Cont.) The Honoble. Wm. **SMITH** Esqr. John **MONTGOMERY** Esqr. John **HODGSON** Esqr Joseph **ANDERSON}** Edmd. **GALE** Henry **BONNER** Thos. **LUTEN** Robt **FORSTER**

The late Church Wardens Being Called on to Make up their Accounts and Mr **HUNTER** One of them appeard But was Not Ready Not having finished his Collection. Whereupon a further day is given them to Monday the 24th day next At Which time they are Ordered to be ready with their accounts to be then Made up.

Ordred that the Clk. serve each of the Sd Late Church wardens with a Copy of this Order.

Orderd that the Same Allowance be Continued to Mrs. **THOMPSON** till the Sitting of the Next Vestrey.

A letter from the Reverend Mr. **BOYD** being Read.

And Ordred that it Lie for a further Consideration at the Next Vestrey.

An Order from the Reverend Mr. **GARZIA** for five pounds payable to Mr. **SLAUGHTER** for divine Service Ordred that Mr. Wm: **LUTEN** the Late Church Warden pay the Same and Charge it in his accounts. *Rev. Mr. GARZIA.*

Ordred that to Contribute towards defraying the Expences of Building a Church at Edenton for Support of the poor and other Contingent Charges of the parish a tax or levey Of twenty Shills. pr pole be levied on Each Tythable in the parish for the Ensuing Year. *Tax for a New Church*

(77) 77) Chowan Prcinct At a Vestry Held at Edenton ye 24th day of May 1736

Mr. Abraham **BLACKHALL** C Warden

John **MONTGOMERY** Esqr John **HODGSON** Esqr Joseph **ANDERSON** Edmund **GALE** Thos **LUTEN** Henry **BONNER**

The Late Church Wardens haveing produced their accounts According to the Order of the last Vestrey.

Ordred that Mr. **ANDERSON** and Mr. **LUTEN** Inspect the Said Accounts and Make Report thereof at the Next Vestry and that the Said Late Church Wardens there attend.

Ordred that the Vestry Meet on Tuesday the first day of June Next and that Such persons as have been Cho___ And Not quallifyed have Notice then to Attend.

At a Vestry held at Edenton the first day of July? 1736.
Present Mr. Abraham **BLACKHALL** C Warden

Wm. **SMITH** Esqr John **MONTGOMERY** Esqr John **HODGSON** Gent. Edmd **GALE** Gent Joseph **ANDERSON** Henry **BONNER** Thos **LUTEN**? Samll **PADGETT**.

Mr **ANDERSON** & Mr **LUTEN** returned their Report of the late Church Wardens Accouts: and Stands dated as follows.
42

(78) No. Carolina September ye 20th 1735

These are to Certifie that William **BADHAM** And Martha **MOONEY** were Lawfully Married pr Me. John **BOYD**

William **BADHAM** the son of Willm **BADHAM** & Martha his wife was Born November. 22-1736

William **BADHAM** Deceasd Octobr: ye? 29-1736.

Thos **ECLESTON** the Son of Thos **ECLESTON** was Born ye 7th day Octobr. 1736. Henry **BONNER** Clk Vestry

May 1736

Mr. W: **LUTEN** late Church Wd: to the No. East Parish Dr?		
For 462 tithls: @ 5 S. pr Tithle due for ye Year 1734	£115 10 0	
For 384 tithls @ 5 pr Tithle due for ye year 1735	.96 = =	
For fines due to Said parrish -- --	..3 10 --	
	215 -- --	
Mr. Isaac **HUNTER** to the above Said parish	£ [blank]	
For 510 tithle @ 5 pr tithle due for ye Year 1734 -- --	£127 10 --	
For 505 tithle @ 5 pr tithle for the Year 1735 -- --	141 .5 --	
For fines Due to the Said parish -- -- --	..8 .. --	
For Money Recd of W: **HINTON** late C. Ward -- --	. 28 17 --	
	520 12 0	
Cr	403 9 3	
The Ball: Due to the parrish is	£117 2 9	

(79) 79) By Crdt.

To the Coms: of £215 s10:d- ? @ 15 pr Cet? -- -- -- £.32 .5 -

1 July? 1736

(79) (Cont.)

To Robt FFULLINGTON for Boarding Chrisn NUTEN -- -- --	.32 .. -
To Mary BUTLER for Boarding Eliz POWERS -- -- --	..6 15 -
To Caleb CALLEWAY & R WATHUM for Burng Danl: WILLIAMS	..8 -- -
To Robt KINGHAM for boarding E: POWERS -- -- --	..3 -7 -
To James POTTER for a Coffin -- -- -- -- -- -- -- --	--3 --
To Doctr: BLACKHALL for Sallevag: C: NUTEN -- -- --	.25 -- --
To Robt FFULINGTON for Boarding C NUTEN In her Saleavgn-- --	.10 --
To Robt KINGHAM for Board of E POWERS -- -- -- -- --	..4 10 -
To Sd KINGHAM for Boarding ye Said POWERS -- -- -- -- --	-- 8 --
To Moseley VAIL for Being Clark of ye Vestery -- -- -- --	..-6 --
To Parson GARZIA -- -- -- -- -- -- -- -- -- -- -- --	..-5 --
To W MACKEY for board of ffrans: FLETCHER -- -- -- --	..-8 -- --
To Parson GARZIA five Pound -- -- -- -- -- -- -- -- -- --	..-5 -- --
To ye preSent C: Warden -- -- -- -- -- -- -- -- -- -- --	.10 -- --
By Credit	100?
To ye Coms: of £305 - 12 @ 15 pr: Cet. -- -- -- -- -- --	.45 10
To John PARKER for Boarding F JONE [sic] - -- -- -- -- -- --	.21 - 5?
To Hanah WALTON for Barding W: WESTON -- -- -- -- --	.18
To John CHAMPIN for Repairing ye Chapil - -- -- -- -- -- --	.15 -
To Hanh [sic] WALTON for Boardg ye Sd WESTON in "? Sickness	..7
To Michl WARD for Boarding ye Sd WESTON 3 Months -- -- --	..6
To Richd RAINER for Boarding ye Sd WESTON 2 Months & ½	..5
To 23 Yds: of Oznebrigs @ 6 Pr Yd for Sd JONES & WESTON	..6
To 3 pair of Shoose pt? @ 25 pr pr for Sd WESTON -- -- --	.._
To Making Two Shirts & two pr Britches for Do -- -- -- --	..1
To 3½ yds kersey 1 dozen butens & 1 Slip hair & pr Stocks for JONES	..3?
To one Qt: of Brandey @ 8s and one Course hatt @ 2¼ for Sd WESTON	..6?
To My Self boarding ye. Sd WESTON 5 Mons & ½ -- -- -- -- --	13
To My Reading In the Uper part of ye parsh: @ 16 pr Year	.32
To John ARLINE for Looking after ye Chapil 2 Year -- -- -- --	.03
To John PARKER Boarding F JONES 1 year & 8? days -- -- -- --	.85
and Making him a Pearsey Coat	
To Money Paid to the prsent C Wrdens - -- -- -- -- -- --	
Cr.	43

(80) *80)* North Carolina ss? May ye 29 1736

    Wee the Subscribers persuant to an Order of ye Vestry for ye No East parish of Chowan held at Edenton ye 24 of This Instant May have duly Examined the Accounts of Wm. LUTEN and Isaac HUNTER Late C Wardens and find that Mr. LUTEN on the Ball: of his account is Indebted to ye parish the Sum of £49:2:6 and that Mr. HUNTER is ye Sum of £81:15.8 Out of which ball. an article in the Said HUNTERs account for ½ of W: WESTON five Monthes & half the allowance of Which When ascartained by the Vestry to be adCleduced?   Jos ANDERSON Thos LUTEN

Which Report being Read & approved of It is Ordd that an Allowance of £13:15:0 be Made unto Isaac HUNTER for the boarding of W WESTON which reduces the ball. of his acct: to £68 -0?:2 and it is further ordd that the Sd Wm LUTEN & Isaac HUNTER Late C Wardens forthwith pay ye Ball. of their Respective accots to the prsant Church Wardens.

    Ordred that ffrancis JONES W WESTON have an allowance of fourty pounds Each pr anum for their Maintainance for this Ensuing Year.

    Ordred that the Constables Summons Mr Henry BAKER and Mr John SUMNER to attend at a vestry to be held on Tuesday the 15 of June Next.

    Mr. Wm LUTEN late C Warden Paid to Mr A BLACKHAL prsant C Warden the Sum of twenty Nine pound five Shill in part of the ball of his accout:

(81) *81)* At a Vestrey held for the No East parish of Chowan ye 19th of August 1736 *A. D. 1736*

    Mr. A BLACKALL C W W SMITH Esqr J MONTGOMERY Esqr J HODGSON Esqr J ANDERSON Gent E GALE Gent H BONNER lt? Thos. LUTEN Gent

19 August 1736

(81) (Cont.) Ordred that Mr Edmund GALE & Henry BONNER Examine & Settle the Accot: of Doctr. George ALLEYN formerly Church Warding [sic] With John RICHARDS Extor: to the Said ALLEYN & Make their Report at the Next Vestrey.

Ordred that Walter DROUGHEN be Allowed reason___ And Nessessary Charges in Cloathing W WESTON for the Ensuing Time.

Ordred that the Church Wardens do demand & Receive of Mr W BADHAM & Mrs Penelope LITTLE Exts?: of W LITTLE Esqr Deceasd the Several & Respective Sums Lodged in his the Said W BADHAMs hands as Also Mrs. LITTLE Decea___? Towards Building a Church At Edenton And that _____ Refusal of Nonpaymt: of the Same Respectively They the Said Church Wardens Comence Suit agt them the Said Mr. BADHAM & Mrs LITTLE or Eyther of them? that the Same May be applyed to the Use that the Same was Intended. *Bldg. Church at Edenton* 44

(82) *82)* At a Vestry held for the No East Parish of Chowan the 11 day of April 1737. *A. D. 17__*

Mr. Abraham BLACKALL C W

W SMITH Esqr J MONTGOMERY Esqr J HODGSON Esqr Jos ANDERSON Gt. Edmd GALE Gent Henry BONNER Thos LUTEN.

Ordred that Mr. John SUMNER be Summonsed to meet At Edenton to quallify As A Vestry Man.

It is Certifyed that Robt FORSTER Esqr Vestry man of this Parrish Is Departed this govermt. And that Mr. Isaac HUNTER be quallifyed As Vestry Man In his Stead.

It being Moved by Mr. A: BLACKALL C Wardn: that an Order passed Last Vestry Impowering the Church Ward. to Call in Such Sums of Money as is Now Due to this parish Towards Building a Church at Edenton, & the Said C Ward Setting forth the difficulty of getting a full Vestry when Need Requirs It is thereupon Ordd that Mr. Edmund GALE be a Com: to Receive & Call in the Said Money he giving good & Sufficient Security to the C Wardens And their Successors for the Same to be for the Use of this Parrish, And further that the Said Comr. be Impowered to Disburse from time to time, Such Part of the Said Money as is Nessessary towards Building the Said Church & that the Said Comr: Accot: with the Church ward. or wardens for the time being for Such Disbursements As AfSaid when Ever thereto Required. *Order to Collect a tax and to disbu___ the Same in building a Church*

Ordd. that Mr. Isaac HUNTER Pay to John PARKER forty Pounds in part of the Ball: of his Accot: for the Maintainance of Francis JONES.

Ordd: that the Six pounds being the Residue of Mr HUNTERs Accot: be paid to Walter DRAUGHON? in part for the Maintainance of Will WESTON.

(83) *83)* At a Meeting of the Vestry held in? the No East Parish of Chowan ye 27 day April __ Mr. A BLACKALL Mr Henry BAKER C W *A. D. 1738* [sic]

W SMITH Esqr J HODGSON Esqr Mr Samll PADGETT} Mr Isaac HUNTER Mr Henry BONNER{

Ordred that Towards defraying the Expences of a Church at Edenton & Repairing the Indian Town Chappell & other Continget Charges of the parrish a Tax or Levey of Ten Shill? pr pole be leveyed On Each Tithable of the parish for the Ensuing Year. *Church __ Edenton*

Ordred that Henr BONNER Continue Clerk of the Vestry for the Same lowance [sic] for the Ensuing yea [sic.]

Ordred that Ten prsent be allowed for Collecting the Said levey Henry BAKER CW 45

(84) *?)* At a Meeting of the Vestry held for the No. East Parish of Chowan the 12 of August 1737 Mr. Abraham BLACKALL C W W SMITH Esqr J HODGSON Esqr J MONTGOMERY Esqr Jos ANDERSON Gt Edmd GALE Gt Henry BONNER Gt

Ordred that the money Arrising from the Parish Leveys the readers Salleryes Money Nessessaryes for the Support of the poor & Other Incident Charges Occruing [sic] deducted be paid into the Hands of Mr Jno HODGSON to be by him Aplyed to the building of the Parish Church at Edenton & the Church Wardens are hereby Ordd. to pay the Same Into his hands for that Purpose.

Easter Monday April 3d 1738 *A. D. 1738 Freemen elect the Vestry*

The freemen of The parish of Chowan Mett at The Court house in Edenton & There Did Elect for Vestrey men Vizt: {Richd PARKER Isaac HUNTER Robt. HUNTER John ALSTON Thos LUTEN John SUMNER} Willm ARKILL Edwd HARE Charles KING Jacob BUTLER John BLUNT Will SPIGHT}

The Same Day the Freemen Did Chuse Will BATTLE & Thos PEARCE Inspectors

To these? _____ appointed Clerk by the ____

(85) *85)* And On the 17th Day of Aprrill 1738 Mett at the Court House in Edenton The Said Mr Richd: PARKER Mr Robet: HENTER Colon. John AULSTONE Capt. John SUMNER Mr Edwd HARE Mr William SPIGHT Mr Isaac HUNTER Mr. John BLOUNT Mr Thos LUTEN Mr Willm ARKEIL? Mr Jacob BUTLER *A. D. 1738*

They being Qalified by Taking the Publick Oaths do appoint and Chuse Mr John BLOUNT and Capt John SUMNER to be Ch Warde___ for this Year.

35

17 April 1738

(85) (Cont.) It is this Day Ordered that the Late Ch Wardens Doctr Abraham **BLACKHALL** & Capt Henry **BAKER** do lay their accounts before ___ Vestry at their Next meeting Which is by appointment to be he__ at the Court house in Edenton on the 12th day of may Next.

Orderd: That Mr John **BLOUNT** Ch Warden Demand of ___ Henr: **BONNER** The Vestry Book and all papers Relai?ting to? The parish affaires Which is in his possession to be had at the Next Vestry

At a Vestry held for the parish of Chowan at the Court hou__ In Edenton the 12th day of May 1738.

Present Mr: John **BLOUNT** Capt John **SUMNER**} Ch W

Mr Richd. **PARKER** Mr. Isaac **HUNTER** Colo John **AWLSTON** Mr Thos. **LUTEN** Mr Edward: **HARE** Mr William **SPIGHT** Mr Robet: **HUNTER** Mr Willim. **AAKELL** [sic] Mr Jacob **BUTLER**

Mr Charls **KING** this day Qalified as a Vestry man and took ___ place accordingly.

Ordered that for and towards the Defraying all Nece?sary Chgs? and Expenses of this parish a tax or Leavey of ten Shillings per p___ Be Leavied on Each Tithable of the parish for the Ensuing Year. 46

(86) *86)* Doctr: Abr: **BLACKHALL** one of the former Ch Wardens produced his accounts to this Vestry and it is Orderd: that Mr. John **BLOUNT** Capt John **SUMNER** Mr Jacob **BUTLER** and Mr Richd: **PARKER** Inspect and Settle the Said accounts and make report of the Same to the Next Vestry.

Ordered that the Ch Wardens be allowed on their accounts fifty Shillings pr Mounth for the Support of Elizath. **THOMPSON** a pore Wooman, till the Next Vestry.

Ordered that the readers Continue till the Next Vestry.

Capt Henry **BAKER** Late Ch Warden haveing failed to Lay his accounts before this Vestry pursuant to an Order of the Last Vestry It is this day Ordered that the Said Henry **BAKER** make up his accounts and Lay them before the Vestry at their Next Meeting

By Consent of the Whole Vestry John **LUTEN** Is appointed The Clark

It is Orerd. [sic] that the Ch Wardens pay him ten pounds Currant Money for this year for his Servises as Clark of the Vestry.

Orderd that there be a Vestry held at the Indian town Chappell on the first Saterday in July Next.

John **AULSTON** Isaac **HUNTER** Robet **HUNTER** Thos **LUTEN** Jacob **BUTLER** Edwd **HAIR** Richd **PARKER** Charles **KING**. *Vestry meet at Indian Town Chapel*

Att a Vestrey held for the prish of Chowan at the Indian Town Chappell on the first day of July 1738

prSent Colo. John **ALSTON**. Mr. Isaac **HUNTOR**. Mr. Robt. **HUNTOR**. Mr. Thos **LUTON**. Mr. Jacob **BUTLER**} Mr. Willm. **ARKILL** Mr. Willm. **SPEIGHT** Mr. Edwd. **HAIR** Mr. Richd. **PARKER**} Mr. John **BLUNT** John **SUMNER**} CW

Persuant to an Ordr: of Last Vestrey Capt. Henry **BAKER** late Ch wardin Laid his acotts befor: the Vestrey and on Examination there appeairs to be dew to this parish £128:S3:d3: He then paid 24£: to Jno. **SUMNER** which Reduceth the Bals. due to the prish to :104:3:3 which he is ordred to pay to the prest. C wardens. - - - - - - - - - - - -

Ordd. that Eliza. **TOMPSON**s allowance of fifty Shillings pr. month be Continued tell next Vestrey = ordd. that Willm. **LUTON** pay to Mr. Jno. **BLUNT** prsnt. C warden his Balls? of actts.due? to Mr. Abraham **BLACKALL** Late C warden - -

Ordered that Willm. **WALTON** be allowed for Keeping Willm. **WESTON** and ffra: **JOANES** [sic] ___rty pounds pr. annum Each one? in perportion pr. month.

___dred: that Jno. **LUTEN** Receive of Mr. Edm?d. **GALE** the Chalis and plate which belongs ___ this prish and present it to the _____

(87) *87)* was ___ered that Mr. John **BLUNT** ___-ohn___ [Remainder of this line is missing.] *1738*
Inspect and Settle the accots. of Abra: **BLACKALE** [sic] one of ___ ___ C wardens and Reporte thereof to the next Vestry & they do Report that they Cannot Settle the Sd. acctts. for ___ the Sd. CWd. hath Given in but part of the Lists of Tythables, on Reading their Report it is ordred that the sd. **BLACKALE** Doe appeair before John **BLUNT** & Thos **LUTON** at the Court hows in Edenton on the 15th day of this Inst. July and their make up his acctts. according to ye Severall Lists of ye Tythables Between **BALLARD**s Bridge & yawpim Reve_ which are for ye years 1736 and 1737 and they to make Report of the Same to the next Vestrey -

ordred that Robt. **RODGERS** be payd five pounds Currt money for Looking after Eliza. **HART** [or **HARE**] one month in her Sickness & Decently Burie?ng her Corps - - - - - - - - - - - - -

Mr. Edmond **GALE** being by an ordr. of a former Vestrey appoynted a Commr. to Receive and Call in Severall Sums of money that was Dew towards Building a Church at Edento_ and by the Same ordr. the Sd. Commr. is obledged to accoumpt with the C wardens for time Being for the Same it is ordred that the present Ch warden or Ch wardens Cal_ upon the Sd. Commr. to Render to him or them an acctt. of all Sums of money Recd. by him and how he hath appld. ye Same - - - - - -

1 July 1738

(87) (Cont.) ordred that the Readers Continue untill the next Vestrey

ordred that the Vestrey meet ye 22d: day of this Instant July at ye Indian Town Chappell

At a Vestrey held for the parrish of Chowan at the Indian Town Chappell ye 22d. of July 1738

present John **ALSTON** ISaac **HUNTOR** Robt. **HUNTOR** Thos **LUTON**} Richd. **PARKER** Edwd. **HAIR** Charles **KING**} John **BLUNT** C wd. John **SUMNER** C wd.

Persuant to an Ordr. of a Vestrey held the first day of July 1738 appoynting us the Subscri____ to inspect and Settle the acctts. of Doct: Abra: **BLACKALE** Late Ch warden and wee have Caref____ Examoned ye Sd. acctts. and find that their is due to ye prish according to ye Severall Lists of Tythables for the years 1736 & 1737 Vizt. for 496 Tythables for the ye__ 1736 at 20S: pr Tyha: is 496 £ and for 496 Tythables in ye year 1737 at 10? pr. Tythe. is 248£ which is in all 744£   Pr.?   Cert.

& By Cash Recd. of Several prsons as pr his acctt   80:10: By ye Commishons 74½Coms?
the Balls which is Dew to the prish 607£: 6s:0}   824:10: is - - -   74:8:
Given under our hands the 22d. day of}   223: 4: By Cash pd. ye prish 148:16:
July 1738 - - - - - - - - - - - - - - - - - £601:06?:0 - - - - £223: 4:

Abraham **BLACKALL**

John **WILLIAMS** preposed to this Vestrey to take and Keep of the pish a Child Born of ye Body of one Mary **VANN** Single woman of this County & prsh She being Dead, for the Consideration of the Sum of fifteen pounds__ him by the prsh and have the Child bound to him till it Cums of age &? it is Considered and ordred that the Ch wardens pay the Sd. **WILLIAMS** Fifteen pounds and bind the Sd. Child to him according to ye Direction of ye Laws in Such Cases made & provided - - -

ordrd. that the Church wardens Collect ye prish Leveys for this prsnt year and that? they be allowed ten pr Ct for the Same

ordrd. that the Late Ch Wardens Abra: **BLACKALL** & Hen **BAKER** pay to this prish forty pounds or Deliver to the prsent Ch wardens a mullatter boy by them___ pretended to be bound to one Sarah **RONDENG** - - - - - - - -

ordrd That the present C wardens Receive and Collect all the money now d__ to the parrish - - - - - -

ordrd that all the moneys that is properly prish moneys after the Just Debts that? is now Dew is payd Except ye Levey for this present year be payd into the hands of Thos **LUTON** to be by him applyed towards Compleating a Church now begun at Edenton he giveing Security to ye Ch wardens in the behalfe of ye prish to Render to the Vestrey an acctt. thereof when Required -

N. B. Church now begun at Edenton

ordr. that Robt. **FFULLERTON** be payd fifty nine pounds two Shillings & Six pence for nursing and? boarding Christian **NUTON** from ye 12th. of febuary 1736 to ye 12: of July 1738 - - - - - - - - - - - - -

ordr. that Mrs. Mary **FREEMAN** be paid Eighteen pounds for Keeping Margrett **RODGERSON** :9 Mont__

ordr. that Willm. **HEWS** be payd 20£ for keeping Margrett **RODGERSON** 18 monthes - - - - - - -

ordr. that the former Readers be Continued

ordr that Eliza. **THOMPSON**s allowance of fifty Shills. pr. month be Continued till next V_____ 47

(88)__) At A Vestrey Held on Easter Munday Aprill The 23: 1739 at Mary **FREEMAN**s Hows prsent *A. D. 1739*

John **ALSTONE** Jacob **BUTLER** Isaac **HUNTOR** } William **ARKEELE** William **SPEIGHT** Robert **HUNTOR**} John **BLUNT**: C Wd Jno **SUMNER** C Wd.

Ord That the Church wardens pay unto William **WALTON** Seventy four pounds fifteen Shillings for Keeping Wm. **WESSON** and ffrancis **JOANES** untell the 10th: day of Aprill 1739

Ordered That the Church wardens pay unto William **SKINNER** fifteen pounds for Reading at three Several places untell This Day Being one year -

Ordred that the Church wardens pay unto Mary **FREEMAN** Twelve pounds for Keeping John **FOARD** a poor man from ye 20th day of January to the 20th: of Aprill 1739 - - - - - - - - - - - - - - - - - -

Ordred that the Church Wardens pay unto Mr. William **ARKEELE** five pounds for Burring of Mr. **WICKS** - - -

Ordred John **SUMNER** and Thomas **LUTON** Serve as Church wardens for this present year 1739 - - - - -

Ordred that Capt.? John **ALSTON** take Joyce Daughter of Mary **BRADDY** and Keep her untill the next Vestrey to be held for this parrish and to Return her to the Sd. Vestrey their to be Dealt with according to Law - - - - - - -

Ordred that the Vestrey Meet at Mrs. Mary **FREEMAN**s Hows The first day of June Next.

(89) 89) At a Vestrey Held at the hows of Mary **FREEMAN** the first day of June 1739 prsent

John **ALSTONE** Jacob **BUTLER** William **ARKEEL** William **SPEIGHT**} Robert **HUNTOR** ISaac **HUNTOR** Edward **HARE** Charles **KING**} John **SUMNER** Ch W

Ordred That the Church wardens Take the Scailes waits and Measures Belonging to this Parrish into their Care and Keep the Same untill further orders -

Ordred that Capt Thos **GARRETT** Take Margrett **RODGERSON** and Keep her at the Rate of Twenty pounds pr year according to a greement [sic] -

Ordred that the Church wardens pay unto Capt Thos **GARRETT** Twenty Eight pounds for Keeping Margrett **RODGERSON** and makeing two Shifts one Coat and Jackett, untill the first day of June 1739 - - - - - - -

Ordred that the Church wardens pay unto Mary **FREEMAN** fifty Shillings for Keeping and Looking after John **FOARD** a poor man and makeing Cloathes for him untill the first day of June 1739 - - - - - - - - - - - - - -

Ordred that the Church wardens pay unto Elizabeth **TOM**___ forty Shillings pr. month from the first Day of June ___ untill further Orders -

Ordred that Benjamin **TALBURT** and William **SKINNER** Continue Reading Devine Service at the Rate of fifteen pounds pr. year according to former orders - - - - - - - - - - - - - - - -

Ordred that the Church wardens pay unto Mary **FREEMAN** five pounds for Charges of the Vestrey at her hows 48

(90) 90) On Easter Munday April ye 7th: Day 1740 A. D. 1740

The Freemen of Chowan County Did Meet at the Court Hows and Chuse Benjamin **TALBOT** as Clark for Takeing the pole for Vestrey men and then and their did Elect and Chuse for Vestrey men the following persons Viz:

John **BLUNT** John **SUMNER** Demsey **SUMNER** Richard **PARKER**} Thomas **WALTON** John **BENBUARY** Jacob **BUTLER** William **SKINNER**} ISaac **HUNTOR** William **SPEIGHT** Edwd. **HARE** Richard **BOND**

And mett on the 18th: day of Aprill 1740 at the Court Hows in Edenton the Sd John **BLUNT** John **SUMNER** Demsey **SUMNER** Richard **PARKER** Thomas **WALTON** John **BENBUARY** Jacob **BUTLER** William **SKINNER** ISaac **HUNTOR** William **SPEIGHT** Edwd. **HARE**

They Being Quallified by Takeing The publick Oaths Do Appoint and Chuse Mr. Jacob **BUTLER** and Mr. Demsey **SUMNER** to be Church wardens for this Insueing year.

It is Ordered that the Church wardens or Either of them Demand the Vestrey Book of Mr. John **LUTON** and all papers Relateing to the prish Affairs which is in his possession To be had at the Next Vestrey - - - - - - - - -

Ordred that the Late Church wardens Make out their Collections and Lay their accounts before the next Vestrey held for this prish

Ordred that the Church wardens pay unto Benjamin **TALBOT** forty Shillings for his Takeing the pole at the Collection

Ordred that a Levey of five Shillings pr pole be Leveyed on all the Tythables in the parrish of Chowan for and Towards the Defraying all Nessary [sic] Charges and Expences of the Said prish for the Insueing year - - - - - - - -

Ordred that the Vestrey meet at Mr. Thos. **WALTONS** at Cathrian [sic] Creek the first Saturday in August Next

- - - - - - - - - - - - - - - - -Jacob **BUTLER** -Ch w. Demsey **SUMNER** Ch w

(91) Att a Vestrey mett and Held at Mr. Thomas **WALTON**s Hows the 10th day of May 1740 present. A. D. 1740

Jno **SUMNER** Richd **PARKER** ISaac **HUNTOR** Thos: **WALTON** Wm **SPEIGHT**} Richd **BOND** Edwd. **HARE** Wm. **SKINNER**} Demsey **SUMNER** Jacob **BUTLER**} Church wardens

Ordred That the Church wardens pay Each and Every person which produces a Sertificate for a Lawfull Claim Relateing to the Vermine act when ye prish money is Collected as the Law Directs - - - - - - - - *The Vermin Act*

Ordred That the Ch wardens pay unto Precilla **PERRY** by ord of Eliza. **THOMPSON** five pounds it being for the Support of the Said Eliza. **THOMPSON**s Maintainence - - - - - - - - - - - - - - - - - -

Ordred that the Ch: Wardens pay unto ISaac **HUNTOR** Sixteen pounds and to Willm. **SKINNER** fifteen pounds for Reading dev___ Service from April 23: 1739 to April 23: 1740 - - - - - - - - - - -

Ordred ISaac **HUNTOR** and Willm. **SKINNER** Continue Reading Devi___ Service from according to former orders -

Ordred that Mr. Jacob **BUTLER** appoynt a Reader for the Lower part of this prish at the Rate of fifteen pounds pr. year

Ordred that the Ch wardens pay unto Thomas **WALTON** Seventy pounds and fourteen Shillings for His Charges with? **WESTON** and **JOANES** in Keeping and Decently Buriing of them - - - - - - - - - - - - - - -

Demsey **SUMNER** Jacob **BUTLER** 49

(92) 92) Att a Vestrey Mett and held at Mr. Thos: **WALTON**s Hows The 25 day of October 1740 prsent

Vizt John **SUMNER** Willm. **SKINNER** Thos **WALTON**} Richd. **PARKER** ISaac **HUNTOR** Edwd. **HARE**} Demsey **SUMNER** Ch Wd.

This Day John **SUMNER** Layd his acctt. Before this Vestrey as Being Late Church warden and it is ordred that Demsey

25 October 1740

(92) (Cont.) SUMNER Richard PARKER and ISaac HUNTOR inspect and Settle the Said acctt. and they Report that the Ballance of the Sd. acctt dew to the Sd. John SUMNER is NIneteen Shillings and three pence which he is ordred to be payd pr. the Present Church warden

....

Ordred that Capt. Thos GARRETT be allowed at the Rate of Thirty Pounds pr year for Keeping Margrett RODGERSON from the first day of June Last -

Ordred That the Church warden be allowed for a Doctors Bill or acctt. for a Cure or Trouble with Fleete COOPER a poor Boy which is now Lame - |- - - - - -

Ordred That Mr. John BLUNT Settle his acctt. as Being Late Church warden at the Next Vestrey to be held for this prish

....

Ordred that Mr. Thos WALTON be allowed and payd forty Shillings for his Trouble and Charge in provideing and Gitting a Coppy of the Vermin act which act Is Ordred to be Kept for the Use of the Vestreys with the Vestr. Book
- -

Ordred that the Vestrey Meet at Mr. Thos WALTONs hows on fryday the 28th: day of November next to appoynt possessioners to possession Every Mans Land in this prish

ISaac HUNTOR Thos. WALTON Edward HARE John SUMNER Willm SKINNER Richd PARKER Demsey SUMNER C wd.

(93) *93)* Att a Vestrey Mett and held at Mr. Thos WALTONs How_ for Chovan prish the 28 day of November 1740 *1740*

prs. John SUMNER ISaac HUNTOR Thomas WALTON Edwd. HAIR William SKINNER William SPEIGHT John BLUNT Richard BOND} Jacob BUTLER-Ch Wd

This Day Mr. John BLUNT Layd his acctt. Before this Vestrey as Being Late Church warden which acctt was Inspected and Settled and the Balls. of the Sd. acctt. dew to the prish is two hundred and two pounds and Eighteen Shillings whereof he pays down to Demsey SUMNER prst. Ch wd. Seventy Seven pounds and to Jacob BUT___ prst. Ch wd. Seventy five pounds whereof there is Remaining Dew to this prish fifty pounds & Eighteen Shillings.

it is therefore Ordred that Mr. John BLUNT pay the Balls. of his acctt Being fifty pounds & Eighteen Shillings into the han___ of Mr. Jacob BUTLER prst Ch wd. for the Use of this prish and that he the Sd BUTLER acctt for the Same With the Vest__

Ordred that the Church wardens pay Mr. Benja TALBOTT Ten poun__ fifteen Shillings for Reading Devine Service from the firs_ day of June 1739 to Easter munday following   Jacob BUTLER C___

- -

Att a Vestrey mett and Held at the Hows of Mr. Thos. WALTON for the prish of Chovan March :30: day 1741 present *A. D.1741.*

Mr. Edwd. HAIR Mr. Willm. SPEIGHT Mr. Thos WALTON} Mr. Isaac HUNTOR Mr. Richard BOND Mr. William SKINNER} Mr. Jacob BUTLER C___

	£ S d
Ordred That the church wardens pay to Lodwick MIRCLER ---	16: 5:0
ordred That the church wardens pay Mr. Isaac HUNTOR for} Reading two years at 16£ pr. anm. - - - - - } ---	32: 0:0
ordred that the Church wardens pay to Mr. Wm. SKINNER for} Reading one year - - - - - - - - } ---	15: 0:0
ordred That the Church wardens pay to Mr. Benja. TALBOT} for Reading one year - - - - - - - -} ---	15: 0:0

Ordred that Mary HAVIT? be alowed and payed by ye Church wds. Twenty Shills. pr. month from march ye 30th: 1740

Jacob BUTLER Church wardin Laid his acctt. before the Vestrey and? was Examined and allowed of 83£: 4S:10d it being moneys disputed? for the use of the poor

ordd. that the Vestrey meet at ye Indian town Chappell the 18th: day of April 1741   Jacob BUTLER Ch wd. 50

(94) Att a Vestrey Mett and held at The Indian Town Chappell the 18th: day of Aprill 1741 pr. *A. D. 1741.*

Mr. Isaac HUNTOR Mr. Thos WALTON Mr. Richd. BOND} Mr. William SPEIGHT Mr. Edwd. HAIR Mr. William SKINNER} Mr. Jacob BUTLER C Wd.

Ordred that Mr. Thos. WALTON and Mr. Richard BOND Serve as Church wardens for this Insueing year 1741 - - -
- -

Ordred That Demsey SUMNER as Late church warden Lay his acctt: Before the next Vestrey to be held for this parrish and acctt. for ye Same

- -

18 April 1741

(94) (Cont.) Ordred That James **EGGORTON** be allowed and payed the Sum of Twenty pounds by the Church wardens for his Trouble and Care in Keeping and Maintaining of a poore child Sarah **LACEY** by name

- -

Ordred That the church wardens pay unto John **SUMNER** Ten pounds for his Trouble in Serveing as clark of this Vestrey for the year 1740

- -

Ordred that the church wardens pay unto Capt. Thos. **GARRETT** the Sum of Twenty five pounds for his Trouble and Charge in Keeping & maintaining Margett **RODGERSON** from ye. first day of June 1740 untell ye first day of Aprill 1741 - -

Ordred That a Tax or Levey of Two Shillings proclamation money be Leved on Every Tythable in This prish for the Insueing year 1741 for And Towards the Defraying the Contengent charges of this prish and Towards the Building of two chappells Each to be Thirty five foot Long and Twenty two foot and a halfe wide and to Stand one at James **COSTAN**s or their a bouts [sic] and the other to Stand at James **BRADDEY**s or near their a bouts - - -- - *Two Chpls. Ordred? to be built*

Ordred That Mr. Richd. **PARKER** Mr. Isaac **HUNTOR** Mr. Thos. **WALTON** and John **SUMNER** doe Inploy or hire work men for to build two Chappels in chowan prish Viztt at James **COSTAN**s or their a bouts as they Shall Think fett and the other at James **BRADDEY**s or near their a bouts and the Dementions as here mentioned Vizt Thirty five foot Long and Twenty two foot and a halfe wide Eleven foot in the pitch betwee [sic] Sill and plate and a Roof workmanlike n?ear a Squear and to be a Good fraim Gott out of Good Timber and coverd with Good Siprus Shingles and weather boarded with feather Edged plank nine inches broad with Good Lapp of two Inches at the Least and Good Sleapers and flowers [floors] of Good plank of Inch and a qtr? thick and Sealed with Good plank with ~~ills~~ three windows Suitable for Such a hows or howses and two Doars Suitable with a pulpitt and all things Suitable according to the ?ew of the Sd. Richard **PARKER** ISaac **HUNTOR** Thos **WALTON** and John **SUMNER** - -

(Turn forrad?) *Description of the Chpls.*

(95) *95)* Ordred that the Church wardens pay unto Mr. Jacob **BUTLER** the Sum of fifty Shillings for the Like Sum payd Robt. **FULERT**__ Towards the maintainance of Christian **NUTEN** - - - - - - - - - - - - - - - - -

Ordred that John **SUMNER** Keep the Vestrey Book this Insuein_ year and act as Clark of the Vestrey and to be allowed Ten Pounds for the Sd. Service untill next Easter munday

Ordred that the Vestrey meet at the Indian Town Chappell the Last Satterday in June next - - - - - - - -

Jacob **BUTLER**

Att a Vestrey Mett and held at Mr Thos. **WALTON**s Hows The 8th: day of August 1741

pst. Mr. ISaac **HUNTOR** Mr. Richd. **PARKER** Mr. Edward **HAIRE** Mr. Demsey **SUMNER** John **SUMNER**} Mr. Thos. **WALTON** Mr. Richd. **BOND**} Church Wds.

Ordred that Mr. Richd **BOND** be allowed and payd the Sum of forty Shillings for the Like Sum pd. by him to Rachell **PERVINE** a poore woman in Great wont of assistance from the prish - - - - - - - - - - - - - - - -

Ordred That Richard **BOND** and Jonathan **PARKER** Be allowed and payd by this prish the Sums of Money by them a greed [sic] for by this Vestrey for the building of Two Chappells when their work is Done according to their a greemt. *Chapels*

Ordred that Precilla **PERRY** be allowed and payd by the Ch: wardens the Sum of Thirty two pounds for her Trouble and Charge in Keeping & maintaining of Eliza. **TOMPSON** Eight months.

Ordred that the Ch wardens pay unto Capt Thos **GARRETT** the Sum of five pounds fifteen Shillings for his Trouble in Keeping Marget **RODGERSON** from the first day of Aprill to the Tenth day of June 1741 51

(96) *96)* Att a Vestrey mett and Held at The Chappell at Meherin The 10th: day of Aprill 1742 *A. D. 1742*

prst. ISaac **HUNTOR** Richard **PARKER** Demsey **SUMNER**} John **SUMNER** William **SKINNER**} Thos. **WALTON** Ch wd. Richard **BOND** Ch wd.

This Day Demsey **SUMNER** as Late Church wardin Laid his acctt. before this Vestrey which acctt. was Settled and the Ball. dew to the prish is Eight pounds which he then pays Down to Richd. **BOND** prsent C wd.

- -

Ordred that the Church wardens pay to Wm. **FREEMAN** Eight pounds four Shillings & Six pence for Keeping Rachell **PERVINE** and helping her a way [sic] to Jno **ROBERSON**s and helping Jno. **MARKUS** to Thos: **WALTON**s

- -

ordred that the Ch wds. pay to Mr. Thos **WALTON** forty five pounds and Three Shillings for Keeping Rachell **PERVINE** ~~and~~ and makeing Cloathing for her Six months and finding four pare of Shews for the poare - - - - - -

Ordred that the Ch wds. pay to Jonathan **PARKER** forty Two Pounds and Ten Shillings proclamation Monney for his Trouble and Charge in Building a Chappell at the Knotty pine - - - - - *Knotty Pine Chapel*

ordred that the Ch wds. pay to James **GOODWIN** Ten pounds and Ten Shillings for Keeping Margett **RODGERSON**

10 April 1742

(96) (Cont.) Three Months & a half

- -

Ordred that the Ch wds. pay to Doctr. Arthur **GOURLEY** forty five pounds for His Trouble and Charge in Cureing Fleete **COOPER** a poore Lame boy -

Ordred that the Ch wds. pay to Mr. ISaac **HUNTOR** Sixteen pounds for Serveing as Reader for the year 1741 - - -

Ordred that the Ch wds. pay to Mr. Wm. **SKINNER** fifteen pounds for Serveing as Reader for the year 1741 - - -

Ordred That the Church wardens pay to John **SUMNER** Sixty Seven pounds and Eleven Shillings for Sundrey Goods Delivered the Ch wds. for the poore and for Serveing as Clark of the Vestrey for the years 1740 and 1741 and Ball. of his acctt. when he was Church warden as pr. Ordr.   Thos. **WALTON** C wd. Richd. **BOND** C wd.

(97) 97) North Carolina Ester [sic] Monday the 19th day of April 1742

The freeholders of the County & Parish of Chowan Mett at the Cou_. House in Edenton, and then & there did Elect and Chose the following Gentlemen, for Vestrymen (Vizt) *A. D. 1742.*

{Mr James **CRAVEN** Mr Peter **PAYNE** Esqr Mr William **LEWIS** Mr Orlando **CHAMPION** Mr John **HALLSEY** Mr William **HOSKINS** Jacob **BUTLER** Esqr John **BLOUNT** Esqr Mr John **BENBURY** Mr Joseph **MING** Mr Peter **ADAMS** Mr William **BENBURY**}

Which said Gentlemen Qualified by Taking the Oaths by Law appointed for the Qualification of Publick Officer and Subscribing the Test, And then Chose Mr Orlendo **CHAMPION** Church Warden for the uper part of County and Parish of Chowan, and Mr John **HALLSEY** Church Warden for the Lower part of the said Parish

And it was then and there Ordred that the Late Church Wardens ____ or whoever has the Vestry Books and papers in their hands deliver up the Same on demand to the Present Church Wardens or Either of them.

Ordred that the late Church Wardens appear at the Court House in Edento_ on the fourth day of May Next then and there to Lay an Exact account of the Money by them Reced and paid as Church Wardens for the County & Pari__ of Chowan, before the Present Vestry.

Ordered that the Tax or Money Levyed by the late Vestry & Collected by the Inspector or Sheriff Remain in their? hands untill the Meeting of and it is farther Ordred that the said Sheriff and Inspector then and there Attend Make up their Accounts, and pay in the Several Sums in their hand.

The Vestry Adjourns untill Tuesday the fourth day of May next & then to Meet at the Court House in Edenton without any further Notice under the Penalties by Law appointed.

Tuesday May the fourth 1742 The Vestry Mett According to Adjourn____ & Present of the Vestry
Mr James **CRAVEN** Peter **PAYNE** Esqr Mr Wm **LEWIS** Mr Jacob **BUTLER** John **BLOUNT** Esqr John **BANBURY** Joseph **MING** Peter **ADAMS** Will? **BANBURY**} Orland [sic] **CHAMPION** John **HALLSEY**} Ch: Wardens 52

(98) 98) Mr William **HOSKINS** appeared and Qualified according to Law by taking the Oaths appointed to be Taken by Publick Officers Subscribing the Test as also the Oath of a Vestryman and Took his place accordingly. On a Motion of Robert **LASETER**'s to this Vestry That John **MARKS** and Sarah the wife of the sd? John now in the Keeping of the late Church Wardens at an Extravigant Rate as this Vestry is Informed Therefore the said Robert **LASETER** being Willing to take the Said John **MARKS** and Sarah the wife of the said John, at the Rate of four Pounds pr. Month It is ordered that the sd Robert **LASITER** have the Keeping of the said John **MARKS** and Sarah his wife untill the Meeting of the Next Vestry at the Rate afsd.

Ordered that Mr. William **LUTEN** Sheriff pay to the Present Church Wardens the Sum of forty pounds for the use of the Poor untill the Meeting of the Next Vestry.

Ordered that the said Church Wardens pay to the Keepers of Such Poor Persons as belong to the Parish out of the afd Sum of forty Pounds, so much as shall be Neccassary for their Suport untill the Meeting of the Next Vestry and that they Return a Just Account of Such Money and to whom Disbursed to the Next Vestry.

Pursuant to an Order of the Vestry Meet at Edenton on the 19th day of april Last for the County and Parish of Chowan Directing the late Chur__ Wardens to Deliver the Severall Books and Papers belonging to the parish to the present Church Wardens and the sd Order not being Complied with as Yet. It is therefore ordered that Mr John **SUMNER** the late Clk do Deliver up the said Books and papers as aforesd to Mr Richd **BOND** & Mr Mr [sic] Thomas **WALTON** the late Church Wardend and that the [sic] Deliver the Sam [sic] Books & Papers to this Vestry at their Next Meeting.

The Vestry Adjourn untill Saturday the 15th. of May Instant

Saturday the 15th of May 1742 the Vestry Mett at the Court House in Edenton according to Adjournment Present
Mr. James **CRAVEN** Mr John **BLOUNT** Mr Jacob **BUTLER** Mr Peter **ADAMS** Mr John **BANBARY** Vestry Men [Written vertically, between the columns.] Mr Wm **BANBURY** Mr Wm **LEWIS** Mr Peter **PAYN** Mr Joseph **MING** Mr Wm

15 May 1742

(98) (Cont.) **HOSKINS}** Mr John **HALLSEY** C Warden

Ordered that a Tax or Levy of one Shilling Proclamation Money be Levyed on Each and every Tithable Person in this Parish of Chowan for the Ensuing Year 1742 for and Towards Defraying the Contingent Charges of the said Parish and it is further Ordered that when the said Levy is Collected, the poor be first Paid the the [sic] Several Readers appointed by the Vestry, and what money shall

(99) *99)* Shall then Remain to be applyed as the Vestry Shall Direct.

Ordered that the Sheriff and Late Church wardens Account with the pr Vestry and Pay the Money Due from them at their Next Meeting.

Ordered that Mr James **CRAVEN** Mr. Peter **PAYNE** Mr John **BLOUNT** & Mr Jacob **BUTLER** be? & is hereby appointed to Inspect into the Accounts of the late & present Sheriffs & Church wardens for the Years 1740 & 1741 & to Make Report to the Vestry at their Next Meeting of their Proceedings.

Ordered That the Late & Present Sheriffs & Church wardens for the Years 1740 & 1741 Deliver in their Respective Accounts to the persons Commissionated and appointed by? the Vestry for that purpos of all the Money by them Received and how they have applied the Same for the sd Two Years on the 29th day of this Instant, on Oath at the Court House in Edenton.

Ordred that William **LUTEN** the Present Sheriff pay to the present Church warden fifty pounds Current Bills to be by them applied towards the Maintaining the Poor of the Parish and that they Render an Account to the Vestry at the Next Meeting.

Ordered that the Church Wardens bring all the Poor of the Parish to the Next Vestry at their Meeting and that the Clerk of the Vestry put up an advertisement that all Persons who have any Claim on the Parish then appear and Put in their said Claims and that any Person or persons who are Inclined to take all the poor of the Parish into their hands for the ensuing? Year may then appear and Put in their Proposals.

Ordered that Mr Robert **LASITER** Keep John **MARKS** and his Wife until the Meeting of the Next Vestry and then to bring them to Edenton at the Charge of the Pari__

Ordered that Benjn **TALBOT** be Continued Reader untill the Meeting of the Next Vestry and it was then and there further Ordered that after the Contingen_ Charges of the Parish for the Ensuing Year is Discharged that whatever Money ___ then Remain out of the Levy already Laid Shall be applied Towards Repairing the Old Chaple at Indian Town Creek or towards Building a New one at Some Convenie__ place thereabouts as the Majority of the people there shall Judge Most Proper *Indian Town Chapel*

Ordered that Richard **MC CLURE** be Clerk for this Present Year 1742 and that he be paid at the End of the Year by the Vestry as they Shall Decide? and think he Deserves, and that he Keep the Books untill that Time.

The Vestry Adjourn untill Saturday the 12th of June and then to Meet at the Court House in Edenton

---

Saturday the 12th day of June 1742. The Vestry Meet at Edenton according to Adjournment Present 53

(100) *100)* Present

Mr Peter **PAYNE** Mr James **CRAVEN** Mr. John **BLOUNT** Mr John **BANBURY** Mr Wm **BANBURY** Vestry men [Written vertically, between the columns.] Mr Wm **HOSKINS** Mr Peter **ADAMS** Mr Joseph **MING** Mr Wm **LEWIS** Mr Jacob **BUTLER}** Mr John **HALLSEY** Ch: Warden

It was then and there Ordered that Mr Jacob **BUTLER** be paid forty Shillings by the present Church Wardens the Same being for Bread & Wine for the Sacrement, for which he produced a Receit to this Vestry that he Disbursed as much for that use Mr Thomas **WALTON** having agreed with the Vestry to take into his Care the Poor of the Parish, to Maintain for this Present Year 1742 Namely Rachl [sic] **PERVINEY** John **MARKS** and Sarah his Wife Elizabeth and Frances **THOMPSON** at four pounds pr Month Each Person and so in proportion for a Shorter or Longer Time provided they be Sent to his house by the present Ch: Wardens. Ordered that the Church send the said Persons to Mr **WALTON**s and that he the said Mr **WALTEN** be paid at the Expiration of the Year in proportion as afd

Ordered That the present Sheriff pay into the hands of the present Ch: Wardens the Ballance Due to the Parish which Remains in his hands and unpaid & that he Account as the Law Directs with this Vestry at their Next Meeting by the List of Tithables to him Delivered with an acot: of the Insolvents by Name

Ordered That Mr Thomas **LUTEN** the late Sheriff Account with the p___ent Vestry in Manner aforesaid and at the Time afd.

Ordered That the present Ch: Wardens Discharge and pay all the Debt Due from the Parish on Account of the Poor and Readers to this day and Account with the Vestry at the Next Meeting And it was further Ordered that the Sheriffs have a Copy of the Order Relating to them Delivered by the Church Wardens

Ordered That Benjn **TALBOT** and all Other Readers that was in this parish the Last Year and Imployed by the Vestry be Continued for this present Year 1742 and be paid fifteen pounds pr Year as usual.

Ordered that the Church Wardens Pay to Mrs: **RICHARDS** Twenty Shillings pr. Week for Keeping Rachl **PERVINEY**

10 July 1742

(100) (Cont.) for five Weeks

The Vestry Adjourn until Saturday the 10th day of July Next & then to meet at Edenton

---

Saturday the 10th of July 1742 The Vestry mett at Edenton according to adjournmt: Present

Mr James **CRAVEN** Mr Peter **PAYNE** Mr Joseph **MING**{ Vestry Men } Mr John **BANBURY** Mr Wm **HOSKINS** Mr Jacob **BUTLER**} Mr Orlando **CHAMPION** Mr John **HALLSEY**} Ch: Wardens

It Was then and there Ordered that the present Church Wardens pay to Precilia **PERRY** Seventy Eight Pounds Ten Shillings (Including an Order which she had from a former Vestry on Mr John **BLOUNT** august the 8th 1741 for Thirty

(101) *101)* Thirty Two pounds

Mr Jacob **BUTLER** Produced a Certificate to the Vestry for Eight Wolf Scalp, _ Wild Catts Scalps & four hundred & Seventy Seven Squirrel Scalps & prayed he mig__ be allowed for the same as the Law Directs.

Ordered that the Church wardens pay to Jacob **BUTLER** Esqr forty Six pound_ Eighteen Shillings and Six pence as a Satisfection for the Eight wolf Scalps & 3 wild Catts Scalps & four hundred & Seventy Seven Squirrel Scalps as aforesd which he has produced and proved according to Law.

Ordered That Mr James **CRAVEN** Search the Records for a Copy of Thomas **CLARK**s will & Other Papers which are Necessary (and if to be found) to produce the Same to this Vestry at their Next Meeting at the Cost of the Parish.

The Vestry Adjourn untill Thursday the 15th Instant then to meet at Edenton

---

Thursday the 15th of July 1742 The Vestry Meet at Edenton According to adjo_____ Present

Mr Jacob **BUTLER** Mr Wm **HOSKINS** Mr Will: **LEWIS**{ Vestry Men } Mr John **BANBURY** Mr Joseph **MING** Mr Wm **BANBURY**} Mr John **HALLSEY** Ch; Warden

It was then and there Ordered, that for as much as the Late C_____ Wardens have (altho often requested thereto to make up their Accounts for the Parish Money Which they have Received During the Time that they were Church wardens And as) Yet Neglected to do the same, which they Ought to have done? On Oath with the present Vestry, Yet a further Day is Given them (to wit) untill Saturday the Eleventh Day of Speptember [sic] Next to make up their Accounts with the present Vestry and pay the Ballance Due to the parish into the hands of the present Chur__ Wardens that now are for the Year 1742

Ordered That Mr Orlando **CHAMPION** be allowed four pounds pr Month for Keeping Mary **WILLIAMS** from the Time he first Took her in untill ___ Meeting of the Next Vestry.

The Vestry Adjourn untill Saturday the 11th Day of September Next & will? Meet at the Court house in Edenton

---

Saturday the 11th of September 1742 The Vestry Mett according to adjournment

Present

Mr Peter **PAYNE** .... Mr William **HOSKINS**.... Mr John **BANBURY**... Mr Jacob **BUTTLER**... Vestry Men [Written vertically, between the columns.] Mr William **LEWIS**.... Mr Joseph **MING**.... Mr William **BANBURY**} Mr John **HALLSEY** Church wd?

Forasmuch as the late Church Wardens (to wit- Mr Richard **BOND** & Mr Thomas **WALTON** have neglected to Mak [sic] up their Accounts with this Vestry & do Still refuse to make up their Accounts and pay the Ballance due from them to the Parish it is therefore 54

(102) _02) 1742_ Therefore Ordered that the Said Richard **BOND** & Mr Thomas **WALTON** Church wardens in the Year 1741 be Immediatly prosecuted as the Law Directs by the proper persons appointed by Law for that purpose & that the said Suit be Carried on at the Charge of the Parish.

Ordered that John **DICKSON** be Sued by the Church Wardens for Twenty Two pounds Sixteen Shillings Which the Vestry have Disbursed to Maintain his Cheldren when he Run away out of the parish.

The Vestry Adjourn untill Saturday the Second Day of October Next.

October the 2d 1742 the Vestry Mett According to Adjournment.

Present

Mr James **CRAVEN**... Mr John **BANBURY**.. Mr William **HOSKINS** Vestry Men [Written vertically, between the columns.] Mr William **BANBURY** Jacob **BUTLER** Esqr Mr Peter **ADAMS** Mr Joseph **MING**} Mr John **HALLSEY** Church Wardn

Ordered that Thomas **LUTEN** Esqr late Sheriff appear at the Next Vestry & Account upon Oath for the Several Parish Levys & Other Parish Money by him Received for the Year 1740 and that the Church wardens Serve him with Copy of this Order.

Mr Thomas **WALTON** & Mr Richard **BOND** late Church Wardens Personally appear and made Oath on the holy

2 October 1742

(102) (Cont.) Evangilests [sic] befor a Justice of the peace that They had? Received no more money of the parish Levies from Thomas **LUTEN** late Sheriff __ an £262..10..0 for the Year 1740 as appears by account Stated here under. [One quarter of the remainder of this page is blank.]

    Ordered that the present Church wardens Commence an Action against the present Sheriff for all the Money by him Collected as Sheriff, or to be Collected Relating to the parish Levis for the years 1741.

    Ordered that Thomas **LUTEN** late Sheriff appear at the Next Vestry and account upon Oath for the Several Parish Levies and Other parish Money by him received for the Year 1740 and that the Church wardens Serve him with a Copy of this Order

    The Vestry Adjourn untill the third Thursday in this Instant October and then to meet at Edenton.

(103) *103) 1742* At a Vestry began & held at Edenton __ Day of Nov?ember Annog Dom 1742.
    Present

    Mr James **CRAVEN** Mr John **BANBURY** Mr Willm **BANBURY** Mr Joseph **MING** Vestry Men [Written vertically, between the columns.] Mr William **LEWIS** {Mr John **HALLSEY** Mr Orlendo **CHAMPION**} Church wardens.

    Ordered that Mr Orlendo **CHAMPION** one of the present Church Wardens have ____ Twenty Shillings pr Week from this Time untill the Meeting of the Next Vestry for Keeping of the po__ of the parish that are now at his House. And that Mrs **PERRY** have Twenty five Shillings __ week for keeping Mrs **THOMPSON** untill the Same Time

    The Vestry Adjourn untill the Saturday after the County Court

---

At a Vestry began & held at Edenton the 5th Day of february Anno Dom 1742.
    Present

    Mr James **CRAVEN** Mr Peter **PAYNE** Mr Joseph **MING** Mr William **LEWIS** Vestry Men [Written vertically, between the columns.] Mr William **HOSKINS** Mr John **BANBURY** Mr Wm **BANBURY**} Mr Orlend [sic] **CHAMPION** Church ward__

    Ordered that Mr Orlando **CHAMPION** Church warden Take [blank] **WILIAMS?** Orphain & under a Lingering Desease And agree with Docter James **FLOOD** at the Rate he Can to Cure her. And it is further Ordered that Mr? **CHAMPION** be allowed for her Maintainance from the 22d Day of January Last? said [blank] **WILLIAMS** is Cured at the Same Rate that he hath for the Others? of the parish, he hath under his Care.

    The Vestry Adjourn untill the 12th Day of March Next then to meet at ___

At a Vestry began & held at Edenton the 12th Day of March Annog Dom 1742
    Present

    Mr James **CRAVEN** Mr John **BANBURY** Mr Jacob **BUTLER** Mr Joseph **MING** Mr Willm **BANBURY** Mr Peter **ADAMS**} Mr Orlando **CHAMPION** Mr John **HALLSEY**} Church Wds?

    The Vestry proceed to appoint precessioners according to the Directions of a ____
Province of North Carolina &c.

    And it was then & there Ordered that John **MONTGOMERY** & John **BLOUNT** Esqr be a ___ hereby appointed precessioners for the Canton from Mr William **HOSKINS**es Mill Dam _ Yawpim River &c.

    And that Joseph **ANDERSON** Esqr and Mr. William **ARKILL** be and? they are hereby appointed precessioners for the Canton from Mr **HOSKINS**s Dam to the Long Bridge and Machaccoma Creek &c.

    And that Mr John **HODGSON** Esqr and Mr Peter **ADAMS** be and they are here__ appointed precessioners for the Canton from the Long bridge aforesaid to

    Tara____ 55

(104) ___) *1742* [Portions of this line appear to be torn away.] Tarripin Hill all? ___an between R_____ock? Creek and _____ &c?

    Ordered that Mr James **CRAVEN** Mr. Edward **CHAMPION** be & they are hereby appointed Possessioners for the Canton from Rockohock Bridge to Luke **WHITE**s Ferry on the South Side of the fferry Road & to the Mouth of Rockohock Creek &c. Ordered that Mr James **FARLEE** & John **ROBINSON** be & they are hereby Appointed Possessioners for the Canton from Luke **WHITE**s ferry to the Sandy Ridge Road to **BALLARD**s Bridge & up the Said **BALLARD**s Bridge Swamp to the head thereof & all Contained within? the County & Canton afd to the Said Sandy Ridge Road Down to Tarripin Hill &c. Ordered that Mr. Williams **LILES** & Thomas **LUTEN** Esqr: be & they are hereby Appointed Possessioners from the Sandy Ridge Road to Bear Swamp & the Long Bridge on the Eastermost Side of the Said Road & up to the head of the Canton & Perquimons in the said County of Chowan. Ordered that Mr: John **PARKER** Mr: John **CHAMPION** be and they are hereby appointed Possessioners for the Canton from **BALLARD**s Bridge to warrick Creek from Chowan River to Perquimons Line &c. Ordered That Mr. Thomas

12 March 1742/43

(104) (Cont.) **WALTON** & Mr: Ralph **OUTLAW** be & they are hereby Appoiented Possessioners for the Canton from the mouth of Warrick Creek to the Mouth of Catherine Creek & all Contained between the said Two Creeks & Swamps of Both up to Perquimons Road? &_ Ordered Mr Richard **BOND** & Mr: **WALTON** be & they are hereby appointed Possessioners for the Canton from the Mouth of **BENNET**s Creek & all between the Swamps of the Said Creeks [sic] up the Perquimons Line &c Ordered that Mr: Demsey **SUMNER** & Mr: Jonathan **PARKER** be & they are Appointed Possessioners for the Canton from the Notty Pine to Perquimons Road at the Loossing Swamp & all Contained between that & **BENNETs** Creek Swamp Down to the Bidge [sic] & the ?? from **BENNETT**s Creek Bridge to the K?notty Pine &c. Ordered that Mr: John & Mr: Richard **PARKER** Senr: be & they are hereby Appointed Possessioners from the Knotty Pine up the Road that Leads to the Virginia Line to the Said Line & perquimons Line & all Contained between that & the Loosing Swamp &c.

Ordered that Mr: Jacob **ODAM** & Mr: Wm. **SKINNER** be and they are hereby Appointed Possessioners for the Canton from **BENNET**s Creek Bridge up to the Road by the Knotty Pine and all Contained between the Two Roads & Meherrin fferry & from thence Down to the mouth of **BENNET**s Creek. Ordered that Mr: Edward **HAIR** & Capt? Charles **KING** be and they are Appointed Possessioners from the afd Road at the Knotty Pine & the Road to Virginia Meherrin fferry & the County Line &c. The Vestry Adjourn untill Eastr Monday   Wm **HOSKINS**

North Carolina ss/?

At a Vestry begun & held at the Court House in Edenton the 4th day of April 1743 being Easter Monday A. D. 1743

Present

James **CRAVEN** Peter **PAYNE** William **HOSKINS** Jacob **BUTLER**{ John **BENBURY** William **LEWIS** William **BENBURY** Peter **ADAMS** Joseph **MING**{ Vestry Men } [Written vertically, to the right of the second column.] {John **HALSEY** Orlando **CHAMPION**{ Church Wardens

Pursuant to the Direction of a late act of Assembly Relating to killing Vermin The following Persons produced Certificates Which was allowed of by this Vestry and the Certificates Destroyed. Ordered that the Said persons be allowed as follows (Vizt) *Wolves & Wild Catts.*

Mr: John **LEWIS** for One Woolf Sculp	- - - - - - -	£ 4: 0: 0	
Mr: Henry **BONNER** one Woolf Sculp	- - - -£ 4: 0: 0}		
Do: Two wild Catts @ 20 S Each	- - - - 2: 0: 0}	6:15: 0	
Do: Thirty Squirrels @ 6/ Each	- - - - - 0: 15: 0}		

(105) *105) 17423.*

Mr: John **BENBURY** Ninety Six Squirrels Sculps @ 6 Each	. .	£ 2: 8: 0	
Mr: John **LUTEN** One Woolf Sculp	- - - - - -	4: 0: 0	
Mr: John **HALSEY** One Wild Catt Do. @	£1: 0: 0} -		
Do: fifty Squirrels @ 6d Each	- - - - 1: 5: 0} -	2: 5: 0	
Mr: William **BENBURY** One hundred Eighty one Squirrels @ 6	- -	4:10: 0	
Mr: Orlando **CHAMPION** five Woolfs Sculps @ 80s £20: 0: 0}			_Wolves_ Wild Cats__
Do: Six Wild Catts Do: @ 20s	- - - - - 6: 0: 0}	26: 0	
Mr: John **BLOUNT** Two Woolfs @ 80s Each £	-- --	8: 0	
Mr: Joseph **MING** Two Woolfs @ 80s	- - - £ 8: 0: 0}		
Do: Twenty Six Squirrels @ 6d	- - - - 0:13: 0}	8:13	
Mr: Thomas **HOSKINS** Two woolfs Sculps @ 80s	- - - -	8: 0	
Mr: Jacob **BUTLER** Eight Woolfs Do: @ 80s	£32: 0: 0}		
Do: Two Wild Catts Do: @ 20s	- - - 2: 0: 0} - -	45	
Do: four hundred & fifty Nine Squirrels @ 6d	- 11: 9: 6}		
		£120: 1	

The Vestry taking into Consideration the Act of Assembly Impowe____ Them to Chuse Two Church wardens and thereupon Made Choice of Mr: Peter **ADAMS** an_ John **BLOUNT** Esqr: and it is thereupon Ordered that they be Sumoned to appea_ __ the Next Vestry to be Qualified as Such.

Ordered that Mr: John **HALSEY** & Mr: Orlando **CHAMPION** Present Church Wardens Appear at the Next Vestry and Account with the Same for the Money __ them received for the Year 1742

Ordered that Richard **MC CLURE** late Clerk of the Vestry be allowed the Sum of Twenty Pounds for his Acting as Such he first Compleating the Minutes of ____ Vestry, Which Twenty Pounds he made a Present of to the Parrish.

Ordered that Benjamin **TALBOT** be paid for Reading Divine}
Servise the year 1742 the Sum of - - - - - - } . . . £15: 0

4 April 1743

(105) (Cont.) Ordered that William **SKINNER** be paid for Reading Divine}
Service the Year 1742 the Sum of - - - - - - - - } . . . 15:0
Ordered that Isaac **HUNTER** be Paid for Reading Divine}
Service the Year 1742 the Sum of - - - - - } 15:0
Ordered that Mr: Benjamin **TALBOT** be Continued as a Reader in Edento_
Ordered that Mr: Isaac **HUNTER** & Mr: William **SKINNER** be Continued as Readers in Chowan Parrish
Ordered that Mr: John **ROBINSON** be allowed the Sum of Thirty Shillings for Services Done for the Parish 56

(106) _06_ _743_ Ordered that Notice be put up for all Persons that has any Demand upon The Parrish to Appear at the Next Vestry, And make Good their Claim.

Ordered that Notice be put up for all persons that is Indebted to the Parrish Appear at the Next Vestry or they may Expect to be Prosecuted as the Law Directs

Ordered that Benjamin **TALBOT** officiate as Clerk of the Vestry for this Present Year 1743 and to be paid Ten Pound at the Expiration of the Sd Year for the Same

Ordered that the Vestry be Adjourned till the 23d day of this Instant April and This Vestry is Accordingly Adjourn'd.

At a Vestry a [sic] held at Edenton on the 23d Day of April 1743 According To Adjournment Present

Mr: Peter **ADAMS** Mr: James **CRAVEN** Mr: John **BENBURY** { Mr: William **LEWISS** Mr: Jacob **BUTLER** Mr: William **HOSKINS** Mr: Joseph **MING**{ Mr: Orlando **CHAMPION** Mr: John **HALSEY**{ Church wardens

Mr: Peter **ADAMS** & John **BLOUNT** Esqr: who was Chosen Church wardens On Easter Monday last for the year 1743 The Said Mr: Peter **ADAMS** Appeared and refused to Act as Such and Jacob **BUTLER** Esqr Appeared and made Oath that he heard John **BLOUNT** afosaid [sic] Declare he would Not Act, It is thereupon Ordered that the Church wardens Proceed to recover their fines According to Law. The Vestry Proceeded to and Made Choice of Jacob **BUTLER** Esqr: and Mr: William **HOSKINS** as New Church Wardens who Accepted of the Same and place Accordingly.

Ordered that the Sheriff and all Other Persons that have Any Money in their hands belonging to the parrish pay the Same into the hands of the present Church Wardens Directly.

Ordered that a Levie of Two Shillings Proclamation Money be laid on Each Tythable in this Parrish for this Present Year 1743 first to Defray the Charge of the Poor of the Said Parrish and Pay the Readers and other Debts Due from the Said Parrish.

Ordered that the Vestry Meet on the Second Satterday In May Next   Pet **ADAMS** Willm. **HOSKINS**

Benjamin **TALBOT** Son of Benjamin & Mary **TALBOT** was born the first day of January In the Year of our Lord 1742/3.

(107) _7 1743_ Att a Vestry held at Edenton the 4th day of June 1743 Present

James **CRAVEN** Esqr Peter **PAYNE** Esqr Mr: Peter **ADAMS**{ Mr: Joseph **MING** Mr: Orlando **CHAMPION** Mr: John **BENBURY** { Jacob **BUTLER** Esqr:{ Church warden

Ordered that Mr: Nathaniel **HOCOTT** take into his Care all the Poor of the Parrish aforeSd: at Twenty Shillings pr: Week (Vizt) Rachel **PURVINE** - Sarah **MARKUS** & Mrs: Elizabeth **TOMPSON**.

At a Vestry held at Edenton the 9th day of July 1743. Present

Mr: John **BENBURY** Mr: William **BENBURY** Mr: Peter **ADAMS**{ Mr: Orlando **CHAMPION** Mr: William **LEWISS** Mr: John **HALSEY** { Jacob **BUTLER** Esqr{ Church warden

Ordered that Mr: William **HUNTER** be allowed for five Woolfs Sculps and three? Wild Catts Sculps Which Amounts to Twenty Two pounds.

Ordered That for as much as the former Sheriffs and Church wardens having neglected to bring in their accounts with the lists and all the Ballancess due to the Parrish That the present Church wardens Proceed against the Sheriffs and all other Persons with? any Parrish money in their hands att the Same time to?

At a Vestry held at Edenton the 15th Day of October 1743 -Present-

Mr Wm. **BANBURY** Mr: James **CRAVEN** Mr: Orlando **CHAMPION**{ Mr: John **HALSEY** Mr: Peter **ADAMS** Mr. Jno. **BANBURY**{ Jacob **BUTLER** Esqr Mr: Willm. **HOSKINS**{ Church wardens

Ordered that the Church wardens Agree with any Person to take Care of the poor of the Parrish at as Reasonable Rates as they Can Till Easter Monday Next

---

Thomas **DAILY** Son of Thomas **DAILY** and Mary **DAILY** was Born the 12th day of December In the year of our Lord 1737.
Elizabeth **JONES** Daughter of Richard **JONES** & Ann **JONES** was born the 9th Day of January 1740/1. 57

11 February 1743/44

(108) __8 1743__ At _ Vestry held at Eden___ the 11th day of February 1743. -Present-

Mr. John BANBURY Mr: Willm. BANBURY Mr: Joseph MING{ Vestry Men [Written vertically, between the first two columns.] Mr: John HALSEY Mr: Orlando CHAMPION Mr: James CRAVEN{ Mr Jacob BUTLER Mr: Wm. HOSKINS{ Church wardens

Ordered that Mr: Richard MC CLURE be paid the Sum of Twenty Pounds for officiating as Clark of the Vestry for the year 1742.

Ordered that the Present Sheriff pay into the hands of the Present Church wardens all the money by him Collected or to be Collected for the Use of the Parrish for the year 1743.

Ordered that the Present Church wardens Discharge the Several Debts Due from the Parrish (Vizt) First wt [sic] is Due to the poor Next the Several Sculps Then the Readers & then the other Debts till they are Discharged

Ordered that Mary HAVIT be paid by the Present Church wardens Ten Pounds for her Support.

Ordered that the Vestry be Adjourned till the Thursday before Easter and According [sic] it is Adjurned.

===

At a Vestry held at Edenton the 24th day of March 1743. Present

Mr: James CRAVEN Mr: John BLOUNT Mr: John HALSEY Mr: Wm. BENBURY { Mr: Joseph MING Mr: Wm. LEWIS Mr: Olando CHAMPION { Mr Jacob BUTTLER Mr: Wm. HOSKINS { Church Wardens

Ordered That Mr: Jacob BUTTLER be allowed for Sixy Six Squirels Sculps Killed in the year 1740 One Pound Thirteen Shillings and for One Wild Catt Twenty Shillings Killed In the year 1742.

We the Subscribers being Ordered by the Vestry to Examine and Settle the Accounts [sic] Mr: John HALSEY and Mr: Orlando CHAMPION and to Make report to th_ Vestry of the Same, And Pursuant to the said Order We have Carefully Examined Upon Oath & Setled the Same and do find that the Ballance due is followeth (Vizt) that Mr: Orlando CHAMPION hath received for the use of the Parrish   £258=10 0?

that he hath payd & Ex?pended for the use of the Same 409 0? So there is Due from the Parish to Mr: Orlando CHAMPION   £155:1 ?

(109) *109 1743* And that Mr: _ohn HALSEY [Remainder of line is illegible.]

And that he hath paid & Expended for the use of the Same _____ [blank]

So that there is Due from the Parrish to Mr: John HALSEY in Ballance £ [blank]

       Test. --   J BUTLER Cwd Wm: HOSKINS Cward__

William LUTEN Esqr: Late Sheriff of Chowan (Vizt) for the year 1741 and 1742 Proov?ed his Accounts Upon Oath Which is as follows (Vizt.)__

Parrish of Chowan Dr: to William LUTEN for the years aforesd. -------
To Bills paid to Sundry parsons as pr Vouchers Produce £935 - 5 --
By Sundry Sums received for 1741 for 806 Tythables @ 15/-- 604 -10 --
By Do: Received for 1742 for 876 @ 7/6 pr Do - - - - 330 15 --
                                                       £935= 5

So that it appears to this Vestry that he hath fully Accounted According to Law

Allowed in the above Account An Order to Robert FULLERTON for £59: 2:? Allowed him at a Vestry held the first day of July 1738 for Boarding Christian NUTON.

Ordered that Mr: Nathaniel HOCOTT is allowed Thirty Shillings for ???? Attendance with his horse and Cart to Ca_ry the poor to his house

Ordered That Jacob BUTTLER Esqr: be allowed the following Sums To wit
The Ballance due of a former Acct: as Appears in this Book   £ 8: 4 10
The Ballance of Thos. EVINS Acct: on Account}   8:15: 0
of a Bastard Child - - - - - - - }
For three Coppys of the Church Act - - - - - -   6 -- -- --
                                                              £22:15: 4

Ordered that the Present Church wardens pay to Jacob BUTTLER the above Sum of £22:15:4}----

Ordered that the present Church wardens pay to Orlando CHAMPION late Church warden the Sum of £155:15:5 Which he has advanced for the Parrish as appears by his Account Stated in this Book.

Ordered that the present Church wardens pay to John HALSEY Late Church warden the Sum of four Pounds which he has Advanced for the parrish as Appears by his Account Stated in this Book.

Ordered that the present Sheriff pay into the hands of the present Church wardens all the Money that is Now Collected or to be Collected for the year 1743. 58

(110) *10 1743* Ordered that Benjamin TALBOT be paid by the present Church Wardens Twenty five Pound for officiating as

24 March 1743/44

(110) (Cont.) Clark of the Vestry and? and as Read~~inger~~ for this Present Year 1743.

Ordered that George **PARRISS** be Paid by the present Church wardens Seven Pounds Ten Shillings for Rent a of [sic] house for Mrs: Elizabeth **TOMSON** to Dwell in from the 5 day of June 1743 to the 24th of this Instant March 1743

J **BUTLER** Cwad? Wm. **HOSKINS** C Warn.

Than? _ ayr.?

Easter Monday the 20th day of March 1744

The Freeholders of the County & Parrish of Chowan Met at the Court house in Edenton and then & there did Elect & Choose the following Gentlemen for Vestry men (Vizt)

James **CRAVEN** Esqr: Richard **BOND** William **WALTON** Jonathan **PARKER** William **HOSKINS** { John **HALSEY** Esqr Thomas **WALTON** John **BANBURY** James: **FARLEE** Isaac **HUNTER** { Mr: John **LEWIS** Mr: Isaac **HUNTER**{

Which Said Gentlemen Qualified by taking the Oaths by Law appointed of the Qualification of Publick officers & Subscribing the Test The Vestry Adjurns till the 21st day of April Next & then to Meet at the Court house in Edenton.

===

At a Vestry held at [sic] the 21st day of April 1744. Present

Mr: James **FARLEE** Mr: Thomas **WALTON** Mr: Jonathan **PARKER** Mr: William **HOSKINS** Mr: William **WALTON** Mr: Richard **BOND**{ Mr: John **WILLKINS** Mr: Isaac **HUNTER** Mr: John **LEWIS** James **CRAVEN** :Esqr: John **HALSEY** :Esqr Mr: James **FARLEE** [sic]{

And Chose Mr: John **WILKINS** & Mr: Isaac **HUNTER** Church wardens for this Present year 1744.

Ordered that Benjamin **TALBOT** be appointed Clerk of this Vestry for this Present? year? and be allowed Twelve Pounds for his so Acting.

(111) *111 1744* Ordered that M_: William **SKINNER** & Isaac **HUNTER** be C_____ Readers at fifteen Pounds pr. Anum.

Ordered that a Levie of Eight Pence Proclamation money be? Levied on Each & Every Tythable Person in this Parrish of Chowan This Present year 1744 for and towards Defraying The Contingen_ Charges of the Said Parrish.

Ordered Mr: **GRANDIN** be appointed Reader of Edenton and to be allowed as other Readers.

Ordered That Benjamin **TALBOT** be appointed Reader and to Read Once a fortnight at Wm. **HOUGHTON**'s & to have fifteen £s Per year for his Such Servise

This Vestry adjourns till the 28th day of ____ next then to meet at the Chapple on Mr: James **CONSTANT**s Plantation.

At a Vestry held at the Chapple on Mr: James **CONSTANT**'s Plantation June the 28th 1744 Present

James **CRAVEN** Esqr: John **HALSEY** Esqr Mr: John **BANBURY** Mr: James **FARLEE** Mr: Jonathan **PARKER**{ Mr: Thomas **WALTON** Mr: William **WALTON** Mr: William **HOSKINS** Mr: John **LEWIS** Mr: Richard **BOND**{ Mr: Jno: **WILLKINS** Mr: Isaac **HUNTER**{ Church wardens

Ordered that Benjamin **TALBOT** be Discharged from officiating - Reader for the Parish of Chowan & to be paid for the Quarter he has officiated.

Ordered that Daniel **GRANDIN** be Discharged from officia____ as Reader for the Parrish of Chowan & be paid for the Quarter he has officiat__ as Such. On the Motion of Mr: Henry **BAKER** that as he has Given One Acre of Land & Timber to Build a Chapple on Knotty Pine Swamp Whereon the Chapple Now Stands, In Consideration thereof it is Ordered That he Shall have Liberty to build a Pew in any Part of the Sd: Chappel he Pleases. *Right to a pew? in ____ ty Pine Chappel*

Ordered that the Church wardens & three of the Vestry to lay off The Pews belonging to the Chapples of this Parrish in a Reguler form, In Order for the Inhabitants to build Pews thereon & to be built in a Reguler form all a like. Ordered that the Present Sheriff and the late Church wardens do Settle their Accounts with the Present Church wardens at Edenton the 12th day of July According to Law & pay their Respective Sums of Money Due to the Parrish. Ordered that John **MATHIAS** be appointed Reader In the Roome of Benjamin **TALBOT** & to Read at Such placess as Shall be Directed by the Inhabitants and be allowed fifteen Pound pr year for his officiating as Such. *59 How to build pews*

(112) Ordered that the old Chapple Standing Near the Sandy Run Shall be Sold at Publick Vendue Giving Ten days Notice by Advertisement by Richard **BOND** & Isaac **HUNTER** Giving Six Months Credit for the Payment thereof & the money arising thereby to be applied to the use of building a Chapple at Tottring Ridge [sic.]

Ordered That William **DANIEL** & Edward **VANN** Senr: Possession all the Lands On the East Side of **COLE**s Creek to where the Road Crosses the Knotty Pine Swamp Thence Down the Said Road to **KITTERELL**s Road Thence along the Road to George **WILLIAMS** and from thence to the head of the White Potts, Then down the Said Swamp to **BENNET**s Creek, Thence Down the Said Creek to the first Station.

28 June 1744

(112) (Cont.) Ordered that Henry **GOODMAN** & Robert **ROGERS** Prosession all the Lands Between the Mill Swamp & the Knotty Pine to the Country Line.

Ordered That J [End of entry.]

N. B. St. Pauls Parish 1744 First Notice of St. Pauls Parish - Not So See ----der 1703/4
Govr. NICHOLSONs gift to the Precinct & Parish of St Paul's.

At a Vestry held at Edenton the 26th day of July 1744. Present

James **CRAVEN** Esqr: John **HALSEY** Esqr: Mr: Wm. **WALTON** Mr: James **FARLEE**{ Mr: Jonathan **PARKER** Mr: Wm. **HOSKINS** Mr: John **LEWIS** { Mr: Isaac **HUNTER** Mr: John **WILKINS** { Church wardens

Ordered by the Vestry that the Present Church wardens and James **CRAVEN** John **HALSEY** and Jonathan **PARKER** meet the 26th day of August Next at Edenton to write a Letter to the Commisory [sic] of South & North Carolina Acquainting him that by an Act of assembly of the Province of North Carolina The Vestry of Each Parish is obliged to Provide for a Clergiman a yearly Stepend of fifty Pounds Proclamation money Per Annum Each & Not less and Not to Exceed five Shillings Proclamation money Per Tythable for that & all other Parrish Charges and on the Arrival of a min____ of the Church of England of the Said Commissiorys Recommendation being of a man of Good Life and Conversation and Indowed with the True Princip__ of Such Profession that the Vestry & Church wardens of the Parrish of Chowan do Promise to Make Such Provision as by Law They are Impowe___ to do besides all other Perquesites Subscriptions & Advantage whatsoe___

(113) *113* [This page is written in two columns, at 90° from the normal orientation.]
Peter **PAYNE** Esqr: Sheriff of Chowan County Exhibated his Account for the Parrish money by him received in Virtue of his office for the year 1743 which is in these words (Vizt.)
Dr. the Parrish of Chowan their Account Current with Peter **PAYNE** Sheriff of Said County

1743   [Left column]

Date	Item	£ s d
Jany 27	To bills paid Jacob **BUTTLER** Esqr as Pr: receipt	13 10
30	To Do: Do: his order to Wm **HOUGHTON**	3 17 6
Do	To Do: Thomas **HOSKINS**	- 8 --
30	To Do: Mr: William **HOSKINS**	34 5..8
Feb ye 11	To bills paid Mr: **BUTTLER**	100 -- --
	To Mr: **HOSKINS** Order to Mr: **CRAVEN**	20 -- --
	To the Church wardens order to Mr **MC CLURE**	20 --
March 20th	To So much Paid Mr: **HOSKINS**	57 18 6
24th	To Mr: **BUTTLERs** Order to Thomas **PEARCE**	3 18 6
	To bills Paid Mr: **BUTTLER**	51 --
26	To Do Paid Mr: Jonathan **PARKER**	15 9 6
	To Do Paid Ms: **PERRY**	41 2 6
July 12th	To Do Paid the Church wardens	60 -- --
	To Mr: **HOSKINS** order on me to Thos: **RAMSEY**	20 18 --
	To Mr: **KIMSEYs** Order on the Church wardens	21 16 3
	To So Much furnished Rachel **PERVINE** as pr Acot:	4 7 6
	To bills paid Mr Orlando **CHAMPION**	26 -- -
	To ballance on Do: Order of Vestry	145 15 5
	To the Ballance of Mrs: **THOMPSON** Acct:	29 11 5
		678 -- 9
26	To Ballance due to this Account	149 14 7
	Edenton 26 July 1744	828 0 4

Errors & Omissions Excepted Peter **PAYNE** Sherff

	[Right column]	Year 1741	1742
1743	By Docr: **BLACKALL**	4 3 --	3 12 6
	By Capt: James **FARLEE**	8 6 --	--8 3 -- --
	By Andrew **OLIVER**	3 2 :5	
	By Elizabeth **HANMER**	1-- 15	1 -- 7 6
	By James **MITCHELL**	-- -- --	3 12 6
	By John **WALBUTTON**	-- -- --	2 -- 15

26 July 1744

(113) (Cont.)

By Wm. HOSKINS		16 -- 6 --
By Richard MC CLURE		1 -- 7 6
By Capt John CAMPBELL	3 2: 5	
By Peter PAYNE	2 1:10	1 7
By John BLOUNT	-- --	9 3 7
By Jonathan PARKER	4 3 --	3 1 2
	£ 18:15	17 12
		18 15
		36
By 1126 Tythables for the year 1743		844 15
		880 17?
Deducting My Comissions @ 6 pr Ct		52 7
		£828

Edenton 26 July 1744 This Day Appeared before Me Peter PAYNE Sheriff of Chowan County & Made Oath on the holy Evangilist that the above Account is Just & True Acct: Nevertheless he Saith that he is hopes to receive Some more money of those People he Present [sic] thinks in Solvents of which ?? he will give a? In a acct. to the wardens. J BLOUNT J P 60

(114) *1744* [Beginning of the first line on this page is missing.] of Chowan County Exhibited his Accoun--for the Parrish money

Ordered that Thomas LUTEN Sheriff of Chowan County for the year one Thousand Seven hundred & Thirty Nine & forty, and William LUTON Esqr. late Sheriff Appear at the Next Vestry to be held for the Parrish of Chowan on the 25th day of August Next at Edenton and then & there to Make up & Settle Their Accounts as the Law Directs Otherwise they May Expect to be Prosecuted According to Law And it is likewise ordered that William HOSKINS & Jacob BUTLER Late Church Wardens Appear at the Same time & Make up their Accounts and pay in the Several Ballances Due from them. It is further Ordered that the Clerk of the Vestry get a Coppy of the list of Tythables for the year one Thousand Seven hundred & thirty Nine, forty, forty one & forty Two at the Parrish Charge Against the Next Vestry so as the Said Vestry May be able to Judge of the Different Accounts Exhibited to them by the Different Sheriffs & Church wardens, And it is Further Ordered that if the afd Sheriffs & Church Wardens do not appear at the Next Vestry & Settle their Accounts According to Law, it is ordered that the Present Church warden Commence Actions in behalf of the Parrish of Chowan agains_ the Several Persons So failing without Further Orders.

On Motion of Rachel PERVINE Praying that Mr Thomas KEMSEY Might be Appointed by the Vestry to take Care of her on Such Terms as Thomas KEMSEY be allowed the Sum of one Pound five Shillings Bills per week for Each week he Shall maintaine her and Carry her to Cosandy Springs and So in Proportion for the Year 1744.

Ordered That the Vestry be Adjourned till the 25th day of August Next at Edenton.

John HOSKINS Isaac HUNTER C. w

(115) *115 1744* At a Vestry held at Edenton [Remainder of line is missing.]

Present

Mr: Isaac HUNTER Mr: John WILLKINS} Church wardens {Mr: Richard BOND Mr: Wm. WALTON Mr: Wm. HOSKINS { Mr Thos WALTON James CRAVEN Esqr

Ordered That Benjamin TALBOT be Appointed Reader of Edenton at fifteen Pound Pr year from the Date hereof.

At a Vestry held at Edenton the Twentyith day of February 1744.

Present Mr: Wm. HOSKINS Mr: John BENBURY Mr: Wm. WALTON { Mr: John HALSEY Mr: Richard BOND Mr: Thoms: WALTON { Mr: Isaac HUNTER Mr: Jno: WILLKINS{ Church wardens.

(Ordered that Mr: John HALSEY be allow'd Ten Pounds for Keeping and burying William COAPS)

Ordered that the Reverend Mr: Clement HALL be Allowed Sixty Pounds Proclamation money per Annum for officiating Two Sundays in three at Edenton and the Next Sunday at one of the Chapples above & to Preach Every Monday at Thomas WALTONs Junr: at Katherine Creek that he Preaches at the Knotty Pine Chapple on the Sunday. Mr. _____ t HALL

Ordered that Mr: John WILKINS and Wm. HOSKINS be Impowered to Agree with any Person for a Plantation and to Employ any Person or Persons to repair the Same if Need require to be fit to receive Mr: Clement HALL to live on and Charge the Same to the Parrish and likewise to hire Persons, and Craft or Vessell to remove the Goods and Chattles of the Said Clement HALL to the place he is to live on in this Parrish. Isaac HUNTER & John WILLKINS Sign as Church wardens _____ HALL

At a Vestry held at Edenton May the 9th 1745.

9 May 1745

(115) (Cont.) Present
Mr: James **CRAVEN** Mr: Richd: **BOND** Mr: Wm. **WALTON** { Mr: Jonathan **PARKER** Mr: James **FARLAW**- Mr: John **LEWISS**- { Mr: Isaac **HUNTER** Church wardn.

Ordered that a Levie be laid on Each Taxable Person within the Parrish of St: Pauls in the County of Chowan for this Present Year of Two Shillings Proclamation Money to Defray the Debts and Charges of the Said Parrish and to be Collected and Levied as the Law directs. Ordered that the Vestry Meet at Mr: **CONSTANT**'s Chappel on the 29th day of June Next. And Likewise Ordered that Advertisements be put for all Persons to Meet the Vestry at **CONSTANT**'s Chapple and bring in their Demands on the Parrish. Ordered that the Sheriff appear at the Next Vestry and Settle his Accts: then & there on Oath or Send the Accts: there with the Ballance thereof Duly Proved.   Isaac **HUNTER** Signs as Church warden 61

(116) _745_ At a Vestry held at Edenton the 19th Day of July 1745
Present Mr: Wm: **HOSKINS** Mr: Thos: **WALTON** Mr: Jas: **FARLOW** Mr: Richd: **BOND** { Mr: Wm. **WALTON** Mr: Jonathan **PARKER** Mr: John **WILKINS** Mr: Jas: CRAVEN } Mr: John **BENBURY** Mr: Isaac **HUNTER** { Church wardens

Ordered that the Church wardens Agree with Doctor **BLACKALL** to Put Margaret **NOWELL** & Christian **NEWTON** into a Salavation in order to Cure them or to take of a Limb if required.

Ordered that No Sheriff for the future Shall Pay any money on any order of Vestry without the Said Order be Signed by the Present Church wardings then in being.

Ordered that the Vestry Meet at the Dwelling house of Cpt: James **FARLOW**'s on the 21st day of September Next
   Isaac **HUNTER** & John **BENBURY** Sign as Church wardens.

N. B. The following Orders of April ye. 15th: 1745, being before omitted are here placed. Vizt.

At a Vestry held at Edenton Aprill ye: 15th: 1745.

Present Mr: Jonathan **PARKER** Mr: John **BENBURY** Mr: Thomas **WALTON** Mr. John **HALSEY** Mr. John **LEWIS** Mr. Wm. **HOSKINS** Mr. Jas. **FARLAW** Mr. John **WILKINS** Mr. Isaac **HUNTER** } Church Wardens.

Order'd that Benjamin **TALBOT** be Clerk of this Vestry for ye present year, & be paid as the year 1744.

Ordered That Mr. John **BENBURY** be Church Warden for this present year In the Room of Mr. John **WILKINS**.

Ordered that Benja. **TALBOT** be paid Twelve pounds for officiating as Clark of this Vestry for ye. year 1744.

Order'd That Robert **FULLERTON** be allowed at ye. Rate of fifty pounds pr. year from ye. date hereof for keeping Christian **NEWTON** In all Necessarys for her Support of ye. year Ensuing.

Ordered That the Vestry meet at the Court House in Edenton on the third Thursday in May
   J **BENBURY** Isaac **HUNTER**.

(117) Dr: The Parrish of Chowan their Acct: Current with Peter **PAYNE**   Contra   Cr
_44_

??t 10th	To Sundrys furnished Rachael **PURVINE** as pr Acot:	20 10 --	By 1151 Tithables for the year 1744 @ 5/ £287 15 --
	To Ballance of Mrs: **THOMPSON**s acct from 22d} June to 24th Novemr? @ 25/ pr week - - - }	20 10 --	
Janry?	To An Order to Jos: **MING** for Sculps & [sic] - -	-- 8 18 --	
	To Do: To Captn: Henry **BONNER** - - - -	-- 6 15 --	
	To Do: To John **LEWIS** - - - - - - -	-- -- 4 -- --	
29	To Bills paid Mr Isaac **HUNTER** as pr ___ [illegible]	23 14 6	
Feby 6th	To Do: Mr: John **WILKINS** - - - - - - -	20 -- --	
___:15	To Mr: **PARKER**s Order on Do: Accepted - -	7 16 --	
Dr?	To Bills paid Mr: **WILKINS** - - - - - -	10 -- --	
	To Do: paid Benjamin **TALBOT** for Mrs: **THOMPSON**s} Board as pr Receipt - - - - - - - - }	18 15 --	
May 10th	To his Order on the Vestry - - - - - - -	22 2 9	
	To Thomas **KIMSEY**'s Order on Do: - - - - -	65 -- --	
	To Bills pd: Mr: **WILKINS** as pr receipt - - - -	4 7 6	
	To Do: Mr: **WILKINS** Order to Mrs: **GREGORY** -	15 --	
		£246 9 3	
	To My Commissions @ 6 pr Cent	17 5 7	
		263 14 10	
	To Ballance due to this Account - - - -	24 -- 2	

51

19 July 1745

(117) (Cont.) Edenton July 19 1745   287 15 : 0
Peter **PAYNE** Esqr: s-- Personally appeared before me and proved the above Acct: On Oath to be Just and True and that he h__ Given Credit for all the Tythables that he hath _____ Abra. **BLACKALL** 62

(118) *118 1745.* C___ an At a Vestry held at Mr. James **FARLOW**s Dwelling house September ye. 21st. 1745.

Present Mr. James **FARLEE** Mr. Richd. **BOND** Mr. Thos. **WALTON** } Mr. Wm. **WALTON** Mr. John **LEWIS** Mr. John **HALSEY** } Mr. Isaac **HUNTER** Mr. John **BENBURY**} Church Wardens

Ordered that, by the Virtue of an order of ye. Vestry made on the 28th: Day of June 1744, the old Chappel Standing Near the Sandy Run be Sold at Publick Vendue. Is this day Sold Accordingly for Nineteen pounds, which Sum is this day paid to ye. present Church Wardens.

Ordered That Whereas Thomas **LUTEN** Esqr. & William **LUTEN** Esqr. Late Sheriffs of Chowan County, for ye. years 1739, 1740, 1741, 1742, Did not appear to Meet ye. Vestry of ye. Parish of St. Pauls in the County of Chowan on ye. 25th: day of August 1744, to Settle their Accounts Due to ye. Sd. Parish, as the Law Directs, We ye. Now Vestry Do now in Consideration of Such Default Impower the present Church Wardens, To Commence Action Directly Against the Said Thomas and William **LUTEN** Late Sherriffs as aforesd., In order to bring & Settle the Ballance of all Accots. Due from them to ye. parish as afd. to a Just Account as ye. Law Directs.

Order'd That the present Church Wardens take into their possession all the plate and other Ornaments, belonging to the Parish of St. Pauls, that Shall be found in ye: hands or Possession of any person or persons whatsoever in the parish aforesd.

Order'd That the Vestry be adjourned till the 19th: Day of October Next; and Then to Meet at Captn: James **FARLEE** [sic] by the Hour of ten of the Clock in ye. Morning.   J: **BENBURY** Isaac **HUNTER** } Ch: W. C: W.

(119) *119. 1745* North Carolina ss.. At a Vestry held at Mr. Willm. **ARKILL**s On the 27th: day of February 1745. Present

Mr. Isaac **HUNTER** Mr. John **BENBURY**} Ch: Wardens} Richard **BOND** John **WILKINS** James **FARLEE**} Thomas **WALTON** Wm. **WALTON** John **HALSEY** Jonathan **PARKER** }

Ordered That the following Drafts be given upon the Sheriff, Vizt.,
To a Draft   [blank]   for [Remainder of page is blank.] 63

(120) *120 1746* ___ :i Ca____ na. ss.

Easter Monday the 31st. day of March 1746

The freeholders of the County and Parish of Chowan met at the Court house in Edenton, and then & there did Elect and Choose the following Gentlemen, for Vestry men. Vizt.

1. James **CRAVEN**, 2. John **HALSEY**, 3. John **BENBURY**, 4. William **HOSKINS**, 5. Christian **REED**, 6. Henry **BONNER**, 7. Joseph **BLOUNT**, 8. John **SOMNER**, 9. Isaac **HUNTER**, 10. Richard **BOND**, & 11. Thomas **WALTON**, and Jonathan **PARKER**, the afsd. Eleven of

Which Said Gentlemen Qualifyed, by taking ye. Oaths by Law appointed for the Qualification of Publick officers and Subscribing the Test, ordered that the Late Church Wardens lay their Accounts before the Next Vestry.

Ordered That the Vestry meet in the Court house in Edenton on Saturday the 26th: day of April 1746.

==

Saturday April ye. 26: 1746. Then ye. Vestry met in the Court House at Edenton, According to appointment Vizt.

1. James **CRAVEN**, 2.. Isaac **HUNTER**, 3. John **SUMNER** 4. Wm. **HOSKINS**, 5. Joseph **BLOUNT**, 7. [sic] Thos. **WALTON** } who chose (then present, by their own Consent) Messrs. John **HALSEY** and John **BENBURRY** Church Wardens for this present year 1746.

Order'd That the Reverd. Mr. Clement **HALL** Clerk be Continued as a Minister for the parish of St. Pauls for ye. year 1746, at Sixty pounds proclamation Money, he attending at Edenton to preach Every other Sunday, and the Same at the Chappels above Vizt. **CONSTANT**s and Knotty pine Chappel.

Ordered That Three Readers be appointed, Vizt. one at Edenton, one at **CONSTANT**s Chappel, and one at knottey pine Chappel And Accordingly that Isaac **HUNTER** be, & is hereby appointed Reader at **CONSTANT** [sic] Chappel and be allowed Twenty Shillings proclamation Money for ye. year; and that William **SKINNER** be & is hereby appointed Reader at Knotty pine Chappel and be allowed the Same Sum: And That Mr. Daniel **GRANDIN** be & is hereby appointed Reader in Edenton & be allowed Two pounds proclamation money for this present year 1746, and that he ye. Sd. **GRANDIN** be, & is hereby appointed Clerk of ye. Vestry   for

(121) ___ ' *1746* for _____ year 1746, and that ____ allowed for the Sum of one pound Seven Shillings & Six pence like proclama____ Money.

Ordered That a Tax be laid of Two Shillings & Six pen__ proclamation Money On Each Taxable person in the Sd. Parish,

26 April 1746

(121) (Cont.) and to be Collected as the Law Directs.

Order'd That the Several Sheriffs, as also the Church Wardens for the County of Chowan & Parish of St. Pauls lay their Accounts before Messrs: James **CRAVEN** and Joseph **BLOUNT** for the_ to Audite & Inspect, and Report to ye. Next Vestry, The Sd. **CRAVEN BLOUNT** [sic] giving Notice, And on their or any of their Refusal be prosecuted as the Law Directs, without further orders.

Order'd That the Vestry Meet the Last Tuesday in May Next at Edenton.

J. **BENBURY** J. **HALSEY** } Ch: Wardens.

Tuesday May ye. 27th: 1746. Then ye Vestry met at ye. Court House in Edenton, According to appointment, Vizt. Messrs. James **CRAVEN**, Wm. **HOSKINS**, Joseph **BLOUNT**, Henry **BONNER**, Isaac **HUNTER**, and Thomas **WALTON**; with Messrs. John **HALSEY** and John **BENBURY** Church Wardens.

Mr. Jonathan **PARKER** (Then appearing) was Qualifyed as a Vestry Man, by taking ye. Oaths by Law appointed for ye. Qualification of Publick Officers, cr. [sic] and Accordingly took his place with his Colleagues.

After Reading of the Entries; Examination made & approbation had of them, from ye. Minutes, wch. were omitted to be Entered? as well by Benjamin **TALBOT**, as ye. Minutes of Last Vestry, Ordered ye. Sd. Minutes be Cancelled, and ye. Entries as in ye. Sd. Vestry Book to Stand.

Whereas in ye. order last Vestry Continuing Mr **HALL** Minister for this year 1746: on Condition of his preaching Every other Sunday at Edenton, & ye. Same at ye. Chappels above, Sd. Mr. **HALL** not being then present, and he now giving his Reasons why he cannot Comply with the Same *It is Therefore Considered & ordered by? this Vestry, That ye. Sd. Mr. **HALL** give his attendance to preach at the places afsd. According to order and appointment last

year *N. B.* __ Messrs. Jas. _**RAVEN** & Jonathan __**RKER** did not ___ sent to this _____ 64

(122) ___6 year, and in _____ to rem_____ plantation where he Now is, as before, till further orders, Together with the Same priviledges in ye. Discharge of his Duty (as a Missionary) as he Enjoyed last year. *122*

Order'd That the Vestry Meet again at the Court house in Edenton the last Saturday in September Next. J **HALSEY** J: **BENBURY** } Ch: Wardens

North Carolina}
Chowan Parish} ss.

At a Vestry held at Edenton March ye. 21st. 1746.

Present John **HALSEY** & Jno. **BENBURY** } Church Wardens.

James **CRAVEN** Willm. **HOSKINS** Jos: **BLOUNT** Isaac **HUNTER** Richard **BOND** Thomas **WALTON**}

Mr. Thomas **WALTON** Exhibited his Account as Church Warden for the year 1741 Which was Duly proved and which follows in These words, vizt. as, on The following Page.

(123) ___ [This page is written in two columns, at 90° from the normal orientation.]
1741. Dr. The Parish of Chowan, Account Current with Thomas **WALTON** [Left column.]

To Bills pd. Richard **BOND** as pr his Credit - - - - -	£ 57: 9:06
To Ditto paid Wm. **FREEMAN** as pr voucher for R: **PURVINE**	8: 4:6
To keeping John **MARCUS** & his wife for 23 Weeks - - - -	45:19:6
To Bills paid Jams. **GOODING** for keeping Margt. **ROGERS** -	10:10:--
To Do. paid Mrs. **PERRY** for Do. Mary **WILLIAMS** 6 weeks	6: --:--
To Do. paid Mary **ANDREW** for Do. Margt. **ROGERS** 5 months	12:12:--
To Do. paid Isaac **HILL** for Two Wolf Sculps - - -	8: --:--
To Do. paid Thos. **TAYLOR** for Do. &? 2 Wild Catts - -	6: --:-- *Wolves Wild Cats*
To Do. paid Moses **HILL** for 1 Wild Catt skin & 8 Squirels	1: 4:0
To Do. for keeping Rachel **PURVINE** - - - - -	45: 3:--
To Do. for keeping Mary **SPIGHT** 7 Months - - - -	20: 0:0
To Do. paid Doctr. John **WILLIAMS** for Ditto - - - -	60: 0:0
To Do. paid Ephraim **BLANSHARD** for a Woolfs Sculp - -	4: 0:0
To Do. pd. Thos: **WALTON** Junr. for 23 Squeril Sculps - -	0:16:6
To Commissn: @ 3 pr Ct. on £186:12:6 - - - - -	5:11:3
Chowan Parish	£291:10:3

Edenton March 21st. 1746 Errors Excepted pr Thos. **WALTON**: Ch: W:

21 March 1746/7

(123) (Cont.) [Right column]ks Cr.

1741 By Bills Recd. from Willm. LUTON Sheriff	£ 44:12:
By Do. from Ditto	100 :--:
By Ditto from Thomas EVENS for a fine	5: 0:
By Ditto from Mary SPIGHTs Estate	32: 0:
By Ditto from John MARCUS Estate	5: 0:
By Ditto from John ALSTON Sheriff	40: 0:
By Ditto from William LUTON Sheriff	36:12
Ball Due to Mr. Thomas WALTON	28: 5:
	£291: 1

Chowan County .ss. Thomas WALTON personally appeared before me, and Made Oath on the Holy Evangelists that the Several Sums Charged in the Account above was Bona fide paid to the Several persons therein Named for ye. within Mentioned Amounting to Two hundred and Ninety one pounds Ten Shillings & three pence Bills, and that he Received No More than what he hath given Credit for in ye. Same Account, from the Severall perso___ mentioned, as Church Warden for Chowan Parish for ye. year one thousand Seven hundred and fo___ one. Sworn before me the 21st. Day of March 1746. J. HALSEY. 65

(124) [This page is written at 90° from the normal orientation.]

Mr: Richard BOND Exhibited his Account as Church Warden for the year 1741 _____ lows in These Words Vizt.

Dr. The Parish of Chowan Account Current with   Richard BOND   Cr. *124*

41. To Building a Chappell near CONSTANTs	-£296:5:0	1741	
N?. B. To Commissn. on 201:17:6 Recd. from}		March 17th: By Bills Recd. of Wm. LUTON Sheriff	-£90:6:
William and Thomas LUTON Late }		By Ditto from Ditto	100:0:
Sheriffs @ 3 pr Ct. - - - }	6:0:10½	By Ditto from Thomas WALTON	57:9:
		By Ditto from Demsey SUMNER	8:0:
		By Ditto from Thomas LUTON Sheriff	11:11:
		By Ditto from John BENBURY	12: 0:
		Ball Due to Mr. BOND	22:18:
	£302:5:10½		£302:5:_

Chowan Parish
    Edenton March ye. 21st. 1746
        Errors Excepted
            Richard BOND Ch Warden

Chowan County.ss. Richard BOND personally appeared before me and Made Oath on the Holy Evangelists That the above Account is Just and True, and that The Credit Contains the Several Sums by him Received, and all, as Church Warden for Chowan Parish, for ye. year one thousand Seven hundred and fourty one.
    Sworn before me the 21st. Day of March 1746. J. HALSEY   Ordered

(125) ___ 7. Ordered That The Vestry Do M___ Easter Monday Next. J: HALSEY: J: BENBURY } Ch: Warden [sic] *125*

North Carolina .ss. At a Vestry Begun and held at Edenton for the Parish of St. Pauls and County of Chowan on the 20th: Day April 1747. Present {John HALSEY John BENBURRY} Church Wardens
    Messrs. James CRAVEN William HOSKINS John SUMNER } Isaac HUNTER Richard BOND Thomas WALTON } Vestry Men.
    Ordered That John WILLIAMSON be allowed the Sum of five Pounds, Bills, for Reading at Knotty Pine Chapel for Eight Months by Past, and that he Be Continued for the Ensuing year at fifteen Pounds Bills pr. Annum, And That Mr. Isaac HUNTER be Contin___ at fifteen pounds pr. Annum.
    Ordered That John ALSTON Esqr. Sheriff of Chowa_ County have Notice To Lay his Accounts before ye. Next Vestry.
    Mr. William HOSKINS Exhibited his Account as Chur__ Warden for St. Paul Parish for ye. year 1743 upon Oath by Which Account, (as on Next page) It appears he hath received £142:4:2 Bills, and hath paid the Sum of £143:13:9 for the Payment of Which Sum he produced Vouchers, So That There is a Ballance Due to ye William HOSKINS the Sum of £1:9:7 Bills, &r H___ 66

(126) [This page is written at 90° from the normal orientation.]
    Dr. The Parish of St. Pauls in Chowan County Acct. with Mr. William HOSKINS
___y 19th:

20 April 1747

(126) (Cont.)

1743	To Boarding Mrs. THOMPSON 5 weeks @ 25s. pr week	£ 6: 5:0	1743.	
	To Boarding Mrs. PERVINE 3 Weeks @ Do.	3:15:0	By money Recd. of ye. Parish	£14:2?___
	To Boarding Mrs. MARCUS 3 Weeks @ Do.	3:15:0	Ball: Due to Mr. HOSKINS	1:
	To Boarding Mrs. MARCUS 21½ Weeks @ Do.	21:10:--		
	To fetching Mrs. MARCUS from Greehall	1:--:--		
	To fetching THOMPSON & PERVINE from Town & Carrying them Back	1:--:--		
	To 4 Load & half of Short Wood to Mrs. THOMSON.	3: 7:6		
	To Burrying Mrs. MARCUS	6:--:--		
	To pd. to Mr. CHAMPION £10: Do. To Mr. TALBOT £14:	24:--:--		
	To Do. pd. to Mrs THOMPSON	14: 5:6		
	To Do. To Mrs. HAVITT	10:--:--		
	To Do. To Mr. TROTTER for Mr. KIMSEY	24: 4:6		
	To Do. To Sarah HARLOE 20s. To Jos: CHAMPION £5:10s.	6:10:--		
	To Do. pd. to Mr. ADAMS	2:16:--		
	To Do. To Mr. KIMSEY	11:01:6		
	To Commissions for £139:10s.	4: 3:9		
		£143:13:9		£143:13:9

Errors Excepted pr Wm HOSKINS ??? April ye 20th. 1747 Then appeared Wm. HOSK___ before me & Made oath on ye. holy Evangelists That ye. above acct. is Just & True and that he Recd. no more? than what as above he hath given Credit for, and all, as Church Warden for ye. year 1743.

Sworn before me this about? 20th. aprill 1747. J. HALSEY   order

(127) *127. 1747.* Ordered That Mr. John [Remainder of line is missing.] be Continued, by their own Consent, as Ch____ Ward____ this year 1747.

Ordered The Church Wardens find Such Necessary Cloathing for Margret NOEL as they or Either of them Sha__ think Reasonable and Charge the Same to the Parish.

Ordered That Notice be put for all persons that have any Demand On the Parish to appear at ye. Nex_ Vestry and Make good their Demand.

Mr. Robert FULLINGTON Agreed to Take and keep ___ Christian NUTON at fourty Pounds Bills for the Ensuing year, he to find her Necessary food and Raiment, &r.

Ordered That the Vestry Meet again at Mr. James FARLEEs the 23d. Day of May Next.

J. HALSEY John BENBURY } Ch: Wardens

May ye. 23d. 1747. Then ye. Vestry Met at ye house of Mr. James FARLEEs, According to appointmt. Present Messrs John HALSEY & Jno. BENBURY Ch: Wardens

Messrs. John SUMNER Thomas WALTON Richard BOND Joseph BLOUNT } Isaac HUNTER Jonathn. PARKER } Vestry-men

John ALSTON Esqr. late Sheriff of Chowan County Exhibited his Account for ye. Parish Money by him Recd. in Virtue of his office for ye. year 1745, which he proved upon oath, as on ye. Next page followeth Viz.

Dr. 67

(128) [This page is written at 90° from the normal orientation.]

___ Th_ Paris__ f St. Pauls in Chowan their Accot. Currt. with John ALSTON Esqr. 128

___5	To Bill Money pd. Mr. HALL pr order	£450 0 00	Contra	Cr.
	To Do. pd. Mr. Jona. PARKER pr Do.	100 0 00	By 1183 Tythables @ 15s pr £ [sic]	£887:_____
	To Do. pd. Wm. SKINNER pr Do.	25 -- --		
	To Do. pd. Thos. WALTON pr Do.	40 -- --		
	To Do. pd. John BENBURRY pr Do.	150 -- --		
	To Do. pd. Isaac HUNTER pr Do.	11 -- --		
	To Do. pd. Richard BOND pr Do.	12 -- --		
	To my Commissions at 6 pr Ct.	53 4 --		

23 May 1747

(128) (Cont.)

To Money pd. Jno. BENBURY	- -	16 5 --
To Money pd. Jno. BENBURY	- -	29 16
Errors Excepted		£887 5 00

£887:5:__

pr Jno. ALSTON

May ye. 23d. 1747. Then ye. above Named John ALSTON personally appeared before Me, and made oath on ye. Holy Evangelists of Almighty God That ye. above Accot. is Just and True and that he hath Given Credit for all ye. Tythables That he hath Received for ye. year 1745.

Sworn before Me J HALSEY   also

(129) [This page is written at 90° from the normal orientation.]
also, Then Mr. Isaac HUNTER Exhibited his? accots as Church Warde_ for ye years 1744 and 1745, wch act. follows in These words Viz.) 129

Chowan Parish Dr. To Isaac HUNTER		Contra	Cr.	
To pd. To Jno. GORDON for work Done		Recd. of Mr. PAIN - -	Bills	£ 50: 0:0
In Meherin Chapel - - - -procl:	£ 2:10:--	---- of Ditto - - - -		23:14:_
To Jonathan PARKER for work Done in}		---- of Do. - - - -		8:-- :_
ye. knotty Pine Chapel - - - - }	2: 2:6	---- of Collol: ALSTON -		11:-- :
To Bread & wine for 2 Comunions -	0:10:--	---- of Eliza. SUMNER -		9: 7:6
To 4 years Salary as Clark @ £15: is -	8:-- :--	---- of Eliza. TUCKER -		9: 7:6
To pd. Jonathan PARKER £50: - -	6:13:4	---- of Eliza. PARKER -		7:10:_
To Wm. HUNTER for Vermin £22: -	2:18:8	---- of Col. ALLSTON for fines, of}		
	£22:14:6	John JAMES & Jas. YOURE for}	*Fines for Swearing*	
To 3 pr Ct. for paying away - -	:13:7¼	Swearing }		5:12:6
To Bread & wine for 3 Comunions}		Recd. of Matthew GUMBS - -		19: 0:_
(one of yem to Come) - - }	--:15:--	The above £143:12:0 in procl:		£143:12:
	£24: 3:1	money at 7½ is £19:2:11 wch makes		
		ye. Ball: Due to Isac HUNTER 5:0: 2		
			£24:3: 1 wch is Bills £37:10:	

Errors Excepted pr Isaac HUNTER

May ye. 23d. 1747 Then ye. above Isaac HUNTER personally appeared before me and made oath on ye. Holy Evangelists of Almighty God, that ye. above Accots. is Just & True, and that he hath Recd. no more than as above in ye Sd. Accot. he hath given Credit for. Sworn before me J. HALSEY.

So that ye. above Ballance of £5:0 2 procl: appearing to be Due to Sd. HUNTER, It is therefore Orde___ That ye. Church Wardens pay ye. Same unto him in Bills £37:10s.   Then 68

(130) *130 1747* Then Coll: John ALSTON late Sher of Chowan County Exhibited his Accot. for ye. Parish Money By him Recd. in Virtue of his office for ye. year 1746. in ye. Manner following viz.

The Parish of St. Pauls in Chowan County their		Contra	Cr
Accot. with John ALSTON Esqr. Sherriff Dr.		By Bills Recd. - - - -	£1072:10:--
1747. To Bill money for 1217 Tythables ye. year 1746}		By Comissions at 6 pr Ct.}	
amounting in ye. whole to £1140:18:9		on £1140:18:9 - - } - -	-- 68: 8:9
May 23d.	£1140:18:9		£1140:18:9
		May ye. 23d. 1747	

Mr. Jonathan PARKER then also Exhibited his Accot. before this Vestry wch. follows in These words, Viz.
The Parish of Chowan To Jonathan

PARKER - - - -	Dr.	Contra	Cr
To Building a Chapel at }	}	Recd. of Mr. HUNTER - -	£ 50: 0:0
Knotty pine pr ordr. of }	}	Do. of Mr. WILKINS - - -	100: --:--
Vestry £42:10. procl: @ 7½ pr is?}	£318:15:0}	Do. of Coll: ALSTON - - -	100: --:--
May 23d. 1747 Errors Excepted		Do. of Mr. PAYNE - - -	18: --:--
pr Jonathan PARKER			£258: 0:0
		Due to J PARKER	50:15:0
			£318:15

23 May 1747

(130) (Cont.) This 23d. day of May 1747. Then appeared prsonally ye. above Sd. Jonathan **PARKER** and made oath on ye. holy Evangelists of Almighty God That ye. above Accots. is Just & True and that ye. Sums in ye. above Credit by him given are all that he hath Recd. & yt. Ye. Ball: of fifty Pounds fifteen Shillings is Justly due to him before me. J. **HALSEY** -- Whereupon It is ordered by ye. Vestry that ye. Church Wardens pay to Sd. Jonathn. **PARKER** ye. Ballance as afd.

Then, the Reverd. Mr. Clement **HALL** appearing, It was & is hereby ordered That he be Continued as a Minister of ye. Parish of St. Pauls for ye. year 1747. at Sixty Pounds proclamation Money, he giving his attendance to preach and perform other Dutyes Required of him, as he performed last year according to ye. order & appointmt. then of ye. Vestry, Always provided, That as he goes to preach to **CONSTANT**s Chapel, from Lady Day to Michaelmas, he preach on ye. Saturday at ye. House of Mr. James **FARLOW**s, &r.

Ordered That a Tax (or Levy) be Lay'd of Sixteen pence proclamation Money on Each Taxable person in the Parrish for this present year 1747, & be Collected as ye. Law Directs. Then

(131) [This page is written, in two columns, at 90° from the normal orientation.]
Then, Mr. John **BENBURY** Exhibited his Accot. in ye. Manner following. [Left column.]
Dr. The Parish of Chowan Their Accot. Currt. with John **BENBURY**

1747. To Bills pd. Mr. J **HALSEY** for burying Wm: **CAPES** £10:-Do. to Mr. **PAIN** & **TALBOT** for Bread &: wine for ye. Comunion ???? £2:9:	£ 12 5 0
April 20th: To pd. Mrs **DENHAM** for keeping **TALBOT**s Children to Ye. 29 Janry: 1745	7 0 0
To **HOWARD** for attendg. Margt. **NOEL** in Salivation £12:-To Wm. **BENBURY** pr ordr. Vestry £4:10s	16 10 0
To pd. Mr. **OSHEAL**s fee Parish Suit agt. **LUTEN** £11:5s. Do. for Bread & Wine for Comunion 40s?	13 5 0
To Job **CHARLTON** on **MATTHIAS** order £10: To Mrs. **GREGORY** in pt. Keeping Rachl. **PERVINE** £25	35 0 0
To Linnin for 4 Shirts, thread & making, for **TALBOT**s Children	5 17 6
To Bills pd. Wm. **BENBURRY** in part Rent for Plantation	25 -- --
To Bills pd. Jos? **DEAR** for keeping **TALBOT**s Children from 29th: Janry: 1745 to ye 6th. May 1746.	15 0 0
To Bills pd Mr. John **HALSEY** for Ballce: of formr. Ch: Wardens Accots.	-4 0 0
To Bills pd. John **LUTON** by ordr. Vestry £4:-To Do. Richd. **HOUGHTON** pr ordr. afsd. £__ [illegible]	6 1 0
To Mr. **ANDERSON**'s fee £12: in ye. Suit agt. **LUTON**, & for wine for Comunion £2:	-14 0 0
To 7 yards of Linnin for Shifts for Rachel **PERVINE** £7:17:6 & pr Shoes 27/6?	-9 5 0
To Bills pd. Mrs. **SHERWIN** for bread & Wine for ye. Communion	--1 5 0
To Bills pd. Mr. **BLACKALL** for Sallivating Margt. **NOELL**	29 -- --
To a? yd: of fine Linen & thread for Rachel **PERVINE** Caps	-1 7 6
To Linen &? Thread & making a Shirt for Benja. **TALBOT**	--1 7 6
To pd. Mr. **HALSEY** for 5 yds. Cloath making a Gourd & moving R. **PERVINE** from Mrs} **GREGORY** to **ROBERTSON**s }	-7 -- --
Easter 1747 To Bills pd. Mr. **HALSEY** by **MATTHIAS** ordr. Ball: of his ordr. Vestrey	-5 -- --
To Bills pd. Mrs. **SHERWIN** for Bread & wine for ye. Comunion	--1 5 --
Nemine? {To Bringing the Parish Suit agt. **LUTEN** and attending ye: Courts	16 -- --
Contras:-{	
cente. -{	
To My Commissions for paying 450 by Draughts & otherwise	12 10 0
	£237 18 6

Contra Cr. [Right column.]
as pr Bills Recd. as follows
Viz.
of Mr. **PAINE** ye. Ballce? of his Accots. £ 24 0 0
of Mr. John **ALSTON** Sheriff - - - 179 16
of Mr. Thomas **LUTEN** part of}
Jean **EVINS** fine for a Bastard }
Child - - - - - - -} 2 10
of Mr. **ALSTON** - - - - - 16 5
222 11
By Ballance Due - - - - - - 15 7 6 69
May 23d. 1747. -- Errors Excepted pr J **BENBURY**

May ye. 23d. 1747. Then appeared personally ye. above Named John **BENBURY** before me who made oath on ye. Holy

(131) (Cont.) Evangelists of Almighty God that ye. above Accot. is Just & true & that he Recd. of ye. above Accots. no more than what he hath given Credit for, So that ye. Ballance as above Due to him is Bills fifteen Pounds Seven Shillings and Six pence. Sworn ye.? Day & year above Sd. before me J: HALSEY   whereupon

(132) *132) N. Carolina 1747.* Whereupon Then the Vestry ordered payment of Sd. Ball. of fifteen pounds Seven Shillings & Six pence Bills to be made unto ye. Sd. John BENBURY and after Motion for as well another Vestry Clerk as Another Reader for Edenton to be Elected for this present year 1747, It was Carryed in ye. Negative till ye. Meeting of ye. Next Vestry, which is left to be at Such a time and place in ye. Parish as ye. present Church Wardens Shall hereafter think fitt to order and appoint.
as pr order   [blank]   }Church Wardens

1748 Chowan County.
Be it rembered that the Sheriff of the Said County, did return that the Freeholders of St. Pauls Parish, in this County met at the Court house in Edenton, on Easter Monday being the Eleventh of April 1748: And, pursuant to ye. Act of the General Assembly, in that Case made & provided; did then & there choose and elect the following Persons for Vestry men To wit, Joseph ANDERSON, Esqr. John BLOUNT, John HALSEY, Joseph BLOUNT, John BENBURY, Willm. ARKILL, Thomas WALTON junr. William WALTON, Isaac HUNTER, William HUNTER, John LUTEN and John BONNER.

And on Thursday the 21.st Day of the afd. Month of April the Sd. Joseph ANDERSON, John BLOUNT, John HALSEY, Joseph BLOUNT, John BENBURY, William ARKILL, Thos. WALTON William WALTON, Isaac HUNTER, William HUNTER, and John LUTEN (John BONNER being absent) met at the Court house in Edenton, and were duly qualified by taking the Oaths by Law appointed for the Qualification of publick Officers and subscribing the Test and Declaration prescribed by the afd. Act of the General Assembly for the due Qualification of Vestry-men. And the said Vestry having taken their Places proceeded to the Choice of Church wardens and unanimously chose John HALSEY and John BENBURY Church wardens for this present Year.

Ordered that William MEARNS, be, and is hereby appointed Clerk of ye. Vestry for this ensuing Year; and that he be allowed the Sum of Twenty seven Shillings and six Pence Proclamation Money for the Same: and also that he be appointed Reader in Edenton, and be allowed, Ten Pounds Proclamation Money for the Year.

It is order'd that a Levy of sixteen Pence Proclamation Money, be laid on every taxable Person within this Parish, for defraying the Expence thereof, for this present Year; to be collected at the usual Times & Places of paying the publick Taxes.

Ordered that the late Church wardins lay their Accounts before ye. Vestry, at their next Meeting.

It is ordered that the Sheriff of the County lay his Accounts befor [sic] the   Vestry

(133) *133.) N. Carolina} 1748* Vestry, at their next Meeting; and that he pay the Money, belonging to the Parish, remaining in his Hands.

The Vestry adjourn'd till the second Mondy in June next being the 13th Day thereof; when, it was order'd that they meet again, at the Court house in Edenton   [blank]   { Church wardens

Saint Pauls Parish. . . . Monday the 13th. June. A. Dom. 1748.
The Vestry met at the Court-house in Edenton, according to Appointment. Present,
John HALSEY John BENBURY} Church-wardens.
Joseph ANDERSON. John BLOUNT} Esqres. Mr. Thomas WALTON. Mr. William ARKILL.. Mr. William HUNTER. Mr. John LUTEN Mr. John BONNER..} Vestry-men.

Capt. James FARLEE, petition'd the Vestry, in Behalf of Himself and several of his Neighbours that John FREEMAN, might be appointed Reader in their Precinct: The Vestry, after having maturely deliberated upon the said Petition,

Order'd, that John FREEMAN, be appointed Reader for the said Precinct, and that he be allowed the same as the other Readers are, by the year, which, the Vestry agrees, shall commence from Easter-monday last.

Joseph ANDERSON, Esqr. one of the Justices of this County paid, By the Hands of Thomas WALTON, into the Hands of John HALSEY, Church-warden, Twenty five Shillings Proclamation, being the Fine he received of Joseph LEDGER, for having a Bastard-child, on the Body of Anne MANN.

Col. John BLOUNT produc'd a Receipt to the Vestry from Timothy YEATS, [or YEALS] for Fifty Pounds, Bill money; which the Vestry order'd to be entered, as it appear'd to them to be the Ballance due in his Hands for the year, One Thousand seven Hundred and thirty eight, being appropriated by Act of Assembly for the Use of the Parish.   Mr. John 70

(134) *North Carolina.*   134.
Mr. John BENBURY, one of the late Church-wardens of this Parish, pursuant to the Order of the last Vestry; laid his Account of the Parish-moneys he had received from Mr. ALSTON, the late Sheriff; for the Year, One Thousand Seven hundred and

13 June 1748

(134) (Cont.) forty six, before the Vestry; whereby it appears to this Vestry, that he hath receiv'd, Five hundred and thirty Six pounds; and that he hath paid, for the Use of the Parish, the Sum of Five Hundred and forty Six pounds, Thirteen Shillings and seven pence, and produc'd the Vouchers for such his Payments; which said Account stands stated as here under neath: and that upon the Same there is a Ballance of Ten pounds, thirteen Shillings and seven pence due to him.

Dr. St. Pauls Parish, it's Accot. Currt. with John BENBURY	Cr.	£.. S. D.
To Bills pd. John SUMNER of his Accot. to 23 May 1747£.	67..11..--	
To ditto pd. Arthur GOLEY?, Ballance of his Accounts to Do. ..	45..--..--	
paid John WILLIAMSON, Ball. of his Accots. to Ditto	5..--..--	
pd. Thomas WALTON the Ball. of his Accots. to Do. ..	28.. 5..3	
pd. Isaac HUNTER, the Ball. of his Accots. to Do. ..	37..10..--	
pd. Daniel GRANDIN, ye. Ball. of his Accots. to Do. ..	37..--..--	
pd. Richd. BOND, in part of his Accot. to Ditto ...	15..--..--	
pd. John ROBERTSON, the Ball. of his Account to Ditto ..	1..10..--	236..16..3
pd. Robert FULLINTON, in part of his Accot. to Do. ..	50..--..--	
pd. Margret NOWAL, by Order of Vestry for ye. year, 1746 ..	10..--..--	
January 29th. pd. Mrs. SHERVIN, for Bread & Wine for ye. Communion..	2.. 5..--	
pd. Wm. BENBURY, in part of Rent for ye. Plantation qr. on ye. Parson lives	81..--..--	
paid John SYMONS in full for keeping Rachel PURVINE to ye. 11th Febry. 1746, and finding her some Cloathing ...	52..--..--	
pd. the Parson in part of his Account	22..--..--	217.. 5..--
pd. Thomas ROBERTSON in part for keeping Rachel PERVINE, from ye. 11th: of Febry. 1746 till ye. 24 of Do. 1747	25..15..--	
pd. Joseph DEER, in part of keeping Ben. TALBOT. ...	8..12..6	
pd. Messrs. ANDERSON & GHEAL, for carrying on Suit agt. LUTEN	12..10..--	
2 Days Expence for Liquors yn. ye. Auditors settld LUTENs Accot.	1..10..--	
pd. KIMSEY for serving Mr LUTEN wth. ye. Order of Court..	--..10..--	
pd. for 6 yds. Oznabs. for Rachels Bed, and Thd. to make it ..	4.. 6..--	
Ozab Thd. & making a Shirt for Ben. TALBOT	1.. 7..6	
Decr. 29. Bills pd. for Wine at the Communion	1..--..--	
To Ballance due to me for last year	15.. 7..6	
To 2½ Days of 2 Negroes & Pettaugre to move the Parson ..	3..10..--	
Easter 1748. To Wine for the Communion	1..--..--	
Whitsunday. To Bread and Wine . . .for Ditto	1.. 2..6	76..11..--
To my Commissions at 3 pr Cent.	16.. 1..4	16.. 1..4
		£546..13..7
Contra. Cr.		
By Half of the 18s9 Parish-tax recd. of John ALSTON Esqr. ye. late Sheriff for 1217 Tithabies amounting to . . .	£536..--..--	
Ballance due to John BENBURY	10..13..7	
	£:546..13..7	

Capt

(135) *North Carolina.*

Capt. John HALSEY, the other late Church-warden of this Parish, pursuant to the Order of the last Vestry, laid his Accounts of the Parish-moneys he had received from Mr. ALSTON the late Sheriff, for the Year One Thousand seven Hundred and forty six before? whereby it appears to this Vestry, that he receiv'd Five hundred and thirty six Pounds; and that he hath paid, for the Use of the Parish, the Sum of Five hundred and thirty seven Pounds four Shillings & nine pence, and produc'd the Vouchers for such his Payments; which said Account stands stated as here underneath: And that upon the Same there is a Ballance of One pound four Shillings and nine pence due to him.

£.. S. D

Dr. St. Paul's Parish It's Accot. Currt. with John HALSEY,	Cr.	
1747.		
May 23rd. To Bills paid Jonathan PARKER, the Ballance of his Accot. for building the Chappel at Knotty pine	£ 50..15..--	
24th. To Bills pd. Willm. HOSKINS, ye. Ball. of his Order of Vestry..	1..10..--	
27th. To Bills pd. ye. Minister in part of his Salary for ye. year 1746..	300..-- ..--	
30th. To Do. pd. Robert FULLERTON, in part of his Order of Vestry		

(135) (Cont.)

for £127..10.. for keeping Christian **NUTEN** .}	50.. --..--	
June 1st. To Bills pd. John **BLOUNT**, as pr. Order of Vestry . . .	8.. --..--	
Novr. 9th. To Do. pd. Willm. **BENBURY**, in part of his Rent due by ye. Parish ..	10.. --..--	
Febry. 10. To Do. pd. ye. Minister, in part of his Salary for ye year 1746 ..	10.. --..--	430.. 5..--
To Do. pd. Willm. **HALSEY**, for Boarding Ben **TALBOT** from} Septr. 28. to Janry. 28.	} 10.. --..--	
March 10. To Bills pd. Thos. **ROBINSON**, in full, for boarding old Rachel} 1748 from ye. 11th ??? of Febry. 1746, to Febry. 24th. 1747, at £49 pr. } Annm.	} 25..15..--	
March 25th To Money pd. Joseph **DEER**, for boarding Ben. **TALBOT**} from May 6th 1746 To Septr. 28th. 1747, at 40s. pr. Month, in full. }	23.. 8..--	
April 2nd To Bills pd. John **SYMONS** toward keeping old Rachel from 11 Febry. 1746.	15.. --..--	
Do. 11th. To Do. pd. Thos. **MARLOW**, for nursing a Child from 3rd. March to 11th April.	3.. --..--	77.. 3..--
To 1 pr Shoes, for old Rachel **PERVINE**	1..10..--	
To Bills pd. Mr. **RICHMOND** for Allom for old Rachel ..	--.. 5..--	
To Cart, Oxen & Leader 2 Days to move ye Minister, at 30s pr. Day	3.. --..--	
To a negroe Fellow 2 Days to help him move his Goods, at 10s pr Dm.	1.. --..--	
To my Commissions for receiving & paying £536. at 3 pr. Ct.	16.. 1..9	
April To Bills pd. Rachel **PETERS**, for boarding Pat **LONG** from the} 15th. of Febry. 1747. to ye. 15th. of April 1748. at £4 pr Month }	8.. --..--	29..16..9
		£537.. 4..9

Contra,	Cr.
By Bills receiv'd of Colo. John **ALSTON** Sheriff,} for the Use of ye. Parish of Saint Paul's . . . . }	£.536..--..--
Ballance due to John **HALSEY**	1..4..9
	£.537..4..9

William skipwith **MEARNS** only lawful Son of William & Dorothy **MEARNS**; was born at **MILLIKIN**s on Roanoke River, in the County of Edgcombe and Province of North Carolina on Saturday the Sixth of July In the year of our Lord Christ, One Thousand Seven Hundred & forty five; about Three of the Clock in the Morning. The 71

(136) *North Carolina.* 1_6.

    The Vestry, having observ'd the Tediousness and great Difficulty that commonly occur'd in canvassing Accounts exhibited to them during their sitting, without previous Notice; have, in Order to facilitate the like Inconvenience for the Future, unanimously resolv'd

    That it be observ'd as a Rule by the Church-wardens henceforward

    That They pay none of the Parish moneys in their Hands, to any of the respective Persons, before the Claimants produce unto Them a Ticket? from the Clerk of the Vestry (For the Time being) which Ticket, having a Receipt upon it, sign'd by the Receiver; Shall be allowed a sufficient Voucher for such Payment, when laid before the Vestry.

    Ordered that the Justices of this County have Notice to account with the Church wardens for the Fines and Forfeitures, by them receiv'd, in Virtue of the several Acts of Assembly, which are appropriate for the Use of our? Parish; so that the Church wardens may be able to render an Account thereof at the next Vestry. J. **BENBURY** J. **HALSEY** { Ch-wardens

---

1749 St. Paul's Parish. ss. At a Vestry begun & held at Ed the Court-house in Edenton, for the said Parish, in the County of Chowan; on the third Day of May, One Thousand Seven Hundred & forty nine. Present. John **HALSEY** John **BENBURY** } Ch-wardens Joseph **ANDERSON** John **BLOUNT** Isaac **HUNTER**, William **HUNTER** William **WALTON**, William **ARKILL** } Vestry-men.

    John **BONNER**, appeared and took the Oaths, &c appointed by law, to be taken by Vestry-men; then took his Place accordingly.

    It is resolv'd, by the Vestry; and it is hereby ordered, that the Reverend Mr. Clement **HALL**, have & receive, out of the Parish tax, for the Year, One Thousand seven Hundred and forty eight, the Sum of Sixty Pounds, Proclamation money, for his per-

3 May 1749

(136) (Cont.) forming   Rev. Mr. Clemt. **HALL**   Divine

(137) *North Carolina. Anno Dom 1749.*   137.

divine Worship and preaching in the said Parish for that Year: and also the Sum of Six Pounds thirteen Shillings & four Pence, like Money, for the Rent of a Plantation, or Farm, in Lieu of a Glebe.

It is ordered that the Revd. Mr. Clement **HALL**, be retain'd as Minister of the Parish of Saint Pauls, for this ensuing Year, One Thousand seven Hundred & forty nine to Easter-Monday next: He, giving his Attendance at the several Places in this Parish, as was enjoin'd him the foregoing Year; to perform divine Service, preach, and other Duties incident to his holy Function, and that he be paid for his said Service, out of this Years Levy, the Sum of sixty Pounds, Proclamation-money: also the Sum of six Pounds thirteen Shillings and four Pence, like Money, for the Rent of his Farm, in Lieu of a Glebe.

Thomas **MARLOE**, having a Claim upon the Parish, for keeping Judah **SHEARS**? an Orphan Child; agrees with the Vestry, to quit the said Claim, and keep the said Orphan, clear off the Parish, untill he arrive at the Age of twenty one Years: and likewise to teach, or cause him to be taught, to read & write? and also to get his Living in an honest and industrious Way, by some lawful Trade or Calling; in Consideration of the Sum of fifty five Pounds, of the late Current Bills of Credit, to be paid him by the Vestry, in the Behalf of the Parish..

Sarah **DEER**, agrees to take and keep Rachel **PURVINE**, in Consideration of the Sum of forty five Pounds, of the late Current Bill-mony [sic] pr. Annum.

Henry **CLAY**, agrees, with the Vestry, to take and keep Mary **HAVIT**, for the ensuing Year, in Consideration of the Sum of, thirty Pounds, of the late Current Bills of Credit of this Province.

Ordered that William **MEARNS** be continued Clerk of the Vestry & Reader for th?-?????? for this ensuing Year, One Thousand seven Hundred & forty nine to Easter-monday next; and that he be allowed the Same, as for the preceeding Year.

It is ordered by the Vestry, that a Levy of one Shilling and eight pence Proclamation mony, be laid on every taxable Person within this Parish, for defraying the Expence thereof for this present Year, to be collected at the usual Times & Places for paying the publick Taxes.

Ordered that Mssrs. John **HALSEY** and John **BENBURY**, be continued Church wardens for this ensuing Year, One Thousand seven Hundred and forty nine to Easter monday next. Ordered 72

(138) North Carolina}   138.

St. Paul's Parish } ss. Ordered that the Vestry meet again, at the Court-house, in Edenton, the third Tuesday in June next ensuing.   **J. HALSEY J. BENBURY**} Ch. Wardens.

1749. Saint Paul's Parish. ss. At a Vestry, call'd and held for the said Parish, at the Court-house, in Edenton, on Wednesday, the Second, of August, in the year of our Lord, One Thousand seven Hundred & forty nine, The Vestry not meeting according to the last Adjournment.

Present. John **HALSY** John **BENBURY**} Ch. Wardens.

Joseph **ANDERSON** Esqr. Mr. Isaac **HUNTER** Mr. William **HUNTER**, Mr. Thomas **WALTON**, Mr. William **WALTON**, Mr. John **LUTEN** Mr William **ARKILL**.} Westrymen. [sic]

Then the Vestry adjourn'd, 'till Three o'Clock in the Afternoon.

The Vestry met according to Adjournment,

Present as before.

Mr. Isaac **HUNTER**, one of the Readers of the said Parish laid his Account before the Vestry, as it stands here underneath stated; and Vouch'd the Same upon his Oath; whereby it appears, that there is due to him upon the Whole, the Sum of fifty one Pounds of the late current Bills of Credit of North Carolina

Chowan, Saint Pauls Parish ss.
July, the 2nd 1749.

	£. S. D.
The Claim of Isaac **HUNTER**, stands thus. Viz.	
To Serving as Reader three years at £15 ..--.. pr. year	45..--..--
And for finding Bread & Wine three Times for the Sacrament} at forty Shillings pr. Time}	6..--..--
	£.51..--..--

(139) *1749.* North Carolina} ss.   139

Saint Pauls Parish}

John **HALSEY** Esqr. One of the Church Wardens of this Parish, laid his Accounts of the Parish Monys he had received for part of the Year One Thousand seven Hundred and forty eight, and the preceeding Part of this present Year, One Thou-

2 August 1749

(139) (Cont.) sand seven Hundred & forty nine, before the Vestry; whereby it appears to this Vestry that he hath received the Sum of Six Hundred & Twenty Pounds five Shillings, of the late current Bills of Credit of this Province and that he hath paid for the Use of the said Parish the Sum of four Hundred and Twenty four Pounds, sixteen Shillings and seven Pence; and produced Vouchers for such his Payments: which said Account stands stated as here underneath: and that upon the Same, there is a Ballance of two Hundred and four Pounds eight Shillings & five Pence, like Money, due to the said Parish from the said John HALSEY.

£. S. D.

June 13th 1748. Saint Paul's Parish, To John HALSEY Dr.

	£. S. D.	£. S. D.
To Bills pd. the Revd. Mr HALL, as part of his Salary for ye. year 1747	£.200.. -- ..--	
To Do. pd. Jno. MIDDLETON, for keeping old Rachel, from Febry. 24th 1747 To May the 24th. (at £45 pr. Annum) 1748	11.. 5..--	
May 2 1749. To Bills paid Mr. PENRICE, in full for keeping old Rachel, from May 24th. 1748, to May 24th. 1749, at £43..... pr. Annum.	28.. 4..4	239.. 9.. 4
To Ditto pd. PENRICE, for Cloathing bought for sd. Rachel	14.. 4..6	
To 3½ yds. Linen bot. for Mary HAVIT, at 13/4 pr. yd.	2.. 6..8	
To Bills pd. Henry CLAY, for keeping Mary HAVIT, from Febry. 2d. 1748 to June 2d. 1749 at 50/ pr Month.	10.. -- ..--	26 11..2
To my Commissions for £130..10..-- Recd. of Willm. LUTEN	3..18..1	
To Ditto on £450 Recd. of Capt. HARRON	13..10..--	
To Ditto on £30, Recd. in Fines	-- ..18..--	
To Bills paid Mr. HALL	130..10..--	
To Ditto pd. Ditto, as pr. Receipt	10.. -- ..--	158..16.. 1
Contra Cr.		£.424..16..7

June 13th. 1748.

By Bills recd. of Capt. Jos. HARRON, for the Use of the Parish	£250.. -- ..--	
By Ditto, recd. the same Day of Mr. ANDERSON, for Anne MANNs Fine	9.. 7..6	
By Ditto, recd. of Mary FORDICE, as her Fine for a bastard Child	9.. 7..6	
By Ditto, recd. as a Fine for the Half of four Oaths swearing	1..17..6	
By two Fines from Susanna AMBROSE, for two Bastards	18..15..--	
June 3rd. 1749.. By Bills recd. of Mr. HENDERSON? HARRON for ye. Parish Tax, in Part, for 1748.	200.. -- ..--	
By Ditto, recd. of Thos. LUTEN Esqr. for Nell OSHLEY's Fine	9.. 7..6	
By Ditto recd. of Mr. Willm. LUTEN, being part of a Judgmt. recovered against him.	130..10..--	
	£629.. 5..--	
Ballance due to the Parish, from Mr. HALSEY	204.. 8..5	
	£424..16..7	John BENBURY Esqr. 73

(140) North Carolina: }   140.
Saint Paul's Parish} .ss.   John BENBURY Esqr. the other Church Warden of this Parish, laid his Account of the Parish Moneys he had received for Part of the Year One Thousand seven Hundred and forty eight and the preceding Part of this present Year One Thousand seven Hundred and forty nine before the Vestry; whereby it appears to this Vestry that he hath received the Sum of five Hundred Eighty five Pounds six Shillings and eight Pence.of the late Current Bills of Credit of this Province;and that he hath paid for the Use of the said Parish the Sum of four Hundred and fifteen? Pounds sixteen Shillings and ten Pence, like Mony; and produced Vouchers for Such his Payments; which said Account stands stated as here underneath and that upon the Same there is a Ballance of One Hundred and sixty ___ e Pounds nine Shillings & ten Pence like Mony due to the Parish, from the ____ John BENBURY.

1749 Dr. The Parish of St. Paul their Accot. Currt. with John BENBURY   Cr.   £. S. D.

August 2nd. To the Ballance due to me by former Account	£ 10..13..7.	
To Bills pd. the Minister in June 23d. 1748	200.. -- ..--	
To Ditto pd. Willm BENBURY, in July 7th. 1748, a Ballance then due to him for Rent of ye. Plantation whereon ye. Minister dwelt	30.. -- ..--	240..13.7
To Ditto pd. Mr. RICHMOND for a Blanket for old Rachel	4..12..6	
To Commissions for receiving £250 of the late Sheriff	7..10..--	
3. To Bills pd. SHELDIN, towards keeping Mrs. HAVIT	1.. 2..--	
April 11th. To Ditto pd. Mr. KING for Bread & Wine for the Communion	3.. 5..--	

2 August 1749

(140) (Cont.) 5th. To Ditto pd. Francis **PENRICE**, in part for Keeping old Rachel   14..15..8   31.. 5..2
May 26th. To Ditto pd. Mr. **KING** for Wine for the Communion . .   2.. -- ..--
       To my Commissions of £130..10..-- recd of Mr **LUTEN**   3..18..1
       To Ditto for receiving £200 of the late Sheriff . . .   6.. -- ..--
   8 To Bills pd. Joseph **BARNES** for a pr Shoes for Mrs. **HAVIT**   1..10..--
       To Ditto pd. the Minister . . . .   130..10..--   143..18.. 1
            Contra   Cr.   £415..16..10
       By Bills recd. of Jos. **HARRON**, late Sheriff 13 June 1748   £250.. -- ..--
 1749 By Ditto recd. of Mr. **ALSTON**, in part of Dinah **SIMPSON**s Fine   4..16.. 8
June 15. By Ditto recd. of Jos. **HARRON**, late Sheriff, in part of that years Tax   200.. -- ..--
       By Ditto Recd. of Mr William **LUTEN**, in part of a}
          Judgment recover'd against him . . . . } . . .   130..10.. --
                                      £.585.. 6.. 8
       Ballance due to the Parish from Mr **BENBURY**   £ 169.. 9..10
                                      £.415..16..10   The

(141) North Carolina}   141

Saint Pauls Parish} ss. The Vestry, in Consideration of the Trouble & Fatigue which Mr. **ANDERSON** had in recovering a Sum of Mony due by William **LUTEN**, sometime Sheriff of the County of Chowan; Ordered that he be allowed the farther Sum of Eleven Pounds five Shillings of the late Current Bills of Credit of this Province, for the Same.

Ordered that the following Pieces of Church Plate Viz. One Cup, & one Plate, now in the Hands of Mr. Miles **GALE**, be delivered into the Hands of the present Church Wardens; where, and in the Hands of the succeeding Church Wardens, they are hereby ordered to be kept for the Use of the said Parish. It is likewise ordered that the Church Wardens collect all the other Pieces of Church Plate belonging to the said Parish, now in the Hands of his Excellency Gabriel **JOHNSTON** Esqr. the Governour; Doctor **PLOMER**, or any other Person or Persons whatsoever, or wheresoever any of the said Church Plate shall or may be found or discovered.

Ordered that the Widow & Relick of William **SKINNER** deceas'd formerly Reader of Sarum Chappel, be paid the Sum of thirty five Pounds fifteen Shillings of the late Current Bills of Credit, being the Ballance due in Arrear to her late? deceased Husband, for Reading, as aforesaid.

Ordered that Israel **SHELDEN**, be allow'd the Sum of ten Pounds of the late Current Bills of Credit, for keeping Mary **HAVIT** four Months.   Paid

The Revd. Mr. Clement **HALL**, laid his Account before the Vestry, which stands S__ted as here underneath, whereby it appears to this Vestry that there is a Ballance of four Hundred & sixty three Pounds ten Shillings & eleven Pence, of the late Current Bills of Credit of this Province due, by this Parish, to the sd. Mr. **HALL**.

1748/9.   £. S. D.
       The Parish of Saint Paul, in Chowan County, to C **H**   Dr.
Janury. 12th. To the Rent of a House & Plantation of Mr. Charles **BLOUNT**,}
         in Leiu of a Glebe . . . . }   £ 50.. -- ..--
1749. To Arrears, due in the years 1747 and 1748 . . . . .   224.. 5..--
March 27th. (Being Easter Monday) To one year's Salary due}
         for the year 1748 . . . . }   450.. -- ..--   724.. 5..--
               1748/9. Contra   Cr.
March 4th. By Money recd. of William **LUTEN** . . . .   £.175.. 7..11
       By a Bond & Note of the said William **LUTEN** . . . . .   85.. 6.. 2
                                                     £ .260..14.. 1
       Ballance due from the Parish, To Mr **HALL**   £. 463..10..11
                                               £. 724.. 5..--

Thomas **MARLOW**, moved the Vestry, that Judah **SHEARS**, an Orphan Child might be bound Apprentice to him by the Church Wardens, pursuant to his Agreement with the said Vestry, at the Court house in Edenton, on the third Day of May last; he giving Security for his Performance as the Law requires in such Cases; and he thereupon produced Richard **SADLER**, of the said Parish, as his Security, who is, by the Vestry approved of. Ordered that the Clerk of the said Vestry prepare the Bond and Indentures. 74

(142) *Anno Dom. 1750* North Carolina}   142.

19 May 1750

(142) (Cont.) Saint Pauls parish } ss. Be it remembred that the Sheriff of Chowan County did return that the free holders of St Pauls parish afore Sd In the County afore Sd. Met at the Court house in Edenton On Easter Monday being the 16 of April in the year of Our lord 1750

And pursuant to the Act of the General assembly in that Case Made & provided did then and there Choose and Elect the twelve Following persons for Vestry Men To Witt--

Joseph ANDERSON Esqr Joseph BLOUNT Mr Wm. HOSKINS} Mr Jas TROTTER Mr Wm BONNER Henry BONNER} Mr Jno LEWIS Mr. Thos WALTON Mr Wm WALTON} Mr Isaac HUNTER Mr Willm FREEMAN Mr Jno FREEMAN

And on Saturday the 19th. of May the Said Joseph ANDERSON _ HOSKINS James TROTTER Henr BONNER Willm BONNER Jno. LEWIS Thos WA____ Will? WALTON Isaac HUNTER & John FREEMAN

Met at the Court house in Edenton and were Duly qua__fied Taking the Several Oaths by Law Appointed for the qual_fication of Vestry Men and others.

And the Said Vestry having Taken there [sic] places proceded to the Choice Of Church Wardens And unanimously chose Mr W HOSKINS and? Mr Thos WALTON Church Wardens for this prsent Year.

O__ered that Henry BONNER be & he is hereby appointed Clerk of the Vestry for this Ensuing Year and that he be allowed the Sum of One Pound Seven Shills. and Six pence proclamation Money for the Same

Resolved agreed that the reverend Mr Clemt. HALL be Retain'd as Clerk? and Arrecter of this parrish to preach and perform Devine Service at times and places as heretofore has been Usual. Rec__

Then the reverd. Mr HALL moved to have his Stepend Enlarged £80 proclam. Money which was Carried in the Negative Nemine Contradicante !!!

Then it was Moved by Mr Isaac HUNTER that the parson be allowed £60 proclamn Money And an Adequate for a Gleabe.

Itt was Objected against by Mr TROTTER and that an allowance of £50 and an adequate for a Glebe was Sufficient and Moved that it Might be put? to the Vote and After Some Debate the question being put the Vestry thereon was divided in Equal Votes.

It is thereupon Resolved that the Question be again put at A fuller Vestry.

(143) *Anno Dom 1750*   143   [Portions of this page are illegible.]

Resolved Nemine Contradicante Ordered that a tax or Levey of Two Shillings & Eight pence proclemn. Money be laid On Every Taxable person within this parish for this present Year for Defraying the Expence thereof and for raiseing the Sum of sixty six pounds thirteen Shill. and four? pence like Money to be applyed towards the ___ __esing ___ Finishing the Church at Edenton and that the said ? Tax? __ Collected by the? Sheriff at the Usual times and places as ___ ___ receiving & paying of said? taxes and that ye Sheriff___ ___ ___ hais___ Sd.? thirty Six pounds? thirteen Shill and four? pence ___ ___ ___ tax do pay the Same __ to me? a ___ ___ Vestry to be by them applyed for ___ ___

Ordred that [Remainder of line is illegible.] the Court house and at Every Chapel in this parish? ___ ___ ___ A man? to undertake the Said work to give? [Remainder of line is illegible.] Vestry to be held at Edenton on the first Tues___ ___ ___ W?ith the C wardes and Vestry for the Same [Remainder of line is illegible.] As they Shall then and there ap___ for that ___ of And it is further Ordred that [Remainder of line is illegible.] all former Taxes after the subscription? ___ ___ ___ ___ Same was Laid be paid into the hands of the ___ ___ ___ Vestry to be by them applyed for & Towards the finishing the Said Church.

Ordred that the Late Church Wardens and all [Remainder of line is illegible.] parish Moneys in there hands do forthwith account ___ ___ Into the hands of the present Church War___.

The Vestry adjourn'd to the first Tuesday in ___ Next, to Meet at the Court house in Edenton.

North Carolina}
St Pauls Parish} ss At a Vestry begun and held at the Co___ H___ In Edenton for the Said parish in the County afore? Said On the fifth day of June One thousand one hundred & fifty. Presant

Joseph ANDERSON Joseph BLOUNT Esqrs. Mr Jas TROTTER Mr Isaac HUNTER Mr Willm WALTON Mr Jno. LEWIS Mr Jno. FREEMAN Mr Wm FREEMAN Mr Wm BONNER Henry BONNER Willm HOSKINS} Thos WALTON} Cwl?   75

(144) *_nno Dom. 1750.* Joseph BLOUNT Esqr. & Mr Willm FREEMAN appeard & Took the Oath by Law requird and Accordingly took there places.

Whereas at the Last Vestry the Sum of 66 pounds 13 Shillgs: and four pence proclamation Money was Ordred to be raised Out of this years Levey for finishing? the Church at Edenton And Notice given for Any person or persons at? ___ willing to undertake the Said Worke to appear at this Vestry to agree for the Same but the Vestry finding it Inconveniant this Sitting being so Short have thought it Necessary to appoint proper? persons to Transact that m___ therefore it is? by the Church Wardens and

5 June 1750

(144) (Cont.) Vestry Resolv'd that Mr Francis? **CORBINE** Mr James **CRAVEN** and Mr John **HALSEY** be and they are hereby appointed And impower'd to agree with Such person? or persons who are ___lling to Undertake the Said _____ and ___ the same finished and __rform for Such workmanlike manner as they Shall contract for ____ So Soon as the Same Shall be compleated they are hereby impowered to draw On the Sheriff or Church Wardens for the paying and Discharging there Contracts and agreements afore Said.

    Mr John **BENBURY** one of the Late Church wardens _____ _____ of? the parish moneys he has? received ____ the year 1749 _____ _____ accots. [Remainder of line is illegible.]

    Dr. the Parish of St. Pauls to Jno **BENBURY**

To Bills pd Robert **SADLER**? ___ pr Order Vestry	£ 52 10 0
To Do pd ye? Widow **SKINNER** - - - - - -	32?
To Do. pd Israel **SHELDING** - - - - - -	1
To Do pd the Minister - - - - - - -	10
To Do pd Mr. **PLOMER** - - - - - - - -	10?
To Do pd Jno? ____ in part for keeping Mrs **PERVINE** } from ye 24 May 1749 till ye 24 of May 1750 }	19?
To Do pr the ____ for keeping Mrs **HAVIT** the Same year	19? __ 6
To Alloum found for Rachel - - - - - -	1 6
	£ 169 3?
By the Ballance Due to the parish pr my former accot: Dr	160. 9 10

(145) *Anno Dom 1750.* [Remainder of this page is illegible.] 76

(146) *146 Anno Dom 1750.* [Remainder of this page is illegible.]

(147) *147 Anno Dom 1750* [Majority of this page is illegible, with the following exceptions:] Joseph **HERRON** The Vestry adj____d _____ July to Meet at the Court house in Edenton.

1750. {North Carolina}
    {St Pauls Parish} ss _____ _____ **ANDERSON** Esqr _____ Presant William **HOSKINS**
    Order to pay to ye Parson & Reader
    Whereas it appearing to the Vestry that the Stipend of ____ proclamation Money and? the Allowance of Six pounds____
    Last year _____ 77

(148) ___th Carolina
    __Pauls Parsh. ___750 [The top one-third of this page is illegible, with the following exceptions:] **HERRON** Wm. **HOSKINS** Thos **WALTON**

    At a Vestry held at Edenton the 17th of January 1750
    Presant William **HOSKINS** & Thos **WALTON** Ch Wardens
    [Isaac **HUNTER** Willm **WALTON** Jno **FREEMAN**} Jos **BLOUNT** James **TROTTER** Henry **BONNER**} John **LEWIS** Willm **FREEMAN** Willm **BONNER**}
    Ordred that Capt John **HALSEY** the presant Sheriff receive The Leveys for this presant year in Old Bills Virga. Curency Or Cuntrey produce according to Act of Assembly.
    Ordred that Nathll **MING** be allowed Sixteen pound Ten shills Late Currat: bills for Boarding Mary **QUARELESS** two Months and Three Weekes.
    Capt John **HALSEY** prsant Sheriff of Chowan County exhibitted His accot: for the parrish money by him received in Virtue Of his office for the year 1749 Which he proved upon Oath And is Stated as follows Vizt.

(149) *(149) Anno Dom 1750*
1749 Dr To? the Parish of Sai__ _____ _____ Their Accts: Currant with Capt? John **HALSEY**   Contra
Novembr 1750 To Bill Money pd Willm **HORSKINS**} -- £774 0 0   By 1300 Tythables @ 12s 0?6D pr Tythl £81_____
        as pr Receipt   }
        To My Commishom @ 6 pr Cent   £ 48 15
                                           £822 15   £822_____
Chowan County ssd [sic]
    Personally appeared before me John **HALSEY** Esqr and Made Oath on the holy Evangeleists that the Above accot Is Just and True   Sworn before me ye 17 Jan: 1750 Peter **PAYNE** J. Peace 78

(150) ____ Caro__na? __ Pauls ___ish ss 1750   (150)
    Ordd that Richd **SMITH** be Allowd. Six pound five Shillings Late Curat Bills for boarding Mary **QUARELESS** One

17 January 1750/51

(150) (Cont.) Month And five Days and finding one pair of Stockings and Two Shirts for her Child.

    Ordd That Capt John **HALSEY** be allowed five pound Tenn Shillings Late Currt bills for Burying Rachel **PERVINE**.

    Nathll **MING** agrees to take & Keep Mary **QUARELESS**' Child In Consideration of Three pounds Old Bills pr month Till Easter.

    Ordd That Mary **QUARELESS** be Allowed Seven yards of Lining for Two Shifts.   Wm. **HOSKINS** Thos **WALTON**

Chowan ___nty__ ls____sh} At a Vestry held at Edenton the 18th day April 1751
    Presant Willm **HORSKINS** Thos **WALTON**{ Jos ~~BLOUNT~~ Church Wardens
April 18th _751 Jos **BLOUNT** Jas **TROTTER** Isaac **HUNTER** Henr **BONNER**{ Jno **LEWIS** Jno **FREEMAN** Wm **WALTON** W: **BONNER**{

    Ordred that Lewis **JONES** be allowed five pounds Old bills for Looking after & burying of Martha **LONG**.

    Ordd That Mr Isaac **HUNTER** be Continued Reader at **CONSTANT**s Chappel & to be allowd. Forty Shills proclemation Money for this presant year.

    Ordd That John **SKINNER** be appointed Reader at Notty pine Chappel in the room & Stead of John **WILLIAMSON** & to be allow__ Fifty? Shillings proclemation Money for this presant [Last line on this page is missing.]

(151) *North Carolina _t Pawls Parish 1751* (151) Ordd that a Tax or Levey of Sixteen pence proclemation Money be leveyed on Each & Every Taxable person in this parish for this presant Year.

    Ordd That the Reverend Mr Clt: **HALL** be Continued as Clerk & rector of This parish to preach & perform Divine Service at time [sic] & places as heretofore has been Usal And to be allowd. fifty pounds proclemation Money for This presant Year.

    Ordd That Mr Willm **HORSKINS** & Mr Thos **WALTON** be Continued Church Wardens for this presant Year Till Easter Next.

    Mr Thos **WALTON** one of ye presant Church Wardens Laid his accots before the Vestry for the year 1750 Where by it app____ To ye Said Vestry that there is a ballance of 31 pound Nine shill____ Due to ye Said parish which accts Stand Stated as followeth

April ye 6 The parish of St Pauls to Thos. **WALTON**	D_	
1750 To Bills pd Isaac **HUNTER** - - -	£ 30	
To Do paid John **WILLIAMSON** -	—	
To Mr William **WALTON** Senr. -	—	
To 1 bushel of Meal for the Widow **CULLEY**	10	
To bills pd Mr Clt **HALL** - - - - - -	170	
To Do paid Do - - - - - - -	160	
To 1 bottle of Wine - - - - - -	1	
	£444 11	
Contra		
By Bills receivd of Capn **HARRON** - -	£176	
By Do recd of Capn. **HALSEY** - - - -	300	
	£476	
	444 11 ..	
Ball Due to ye Parish	£..31.. 9	
Wm **HOSKINS** Thos **WALTON**	79	

(152)____ *Carolina___Pauls Parish ss 1751*   (152)

    At a Vestry held at the Court House in Edenton the 17 of October 1751

    Presant Willm **HOSKINS** Thos **WALTON**{ Ch: Wardens John **LEWIS** John **FREEMAN** Henry **BONNER** James **TROTTER** Wm: **FREEMAN**

    Ordred that James **WORDAN** have five pounds Virga Currency for Boarding of Joseph **HACKETT** for this Insuing Year

    Ordred that John **FREEMAN** be allowed Five pounds Old Bills for Boarding James **PHELPS** Three Months

---

Chowan County St Pauls Parish 1752} ss Aprile the 23 1752

    Be it Remmenbered [sic] that the Sheriff of the Said County Did Return, That the Freeholders of St. Pauls Parish in the County afore said, Mett at the Court House in Edenton, on Easter Mundy being the 29th Day of March, 1752, and Pursuant to An Act of the Generall Assembly, in that Cace Made, and Provided, Did then and there, Chose and Elect, the Folowing Persons for Vestry Men, Viz Francis **CORBIN**, Peter **PAYNE**, Joseph **BLOUNT**, Thomas **BARKER**, and James **CRAVEN**, Esqrs., Demcy

23 April 1752

(152) (Cont.) SUMNER, Robt. BEZLEY, Thos. BONNER Joseph SPIGHT, Henery BONNER, John LUTEN, & John LEWIS. And on Thursday the 23d Day of Aprile, Folowing, Francis CORBIN, Peter PAYNE, Thomas BARKER, James CRAVEN Robert BEZLEY, Henery BONNER John LUTEN & John LEWIS, /Demcy SUMNER, Joseph BLOUNT Thomas BONNER and Joseph SPIGHT being abcent/ mett at the Court House in Edenton, and were Duly Qualified, by takeing the Oaths by Law Appointed, for the Qualification of Publick Officers, and Subscribing the Test and Declaration precribed by Law and then Proceeded as Folows Viz. . . . .

    Joseph SPIGHT not being Willing to Qualify, James TROTTER, is by the afore Said Vestry Chosen in his Room, and Qulified as afore Said

    Ordered That John MC. KILDO be, and is hereby Appointed Clerk of the Vestry, and Reeder at Edendon for this Present Year, and that he be Allowed the sum of Six Pounds Proclamation Money for the Same

    Robert BEZLEY and Henery BONNER is by the Said Vestry Chose as Church Wardens.

    It is Ordered that a Levy of five Shillings Procklamation Mone_ be laid on every taxable Person Within this Parish for Defreying   T__

(153) *St. Pauls Parish, ss 1752*   (__)

The Expence thereof and Finishing the Church at Edenton as far as Such Moneys will go for this Present Year to be Colected at the Uswal times, & Places of paying the Publike Taxes.

    Ordered that the Money Appointed for the Finishing the Church be paid to the Order of the Comissioners appointed for Building, and Finishing the Same

    Ordered, That the Revd. Mr HALL Minster of the Parish Afore Sd. have as a Selary, the Sum of fifty Pounds Procklamation Money for this Present year, and no more Other Alowance. And that the Remaining Part of the Taxes be for the Finishing the Church, and Other Nececery [sic] Charges.

    Ordered that the Former Church Wardens Account With this Present Vestry, and pay the Ballance in their Hands at the Next meeting of this Vestry.

    These Proceedings, and Orders were Made, at a Vestry Held at House? the Court House in Edenton one the 23d Day of Aprile 1752 Present Henery BONNER Robert BEZLEY} Church Wardens} Francis CORBINE Peter PAYNE Thomas BARKER James CRAVEN} Esqrs. John LEWIS John LUTEN James TROTTER Vestry Men

    The Vestry Adjornd [sic] till the Last Day of the Next County Court in July at the Court House in Edenton.

St. Pauls Parish sc Chowan County 1752 At [sic] Vestry begun and held at the Court House in Edenton for ye Parish aforesaid, on ye 24th. Day of August Anno. Domini 1752

    Present Robert BEZLEY Henry BONNER} Church Wardens Francis CORBIN Peter PAYNE Joseph BLOUNT} Esqrs Thomas BARKER James TROTER John LEWIS John LUTEN William BOYCE} Vestry Men

    Ordered that William WILSON - - - keep Joseph HECKET, in the room of James WORDAN, and that he be Allowed the sum of five Pounds Virginia Currancy for this Present year, for the same. 80

(154) *N. Carolina St. Pauls Parish} ss 1752.*   (154)

The Petition of John PARISH being Read in full Vestry Praying Releif from ye Parish towards Maintaining his son Who is a Criple

    Ordered that he be Allowed the sum of fifty shillings, Procklamation Money for one year, from ye date hereof.

    James GORDON, is herby Appointed Redar at FARLEEs Chaple

    Ordered that he be Allowed the sum of forty shillings Procklamation money for one year, from ye Date hereof, for ye same.

    John HALSEY Esqr. the Late Sheriff Laid his Accts. for ye year 1750 before this Vestry which being Duly Examined, their Appears to be ??? a ballance of twenty Eeight Pounds forteen shillings and one peney, old Tenor Due to ye Parish; which Acct Stands thus. - - - - - - - - - - - - - -

	s	d
1750 Dr. The Parish of St. Pauls, To John HALSEY		
February 1st To old Bils paid Mr. Thomas WALTON, C. W. £3	00	.. ..
27 To old Bills paid Mr HOSKINS, for ye use of ye Church . . 5	00	.. ..
March ye 10 To old Bills paid Mr HOSKINS, as pr. Receipt 124	17	..
May ye 22d. To old Bills paid Mr HOSKINS as pr. Receipt 164	14	6
July 1751 To old Bills paid Mr HOSKINS as pr. Receipt 76	12	..
Octobr 29 To Do paid Mr HOSKINS, as pr. Receipt 14	2	6
To my Commissions for the Receipt of £1306 @ 6 pr Cnt. 78	6	2
To Bills over paid in my former Accounts 10	5	..
To Bills paid Henry BONNER for serving as Cleark 8	8	9

24 August 1752

(154) (Cont.)   Errors Excepted pr Jno **HALSEY**   £1277 5 11
1750 Contra   Cr.
Janwary By Old Bills Receivd of 1306 Taxables @ 20/S pr Taxab:
    for ye use of ye Parish and Church . . . .   £1306.. .. .
          Ballance Due to ye Parish, in old Bills   028 14 1

The above Account was proved in full Vestry, in due Cource of Law. Before me Peter **PAYNE** J. P.

(155) *N. Carolina St: Pauls Parish ss 1752}*   (155)

William **LUTEN** produced an account, of Fines Receivd. at Sundrie times, for ye Crime of Fornication, and stands thus

From Ann **DILDE**, Receivd. of William **BOND** in part old Bills	£ 2-10-6
From William **BOND** - - - - - - - - - - - - -	9 7-6
From Judith **SHIVE** - - - - - - - - - - - - -	9- 7-6
From Margreat **ASHLEY** - - - - - - - - - -	9- 7-6
From Mary **GRIFFEN** - - - - - - - - - - -	4-13:9
in old Bills	£35- 6.5

The Vestry Adjurned to ye 13th of October Next

St. Pawls Parish 1753} At a Vestry begun and held at the Court House in Edenton On Saterday the fifth Day of May 1753.

    Present Francis **CORBIN** James **CRAVEN** Thomas **BARKER** Peter **PAYNE** Joseph **BLOUNT** John **LEWIS** John **LUTEN**} Vestry Men {Henery **BONNER** Robert **BEZLEY** } C Wardens

    Ordered that the present Church Wardens be Continued Another Year.

    Ordered that the late Church Wardens Account with, and pay the Ballance in their Hands to the present Church Wardens, and that they Render their Accounts to the Vestry on the 28th Instant.

    Ordered Also that the Sheriff pay out of his Colection of the Parish Tax the Ballance in his Hands to the Church Warden.

The Vestry Adjorned to the 28 Instant.

St. Pauls Parish 1753} At a Vestry begun and held at the Court Hous [sic] in Edenton, on Mundy [sic] the 28 Day of May 1753

    Present The Honourabl. James **CRAVEN** Frances **CORBIN**} Esqrs Peter **PAYNE** John **LEWIS** Joseph **BLOUNT**} Esqrs. Thomas **BARKER** John **LUTEN** William **BOYD** Miles **GALE**} Henry **BONNER** C Wd. 81

(156) *North Carolina St. Pauls Parish 1753}*   (156)

    The Honourable John **RIEUSEET** Esqr. on [sic] of the persons Appointed to fill up a Vacancy, not being Willing to Qualify: The Revd Mr. Clement **HALL**, by Writing under his Hand and Seal, appinted Mr Miles **GALE**, Who Accordingly Came in full Vestry and Qualified, by takeing the Oaths Apppoin_ed by Law, and Subscrib'd the Test.

    Ordered That John **MC KILDO** be Contenued Clerk of the Vestry and Reader at Edenton, and to be paid According to his first Agreement with this Vestry

    John **MC KILDO** Produced his acct. against the Parish for his Acting as Clerk of the Church and Other Services don [sic], and ??? amounting to six pounds sixteen Shillings which is allowed, and stand thus - in Proclamation Money

Aprile 1752 St. Pauls Parish To John **MC KILDO** Dr	£ s d	
To my Attendance on Easter Munday at ye Election of Vestry Men} taking ye Pole &c - - - - - - - - - - - - -}	5 4	
To sending Notice in Writeing to the late C. Wardens to lay their} Accts. before this Vestry. pr order of ye Vestry - - - }	2 - 8	
To Summonses Isued out to ye Constabl, to Summons ye Vestry Men &c	2 : 8	
Septr 25 To Diging a Grave and Burieng a Sailors who Died at John **ASTIE**'s	5 : 4	
Apl 23 1753 To my Service as Clerk of the Church & Vestry, for one Year	6 0 : 0	
	£6:16: 0	

    John **SKINER** made a Clame on the Parish, of £4.0.0 Proclamation Money for acting as Reader at Knoty Pine Chapple two Years, which Was Allow'd

    Ordered that he be Contenued Another Year Viz. for ye year 1753.

    John **ASTIE** produced an acct. against the parish for Nursing, Doctors Charge and Funerall Charge, and other Expencees of a poor Man, amounting to £2.3s.9d proclamation, which is alloued. and stands in these words, towit,

August. 1752 The parish of Saint Pauls - - To John **ASTIE** -   £ s d

28 May 1753

(156) (Cont.)

To Boarding and Nursing Thomas **WOOD** Deces'd Eleven Days	0..15..0
To Doctors Charge	0.. 7..6
To a Coffen	0..10..0
To a pair of Draus [sic] and a Winding Sheet	0.. 7..6
To half Gallond Burnt Rum	0.. 3..9
Errors Excepted pr John **ASTIE**	£2: 3: 9

St. Pauls Parish ss 1753 At a Vestry bgan [sic] and held at the Court House in Edenton on Thursday the 31st Day of May 1753
  Present The Honbl. Francis **CORBIN** Peter **PAYNE** Joseph **BLOUNT**} Esqrs. Thomas **BARKER** John **LEWIS**} Vestry Men Miles **GALE** William **BOYD** John **LUTEN**} Henry **BONNER** Robert **BEZLEY**} Church Wardens

(157) *North Carolina Chowan County St. Pauls Parish 1753}*   (157)

Ordered that a Levey of one Shilling and six pence Proclamati___ Money be laid on every Taxable within this Parish for this present Year for paying the Minister his Salary and the Readers, and Parish Clerks for Maintaining the poor & for finishing such Chappels as are built by Order of Vestry in Such Maner and Such proportions as Shall be Ordered by the Vestry. - - - - -

Ordered That James **SURRENGAR** be Appointed a Reader for this present Year to Attend at **FARLEE**s Chapple, and that he be Alowed forty Shilling Proclamat___ for the year

Ordered that a Levy of two Shillings Proclamation Money be Laid on each Taxable within this parish, to be Applyed towards the finishing the Church already begun att Edenton.

Ordered that the late Sheriff do Acct. with the Church Wardens for such Money as he is accountable to them for, and to pay the Ballance Coming to them. And that he render an Account to the Comisioners for finishing the Church, for such Moneys as he is accountable to them for, That is to say: Eeigteen [sic] pence (Deducting Comissions) for each Taxable for which he is by Law Accountable for: to the said Church Wardens, and the Remainder? of his Colection of the Parish Tax, to the Comissioners for Finishing the Church.

Ordered allso that all former Sheriffs do Acct. with the Church Wa_____ and Comissioners of the Church Respectivly for all such Moneys as they are Respectivly accountable to them for

Ordered that the Fines Colected by every person now or heretofore as Justices Within this County payable to the Church Wardens, be by him paid to the Chch. Wardens that the same may be applyed agreeable to Law

David **MARSHEL** produced his Acct. against the parish for Boarding Nursing and Burying a poor Man amounting to £3 11 s 7¼d.. proclamation Money which was Alowed, and foloweth in these Words, to wit &c

St. Pauls Parish to David **MARSHEL**		Dr	
To Board and Attendance of Stephen **BROWN** from ye 19th of Decem 1752} to ye 5th Day of February 1753 @ 8s pr week, att sick Quarters }			2..16..0
To ye Doctors Charge			0 7:6
To a Coffin for him			0:10..0
To a Winding Sheet			0.. 5..0
To Rum and Suger at the Funerall			0.. 5..7¼
To Diging his Grave			0 1:3
			£4: 5:4¼
Cr. By Cash on Acct.	10/S-Take out		0: 13:9
By pair of Treusars [sic]	3/9 Ball Due		£3 11:7¼

John **FREEMAN** produced an Acct. against the parish for Boarding Nursing and Burying Rachel **PURVINE** amounting to 2£ 12s:6 Virgin. Currancy Which was Alowed and Stands in these Words to wit &c 82

(158) *North Carolina St Pauls Parish 1753}*   (158)

The Parish of Saint Pauls To John **FREEMAN**	Dr		
	£	s	d
To Boarding Rachel **PURVINE** 2 manths	1..10:0		
To Carting ye Said **PURVINE** to my House	0: 10:0		
To Burying ye said **PURVINE**	0 12:6		
In Virgina Currancy	2: 12:6		

Ordered that the Revd. Mr **HALL** be Allowed fifty Pounds Proclamation Money, for performing Devine Service, and of-

31 May 1753

(158) (Cont.) ficiating as Clerk and Rector of this Parish, this present Year; and that he officiat [sic] 21 Sundays at Sarum, **CONSTANT**s, and **FARLEE**s Chappels, and the rest of his time at Edenton, Except when absent on the Duty of his Mission. *Sarum CONSTANTs &? FARLEEs Chapels*

Ordered that fifteen Pounds proclamation Money be Allowed out of the Parish Taxes for building a Chappel on some part of Mr Robt **BEEZLEY**s Land, he Making a Conveyance in fee simple to one Acre thereof to the Church Wardens for the time being to have and to hold, to them, and there Successors forever, for the Use of the publick of ye Said Parish. *Robt. BEASLEY Gives 1 Acre of Ground for a Chappel}*

Ordered Mr. Thomas **WALTON**, one of the late Church Wardens, do Satle [sic] with the present Church Wardens, and pay the Ballance in his hands Imediatly [sic] to the present Church Wardens, and that he have Notis of the same ~~Time~~

The Vestry adjurned to ye Last Saterday in June

Chowan County St Pauls Parish 1754} Aprile 15th 1754

Be it remmembered that the Sheriff of the said County did Return That the Freeholders of St Pauls Parish in the County af Sd, Mett at the Court House in Edenton on Easter Munday being the 15th Day of this Instant Apl. and pursuant to an Act of Generall Assembly in that Cace Made and provided, did then and there Chuse and Elect the folowing persons to serv [sic] as Vestry Men for the two Insuing Years Viz.

Francis **CORBIN** Esqr Henry **BONNER** Thomas **BONNER** Thomas **BONNER** [sic]} William **HOSKINS** Robert **BEASLEY** Job **CHARLTON** William **BONNER**} Charles **ROBERTS** John **LUTEN** John **SIMONS** Nathaniel **HOWKOTT**}

And on the first Day of May following Mr Henry **BONNER**, Thomas **BONNER**, William **BONNER**, Thomas **BONNER**, Nathaniel **HOWCOTT**, Charles **ROBERTS**, Job **CHARLTON**, John **LUTEN**, John **SIMONS**, & William **HOSKINS**, ten of the afore Sd. twelv [sic] Mett at the Court House in Edenton and were duely Qualifyed by taking the Oths by Law Appointed for the Qualification of Publick Officers, and Subscrib'd the Test And then proceeded to the Chois of a Clerk and Reader, and Church Wardens;

(159) *North Carolina St Pauls Parish 1754}Sc*   (159)

Henry **BONNER** & William **HOSKINS** wer Duely Chosen to serve as Church Wardens for the Insueing Year.

Ordered That John **MC KILDO** remain Clerk of the Vestry & Reader at Edenton for the Insueing Year, and that he have the sum of Six Pounds Proclamation for the same.

The Petition of Serah **RUTTER** Red in these Words Viz; and so forth Praying some Releef towards Maintaining her Daughter who is Lame and Otherwise Destracted that she is not Able to maintain her Any Longer without Some Assistance

Ordered that she be Allowed the sum of three Pounds Proclamation Money Towards the same.

On Motion of Robert **MC CLELAND** praying that Jean **PARKER** may have a Maintainence from this Parish.

Ordered that the said Robert **MC CLELAND** be Allowed the sum of Six? Shillings Proclamation pr Mounth for keeping the said Jean **PARKER**.

Ordered that the Former Church Wardens and Former Sheriffs lay their Accoumpts befor this Vestry at their Next Setting on the tenth Day of this? Instant And pay the Ballance in their Hands to the present Church Ward___

The Vestry Adjurn'd till the tenth of this Instant Wm. **HOSKINS** Henry **BONNER**

St Pauls Parish 1754} sc Att a Vestry begun and held at the Court House in Edenton, on fryday the tenth of May 1754 Present

Nethaniel **HOWKOT** Charles **ROBERTS** William **BONNER** John **LUTEN**} Job **CHARLTON** John **SIMONS** Thomas **BONNER**} William **HOSKINS** Henry **BONNER**} Ch Warn.

Henry **BONNER**, one of the late Chch Wardens Produced an account agst. the Parish amounting to £25..0s.5d proclamation which was alowed, And? their Appears to be a Ballance due to the said Henry **BONNER** of £4:14 2? the Like money and Stands thus to Wit &c

	£
July 1752 The Paris of St Pauls to Henry **BONNER** Dr	
To Acting as Clerk of the Vestry for ye Year 1737	4..0..0
To 12 yds of Oznabrigs for Joseph **HECKET** for 2 Shirts & 2 pr Trousars	15. 0
To making 2 Shirts & 2 pr Trowsars and finding Thread	.. 1 8
To 1½ Yds of Duffels for Jos: **HECKET**	.. 9..0
To making his Jacket & finding Thread	.. 2.0
To Spining & Kniting a pair of Stokings for Do	.. 1..6
To 6 yds of Oznabrigs for Old **PHILPS**	.. 6..0
To a pair of Shoes for Josh: **HACKET**	.. 4..6
To Boarding **HACKET** from ye 6th. of Aprile 1752 to ye 6th of Feby 1754} @ 5£ Virginia Currency pr Year	9. 15.9?

10 May 1754

(159) (Cont.) To Acting as Clek of ye Vestry for the Year 1751   1. 7. 6
    To Money paid James **LUTEN** on Acct of Jno **PARISH** - -   2. 10.. 0
    To Do paid Thoms **FREEMAN** as pr Order of ye Vestry - -   3. 9. 4
    To looking after Jos. **HACKET** in his Sickness, & his Funerl Charges   1- 0- 6?
    To my Comissions - - - - - - - - - - -   .. 12 6
                                                            £25: 0: 5
                Cr on the Other Side   83

(160) *North Carolina St Pauls Parish} sc Anno Dom 1754.*   (160)
                 Contra - - - - - - - -Crrt to H. **BONNE** Acct.
Jan 1752 By Money recev'd of John **BENBURY** - - - - -   £ 3. 0..0
Aprile 1753 By Do receved of Do - - - - - - - - -   2..10..
         By Money Recevd of Do - - - - - - - - -   7.. 0..
May 15 By Money Recev'd of Do - - - - - - - - -   5. 1..3
May 18 1753 By Do recevd of William **HOSKINS** former Chch Warden   2 15..
                                                          £20.. 6..3
                       Ballance Due to Henry **BONNER** is   4 14 2
                                                         £25: 0.. 5

    The Debt on the Other Side, & the Above Cr. Was prov'd in full }
    Vestry, in Due Curce [sic] of Law before Thomas **WALTON** Esqr.}

Thomas **WALTON** Esqr on [sic] of the late Church Wardens produced his Accounts against the parish for the Year 1751 and their Appears to be due to the Said Thos. **WALTON**, the sume of ten pounds fouer Shillings old Bills, which Was proved in full Vestry in due Cource of Law, before John **HALSEY** Esqr. and stands in these Words to wit &c

[This account is written at 90° to the normal page orientation.]

Dr St. Pauls Parish in Acct Currant with Thomas **WALTON**   Cr
1751   £   s   d old Bills   £
June 24? To Bill money paid Mary **PHILPS** for }   By Cr given, for Bills Receivd. in the}
         Boarding James **PHILPS** @ 40/s. pr month}   4: -0--0   Year 1750, as it is already Steated in}
1752   To 3½ yds of Checks for Sd Jas **PHILPS**   2:..2--0   this Book - - - - - } 476..0..0
Jany 23d To 3½ Do for Do @ 20/s pr yd   3 10 0   Ballance due to Thos **WALTON**   - 10..4 0
         To 2 yds half thicks for Do @ 18/s - -   1. 16 0   £486 4 0
1753   To 40/s Cash paid Christian **WARD** for
February 10th Boarding James **PHILPS**; In old Bills   16 0 0
         To my Commissions, on £471..19s for 2}
         Years as Church Warden, @ 3 pr Ct.   }   14. 5. 0
                                         £41..13..0
    To the amount of my Acct given in for
    the Year 1750 as it is Stated in this Book.   444..11..0
                                         486: 4: 0   £486 4

(161) *Noth. Carolina St Pauls Parish 1754.*}sc   (161)

    John **HALSEY** on of the late Sheriffs appeard in full Vestry and paid into the Hands of William **HOSKINGS** on of the present Chch. Wardens an Account for a Comunion Cloth, and the sume of forty fouer shillings and six pence proclamation, being the amount of a Ballance due to the Parish from the said John **HALSEY** in the year 1750.

    John **BENBURY** the Late Sheriff produced his Accounts for the Yea_ 1751 as his Colections for that Year, Also, his disbursments sinc [sic] that time Which Stands in these Words to Wit &c.

1753 Dr The Parish of St Pauls in Acct. Currant with Jno **BENBURY**
Aprile 22 To prock, paid William **HOSKINS** as pr Receipt - -   £58 0:0
         To Do paid Henry **BONNER** as pr Do - - - - -   5 11:0
         To Do paid Robert **BESLEY** @ pr Do - - - -   5. 0.0
         To Do paid Henry **BONNER** @ another time - -   7. 0.0
         To my Commissns. for Receiving 85 £ 16 Shills   5. 3.7
                                                  £80 14.7
                     Ballance due to the parish   5   1 5?
    Which Balance has since ben paid to Mr Henry **BONNER**   £85:16 0

10 May 1754

(161) (Cont.) as appears ~~in~~ by his acct Stated on the Other side
    Contra - - - - - - - - - Cr.
    By a 1s/4d Tax Receivd. of 1287 Taxables for ye Year 1751 Amting. to £85..16 0

Ordered that John **MCKILDO** the now Clerk of the Vestry and Reader at Edenton take in his Possession all the plate and Peuter and Linen belonging to Edenton Church; and Also that he provide Bread and Wine for the Comunion at the Charge of the Parish.

    On Motion of John **PARISH** praying some Assistance towards Maintaining his son who is a Criple.

    Ordered that he be allowed the sume of twenty five Shillings prock, for ye same

    Ordered that a Levy of one shilling and fouer pence procklamation be Laid on every Taxable person Within this parish for paying the Minester Clerk and Readers and towards Maintaining the poor of the said Parish.

    The Vestry adjurn'd till the 3d Day of June Next. Wm. **HOSKINS** Henry **BONNER** C Ward

---

St Pauls Parish 1754 sc At A Vestry begun and held at the Court House in Edenton on Munday the third Day of June 1754 Present
    Thomas **BONNER** Thomas **BONNER** John **LUTEN** Job **CHARLTON**} Nethaniel **HOWCOTT** Charles **ROBERTS** John **SIMONS** William **BONNER**} William **HOSKINS** Henry **BONNER**} Chch Ward

    Thomas **FREEMAN** produced an Acct. against ye Parish for Boarding James **PHILPS** 3 Months, and for Burieng the Said **PHILPS**, Amounting to 1£7 6 Virginia Currancy which is Allowed and Stand in theses Words to wit &c.
                                Turn Over 84

(162) *Chowan County St. Pauls Parish 1753*} sc   (162)
    The Parish of St Pauls to Thos **FREEMAN**   Dr   £
    To Boarding James **PHILPS** 3 Months @ 5S Virga Curcy pr Month   0..15..0
    To his Funerall Charge - - - - - - - - - - - -   0..12 6
                                                     £1: 7:6

Anno Dom 1754 An acct. of Mr Isaac **HUNTER**s was produced to the Vestry for finding Bread and wine for 3 Sacraments amounting to 15 Shillings prock: wch. is allowed.

    Ordered That Abraham **NORFLET** be Reader at **FARLEE**s Chaple for the Insuing Year, and that he be allowed 40S proclamation for the Same. *FARLEEs*

    Ordered that Moses **HAIR** be Reader at Sarum Chaple for the Insuing Year and that he be allowed 40 Shillings proclamation for the same *Sarum*

    The Honorable Francis **CORBIN** & Mr. Robert **BESLEY** Not being Qualified in due Time according to the Act of Assembly in that Case made and provided The Vestry did, according to the aforesaid Act, Chuse and Elect the afsd. Francis **CORBIN** Esqr. and Mr Robert **BESLEY**, Who were duly Qualified by takeing the Oaths by law appointed for the Qualification of publick Officers and Subscrib'd the Test.

    Ordered that Jacob **HUNTER** serve as Reader at **CONSTANT**s Chaple for the In Suing Year, and that he have 40 Shillings proclamation for the same.

    The Vestry adjurn'd till Munday ye 17th Instant Willm. **HOSKINS** Henry **BONNER**} Chch. Ward.

St Pauls Parish 1754.} sc At a Vestry begun and held at the Court House in Edenton on Munday ye 17th of June 1754 Present.
    The Honourable Francis **CORBIN** Robert **BEASLEY** Thomas **BONNER** Job **CHARLTON** Nethaniel **HOWKOT** [sic]} Charles **ROBERTS** John **SIMONS** William **BONNER** Thomas **BONNER**} Willm **HOSKINS** Henry **BONNER**} C Wd:

    On the Representation of Mr Robert **BEASLEY**, That a More Conveniant Acre of Land for Building a Chaple for the Benefit of the Inhabitant's of the of the [sic] Loer part of this Parish could be had of Mr Christopher **BUTLER** for that Purpose.

    It is Ordered on the Deed being produced for the said Land That the said Intended Chaple shall be Erected on the Land to be Granted by the said **BUTLAR** and the sume of fifteen Pounds Proclamation be paid into the Hands of Mr. Robert **BEASLEY** on of the Church Wardens of the said Parish for the purpose aforesaid. *Chapel*

    John **ROSS** produced an Acct. against ye Parish for Nursing and Burieng Elizabeth **HANNAH** & finding a Coffen for the said **HANNAH** Amounting to forty Shillings Virginia Money Which is Allowed.

    Ordered That William **LUTEN** pay to this Vestry at their Next Sitting What Money is in his Hands due to the said Vestry Otherwise, that he be delt With as the Law Directs.

(163) *Chowan County St. Pauls Paris* [sic] *1754*}sc   (163.)

    Mr William **HOSKINS** on of the late Church Wardens for the Year 1750 Produced his Accts. for that Year Amounting to 778£ 4s 6d old Bills with a Cr. 774£ and a Ballance due to him of £4.4..6 Like Money, Which was duely proved in full Vestry be-

17 June 1754

(163) (Cont.) fore the Honourable Francis **CORBIN**, and Stands thus to Wit &c.
[This account is written at 90° to the normal page orientation.]

The Parish of St Pauls To Willm? H__K___	Dr?		Contra	Cr
February To money Paid Mr **HALL** - - - -	561 6 11		By Money Reced of Mr **HALSEY** Late}	
ye 5th 1750 To Do paid Mr. **MEARNS** - - - -	44.12 5		Sheriff for ye Year 1749 - - - }	774 s d
To Do paid Mr John **FREEMAN** - -	15. 0. 0		Ballance due to me - - - - - -	4.4.6
To Do paid Mary **QUARLES** - - -	5 0..0			£778:4:6
To Do paid Thomas? **ROBINSON** - -	3..0..0			
To Do paid Phillis **BROWN & TROTER**	5..0..0			
To Do paid for 3 Bottles of Wine - - -	3..0..0			
To Do paid to Francis **PENRICE** - -	2..0..0			
To Do paid to Mr. **WARD** - - - -	16..7..6			
To Do paid to Mr. **CAMPBELL** - -	4..0..0			
To Do paid to Mr. **HALSEY** - - -	56. 0..10			
To Do paid to Mr. **MIDLETON** - .-	11. 0..0			
To Do paid to Mr **DEAR** - - - -	1 17 6			
To Do paid to Mr **CRAVEN** for Linnen	1.15. 0			
To Do paid to Mr John **BENBURY** -	3.. 0..0			
To Do paid to John **WARE** in his Sickness	1 18. 9			
To Do paid to Mrs **PARKER** - - -	2 5 0			
To Do paid to Mr **DAVIS** for mending ye Court House Windows - - - -	1 10 _[blot]			
To Do paid for keeping & Burieng Henry **BULLY** - - - -	10.. 0. 0			
To Do for ½ pound of Suggar & half thowsan Pins	0 12: 6			
	£755 6 6			
To my Comissions on ye Whole @ 3 pr Ct:	22 18: 0			
	778 4: 6			£778:4:6
85				

(164) *Chowan County St Pauls Parish 175?} * (164)

Ordered That the present Sheriff pay to the Present Church Wardens, What Money is in his Hands belonging to the Parish, towards ??????? Defreying the Charges thereof.

The Vestry adjurn'd till Saturday ye 6th Day of July Next. Wm. **HOSKINS** Henry **BONNER**} Chch Wardens

==

1755. Att a Vestry begun and held at the Court House in Edenton Saturday ye 10th Day of May 1755 --Present--
William **BONNER** Charles **ROBERTS** Robert **BESLEY**} Nethaniel **HOWKOT** Thomas **BONNER** Job **CHARLTON**} {William **HOSKINS** Henry **BONNER**} C. W.

Mr Henry **BONNER** one of the Chch. Wardens Mov'd that som Allouenc [sic] might be mad by this Vestry for a Child left on this parish by Christopher **WEST** who went on the Expodition to Ohio,

Order That the sume of Nine Shillings pr Mounth be Allowed for the same

William **HOSKINS** the Other Chch. Warden Mov'd that some Allowance be made by the Parish for keeping William **DIKSON** an Orphant Boy being Unable to Work for his living.

Ordered that the sume of ten Shillings pr Mounth be Allowed him for the same.

Mr. Robert **BESLEY** produced an account against the Parish for Sundries Which having ben prov'd according to Law is Allowed and Stand thus to witt &c.   On the Next Sheet.

(165) *Anno Dom. 1755}* (165)
[This page is written at 90° to the normal page orientation.]

1752 Dr The Parish of St: Pauls in Acct. Currant with Robert **BEASLEY** Chch: Warden for ye Year 1752

Octobr 10 To 10 lb of Bacon to Jean **PARKER**	0 3. 2	Contra	Cr
To 2 Bushels of Corn - - - -	0 3. 0	Apl 1753	£
To 1 Qt: of Molasses - - - -	0 0 8	2d Recevd. of Mr. Jno. **BENBURY** -	5:0:0
To 2 Bushels of Corn - - - -	0 3..0	Augst 15 Recevd of Do - - - -	12 3 4
To ½ Bushell of Wheat - - - -	- 1. 10½		17:3:4

10 May 1755

(165) (Cont.) To 9 lb of Hogs Lard		0 3 0
To 10 lb of Baccon		- 3 2
To proc		0 7 0
1753 To 35 lb of pork		- 5 4
Feb 3 To 2 Bushels of Corn		0 3 0
To 10 pounds of Baccon		0 3. 2
To 10 lb of Beef		0 2 6
To 1 Bushell of Corn		0 1 6
To 1 Qt of Brandy		0 1 0
To 22 lb of Baccon		-- 7 0
To 5 lb of Lard		- 2 0
To 1 Bushell of Corn		- 1 6
To 1 Qt of Molasses		- - 8
To 6 lb of Baccon		- 1 7
To 1 Bushell of Corn		- 1 6
Septem 8 To paid John **ASTIE** by Order of Vestry		2 3 9
12 paid Joseph **DEAR**--(for Childrens Board)		3 10 0
25 paid John **MC. KILDO** for acting Clerk &c		6 0:0
To Sundrie Charges for keeping & Burying} Margret a Woman left by Capn: **POLLAK**		1: 5:0
To my Comissions on 17£:3s:4d		0 10 3½
		£16 4 8
Due to the Parish from Robt **BESLEY**		0 18 8
		17 3: 4

1734   86

(166)   (166)

By virtue of an Act of The General Assembly of North Carolina, begun and held at Newbern on The Twelfth Day of December in The year of our Lord One Thousand seven Hundred and Fifty Four, Intitled an Act. for Appointing Parishes. and Vestries. for The Encouragement. of an Orthodox Clergy. for. The Advancement. of The Protestant. Religion, and for The Diretion of The Settlement. of Parish Accounts.

The Freeholders of Saint Pauls Parish, in Chowan County did Meet The Sheriff at The Court House of The said County, on Monday The Sixteenth day of June in The year. of Our Lord Christ. One Thousand Seven Hundred and Fifty Five. and Then and There According to The Directions of The said Act, in due forme did Choose and Elect. The following Persons. To. Serve as. Vestry men for The Three Insuing years. To wit. Demsey **SUMNER**. Esqr: Luke **SUMNER**. Henry **KING**, Elisha **HUNTER**, Timothy **WALTON**, Richard **BOND**, Josiah **GRANBERY**, Jethro **BENTON**, Henry **BONNER**. Peter. **PARKER**. John **LUTON** and William **WALTON**. who were Summoned by The Sherriff to Meet and Qualifie at The Court House on Tuesday the 17th day of June. 1755.

1755. On Tuesday. The 17th day. of June 1755. The said Demsey **SUMNER**. Esqr: Luke **SUMNER**, Henry **KING**, Elisha **HUNTER**, Timothy **WALTON**, Richard **BOND**, Josiah **GRANBERY**, Jethro **BENTON**, Henry **BONNER**. Peter **PARKER**, (John **LUTON** Excepted.) and William **WALTON** Eleven of The Twelve Vestery Men met. at The Court House in Edenton and were duly Qualified according to Law by. Takeing The Oaths. Prescribed by. Act. of Parliament and Subscribing The Test and Declaration. Pursuant to. The aforesaid Act. of General Assembly, for The due Qualification of Vestry Men.

And The said Vestry having Taken Their Places accordingly. Proceeded to The Choice of Church Wardens. and Unanimuly. Chose Demsey **SUMNER**. and Henry **BONNER**. Church Wardens for This Present Year.

(167) *North Carolina Chowan County. Saint Pauls Parish 1755}* (___)

At a Vestry begun and Held at The Court House in Edenton. on Tuesday The 17th Day of June Anno Dom 1755 Present.
Demsey **SUMNER** Henry **BONNER**} Church Wardens.
Luke **SUMNER**. Henry **KING**, Elisha **HUNTER**. Timothy **WALTON** Richard **BOND**} Vestry men {Josiah **GRANBERY** Jethro **BENTON** Peter **PARKER** William **WALTON**.

Ordered That Luke **SUMNER**. be and he is here by appointed. Clerk of The Vestry. and That he Take the Vestry Book into. his care and Possession.

Ordered. That. The several Readers. in This Parish be continued Readers. for The Insuing year. and That They be Allowed The Sum of Forty Shillings Proclamation Money Each for the same. to wit. John **SKINNER**. Continued a Reader at Sarum

17 June 1755

(167) (Cont.) Chappel, Jacob HUNTER. at CONSTANTs Chappel Abraham NORFLEET at FARLEEs. Chappel, and That. Mr. Henry BONNER. one of The Church wardens. do. Agree with Some Person to be Reader. at Edenton for The Insuing Year. in The Room of John MC: KILDO.

Issd.. Ordered. That the Reverend Mr: Clement HALL be Allowed Eighty. Pounds. Proclamation Money. for Performing Devine Servis and Preaching and Officiating. as. Clerk and Rector. of This Parish This Insuing year Provided That he attend and Officiate in The following Manner, (that is to say.) On Sunday the Twenty Second day of June at FARLEEs. Chappel and on the next sunday being the 29th. at CONSTANTs Chappel on Sunday the 6th day of July at Edenton and The next Sunday following being the 13th of July. at Sarum Chappel & so on in that Course & Manner to Proceed & Continue all the Remaining Part of The year. or in Proportion There__ for the Sundays that he shall so. Officiate he being a Missionary 87

(168) _orth Carolina Chowan County St: Pauls Parish 1755} (__)

Ordered That the Reverend Mr: Clement HALL be Allowed The sum of Six Pounds, Thirteen Shillings and Four Pence. Proclamation Money. in Lieu of a Gleeb for This Present Year.

Ordered That an Order. of Vestry made The 10th day of May Last Allowing Nine Shillings pr. Month. for The Mentainance of a Child Left in This Parish by Christopher. WEST who. went on The Expedition To. Ohio. be Still Continued.

Ordered. That Mr: Henry BONNER. one of The Church wardens Take into his Care and Possession all The Plate. Pewter. and Linnin Belonging to This Parish That is now in The Hands of John MC: KILDO.

Ordered That every Justice of The Peace; The former Sheriffs; and every. other Person or Persons. within this County; That have. any of The Parish Money in Their hands. do appear and Account. for The same according to Law. with The next Vestry to be held for This Parrish on Satterday the fifth Day of July next at CONSTANTs Chappel. by Twelve of The Clock. and That They have Timely Notice Thereof. it is Further Orderred That a Copy of This order. be set up at The several Chappels in This Parish.

The Vestry. adjourned. Till The first Satterday in July next To. Meet. at. CONSTANTs Chappel. Demsey SUMNER Henry BONNER} C W

At a Vestry begun and held at CONSTANTs Chappel on satterday The 5.th Day of. July 1755. according to Adjournment.
-Present- Demsey SUMNER. Church warden.
Luke SUMNER Henry KING. Elisha HUNTER.} Timothy WALTON Richard BOND Josiah GRANBERY {Jethro BENTON Peter PARKER William WALTON

And whereas. John LUTEN Failed to Meet and Quallefie at. The Last Vestry According to Law. and not Appearing now,

(169) _____lina Chowan County St: Pauls Parish 1755.} (__)

The Vestry. Proceeds. To Choose another Person _____ as a vestry man in his Room And accordingly did Ele__ John GORDON. in his Stead. who being Present. is at th_ Same time duly. Quallefied by. Taking The Oathes by Law. Appointed for The Quallefication. of. Vestry Men. subscrib___ The Test. and Took his Place Accordingly. 169

On The Motion of Abraham NORFLEET a Reader. at. FARLEEs Chappel. Praying That he may Read every other sunday at the said Chappel and the other sundays. at The House of Mr. Thomas LUTEN Esqr. which he says will be very agreeab__ and Convenient for The People. Granted and Ordered That he do. Read at. The said LUTENs House every Second Sunday untill it appears to be otherwise Then [sic] Then his Allegation. And it is also. Considered and Ordered tha_ The other Readers. in This Parish may Likewise Read at Such Places as Shall be Most for The Ease of The People not Exceeding every Third. Sunday from Their Respective Chappels.

Ordered That The several Readers. in This Parish do. keep an Exact and True Account of all The sundays That The Parson shall omit Preaching at Each of the Respective Chappels. according to an Order of Vestry made The 17th day of June Last and Produce the Said Accounts. to The First Vestry That shall be held after next Easter. Sunday.

Ordered That a Warrant be Issued to. summon Joseph HERRON, John BENBURY, John HALSEY Miles GALE William LUTEN and The Executors of Peter PAYNE decd To. meet. and Lay Their Respective Accounts. of the Parish Moneys in Their Hands. before The Next Vestry to be. Held. for This Parrish at CONSTANTs Chappel The Second Satterday in August next by. nine o Clock in The Morning. and on Their Refusal or Neglect That the Church wardens do. bring suite against Those That fai_ to appear. As well for the Penalty by Law inflicted, as for a Settlement of Their Respective [Remainder of line is missing.] 88

(170) _____Carolina. _owan County __: Pauls Parish 1755

Issd. Ordered That Sarah RUTTER. a poor. woman be Allowed The sum of Five Pounds. Proclamation Money. for The Mentainance of her daughter. who is an Ideot.. for The Insuing year or at the Rate Thereof. for. any Less Time . . . 170

Issd. Ordered. That. Mary HOLMS a widow woman in This Parish be Allowed The Sum of Forty Shillings Procn. Money. to be paid out of The Fines due to This Parish. towards The Mentainance of Her Young Child. . . . . . .

75

5 July 1755

(170) (Cont.) _____ *Issd 1757 Issd. 1758. Issd. 1760.* Ordered That John **WILLIAMSON** be Allowed the Sum of Six pounds pr. Year forThe Board and Mentainance of James **HOMES** a Poor Old Man in This Parish or at The Rate Thereof for The Time he Shall keep him. . . . .

      Jacob **HUNTER,** Prodused an Account against St: Pauls Parish for fifteen Shillings Proc. which is Allowed and Stands. Stated. as. followeth.

      Viz. Dr. Saint Pauls Parish to Jacob **HUNTER** for. Bread & Wine &c. for Three Communions at. **COSTEN**s Chappel at five Shillings. Each Time is Fifteen Shillings . . . .£.0:15:0.

July 5th 1755.   Errors Excepted pr. Jacob **HUNTER**

Chowan. To wit. Proved in Open Vestry before me Demsey **SUMER**.

Issd.   On the Petition of John **PARRISH**. seting. forth. That his son is. helpless. Cripple. and praying some. relief Towards his supp_rt and Mentainance. Granted and Ordered That he be Allowed? Twenty Five Shillings for the Insuing Year. . . .

      Ordered That The Vestry be Adjourned. Till the second Satterday in August next. To. Meet. at **CONSTAN**s [sic] Chappell by Nine of the Clock in The Morning. . . . . Demsey **SUMNER**

(171) _____ *t: Pauls Parish1755.* At a Vestry begun and Held at **CONSTANT**s Chappel __ August the 9th: 1755. According to Adjournment. Present.

      Demsey **SUMNER.** C. W. Elisha **HUNTER.**. Timothy **WALTON**} Henry **KING** Richard **BOND** Jethro **BENTON**{ John **GORDON** William **WALTON** Josiah **GRANBERY**

      Abraham **NORFLEET** Appeared and made Return That he has Personally Summoned. Joseph **HERRON**. John **BENBURY**. John ____ Miles **GALE** William **LUTEN** and The Executors of Peter _____ deceased. who are. Thomas **BARKER.** and John **CAMPBELL**. To. M___ The Vestry This day in Order. to Settle Their Several Resp_____ Accounts. Pursuant to the Warrant For That Purpose to him Directed?.. Ordered that he be Allowed Fourteen Shillings Proc. for ___

Issd.   Ordered that Abraham **NORFLEET**. be Allowed five Shillings for ____ The Elements for a Communion at **FARLEE**s. Chappel Last Y___

Issd.   Ordered. That. Josiah **GRANBERY**. do Purchase for. the Three Ch-_____ That is not already Supplyed. with Books. Three Bibles ____ and Three Prayer. Books. in Folio..well Bound and that __ be. paid. according To. his Accot: for Them.

Issd.   Ordered. That Jacob **HUNTER** be Allowed. forty Shillings Proc: for Reading at. **CONSTANT**s Chappel the Year. 1753. as pr. Proved Accot:.

Issd.   Ordered That five Pounds. be Given to. John **WATERS** a Poor Old ____ man in This Parish. and That it be paid Out of the Fines due? To the Parish for this Present. Year.

Issd.   Ordered That Moses **SPEIGHTS** [sic] be Allowed Six Shillings and Eight pence per Month for the Time he Shall Keep Rob___ **ALPHIN** a poor Old man.

issd.   Joseph **ALPHIN** came into Vestry and Agreed to. Give Six? Shillings and Eight Pence a year. towards the Support of ___ father Robert **ALPHIN**. to be Deducted Out of the afore____ Sum of Six Shillings and Eight pence per Month

      Ordered that The Church Wardens or Either of Them do Give __ order on John **MC: KILDO** Who has. Some parish Money _____ ____ The Reverend Mr. Clem__t H_LL _____ 89

(172) John **HALSEY**. appeared. and Produced his Accot: of The Parish Money in his Hands., and Proved The Same in Open Vestry. The ballance is five Pounds. Thirteen Shillings and Nine pence Due To the Parish Which he paid into the Hands. of. Demsey **SUMNER** One of the Church Wardens. at The Same Time. and his Accot. Stands Stated. as Follows. *172*

      The Parish of St: Pauls. in Accot. with John **HALSEY**. Cr.   £. S D.

      1754. October: 15. By a Fine from Hannah **CLAY** for a

            Bastard Child . . . .   1:5:0.

      By. a Fine from William **WILKINS** for Profane Swearing   1:5:0.

      By a Fine from Elizabeth **FORD** for a Bastard Child . .   1:5:0.

      By. a. Fine from Sarah **HUNTER** . . . . .   1:5:0.

      By. a Fine from Francis **ROBINS** for Swearing . .   0:3:9.

      By. a Fine from Mary **JONES** for a Bastard-Child   1:5:0.

                                   £.6:8:9

      Dr. the Parish of St. Pauls. with John **HALSEY**   .£. S D.

      To. Cash Paid for Burying Jean **PARKER** . .   0.:15:0

      Ballance Due to ye Parish 5:13:9   6:8:9

      Errors Excepted pr. J. **HALSEY**.   £6: 8:9   0

      August 9.th 1755. Sworn before me. Demsey **SUMNER** J P.

      Miles. **GALE** who. Succeeded Peter **PAYN** in his Last Years Sherifalty. Appeared in Vestry. and Paid Thirty five

(172) (Cont.) Pounds. Procn: Money in Part in Part of his Parish Collection.

Thomas. **WALTON** Produced his Acco't: and Proved the same on Oath and. Paid the ballance of The same. being. Twelve Shillings and Two pence which Stands Stated as follows..

_755._ St. Pauls Parish Dr.. To Thos: **WALTON**. Contra Cr   £. S. D.

To Bills pd: Elizabeth **HINTON**}		{1755. By a Fine from Isaac **HILL**}	
for Curing Robt. **ALPHIN**s hand}	12:9:½	{For having a bastard sworn to him}	1: 5: 0
Ballance due the Parish	12:2:½		
	1:5:0		

August 9th. 1755. The Above Accot. was proved in Open Vestry by the Oath of Thomas **WALTON**. & That he has no more Parish Money in His hands. Sworn before me. Demsey **SUMNER**.

Ordered That the Church Wardens or either of Them Pursuant to An Order made The 5th day of July 1755. do. Imploy an Attorn__ to. bring Suit against. Them That Have failed to Appear and Settle Their Accots. Vizt. Joseph **HERRON** John **BENBURY**. and the Exrs [Next line is illegible.]

(173) ____ Pauls. Parish 1755.:}   (__)

Ordered? that? William **LUTEN** pay The Reverend Mr. Clem: **HALL** Four Pounds Fourteen Shillings and a Penney. Proc___ation Money. As. Appears to be Due From Him to The Parish as pr. an Accot:. stated in The Vestry Book the 24th of August. in The Year. 1752. And That Mr. ____ Account with The Vestry for The Same. _173_

Ordered That. The Vestry be Adjourned Till Satterday ___ Sixth Day of September Next To. meet at **CONSTA**___ Chappel. Demsey **SUMNER**

At a Vestry. Met. according To. Adjournment. at **CONSTAN**__ Chappel. on Satterday The sixth Day of September 1755. Present. Demsey **SUMNER**. Church Warden

Luke **SUMNER**. Elisha **HUNTER** Timothy **WALTON** Richard **BOND** Jethro **BENTON**} Vestry Men { Josiah **GRANBERY** John **GORDON** Peter. **PARKER**. William **WALTON**.

On the Motion of the Reverend Mr. Clement **HALL**. it is Or_____ That John **MC: KILDO** be and he is hereby Appointed Cler_? or Reader. of Edenton Chappel. and That he be Allowed T__ Same. as. the Other Readers. are. or in Proportion thereto It being Forty Shillings Proclamation per. Annum.

Issd. for HARRIS Isd. for HALSEY. Isd. 5 Wolves Isd. Isd. Copys. Issd. Certificates. is Produced To The Vestry This Day. for Five Wolves Scalps Killed in This County. Vizt.. George **HARRISS** killed one Wolf. Miles **HALSEY**. Killed. one Jacob **HUNTER** &? John **GORDON** One. Daniel **HUNTER**. One for Which They are Allowed According to Law. Ten Shillings Each?

Ordered That. William **HORSKINS** and Charles **BLOUNT** Exrs. of James **TROTTER** Deceased Pay. to The Reverend Mr. Clement **HALL** The M____ Due. to The Parish from The said James **TROTTER**s Estate for Two Ye___ Hire of Negro **DUBLIN** at the Rate of 50£ old Bills pr Annum being A Legacey Left to The Parish by The Last Will & Testament [Next line is illegible.] _90_

(174) _____ish_755.}   (__)

John **MACKILDO** Sent to the Vestry by _____t **HALL** The Sum of. Thirteen Pounds. Eight Shillings and Eight Pence Proc. being Part of The Parish Money in His hands. pursuant to an Order of Last Vestry. . . . . . _174_

Ordered That. Warrants be Issued. against Each and every Person or. Persons. That are in Arrear To this Parish for their Respective Leveys That are Unpayed Unless they do. appear. and pay the same at the Next Vestry to be Held at **CONSTANT**s Chappel on Satterday the 18th Day of October Next and That a Copy of This Order be Set up. at Each of The Chappels in This Parish

Ordered That a Tax or Levey of Two shillings and Eight Pence Proclamation Money. be Leveyed. on. Each and Every Taxable Person in This Parish. for. This Present year to Defray the Contingent Charges. Thereof. and That The Same be Collected by some person To be Appointed by The Vestry.. at some Meeting before January next which person. so. Appointed shall. Appear. and Give Bond and Security. according to Law. in full Vestry.

Ordered That The Church Wardens. or either of Them do. Advertise. The Tobo: That was. Received at **BENNET**s Creek by the Sheriff on Accot. of The Parish and sell it at Publick Sale To The highest Bidder For The Use of The Parish and Accot. with The Vestry for The Same.

Ordered The Vestry. Meet again at **CONSTANT**s Chappel on Satterday The Eighteenth Day of October Next to which Time & Place they adjon: Demsey **SUMNER** C. W.

At a Vestry begun and held at **CONSTANT**s Chappel on Satterday The 18th Day of October. 1755. -- 1756.. [sic] according to Adjournment Present.

18 October 1755

(174) (Cont.) Elisha **HUNTER**. Jethro **BENTON** Peter **PARKER**.} Henry **KING** John **GORDON** Josiah **GRANBERY**{ William **WALTON** Richard **BOND**. Vestry Men

The Vestry Adjourned. To. Meet again on Satterday the Twenty fifth day of This Instant October at **CONSTANT**s Chappel . . . .

(175) _____. *Parish 1755.*} At. A Vestry Met and Held at **CONSTANT**s Chappel. On saterday. The 25th Day of October. Anno Dom 1755. Present. Demsey **SUMNER**. Church warden

Luke **SUMNER** Elisha **HUNTER**. Richard **BOND**. Jethro **BENTON**.} Vestry Men { John **GORDON**. Henry **KING**. William **WALTON**. Peter **PARKER**.

The Vestry Takeing into consideration The Law for Settleing the Title and Bounds. of Peoples Lands. by. freeholders. appoind.? To. Procession The Same. On Oath &c. Accordingly Proceed to. Divide The Parish into Convenient Cantons. and to Appoint Two. Freeholders in Each Canton Processioners. to procession The same according To. Law. as Follows.

Ordered. That Francis **SANDERS** and John **MINSHEE** do. Procession all The Lands. from Abraham **ODAM**s. as The Road runs to Mehe____ Ferrey. which is bounded between The Road and The River

Ordered That Edward **HAIR** Juner [sic] and Joseph **SPEIGHT** Do. Procession all The Lands. from the Road that Leads to- by Abraham **ODAM**s to. Meherin Ferrey. begining at the Cuntry Line. so along Sarum Road. To. **PUGH**s Road and so a Long that Road to the Ferrey. . . .

Ordered That Jacob **ODAM** and James **BRADDY**. do. procession All The Lands. from **PUGH**es. Road, begining at the Plantation of Robert **RODGERS**. so along Sarum Road to. the Notty Pine Swamp. down the Said Swamp. to Henry **BAKER**s Mill. so along The Road That Leads by. William **UMPHLET**s. to **PUGH**s Road

Ordered That Jethro **HARRIL** and John **SKINNER**. Procesion All The Lands. from Henry **BAKER**s Mill begining at the Mill down **COLE**s Creek to the River, up the River to. **COTTON**s Ferrey. then a Long the Road to Henry **BAKER**s Mill

Ordered That. Robert **RODGERS** and John **ARLINE** do Procession all The Lands. from The Cuntry Line begining near Moses **PARK**___ on The New Road _____ the Said Road _____ at 91

(176) __*auls. Parish. 1755.*} [Approximately four words missing.] Saru_ Road to The Cuntry ____. *176*

Ordered. That William **POWELL** Juner. and Richard **FELTON**. Senior. Procession all The Lands from the New Road begining at The head of **BENNET**s Creek. down The said Creek To the Mouth of The Honey pot Swamp, up the said Swamp to The Head of it, & so a Cross to the head of The knotty Pine Swamp. and down The said swamp. to. To [sic] The New Road.

Ordered. That William **DANIEL** and James **PILAND**. do Procession All The Lands from The new Road begining where The new Road crosses The Notty Pine Swamp. Thence up the said swamp to the head there of Then a Cross from That to the Honey pot. Swamp. and then down the Same to **BENNET**s Creek & Down the said Creek to The River thence up the River to **COLE**s Creek and up the said Creek to the Notty Pine Swamp. and up the Swamp to The New Road.

Ordered That. William **POWELL** senior and Edward **ARNELL** [sic] Procession all The Lands. from The Head of **BENNETT**s Creek begining at the Cuntry Line up Chowan Road to The Loosing Swamp. & up the said Swamp. by The flat Branch across. to **BENNET**s Creek and up the said **BENNET**s Creek to The Cuntry Line and a Long the Line to. Chowan Road. .

Ordered That. Samuel **HARRILL** and John **RICE** Procession all The Lands. from The Loosing Swamp. down Perquimons Road to. **SPEIGHTS**s. Plantation Thence by the Cart Road That. Leads to Elisha **HUNTER**s. Then down by Meherin Swamp To. **BENNET**s Creek and up the Creek to The Flat Branch then by the Loosing Swamp to. Perquimons Road..

Ordered. That Robert **LASITER** and Moses **LASITER**. Procession all The Lands. Included from Meherrin Swamp. begining at Jacob **HUNTER**s. Mill. up. the said Swamp to The piping Branch so along The said branch to The Main Road and Down The said Road to Aaron **BLANSHARD**s. Old Road and a Long the Said Old Road To **BENNET**s Creek road up the said Road to **BENNET**s Creek Bridg_ and thence up **BENNET**s Creek To the Mill. on Meherrin Swamp

Ordered That Jesse **HUNTER** and Benjamin **BLANSHARD**. do. Procession all The Lands included from **BENNET**s Creek Road

(177) __: _____ *Parish 1755*} Begining at **BENNET**s Creek Bridge _____ _____ Creek ____ Catherins Creek Bridge, Down Catharins Creek to The River up. The River, to. The. Mouth.. of **BENNET**s Creek. and up **BENNET**s Creek to **BENNET**s .Creek Bridge. *177*

Ordered That. Abner **EASON** and Guy **HILL** do. Procession all The Lands Included. Begining at. **SPEIGHT**Ses Plantation so along the Road to James **SCOTT**s. Thence Down Catharin Creek to The Road at Thomas **WALTON**s. Thence along **BENNET**s Creek Road to. **BLANSHARD**s. Old Road so along. the said Road to Chowan Road & so. to The Piping Branch. then down ye Branch to. meherin Swamp. and. down ye Swamp to Elisha **HUNTER**. and from thence by his Cart Road to **SPIGHTES**s [sic] Plantation.

Ordered That. James **SUMNER** and Richard **FREEMAN** Procession all The Lands. included Between Catharins

25 October 1755

(177) (Cont.) Creek, The Sandy Run and Perquimons Road. begining at James SCOTs Plantation.

Ordered That William COUPLAND and Nathan PARKER do. Procession all The Lands included between The Sandy Run and Indian Town Creek, Chowan River and Perquimons.

Ordered. That William BOYD and Luke WHITE. do. Procession All The Lands. Included. between. Indian Town Creek and. Rockahock Creek between the Main Road and Chowan River and make Return Thereof To April Court.

Ordered That William BOND and Charles ROBERTS do. Procession all The Lands. Included Between Indian Town Creek and. Machacoma Creek alis. Garbacon between the main Road and Perquimons County. and make Return there of To. Aprill County. Court.

Ordered That. William LUTEN and William WESTEN do Procession all The Lands. That are Included between Rocahock and Machacoma Creek on the West side of the Main Road between The Road and Chowan River. and That They make Return There of to April Court next

Ordered that Thomas BONNER and Nathaniel HOCOTT do. Procession all The lands That are Included between Machacoma Creek alis Garbac__ and William? HOSKINS? _____ to the River _____ 92

(178) __ ____ _arish 1755 Ordered __ _ohn BENBURY. and. Robert BEASLEY. __. Procession all The Lands. That are Included between William HORSKINSes. Mill Swamp. The Sound side and Yeopim River. and make Return There of To. April Court Next. according To Law. *178*

Ordered. That. The Clerk of The Vestry. do Set up Advertisements. at the Chappels. That the Vestry will Meet. on The Last Saturday in December Next. at CONSTANTs Chappel to Appoint a Collecter of The Parish Tax,. and That any Person Inclinable To Take the Collection of The Same, may Meet the Vestry at That Time and place Provided with Their Securitys.

____ *The Orders. For Processioners are all made out pr L. S.* Ordered That The Vestry be Adjourned Till The Last Saturday in December Next to Meet at CONSTANTs Chappel. Demsey SUMNER.

St. Pauls. Parish *1755.*} At a Vestry. held for. St: Pauls Parish at CONSTANTs Chappel on Satterday the 27th Day of December. Anno. Dom: 1755. According to Adjournment. Present.

Mr: Luke SUMNER Mr: Josiah GRANBERY. Mr: Elisha HUNTER Mr: John GORDON. } Vestry Men [Writen vertically, between the columns.] {Mr: Richard BOND. Mr: William WALTON. Mr: Jethro BENTON.

Ordered That Mr: Jesse HUNTER be, and he is accordingly Appointed. Collector of The Parish Taxes now due on his Giving Bond and Security. in. The Sum. of One Thousand Pounds Proclamation Money. for his duly Collecting and Settling with the Vestry for The Same which is Accordingly Given by Mr: Elisha HUNTER and Mr: John GORDON his securities, it is therefore Ordered. That he do Collect from Each and Every Taxable Person in This Parish, The sum of Two Shillings and Eight Pence Proclamation Money being The Parish Tax Leveyed. for This Present year. and whereas. it appears. That by Reason of The Sherriffs. Death a great Part of The Last years. Parish Levey of One Shilling and four

(179) (179.)
Pence Proclamation Money. per. Pole. Still Remains due and unpa__ it's Therefore Ordered That The said Collector. do. Collect and Receive The same from each and every Delinquent. Together with The Tax for This Present year. and That. he Account and Settle with The Vestry for The same on or before Easter Monday next.

Ordered That The Vestry be Adjourned. Till The Last Satterday In March Next, To. Meet at CONSTANT's. Chappel.

Satterday March ye. 27.th Day. 1756. There not meeting of a Vestry The Vestry, is To. meet by Appointment. at CONSTANTs Chappel on Satterday The 24.th Day of April next.

At a Vestry. met at CONSTANT's. Chappel on Satterday the 24th. day of April 1756, According to Appointment when was. Present. Demsey. SUMNER. Church warden

Mr. Henry KING Luke SUMNER. Richard BOND.} Vestry Men { Jethro. BENTON Peter PARKER. William WALTON.

The Vestry Proçeeds To. The Choice of. Church wardens for The Ensuing Year. and accordingly chose Mr Josiah GRANBERY and Mr. Timothy WALTON. who are accordingly. Appointed Church wardens

Ordered That They the said Church wardens. or Either of Them do. Imploy an Attorney to bring Suits. against The Executors. of Peter PAYNE. The Executors. of. James TROTTER deceased and. Joseph HERRON & The Exrs: or Admrs: of Abraham BLACKALL.for a Settlement of Their Several Respective Parish Accompts And also for? The Penalty by. Law Inflicted. against Joseph HERRON for Refusing To settle his Parish Accompts with The Vestry. when Summoned for That Purpose.

Issd. Isd. to A N Isd. T. H Ordered That William UMPHLET. be Appointed Reader at the Knotty Pine Chappel in The Room and stead of John SKINER and That he be Allowed forty Shillings pr. Annum for ye Same and That The several Other Readers be

24 April 1756

(179) (Cont.) Continued at the Same? Rate. and That each of The Respective Readers 93

(180) __ Pauls. Parish *1756}* in This Parish may. Read at Some Convenient House. From. Their Chappels which may be The Most for The Ease of The people. not Exceeding every Third Sunday According to the Like Order. of Vestry. made Last year. *Isd. to Jno.?* William **HUNTER**. Produced a Certificate according to Law for a Wolfs. Scalp. Killed in This Parish. Ordered That he be Allowed Ten Shillings for the Same out of The Next Levey & ye Certificate Destroyed. *Wolf*

    Mr: Demsey **SUMNER** One of The Late Church wardens Produced his Account with The Parish for The Last year. which was read Examined and Allowed. by which it appears. That The ballance is Three Pounds. Twelve Shillings and a half Penney due from The Parish. Ordered That the said Accot. be. Entered in The Vestry book, which stands stated as follows

[This account was written at 90° to the normal page orientation.]

1755. St: Pauls Parish in Chowan County. Dr.: to Demsey **SUMNER**.   Cr.

8 yds?. 7/8 Check Lining for James **HOLMS**. 2/	0:14:0	By. Mildred **BENTON**s fine for Fornication	1: 5:0
To Cash paid Abraham **NORFLEET** . . .	2:19:0.	By. Cash of Capn Miles **GALE**.	35: 0:0.
To Cash paid for Registering **COSTANT**s Deed .	0: 5:4	By. Do. of Colol: John **HALSEY**. . . .	5:13:9.
To Cash paid Widow ___ alias **RUTTER** . . .	6: 0:0.	By. Do. of Thomas **WALTON**.	0:12:2½
__ Cash paid Jacob **HUNTER**	2:15:0.	By. Thos. **SMITH** a fine for not Voting a Elecn.	1: 0:0.
__ ¾ yds Bearskin for Robt. **ALPHIN** @9/ . .	1: 4:9.	By. Timothy **LILLEY** for Do.	0:17:6
_ o 3½? yds. 7/8 Checks for Do. . . . . . 2/. . . .	0: 7:0.	By John **LINCH** for a fine for Fornication	1: 5:0.
__ 8 yds. Oznabriggs for Do . . . . . . 1/3 . .	0:10:0.	By. Iaac [sic] **BENTON** for Do.	1: 5:0.
_ 2 Sticks Twist for Do. . . . . 6d.	0: 1:0.	By. Mary. **TREVATHAN** for Do.	0 12:6.
_ o 2. doz Buttons for Do. . . . . .7 _ .	0: 1:3.	By. Cash of John **MC. KILDO**	13: 8:8.
__ 1 Linin Handkr. for Do.	0: 2:0.	By. Do. of William **HORSKINS**	8:13:8.
Cash Paid William **HARRILL** for Constables fees	0:10:0	By. a Horse Taken from a Negro	0:10:9
To Cash Paid Mr. **HALL**.	40: 0:0	By. Moses **BENTON** for Fornication a fine	1: 5:0
__ a pr. Shoes for Robt. **ALPHIN**.	0: 5:6		71: 9:0½
_ o 1 Doz Coat buttons for James **HOLMS**. . .	0: 1:3.	Ballance Due to Demsey **SUMNER**.	3:12:0.½
To Cash Paid John **SKINER** pr. accot. . . .	8: 0:0.		75: 1:1
To Ditto to John **WALTERS**, a Parish Clame .	5: 0:0.		
To Cash to John **WILLIAMSON** a Clame. . .	4: 0:0.		
To finding ye Eliments for one Communion	0: 5:0.		
To Cash paid Mary **HOLMS** Widow. . . .	2: 0:0.		
	75: 1:1.		

    Errors & Omittions. Excepted pr. Demsey **SUMNER**
    April 24. 1756.

(181) *St. Pauls Parish 1756}*   (181.)

    Ordered That The Vestry be Adjourned To meet at **CONSTAN__** Chappel on Satterday The 22 day of May next being the Fourth Satterday in The Month.

    At a Vestry. met at. **CONSTANTs**. Chapel on Satterday. ye 22d day. of May. 1756. according To. Adjournment.

    Present. Mr. Demsey **SUMNER** Mr. John **GORDON** Mr. Luke. **SUMNER**. Mr Peter **PARKER**.} Vestry Men [Written vertically, between the first two columns.] {Mr. Elisha **HUNTER** Mr. Richard **BOND**. Mr. William **WALTON** {Mr Josiah **GRANBERY** Mr. Timothy **WALTON**} Ch. W.

Isd   Ordered That. Josiah **GRANBERY**. be Allowed his Accompt for. Three Quarto. Bibles Purchased for. the Three upper. Chapels. in Lew of The Folio. Bibles Ordered. ??? be Puchased by. him his Acot.? being. Four Pounds. Two. Shillings and Six pence Proclamation Money.. & The Bibles is Received at ye Same Time. *Bibles for 3 upper Chapels.*

Isd   Nicholas. **FERRILL**. Produced a Certificate for a Wolfs Scalp killed in This Parrish. which is Destroyed & Ordered that he be Allowed. according to Law Out of the Next Levey. 10s. Proc. *Wolf*

Isd   Ordered That. The Collector. of The Parish Tax pay to the Reverend. Clement **HALL**. The Sum of Forty Seven Pounds. fifteen Shillings Proclamation Money. for his Last Years. Servises he having Failed to Officiate Twenty one Sundays in the Last year.. and Also. The sum of Six pounds Thirteen Shillings. And four pence Allowed him for the Rent of a Glebe, And the Further Sum of. Thirty Three Pounds. Six Shillings and Eight Pence towards Arrears. due to. him before the Election of This Present Vestry. being in The whole Eighty Seven pound_ Fifteen Shillings Proclamation. Money. *Rev Mr. HALL failed to preach 21 Sundays this year.*

    Ordered. That. whereas The Reverend Clement **HALL**. hath Failed To. meet The Vestry To agree with Them for a Sallery for the Ensuing Year. and as. he Failed to Officiate a great Part of The Last Year. according to. Order of Vestry. he being a

22 May 1756

(181) (Cont.) Missionary. it is Therefore Ordered. That he be Allowed The sum of. One Pound. Ten Shillings and Nine Pence Farthing 94

(182) _t Pauls. Parish 1756   (182)
For. each Sunday. That. he shall Preach and Officiate in this Parish ye Insuing Year. in the Following manner. That is to Say begining at the Knottey Pine Chappel on Sunday the 23d Day of May. at Edenton on Sunday the. 30th. day of May. At **CONSTANT**s Chappel on Sunday the 6th day of June. and at **FARLEE**s Chappel on Sunday the 13th day of June and in that Order and Course. to Continue the Year. about. if he Thinks propper. to Comply therewith. but if he neglect or Refuse to Comply with the above Order. That That he be Discharged from the Cure of. This Parish. *Rev Mr HALL allowed £1.10s.9d for each Sunday*

Ordered That. The several Readers. in This Parish do keep a True Accompt of. The. Several Sermons. That. The M___ster [blot] shall Preach at Their Respective Chappels. for the Ensuing Year and Produce The same to The Vestry. at the Years End with the Date of Each Time.

Ordered That Archbishop **TILLOTSON**s. Sermons. be sent for or. Purchased for The Use of The Chappels. in This Parish either in Pocket Vollums. [sic] or. in Folio. by Luke **SUMNER**. and that he be paid his Accompt for The Same. by the Collector of. The Parish Tax. To be a Set for Each Chappel. *TILLOTSONs Sermons Ordered*

Ordered. That The Vestry be Adjourned. To. meet at **CONSTANT**s Chappel on Satterday. the 3d. day. of July. next
                    Timothy **WALTON** Josiah **GRANBERY**} Ch: War.

At a Vestry. met at **CONSTANT**s Chapel. on Satterday. the 3d. Day of July. 1756. Present.
Mr: Demsey. **SUMNER**. Mr. Elisha **HUNTER**. Mr. Luke **SUMNER**. Mr. John **GORDON**.} Vestry Men [Written vertically, between the first two columns.] { Richard **BOND**. Peter **PARKER**. Henry. **KING** William **WALTON**} Timothy **WALTON**. CW Josiah **GRANBERY**. CW

Isd.   Ordered That Mary? **MACGUIRE** keep the Child of Christopher **WEST**s. at The Rate of four Pounds a Year Till further Order.

(183) *St. Pauls Parish. 1756*   (183)
Pursuant To a former Order. of Vestry. The Parish Tobacco. in the Hands. of Mr. James **WILSON**. for which John **MACKILDO** Accounted with The Vestry. Sold This day by the Church Wardens. for the Sum of. Seven pounds. Ninteen Shillings and Six pence Procn: Clear of Charges. & ye deduction of 6 pr Ct. for Shrinkage To Mr. Richard **BOND**, who. Paid the Money into the Hands. of The Church Wardens. . .   1163 lb - NB. it sold @ 15s pr: Ct.

Ordered. That The Vestry. be Adjourned. to Meet at. **CONSTANT**s Chapel on The Last Satterday in September. Next. by 10. of The Clock in the forenoon.   Josiah **GRANBERY**. Timothy **WALTON**} C W Sign as. Church wardens

At a Vestry met at **CONSTANT**s Chapel. on satteredday [sic] the Twenty Fifth Day of. September. 1756. when was Presen [sic] Demsey **SUMNER** Esqr. Henry **BONNER**. Luke **SUMNER**. Elisha **HUNTER**. Peter **PARKER**.} John **GORDON**. Richard **BOND**. Jethro **BENTON** Henry **KING**. William **WALTON**{ Timothy **WALTON**. CW.

Issued Certifi Ordered. That. Edward **TROTTMAN** be Allowed according to Law for a W~~olfs Cat~~. Scalp killed in This Parish (The Certificate is destroyed) *Wolf*

Ordered. That. William **SIMSON** be Allowed. 2/8 for a Wild Cats Scalp. Killed in This Parish (& ye Certificate Destroyed). *Wild Cat.*

Isd: to Dr? Ordered. That William **SPEIGHTS** be Allowed out of the. Next Parish Levey. According to Law. for. Three wild Catts. Scalps. Killed in This Parish 2/8 Each. (the Certificates Destroyd *3 Wild Cats.*

Ordered. That Richard. **WALTON** be Allowed. 10/. for. his Claim on this Parish for Carrying Ralph **RIMINGTON**. a poor man To. the Doctors. in Edenton.

Ordered That William **FRYER** be Allowed according to Law 2/8 for a Wild Catts. Scalp. Killed in This parish to be paid out of The next Levey. The Certificate is Destroyed *Wild Cat 2/8.* 95

(184) *St. Pauls. Parish. 1756.*   (184)
Mr. Henry **BONNER**. one of The Late Church wardens Produced ye. Accounts. of. his wardenship Proved before a Justice of The peace. and also. produced Propper Vouchers. for. The money By him paid. and the Ballance Appears to. be. Eight Pounds. Seven Shillings and Ten pence Procn: Due to him from The Parish. which is paid by. the Collector in Open Vestry. and his Accounts. Stands Stated as follows. [This account is written at 90° to the normal page orientation.]

1754. The Parish of St. Pauls. To. Henry **BONNER**. C. W. Dr.   Contra Credit   Cr.
May ye 18th. To. money. Paid John Benbury **WALTON**s}
   Order . . . .}   1: 5:6.   1755. June ye 16th By Money Recd: of Jno.
   To Ditto paid Elisha **HUNTER** pr. Order}   **BENBURY** .   8:15:2

25 September 1756

(184) (Cont.)

of Vestry . . . . }	4: 0: 0.	By. Ditto Received of. Ditto	. .	3: 0:0.
To ditto paid Thos: **FREEMAN** for burying Jas. **FULKS**	1: 8:10.	By. Ditto Received of Wm..		
To Do. paid Jno **RODGERS** in part for bording Christr **WEST**s		**HORSKINS**		3: 0:0.
Child.	1:15: 0.			14:15:2
To. 10. Yds. Oznabriggs for Wm. **DIXON**. . . .	0:13: 4.	Ballance Due H B	. .	4:16:6.
_ making 2. Shirts & 2. pr. Trowsers for Do.	0: 4: 0.			£19:11:8
To Money paid Charles **ROBERTS** pr. Jno **RODGERS**s Order	0:15:10.			
_ Boarding william **DIXON** Nine Months & ½ @ 10/.	4:15: 0.			
To a ballance due me as pr. my Accot Enterrd in ye Vestry book	4:14: 2			
	19:11:8.			

1755. Dr: The Parish of St. Pauls. To. Henry. **BONNER**. with. Contra	. . . .			Cr.
July --. To. the above Ballance due me.	.4:16:6.	By Money Received of Jno		
To. Money Paid James **LUTEN**	3:11:7½	**BENBURY**		4: 0: 3.
To. Money Paid William **HORSKINS**	2: 0:0.	By Ballance Due H B. . .		8: 7:10.
To. Ditto Paid William **HORSKINS**	2: 0:0.			£12: 8: 1
	£12: 8:1.			

Personally Appeared before me Henry **BONNER** one of The Late Church wardens & made Oath on the Holy Evengelist of Almighty God. that The above account of Dr. & Credit is Just and True and That he hath Received no part nor parcell there of but what is herein Given Credit for. Sworn too. [sic] before me this 23d September 1756. James **LUTEN** J. P.

(185) *St. Pauls. Parish 1756* (185)

Ordered That William **HORSKINS**s: [sic] one of The Late Church warden_ whose Accounts. was Rejected. at a former Vestry for want of Credit to be Given for Money Received from Robert **BEASLEY**. which being now Paid to the Present Church wardens. and Etered in his Accounts.. it is Ordered that The Accounts. be Entered in The Vestry Book which being Proved before a Justice of The Peace Stands Stated as follows. [This account is written at 90° to the normal page orientation.]

1751. Dr: The Parish of St: Pauls in Account with William **HORSKINS**. Contra			Cr.	£ S D.
March 28. To. Bills Paid the Reverend Clement **HALL** . .	311: 1:3.	1751. By Bills Recd: of John		
To. Bills paid Nathanl: **MING** for Keeping Mary **QUARLES**	69: 0:0	**HALLSEY HALSEY** . .		880:6:0
To Do. paid Elizabeth **MIDDLETON** for Do. Rachel		By. Bills Received of Joseph		
PERVINE	77: 0:0.	**HERRON**		60:0:0.
To. bills paid James **LUTEN** for Clothing Do . .	17: 2:8.	NB. of The above Sum I am to.}		940:6:0
To. bills paid Jane **PARKER** in her Distress. .	13: 4:0.	Account with the Commissioners }		492:0:0
To. Do. paid Lewis **JONES** for burying mathew **LONG**.	5: 0:0.	of The Church for 492: pounds.}		
To Bills paid James **TROTTER** for a Yd of fine Lin.	1: 0:0.	The Sum Remaining is . .		448:6:0.
To. Do. paid for Four Bottles of Wine . . .	4: 0:0.	Ballance due me in Old bills is.		103:0:5.
To. Do. paid Robt. **KINGHAM** for keeping Rachl: **PERVINE**	6: 5:0.			551:6:5.
To. fetching & keeping Do. at my house 6 weeks .	11: 0:0.			
To bills paid John **FORD** keeping Joseph **HACKET** 28 days	3:15:0.			
To. ballance Due me for the Year 1750 . . .	4: 4:6.			
To. my Comissions 3 pr. Ct. on 940:6:0 is.	28: 4:0.			
	£551: 6:5.			
1752. To Proclamation money paid Revd. Clement **HALL**	30: 0:0.	1752. By Proclamation Received}		
To money paid James **WORDEN** keeping Jos **HACKET**	5:13:2.	of John **BENBURY** £58:0:0. }		58:0:0.
To Do. paid John **HALSEY** on Henry **BONNER**s Accot.	1: 7:6.			
To. Do. paid John **RUMBERG** for a Coffin for a Traveler	0:13:0.	The ballance due to me in Old Bills being}		
To money paid Jane **PARKER** in her Distress . .	1: 0:0.	Redused to Proclamation Leaves the balle.}		
To. Do. paid John **HALSEY** for burying Mary **HAVIT**	0:16:0.	Due to the parish 3:0:8		
To my Commissions 3 pr. Ct. on 38:0:0 is.	1:15:0.			
	£41: 4:8			

Chowan County ss. Personally came before me Mr. William **HORSKINS** and made Oath That the above Account is Just & True and That he hath Given all Just Credits Sworn to before me This 5th Day of September 1755.
Jos.. **BLOUNT**. J. P.   Wm.. **HORSKINS**   96

(186) *St. Pauls. Parish 1756* (186)

William **HORSKINS**. Church Warden Accounts. from The years? 1753. to The Year. 1755. Stand Stated as follows. Vizt.

25 September 1756

(186) (Cont.) [This account is written at 90° to the normal page orientation.]
Dr: The Parish of St: Pauls To. William **HORSKINS** with Contra Credit . . . . Cr.

1753 Decbr: 10. To money paid Jane **PARKER** before she was on ye Parish	1:11:0.	1753. By. Proclamation money Received} of John **BENBURY** for the year 1753. }	65: 0:0.
Novbr: 5. 1754 To. Do. paid Robert **MC CLAYLAND** for bording Jane **PARKER**	1:16:0.	By Money Received of Henry **BAKER**.} For a Fine . . . . . .25/. }	1: 5:0.
July 14. To. Money paid Sarah **RUTTER**	3: 0:0.	By. money Received for Two Barrils..} of Pork That was. Condem'd 31/6 }	1:11:6.
May 10. To. Money paid the Reverend Clement **HALL**.	3:10:0.	By Money Received of. John **HALSEY**} The Ballance of His Account }	3:16:6.
Sepr.? 4.1755. To. money paid Robert **MC CLALAND**. for} bording **CAMPBELL**s Child . . . . . }	4:10:0.		£71:13:0.
__br 20. 1755. To. money Paid the Reverend Mr. **HALL** . .	40: 0:0		
To. money. paid Henry **BONNER**	8:15:0.		
To my Comissions for 72:3:0. Proc	2:18:0.		
	£66: 0:0.		
Ballance Due To the Parish . . is	5:13:0		
	71:13:0.		

Chowan County ss. Personally came before me. Mr. William **HORSKINS** and made Oath That the above Account is Just and True. and That he hath Given All Just Credits Sworn before me
This 5th Day of September. 1755. William **HORSKINS**:
    Joseph **BLOUNT** J. P.

1756. Sepr 25. To. 18/8.. Proc. pd: Elisha **HUNTER** ye Error.} For money Recd. of Robt. **BEASLEY** and not Entered in ye } above Account }	0:18:8.	By Money Recd: of Robert **BEAZLEY** his} Ballance and Omitted in ye above Account } Entered pr. Order. Luke **SUMNER**.	0:18:8.

(187) *St.. Pauls. Parish 1756*   187.

Isd, Ordered. That. ~~Mary.~~ Sarah **RUTTER**. be Allowed. at The Rate of Five Pounds. a Year. for The keeping her Daughter. a Poor Helpless. Girl in This Parish.

Isd. 1757 Isd. 1758. Isd.. Ordered. That John **WALTERS** and his. wife Two poor Old People. in This Parish be Allowed. Five Pounds. a Year. for Clothing.

Ordered That a Tax or Levey of Sixteen Pence Proclamation Money. be Leveyed. on Each and Every Taxable Person in This. Parish for. This Present. year. To.. Defray. the Contingent Charges There of.

Ordered That. The. Vestry. be Adjourned. to meet at. **CONSTANT**s Chapel on Satterday. the 18th Day of December next. Timothey **WALTON**. sign as Church Warden.   Timothy **WALTON** CW.

At. a. Vestry. met at. **CONSTANT**s Chappel on Thursday the 20th day of January. 1757.. Present.
Demsey **SUMNER** Esqr: Elisha **HUNTER** Luke **SUMNER**. Richard **BOND**} Jethro. **BENTON** Peter **PARKER**. John **GORDON** William **WALTON**{ Josiah **GRANBERY** Timothy **WALTON**} CW:

Isd. Ordered That. James **JONES** a Constable, be Allowed for Summoning Three? Vestry men by a summons according To Law. @ 12d Each is Three Shillings

Ordered That John **LEWIS** of Sarum be Collector of The Parish Tax For This Present Levey of one shilling and four Pence Proclamation money. and That he Give Bond and Security in The Sum of five hundred Pounds. Like Money. which is accordingly done. by Demsey **SUMNER** Esqr: his Security.

Ordered That The Reverend Mr. Clement **HALL** Take The Church Plate, Pewter, and Linen, at Edenton into his care, and That he be Allowed a Reasonable charge for. The same.

Ordered That Mr. Daniel **EARL** be Appointed Reader at Edenton and That he be Allowed forty Shillings per Annum for. The same. *Dan. EARL Reader.*

Jesse **HUNTER** Collector of The Last. years Parish Tax Prodused his Account. with This Parish which is Examined Proved and allowed. and Ordered That The same be entered in The Vestry Book. which is accordingly. done   97

(188) [This page is written in two columns, at 90° to the normal page orientation.]   (188.)
Mr: Jesse **HUNTER**. Exhibited his Account as. Collector. of The Parish Tax for The year. 1755. duly Proved which Follows. and is in These words. Vizt..
Dr:. The Parish of St: Pauls. in Account Currant. with Jesse **HUNTER**. Collector   [Left column]

1756. To. 20/. Paid to Mr:. Luke **SUMNER** for 2. Wolfs. scalps. pr: Order	1: 0:0.	*2 Wolves*
To. 40/. Paid to Mr. Abraham **NORFLEET** as Reader	2: 0:0.	
To £5. Paid to. Mr. Jacob **HUNTER**. as. pr. Order of Vestry . .	5: 0:0.	

20 January 1757

(188) (Cont.)

To 10/. Paid to. Mr. John GORDON for 1. Wolf Scalp. pr. Order . .	0:10:0.
To £4:2;6 Paid to. Mr. Josiah GRANBERY pr. Order for Books . .	4: 2:6.
To £87:15:0. Paid to. Mr. Clement HALL. for his Sallery & part of Arrears.	87:15:0.
To £6:0:0 Paid to Mr. John WILLIAMSON for Keeping James HOMES.	6: 0:0.
To £4:16:0. Paid to Ann MACKGUIRE. for keeping an Orphan Child .	4:16:0.
To. 4. Wild Cat Scalps. Taken in for Leveys. as. pr Law	0:10:0. *4 Wild Cats*
To £3:12:0. Paid to Capt: Demsey SUMNER. pr. Order for ballance of his Accot:	3:12:0.
To £30:0:0. Paid to. Mr:. Clement HALL	30: 0:0.
To £8:7:10. Paid to. Mr. Henry BONNER. pr. Order for his ballance	8: 7:10.
To £3:6:8: Paid to. Moses SPEIGHTS. pr: Order. for Keeping Robt: ALPHEN	3: 6:8.
To. £41:3:0. Paid to. Mr. Josiah GRANBERY. Church Warden	41: 3:0.
To. My. Commissions @ 5. pr. Ct. For Receivi?ng	10.:10:0.
	£208:13:0.
To 52 Taxables. @ 2/8 as. by a List Rendered of Insolvents and. } Such other Persons. as. I could not get the Leveys. of. }	7:18:4
	£216:11:4

[Right column] Cr:.

1756. Cr? By. 1591. Taxables at 2/8. Each. due}
For The year 1755. ..is £212:2:8.. }   212:2:8.
By 63 Taxables. @ 1/4. for ye year 1754. is 4:8:8.   4:8:8.
                    Errors Excepted   £216:11:4
                    pr:. Jesse HUNTER

Chowan County ss. Jesse HUNTER came Before me and made Oath That The above is a just and True account. of His Collections. as. Parish Collector Certified pr. me Demsey SUMNER. JP. January 20th 1757.

(189) *St: Pauls. Parish 1757.}*   (189.)

Ordered That The Vestry. be Adjourned. To. meet. at CONSTANTs. Chapel. on the Last satterday in April next by 12. of the Clock. N. B. Church wardens Chargeable with Possessioners Fine. Josiah GRANBERY Timothy WALTON} CW. Sign as Church Wardens.

NB: There was not a full Vestry the Last Satterday in April its. Appointed To. meet at CONSTANTs Chappel the first Satterday in May.

At a Vestry met at CONSTANTs Chapel on Satterday. the 7.th. day of May. 1757. at which Time and Place was. Present.
Mr. Demsey SUMNER. Mr. Elisha HUNTER Luke SUMNER. Richard BOND. Henry KING.} Jethro BENTON Peter PARKER. John GORDON William WALTON{ Josiah GRANBERY Timothy WALTON} Chh: Warde__

Ordered That Luke SUMNER and Elisha HUNTER. be and they are accordingly. Appointed. Church wardens for This Present year.

Isd.   Ordered That five pounds. eleven Shillings and Three pence Due to Robert MACKCLAYLAND for Boarding Thomas CAMPBELLs child Be allowed.

Josiah GRANBERY. one of The Late. Church Wardens Prodused his. Accot: of his wardenship which being Proved & Allowed is Ordered To be Entered in The Vestry Book.

Timothy WALTON the Other. Church warden Produced his Account of his wardenship. Proved. Allowed & Ordered to be Entered

Ordered That Thomas MING be Allowed 10/. for a Wolfs Scalp killed in This Parish as pr. Certificate which is Destroyed.
Isd. to Jo ALPHIN Ordered That Tobias LASITER be Allowed 10/. out of The Next Levey for a Wolfs Scalp killed in This Parish. . . . .
Isd. To R: BOND. Ordered That Joshua STEVENS be Allowed 10/. out of The next Levey for a Wolfs Scalp Killed in This Parish. *3 Wolves* [Written vertically.]

Ordered That Mr. Elisha HUNTER. Repair and Tar. The Three. Chapels. Vizt. CONSTANTs. FARLEEs. and Notty Pine. Chapels. and That he cause good Glass Windows. in Sash to be Fixed. To. each of Them and That. he. be Allowed a Reasonable Charge for The Same

7 May 1757

(189) (Cont.) *Isd. To Abm: NORFLEET Isd. To Jacob HUNTER* Ordered That The several Readers. be continued for The insuing Year & That They be Allowed as for The Last year 40/ a yr?   98

(190) [This page is written in two columns, at 90° to the normal page orientation.]   (190.)

1756. Saint Pauls Parish   Dr:. To Josiah GRANBERY Church Warden   [Left column]

		Procln. money
May 28th.	To. 1. Stock Lock, for ye Door of CONSTANTs Chapple	£ 0: 3: 4.
June 22nt?	To. 1. Bottle Red Wine for the Commn: at Notty Pine	0: 3: 0.
July 3.	To £8:9:10. Proc. pd: Clement HALL	8: 9:10.
	To. 2/8. Procn: pd Richd BOND. for sending for the Vestry Book to the Clk	0: 2: 8.
16.	To. 3½ yds Ozs. 16. 1. Felt Hatt 2/6 for Robt. ALPHEN . .	0: 9: 2.
22.	To. 7. yds: 7/8 Chex 2/4. 3. yds: Ozs: 16. for James HOLMES	1: 0: 4.
Augst. 18.	To. 5¾ yds Ozs: for Robt ALPHEN, Shirt &c	0: 7: 8.
Octor. 25th.	To. 1. pr: hose for Robt ALPHEN	0: 2: 8.
Novr. 5.	To. 2½ yds: Flannel 3/6. 3¾. yds Linen 2/10. for WESTs Child. at MCGUIREs	0:19: 4½
16.	To. 1. Felt Hatt 4/6. 1. pr: Shoes 5/. for James HOLMES . .	0: 9: 6.
Decr: 15.	To. 3. yds Cloth 4/. 1. yd Ozs: 1/4 for Robt. ALPHEN . .	0:13: 4.
18.	To. 20/. Proc pd: Robt MC. CLALAND in part of his Acct: for keepg Mr CAMPBELL	1: 0: 0.
30.	To. 1. pr. Hose & 1. Clap Knife for James HOLMES . .	0: 5: 8
_57. Janr 5.	To. Procn: Bills pd: Dr: Robt LINOX for Boardg. Doctorg.} & burying of Ralph REMINGTON . . . . }	27:10: 2.
	To. Procn: Bills pd: Thos JONES Clk: of the Coart. for Copies.} of BLACKHALLs, PLOMMERs, & TROTTERs Wills. }	0: 9: 0
17.	To. Proc Bills pd. Clement HALL	6: 0: 0.
28..	To. Ditto	2: 1: 0.
Febr. 22d.	To. Ditto. pr: Mr: GALE	2:10: 9.
	Ballance due St. Pauls Parish	2: 8: 6½
		55: 6: 0

                [Right column]   Cr:

1756. May. 22nd.	By. Proc Bills recd. from Jacob HUNTOR. } for a horse sold him by Demsey SUMNER Chh Warden}	1. 2.9.
July 3d.	By. Proc Bills recd: from Richd BOND for Tobo. } Sold him, that was in the hands of Jas. WILSON recr.}	7.19.6.
Decr. 18.	By Proc Bills for. 2 fines recd. from Jno LEWIS Esqr.	2.10.0.
	By. Proc. recd: from Jesse HUNTOR Collector of Parish Taxes	41. 3.0.
Febr: 22	By. Proc: Bills recd. from Miles GALE former Sherr	2.10.9.
1757		£55. 6.0.

        May 7th 1757. Errors Excepted.   pr. Josiah GRANBERY

Chowan County}
May 7th 1757 } Josiah GRANBERY made Oath That the above Accot: was Just and True Before me.
                Demsey SUMNER. JP.

(191) [This page is written at 90° to the normal page orientation.]   (__)

Dr: St: Pauls Parish in Account. Currant with Timothy WALTON Church Warden & Contra   Cr:

_756. Sepr. 25.	To proc paid Elisha HUNTER for a Clame due} To Isaac HUNTER Deceased .15/. }	0:15:0	1756: Sepr: 25th By Proc Recd: from } William HORSKINS By the Hands of } Elisha HUNTER . . . . . }	0:18:8.
_757 Apl:	To 1. bottle Wine for The Communion . . .	0: 3:0.		
	Ballance due St. Pauls Parish	0: 0:8	Errors Excepted pr. Timothy WALTON	
		18:8.	May 7th 1757.} Timothy WALTON made Oath. Chowan County} before me that the above Account was Just & True. Demsey SUMNER	

7 May 1757

(191) (Cont.)
John MACKILDOs: Account. sent to The Vestry. but not Entered before stands stated as Follows.
Dr. St. Pauls Parish in Account Currant with John MC: KILDO . . & . . Contra . . . Cr..

1753. Apl: 23. To the amount of my Accot: as it Stands on ye Vestry book	6:16:0	1753. By Proc Recd: of Robt: BEASLEY. C. W.	6: 0:0
1754. Apl: To my Servis one year as Clerk & Reader	6: 0:0	1755. By. 520 Taxables @ 1/4. pr. Tax Received} at BENNETs Creek for the year 1754 .is. }	34:13:_
1755. Apl. To. Ditto: Do.	6: 0:0	pr John MC: KILDO	£40:13:_
To. 1274 lb. Tobo: at bENNETs Creek Ware house Inspected & Recived for Taxes @ 10/ pr. Ct}	6: 7:5.	Chowan County. Personaly. Appeared before m_ John MC: KILDO. and made Oath on the Holy. Eva?ngel___ of	
To. my Commissions for Receiveing 34:13:4 @ 6 pr Ct	2: 1:4.	Almighty God. That The above Account again___ St. Pauls Parish	
To. proc paid the Reverend Mr. HALL at } Demsey SUMNERs Order 13:8:8 }	13: 8:8	is Just & True, and that he Hath given all Just Credits to The Same. Sworn before me This Third of September 1755.	
	£40:13:5.	Joseph BLOUNT. J: P	99

(192) _t: Pauls. Parish 1757.}   (__)
    Ordered That The Church Wardens Provide for. The Three Chapels in this Parish, Three Quart Tankard_ Three Pewter. Pint Cupps or Canns. Six Pewter Plates Three Diaper Table Clothes and Three Diaper Napkins and That They be Allowed a Reasonable charge for the Same
Isd: Do. Do.   The Petition of John PARISH a poor helpless Cripple praying An Allowance from the parish for his support. is Granted Ordered That he be allowed at The Rate of Six pounds a year. for his Mentainance.
Isd.   Ordered That Jeremiah MITCHENER be Allowed Twenty Five Shillings. for Burying. Mary GEELSTONE a poor Woman in This Parish
    Ordered That Francis BROWN a poor Lame man in This Parish be supplyed. with cloathes, and be sent to Mrs. Elizabeth HINTONs. in Order to get his Legg Cured.
    Ordered. That The Reverend Mr: Clement HALL be continued Clerk and Rector. of This Parish on The Same Terms. and Conditions, and. to. preach at The Same Times and Places. as. by The Order of Last Year and Copy Delivered him More Fully. is Expressed.
    Ordered. That The Account Currant. Settled with The Reverend Mr. Clement HALL. According to. All The several Former Orders and Agreements. of The several Vestrys with him Since his first coming into. This Parish be Entered in the Vestry Book.
    Ordered That The Vestry be Adjourned to meet at CONSTANTs. Chapel on The first Satterday in September: Next.
        Luke SUMNER Elisha HUNTER.} Chh: War_s
Memorandom The Entering of The account Currant with Mr: Clement. HALL and St. Pauls. Parish is Postponed at his Request. for a Further Examination at The Next Vestry   Certified. pr. Luke SUMNER

(193) __ Pauls. _arish 1757}   (193.)
    At a Vestry met at CONSTANTs. Chapel on Satterday. The Third Day of September. Anno Dom: 1757.
Present. {Luke SUMNER Elisha HUNTER} Church Wardens.
Messrs: { Demsey SUMNER. Esqr: Josiah GRANBERY. John GORDON. Richard BOND. Timothy WALTON. William WALTON} Vestry Men.
Isd: Ordered That Christian WARD be Allowed her Accot Two. Pounds seventeen Shillings and Six pence Procn. For. The Board and Burial of Richard FERRILL a. poor. Man That Died in This Parish. And That She be Paid The same out of The next Levey
    Whereas The Reverend. Mr: Clement. HALL hath Frequently Suggested To. The Vestry. That he hath a Large sum of money. due To him in Old Arrears. From This Parish it was. Therefore Ordered That an Estimate of The Several Sums of Money That hath been Leveyed for him from The year One Thousand Seven hundred and forty Four; Till The Year. One Thousand seven Hundred and fifty Six. be made over Together. with an Account of The several Sums. of Money by him Received. with in The Time afore said, and on Stateing The said Account it Appears. That the said Mr: HALL hath Received. Nineteen Pounds Ten Shillings and four Pence Three farthings More Then was due to him for his Minesterial Servis in This Parish It is therefore Ordered That the said Sum of £19:10:4¾ be Deducted out of The Money. That will be due To him for his Servises. for the Year 1757. And on Motion it is further Ordered That the said Account. be Entered in The Vestry Book to Prevent any Further. Disputes. of the Like Nature. And Stands Stated as Follows. .Turn Ove_   100

(194) [This account is written at 90° to the normal page orientation.]   (194)
Dr: The Reverend Mr: Clement HALL in Acct: Current wth: Saint Pauls Parish. as pr. vestry Book

3 September 1757

(194) (Cont.)

	Procn: money		Procn. mo__
1745. To. £450:0:0. Old Bills pr. Jno: **ALSTON**	£60: 0: 0.	1745. By. yr: Sallery Allowed You this Year	£60: 0:_
1747. To. 310:0:0. Do: . . pr: Jno: **HALSEY** . .	41: 6: 8.	1746. By. yr: Sallery Allowed	60:
1748. To £22:0:0. Do: . . pr: Jno: **BENBERY** .	2:18: 8.	1747. By. yr: Sallery Allowed	60: 0:_
To £340:10:0. Do: . . pr: Jno: **HALSEY** .	45: 8: 0.	1748. By. yr: Sallery Allowed	60: 0:_
1749. To. £330:10:0. Do: . . pr: Jno. **BENBERRY**	44:13: 4.	1749. By. yr: Sallery £60. & for a	
To. 260:14:1. Do: . . pr: Wm: **LUTON** V...V..	48:13:11.	Glebe 6:13:4 procn:	66:13:_
1750. To. £20:0:0. Do: . . pr: Jno **BENBERRY** .	2:13: 4.	1750. By. yr Sallery as by Law £50. & for	
To. £129:11:6. Do . . pr: Jno **HALSEY** . .	16:12: 2½	Rent 6:13:4	56:13:_
To.376:0:0. Do: . . pr: Thos: **WALTON** .	50: 2: 8.	1751. By. yr: Sallery Allowed £50 & yr Rent	56:13:_
To.£561:6:11. Do . . pr. W **HOSKINS** . .	74:16:11.	1752. By yr: Sallery Allowed pr: order of	
1751. To. £311:1:3. Do: . . pr: Do	41: 9: 6.	Vestry, only .	50: 0:_
1752. To. £30:0:0. Procn: Bills pr: Do:	30: 0: 0.	1753. By. yr: Sallery Allowed	50: 0:0
1754. To. £3:10:0. Procn: . . pr Do:	3:10: 0.	1754. By. yr: Sallery Allowed	50: 0:0
1755. To. £40:0:0. Procn: . . pr: Do:	40: 0: 0.		£ 570: 0:0
To. Ballance Due	67:14: 9½		
	570:0:0.		

Dr: The Reverend Mr: Clement **HALL**. In. Acct: Current wth: Saint Pauls Parish as pr. Vestry Book   Cr:

1756. To. £40:0:0 Procn Pr: Demsey **SUMNER** &		1756. By. Balle: of the above Account	67:14:__
MC: KILDO	40: 0:0.	at Eastor By. 31. Sermons Last yr: @ £80	
To. £87:15:0. Procn: pr: Jesse **HUNTOR**		pr Ann: is 2?7:13:1. & Rent is	54: 6:5
as pr: order	87:15:0.	1757. Eastor By. 47. Sermons @ 30/9¼ is	
To. £30:0:0. Do: pr. Jesse **HUNTOR** . .	30: 0:0.	72:6:2¾ & Rent	78:19:__
1757. To. £19:1:7. Do: pr Josiah **GRANBERY** Acct.	19: 1:7.		201: 0:9
To. order on Wm: **LUTON** for £4:14:1 . .	4:14:1.	By. Balle: due ye Parish	19:10:__
To. £39:0:6. Procn: pr: John **LEWIS**	39: 0:6. £ s D		£220:11:__
	220:11:2		

(195) *St: Pauls Parish 1757.}* Ordered That a Levey. of Two Shillings Proclamation _____ be collected from Each and every Taxable Person in This P_____ To defray The Contingent Charges Thereof for This Pres___yea_
  Ordered That The Vestry. be Adjourned. To. Meet at **CONS**____s Chapel on The First Satterday in January next.
       Elisha **HUNTOR** Luke **SUMNER**.} Ch_____

St: Pauls Parish 1758.} At a Vestry. met. at **CONSTANT**s. Chapel on Satterday The seventh Day of January 1758. Present
       Demsey **SUMNER**. Esqr: Josiah **GRANBERY**. Jethro. **BENTON**. Richard **BOND**. John **GORDON**.} Luke **SUMNER** Elisha **HUNTOR**}_____
       Ordered That James **BOND** be Appointed. Collector of ___ Parish Tax due for The Year. 1757. and That he give ____ and Security in The Sum of Five Hundred Pounds _____lamation Money which is Accordingly Given & Mr. Ric____ **BOND** is Security. That he the said James **BOND** Collect ____ Same from Each and Every Taxable Parson in This _____ And on Their Nonpayment to Distrain for The same _____ing To. Law. in Order To Settle Fully with The Vestry __ The second Satterday in March Next.
       Ordered That Joseph **PARKER** son of Thomas **PARKER** ___ Allowed. at The Rate of Six pounds. Proclamation Money a year. for The Mentainance of his Brother Peter **PARKER**. a Poor helpless. man in This Parish.
Isd: Ordered. That Moses. **LASITOR** senior be Allowed six? Shillings Proclamation Money. for making Clo____ for Robert **ALPHEN** a Poor. Parishoner.
       Ordered That The Vestry be Adjourned to Meet? ___ **CONSTANT**s Chapel on The second Satterday __ March next: Luke **SUMNER** Elisha **HUNTOR**.} C W?   101

(196) _____ *Parish 1758.}* At a Vestry Met at **CONSTANT**s Chapel on satterday The 11th Day of March. 1758. Present. *196*
       Demsey **SUMNER**. Esqr. Timothy **WALTON** . . Peter **PARKER** . .}Richard **BOND** John **GORDON** William **WALTON**} Luke **SUMNER** Elisha **HUNTOR**} C. W.   196
       Luke **SUMNER**. One of The Church Wardens Produced his Account with St: Pauls Parish which is Examined. Proved. and Allowed. by which it App____ There is a Ballance of Seven Pounds Eleven Shillings and Ten Pence Proclamation Money. Due To. him Ordered That The Same be paid by The Collector of The Parish Tax. and That The Account be entered in The Vestry Book. and is Stated on the next Side.

11 March 1758

(196) (Cont.) Elisha **HUNTOR** The other Church Warden Produced his Account. with The Parish Proved and Allowed by which it Appears. There is a ballance Due to him of Three Pounds Seven Shillings and Two pence Procn.

Ordered That The same be paid to him by the Collector of The Parish Tax and That The Account be Entered in The Vestry Book which is as follows

Dr: St. Pauls. Parish in Account with Elisha **HUNTOR**. Church Warden

		£ S D
1753. march 11. To. making 2 Shirts. & 2. pr. of Trowsers. for Poor Parishoners	@ 1/ pr.	0: 4:0
To. making 3. Table Clothes & 3. Napkins. for the Chapels	@ 10d	0: 5:0
To 6½ yds. Oznabriggs. for Francis **BROWN**	@ 1/4.	0: 8:8
To 1½ yds. frize for britches for Do. @ 6/. pr yd		0: 9:0
To. Thread and Making		0: 2:6
To. 5.½. Yds. Oznabriggs	@ 1/6.	0: 8:3
To. Making one Shirt		0: 1:0
To. Boarding Francis **BROWN** 2 months & 20. Days. @ 12		1:11:3.
To. 6. yds. Oznabriggs for Robt. **ALPHIN**	@ 1/6	0: 9:0
To. 1. Handkerchief. for Do		0: 2:0.
To. keeping Robt. **ALPHEN** Two Months and Eleven Days @ 15/		1:15:0
		£.5:15:8

Cr: *St: Pauls* Parish in Account with Elisha **HUNTOR**	Cr	£. S. D
By. Procn. Received of Josiah **GRANBERY**		2: 8:6.}
Ballance Due to Elisha **HUNTOR**		3: 7:2.}
		£5:15:8.}

Chowan County. ssr.? Elisha **HUNTER** came before me and made Oath That The above is a Just Account of his Actings and doings as a Church warden to This Day. Certified This 11th Day of marc_ 1758..   Demsey **SUMNER**

(197) [This page is written at 90° to the normal page orientation.]
St: Pauls Parish in Account Currant with Luke **SUMNER** Church Warden C_

	£. S. D	1757. September the 30th Cr.	£. s. _
May 25. To. 7. yds. 7/8. Chex for James **HOMES** @ 2/8	0:18:8.	By Thomas **WIGGINS**s Fine for Prophane}	
_y. 5.th. To. 6. yds. Linen for Robert **ALPHEN** @ 1/4 ..	0: 8:0.	Swearing 10/. Proclamation Money }	0:10._
To 1. Felt Hatt for. Do.	0: 3:6.	Ballance Due Luke **SUMNER**	£ 7:11:1
To. 1. Linen Handkerchief for Do.	0: 1:6.		£8: 1:1
To. 3. Copys. of The Sunday Law for The Readers .	0:17:3.	Errors and Omissions Excepted	
_ 30th To. a Copy of The Sunday Act for Sarum Chapel	0: 5:9.	pr. Luke **SUMNER**.	
_br: 15. To 2¼. yds. Cloth for Robt. **ALPHEN** . @ 3/.	0: 6:9.	Chowan County ss.? Luke **SUMNER** came before	
To. 1. Doz. Buttons & 1. Slip Twist for Do.	0: 1:6.	me and made Oath That The above is a Just Accot: of	
To. 1. pr. Shoes for James **HOMES** . . .	0: 5:0.	his Disbursments as. Church warden to this Day.	
To 3½ yds. Cloth for Ditto . . . .@ 3/	0:10:6.	Given Under My Hand This 11th day of March 1758.	
To 1 Doz Buttons for Do	0: 1:0.	Demsey **SUMNER**	
To. 3½. yds. Oznabriggs for Do . . .15d.	0: 4:4½		
To 1 Slip Hair and 8. Skanes Thread for Do. . .	0: 1:6.		
_mbr: 4. To 1. pr. Stockings for Robert **ALPHEN** .	0: 3:0.		
To. 1. yd. Oznabriggs for Do	0: 1:3		
To. 1. Worsted Cap. for Do	0: 1:6.		
_ 1. To. 2. yds. Cloth for **WEST**s Child . .@ 2/10.	0: 5:8.		
To. ½ yd Linen for Ditto . . . .@ 2/	0: 1:0.		
_ 1st. To 3. fine Diaper Table Clothes for The Chapels @ 14/.	2: 2:0.		
To. 3. Diaper Napkins for Ditto . . .@ 4/	0:12:0.		
	£7:11:8½		
To The difference in Exchange for Procn on the above is	10:1½		
	£8: 1:10	103	

(198) _____ch 11th} Luke **SUMNER** produced his Accot. of Servises done as Clerk? of This Vestry. which is Examined Approved and Allowed.

Ordered that he be allowed four pounds a year. being the same as was Allowed to the. Last Clerk of the Vestry. the amount of his Accompt. is Thirteen pounds. four Shillings. Proclamation money. to be paid. by the Collector of the parish Tax. and that The

11 March 1758

(198) (Cont.) Accompt be Entered in the Vestry Book. and is as. Follows. vizt.

_r: St. Pauls Parish in Accot. with Luke **SUMNER**. Clerk of the Vestry   £ s d Cr

__55. June 7. To writing 4. Advertisements pr. Order for Persons to meet and} Settle their Parrish Accompts with the Vestry .@ 8d }	0:2:0
July 5th. To writing a Warrant & Summons per Order for those} That Failed to meet & Settle their parish Accots. }	0.1.4
To. writing **COSTANT**s Deed for the Chapel Land. pr. Order	0:2:8?
Sepr. 6th. To. writing 4. Advertisements pr. Order for the Delinquints} To meet The Vestry and pay their Leveys in Arrear }	0:2:8?
To an Order drawn on **TROTTER**s Executors for the Money} Due to this parish for negro Hire . . . . . . }	0.0.6?
Octobr. 25. To 19 Copys & Orders for possessioners as per Law	0.0.0
To 4. Advertisements. per Order to Let Ye Collection of} The Parish Tax for this present y_ar @ 8d. }	0.2.8?
Decbr. 27. To a bond Taken of Jesse **HUNTER** Collector of the parish} Tax, with a Copy of The Order and Certificate }	0 1.4
_757. Janr 20. To a Bond Taken of John **LEWIS** Collector of the parish} Tax, and Copy of the Order and Certificate }	0. 1.4?
Sepr. 3d. To an Accot. Currant drawn pr. Order, with St. Pauls} Parish & the Reverend Mr. Clement **HALL** since his } first coming into this parish . . . .}	0. 1.4
1758. Janr 7. To a bond Taken of James **BOND** Collector of the Parish} Tax. and a Copy of the Order & Certificate . . . . }	0. 1.4
To 27. Certificates per. Order for. Claims &c due from} The parish & to be paid on ye same per ye Collectors. }	0. 6.0
To. 2. years & nine months Servis as Clerk of this } Vestry pr. Order. at 80/. per year being The same as was } allowed to John **MC. KILDO**. the Clerk of the former Vestry.}	11.0.0
	£13:4:6?

Errors & Omissions Excepted. pr. Luke **SUMNER**

Ordered that Mr. Demsey **SUMNER**. & Mr. Timothy. **WALTON** do move? to the next Assembly by petition for an Allowance for the Value of? Negro **DUBLIN** a Slave belonging to this parish and was Ex___ted for felloney at Edenton & Valued at forty pounds proc. and that they be. paid a Reasonable Char_____ their Trou__

(199) ___8? June 6.} Be it Remembered That the Freeholders of St. Pauls Parish met the Sherril ef at the Court House in Edenton on Monda_ the Twenty Sixth day of June 1758. and did then and the__ Pursuant To an Act of assembly. Chuse and Elect the fo___wing persons. to serve as Vestry men for the Three Insui__ Years. Vizt. Demsey **SUMNER**. Esqr. Josiah **GRANBERY**, Lu__ **SUMNER**, John **GORDON**, Elisha **HUNTER**. Timothy **WALTO_** William **WALTON**: Richard **BOND** Jethro **BENTON**, Peter **PARKER**, Willis **RIDDICK** Jacob **HUNTER**, who were Summoned by the Sherriff to meet at the Court house In Edenton. at 3 of the Clock in the Afternoon of the same Day. At which Time and place the said Twelve. Accordingly met and were Duly Qualified by Taking the Oathes. by Law Appointed for the Qualification of V vestry [sic] men and subscri___ the T___ &? Declaration. And then proceeded to the choi__ of. Church Wardens for this Insuing Year.

Ordered that Willis **RIDDICK** & Jacob **HUNTER** be and they are Accordingly Appointed. Church War____ for this year.

The Vestry Adjourned til the Last Satterday in July Next. to meet at.**CONSTANT**s Chapel   Willis **RIDDICK** Jacob **HUNTER**} C W

At a Vestry. met at **CONSTANT**s Chapel on Satterday the 29th Day of July. 1758. Present.

Demsey **SUMNER**. Luke **SUMNER**. Josiah **GRANBERY** John **GORDON** Elisha **HUNTER**.}{Timothy **WALTON** William **WALTON** Richard **BOND**. Jethro **BENTON** Peter **PARKER**. Willis **RIDDICK** Jacob **HUNTER**.} C W.

Ordered that the several Readers. be continued. for the present Year.

Ordered that John **PARRISH** be Allowed six pounds proc. for the Mentainance of his son who is a poor Helpless Cripple in this parrish.   104

29 July 1758

(200) *1758.* [The first line on this page is illegible.] ed his Accompt of Five Sermons Omited? by the Parson in the Last Year.. which proved in Open Vestry.

Ordered that Demsey **JONES** be Allowed at the R___ of. Six pounds proclamation Money per Yea_ for the Board & Keeping of Robert **ALPHEN** a poor Old Man in this Parish.

Ordered that Luke **SUMNER** be Allowed seven pou___ One Shilling. proc. for the Purchas [sic] of Twenty fou_ Volums. of Bishop **TILLOTSON**s Sermons for the Use of the Chappels. and that the same be paid him by the Collector of the parrish Tax

The Vestry Adjourned to meet at **CONSTANT**s Chap__ on Satterday the 9th Day of September next Willis **RIDDICK** Jacob **HUNTER**} C W

At a Vestry met at **CONSTANT**s Chapel on Satterday the 9th Day of September 1758. present.

Demsey **SUMNER** Esqr Luke **SUMNER**. Jethro **BENTON** Josiah **GRANBERY** Richard **BOND**} {Elisha **HUNTER** Esqr Timothy **WALTON** Esqr John **GORDON** Peter **PARKER** William **WALTON** Jacob **HUNTER** C W.

Ordered That Joseph **PARKER** be Allowed forty six Shillings proc for his charge in keeping his brother Peter, a poor man in this parish, three months and Burying him.

Issd. Ordered that Everard **GARRET** be Appointed Reader at **FARLEE**s Chapel in the Room of Abraham **NORFLET** and that he be Allowed at the Rate of forty Shillin__

The Vestry Adjourned to meet. at **CONSTANT**s Chapel on Satterday ye 23 of December next.

(201) _____ *1758.* (__)

At a Vestry met at **CONSTANT**s Chapel on Satterday The 23d Day. of December 1758. when was present The following Vestry men. Elisha **HUNTER**. Esqr. Luke **SUMNER**. William **WALTON**} {John **GORDON** Josiah **GRANBERY** Richard **BOND** Jacob **HUNTER** C W.

Ordered That the Church Wardens Apply to the Honorable Francis **CORBIN** for the Money in his hands Due to? This parrish for Hire of Negro **DUBLIN**

Ordered that the Church wardens get warrants for John **THACH** and for the Executors of Thomas **PEARCE** and Isbell **PEARCE**, Decd. in Perquimons County for the Recovery of Taxes Due to This parish & That They be payed for Their Trouble.

Ordered that whereas it Appears by the Vestry Book That there is a Large Sum of money due to the parish from the Estate of Doctor Abraham **BLACKALL** Late of Edenton Deceased, which forwant [sic] of an Administration on the said Estate The same is Like to be Lost. to the parish it is Therefore Ordered That the Church Wardens do Agree with some person to Take Administration on the Said Estate. for which the said Administrator Shall be Allowed For his Trouble the sum of Fifteen pounds Proclamation Money.

The Vestry Adjourned to meet at **CONSTANT**s Chapel on Easter Monday Next. Jacob **HUNTER**. CW. Sign as Church Warden   105

(202) *St. Pauls 1759.}* (202.)

At a Vestry met at **CONSTANT**s Chapel on _____ The 24th Day of February 1759. when was Presen_ Demsey **SUMNER** Esqr. Josiah **GRANBERY**. Luke **SUMNER**. John **GORDON**...} {Elisha **HUNTER** Esqr Richard. **BOND** Peter **PARKER** Jethro **BENTON** Jacob **HUNTER** C W.

Ordered That the Church Wardens Imploy an Attor___ To. bring Suits a gainst [sic] Penelope **BLACKALL** Adm? of Abraham **BLACKALL** Deceased. for the ballance of His Accompt as it Stands Stated in the Vestry Book Due to this parish.

And Also to bring Suit agains [sic] Joseph **HE**____ for a Settlement of his parish Accompt and for the? Penalty by Law Inflicted for Refusing to Settle Same. when Summoned so to do.

Ordered That the Reverend Mr: Daniel **EARL** be Allowed The sum of One hundred pounds proclamation Money for preaching and Officiating in This Parish for This Insuing Year. in The Following manner that __ To say. Beginning at Edenton on Sunday the fourth of ___ at **CONSTANT**s Chapel on Sunday the Eleventh day of ____ at **FARLEE**s Chapel on Sunday the Eighteenth and at the Knotty Pine Chapel on Sunday the Twenty fifth and so in that Maner and form to continue the year about, and That he be Allowed the Further Sum of Twenty pounds Proclamation. Money in Lew of a Gleeb for this insuing year Rev_____ **EARL** *duties Rev____ ___having___*

Ordered That Advertisements be set up At ye Chapels The Vestry. Propose to purchas a Plantation for a Gle__ in this parish. That any Person that has a good plant___ on Conveniently situated. to Dispose of may Apply to ___ next. Vestry. *Order to purchase a Glebe.*

The Vestry Adjourned to Meet at **CONSTANT**s Chapel. on the Last Satterday in April Ne__ Jacob **HUNT**__

(203) *St: Pauls. 1759.* (203)

At a Vestry met at **CONSTANT**s Chapel on Fryday the 25?th Day of May. 1759. Present.

25 May 1759

(203) (Cont.) Demsey SUMNER Esqr. Luke SUMNER. John GORDON Peter. PARKER} {Elisha HUNTER Esqr. Josiah GRANBERY. Jethro BENTON   Jacob HUNTER CW

Ordered That Mr. Jethro BENTON and Mr John GORDON be and they are according_y appointed Church Wardens for ____ Present year and that The Former Church Wardens settle Their Respective Accompts and pay the ballances in their? Hands.

Ordered That The parish Accompts with the Estate of the Reverend Clement HALL Deceased be Settled ____ being Done it. Appears That there is a balance of Sixty _____ Seven Shillings and three farthings proclamation Mo____ to the Estate. from this parish it is therefore Ordered ____ ___ Church Wardens pay the said Ballance to The _____ of Said Clement HALL Decd. and Take their Receipt ____ and That a Copy of the said Accompt be Entered __ The Vestry book.

Ordered that Mrs. Elizabeth HINTON be Allowed Seventeen? Shillings. proc. for. Doctering Francis BROWN a poor Man in This Parrish.

Ordered That Mr. Elisha HUNTER be Allowed forty Shillings proc. for his Trouble and Expence ____ ___ The Administration on Docter Abraham BLACKALLs Estate for the Benefit of the parish.

Ordered that the Several Readers in This parish be Continued for this year and that they be Allowed. as Usual.

Ordered that The Vestry be Adjourned to meet at CONSTANTs Chapel on the first Satterday in September next. Jethro BENTON John GORDON} __ 106

(204) [This account is written at 90° to the normal page orientation.]   (__)
Dr: The Reverend Mr Clement HALLs Estate in Accot: Currant with Saint Pauls Parish &. Cr.

1757. To. ballance of Accot. as per vestry book	5:11.11¾	Easter 1758. By 45. Sermons @ 30/9¼
1758. To money paid by James BOND . .	36. 4. 8.	Each in Proc — 69: 4:3
1759. To. Money paid by Jacob HUNTER.	24. 0. 0	By 6.13.4. for Rent of a Gleebe — 6.13.4
To. ballance Due ye Estate if no Sermons } was Omitted at FARLEEs Chapel Last year}	61. 7: 0¾	Easter 1759. By 29. sermons in 10. Months @ 30/9¼ — 44.12._
	£127: 3: 8½	By Allowance for a Gleebe — 6.13._
		£.127: 3: 4

N. B. The Rev Mr HALL ____ ____ named? as the Minister of this parish Feb 25? 1745. ____ ____ died before East. 1759- Having? ____ Officiated in the Parish about 14 years.

Rev Daniel EARL Replaced? him Feb 22, 1759.

N. B. The Rev. Dan EARL ____ ____ the Minister of this Parish until? the Revolution - ____ ____ ____ Oct. 16 1776 - [Remainder is completely illegible.]

(205)   (205.)
St: Pauls 1759.} At a Vestry Held at CONSTANTs Chapel September ___ Day 1759. Present. John GORDON Jethro BENTON} Church Wardens Demsey SUMNER Esqr. Josiah GRANBERY Jacob HUNTER. Richard BOND. William WALTON} Vestry Men

Jacob HUNTER former Church Warden produced his Accot. proved according to Law whereby it Appears there is a ballan__ of 104:18:3½ proclamation Bills Due to the parish which he payed this Day to the present Church Warden John GORDON.

Ordered That a Tax of Two Shillings and four p____ proclamation Bills be Leveyed on every Taxab__ per___ within This parish to Defray the Charge of the parish for this present year

The Vestry Ordered to meet. The first Satturday in Nov. next at. CONSTANTs Chapell. John GORDON Jethro BENTON} C_   [Remainder of page is blank.]   107

(206) [This page is written, in two columns, at 90° to the normal page orientation.]   (206)
Dr. Saint Pauls Parish in Accot. Currant with Jacob HUNTER Church Warden. per Contra Cr.

	£ S D	[Left column]
1758. To. proc. paid Elizabeth HINTON for Doctering, & boarding} Ralph RIMINGTON 113/	5.13. 0	
To. Cash paid Demsey JONES for Boarding Robert ALPHEN} a parishonar	5.12. 8	
To Cash paid on Acct. of Nicholas FERRIL} for a Wolfs Scalp. to Josiah GRANBERY }	0.10. 0	
To. Cloathes for Robert ALPHEN	1: 5: 0	
To Cloathes for Christopher WESTs Child	0.13. 0.	
To. Cash paid Solomon ALPHEN for Board} and Burying Robert ALPHEN. }	4. 0. 0	
To Cash paid William JACKSON Exr.}		

1 September 1759

(206) (Cont.) of the Reverend Clement **HALL** Decd. }   24: 0: 0.
    To Cash pd. Lemuel **RIDDICK** for fees & Comsn: 7: 0: 0
    To. Cash paid James **JONES** for Summoning}
    The Vestry to meet . . . . . . }   0: 2: 8.
    To Elements for the sacrament &c . .   0.12. 0.
    To Reading for the year 1758 . . . . . .   2: 0: 0.
    To my Trouble & Expences at Edenton   1.10. 0
                                                            £52:18: 4
    Ballance Due the Parish 104.18. 3½
                                                            £157:16: 7½

                                                            £ S D   [Right column]
1758 By cash Recd. from John **LEWIS** Collector}
    of the Parish Tax. July 29th. 1758   }   7.19. 8.
    By Cash Received from James **BOND** }
    Collecter of the parish Tax. Sepr 9 1758}   5. 1. 4
    By John **LEWIS** for cash Recd. Decbr. 23. 1758.   2.18. 8
    By Cash Recd. from James **BOND** Decbr. 23. 1758.   8..11. 6
    By. Cash Received from Leml. **RIDDICK** }
    on Acct. of Thomas **BARKER** Executor to.}   131: 8: 5½
    Peter **PAYNE** at ye Suit of ye Parish   }
    By Cash Recd. of John **THACH** for 6 Taxables   0.12. 0.
    By Cash Recd. from Joseph **HERRON**}
    for Mary **BACCO**s fine for fornication }   1. 5. 0
                                                            £157:16: 7½

Sepr. 1. 1759 The above Accot was proved before me According to Law Demsey **SUMNER**

(207) *St Pauls 1759.*   207.
    At a Vestry Held at **CONSTANT**s Chapel on Saturday the 17?__ Day. of. November 1759. Present.
    Elisha **HUNTER** Jacob **HUNTER** Josiah **GRANBERY** William **WALTON** Luke **SUMNER** Timothy **WALTON** Richard **BOND** John **GORDON**-C. W.
Isd.   Ordered that Thomas **BURKET** be Allowed at the Rate of four pounds. proclamation per Annum for the keeping & Mentaining of Martha **CLENNEY** a poor Lame Girl in This parrish.
    Ordered that Mr. John **MCKILDO** be Appointed Collector. of the Parish Tax of Two Shillings and four pence, proclamation Money and that he Give Bond. and Security for his Collecting and paying the same to Such persons as the Same is Due to. in the Sum of Four Hundred pounds which is done, Elisha **HUNTER** & John **GORDON** are his Securityes.
    Ordered That the Church Wardens Advertise the Leting the Ceiling of The Chapel at **CONSTANT**s to the Lowest Undertaker to be done with Good seasoned ¾ Inch? Pine plank. and Rabeted.
    Ordered that the Vestry be Adjourned to meet at **CONSTANT**s Chapel on Easter Monday Next
                                    John **GORDON** C W Sign as Church Warden   108

(208) *St. Pauls Parish 1760.}*   (208.)
    At a Vestry Held at **CONSTANT**s Chapel on Satterday the. 26th Day of January 1760.
    Present. Demsey **SUMNER**. Elisha **HUNTER** Luke **SUMNER**. Timothy **WALTON** Peter **PARKER**.} Jacob **HUNTER** William **WALTON** Richard **BOND**. Josiah **GRANBERY** John **GORDON**-CW.
    Ordered That the Reverend Mr. Daniel **EARLE** be Taken in Incumbent of this parish and that he preach and perform Divine Servis at The Church and Chapels. Alternately and that he be Allowed a Sallery of One Hundred pounds proclamation money per Annum and. Twenty pounds Like money in Lew of a Gleebe till Till [sic] one shall be. provided. Provided never the less that If any future Law shall Alter the Menesters Sallary in This Goverment. in Such case the above agrement as to the Sallary Shall not be binding, but such Law shall be complyed with Annually. *Agreement with___Da___* **EARL**
    The Vestry Adjourned to meet at **CONSTANT**s Chapel. on Easter Monday Next.   John **GORDON** C. W.

(209)   (209)
    At a Vestry Held at the Church in Edenton the 10th Day of April 1760. Pursuant to a Late Act of Sembly [sic]
    Present. Majr. Demsey **SUMNER** Timothy **WALTON** Josiah **GRANBERY** Richard **BOND** Jacob **HUNTER** John

10 April 1760

(209) (Cont.) GORDON Luke SUMNER Jethro BENTON William WALTON

Ordered That The several Readers in This Parish be continued for The Insuing Year at four pounds proc the Year or untill Some Others. will do it for Less.

Ordered That Majr. Demsey SUMNER and Capt. William WALTON be Appointed Church Wardens for this Year.

Adjourned To meet at The Church at July Court　　　Demsey SUMNER William WALTON} CW.

Be it Remembered That Ten of The Vestry Met at the Church in Edenton On Monday the 15.th Day of September. 1760. According to Summons. and. Then and There Took the Oathes prescribed by Law for the Quallification Of Vestry men Subscribed the Declaration & Test. when was Present Demsey SUMNER Luke. SUMNER. Josiah GRANBERY Elisha HUNTER. William WALTON.} John GORDON Richard BOND Timothy WALTON Jacob HUNTER Everard GARRET

NB. The Vestry Adjourned to meet at CONSTANTs Chapel on Satterday the 27th Day of this Instant September 1760.
109

(210) *Pauls P. 1760.}*　　　　　　　　(210)

At a Vestry met & Held at CONSTANTs Chapel on Saterday the. 27th Day of September 1760.

Present. Elisha HUNTER Esqr. Luke SUMNER. William WALTON. John GORDON. Josiah GRANBERY Everard GARRET. Jacob HUNTER.

Whereas Mr. Henry BONNER. who was Elected as a Vestry Man for this Parish and Refused to Quallifie according to Law, The Vestry there fore now proceed to Elect a nother [sic] person to serve in his Room, and accordingly made Choice of. Mr. James SUMNER. Ordered that he be Notified to meet at The Next Vestry to Quallifie according to Law.

And as Mr. Jethro BENTON failed to meet at the Church within Twenty Days after the Election of Vestry to Quallifie accasioned by Sickness. The Vestry Therefore proceed to Re Elect [sic] Mr. Jethro BENTON a Vestry Man for this parish. Ordered that he be Notified to meet at The next Vestry to Quallifie according To Law.

Ordered that Demsey SUMNER Esqr. and Mr. William WALTON be and they are Accordingly Appointed Church Wardens for This year.

Ordered that the Vestry be Adjourned to meet at CONSTANTs Chapel on Monday the 20th Day of October Next. William WALTON. C W

Ordered That Mr. Abner EASON be and he is accordingly Appointed Clerk, of This Vestry. to keep the Vestry Book and to Attend. The several Meeting [sic] of the Vestry therewith and that he be Allowed. The sum of. forty Shillings Proclamation Money a year for. Attending and Acting as Clerk of The Vestry.

Ordered that the Vestry Meet at CONSTANTs Chapel on Monday the 20th Day of October Next　William WALTON. CW

(211)　　　　　　　　(211)

At a Vestry & Held at CONSTANTs Chapel on Monday The 20th Day of October. 1760. Present
Demsey SUMNER William WALTON} Church Wardens
Elisha HUNTER John GORDON Richard BOND} Jacob HUNTER Josiah GRANBERY

John GORDON former Church warden produced his Accot.. proved according to Law. Allowed and order'd To be recorded.

Ordered That FARLEEs Chapel be sealed, with inside [sic] with Such plank and in the same Maner as CONSTANTs is and that The Church Wardens do Advertise The same and set it up to be done, To the Lowest Bidder On the Last Satterday in November Next at. The said . Chapel.

Ordered That a Tax of Three shillings and four pence proclamation money be Leveyed on Each Taxable person in This Parish to Defray the Contingent Charges of the Parish, to be Collected The Insuing year.

Ordered that the Vestry Meet at CONSTANTs Chapel on the first Saterday in December next
　　　　　　　　Demsey SUMNER William WALTON} CW　　　110

[Remainder of page is blank.]

(212)　[This page is written at 90° to the normal page orientation.]　(212)

Dr. Saint Pauls Parish in Accot. with John GORDON Church Warden　　　　　　　　Cr.

_759. To proc Bills paid Wm. JACKSON}		1759? June. By proc Bills. Recd. of}	
Exr. to Clement HALL June 26th }	60. 8. 0	Jacob HUNTER. former }	
Sepr. 1. To. Ditto paid Ditto . . .	0.19. 0.	Church warden . . . . .}	104:18:3½?
To Proc Bills pd. John WALTERS . .	2.10. 0	By Proc Bills Received from}	

20 October 1760

(212) (Cont.)

To Do. paid John **WILLIAMSON** per Demsey **SUMNER**	6. 6. 0	
Novr 17. To Do. paid John **PARRISH**	6. 0. 0.	
Decbr. 6. To. Proc. Bills pd. Ann **MC. GUIRE**	2. 0. 0.	
To Do. pd. Ditto for Clothing	0.10.10	
60 Ap. 17. To. Do. pd. Everard **GARRET** for Reading	2. 0. 0.	
To Do. paid Sarah **RUTTER** for Keeping her her [sic] Daughter	2. 0. 0.	
To. Bread & Wine for the Sacrament	0. 6. 0.	
To 40/ proc paid Wm. **UMPHLET** per Jethro **BENTON** ye 25th May 1759 for. Reading	2. 0. 0.	
To 20/ pd. Elizabeth **HENTON** pr. Jethro **BENTON** The 15th June 1759.	1. 0. 0	
To £5. paid Willis **RIDDICK** per Do. for Sarah **RUTTER** ye 22 of June 1759	5. 0. 0.	
To 18./. proc pd. Elisha **HUNTER**	0.18. 0.	
To 7. yds Chex & thread pr. John **WILLIAMSON**	0:18: 9.	
tobr 20. To. pd. Demsey **SUMNER** Church warden	3:19: 8½	
	113:18: 3½	

The Exrs. of James **TROTTER**} 9: 0: 0
£113:18: 3½

Octobr. 20th. 1760. Sworn to before me
Demsey **SUMNER**

(213) (213)

At a Vestry Held at **CONSTANT**s Chapel on Saturday the 6th of December 1760. Presen_
Elisha **HUNTER** John **GORDON** Josiah **GRANBERY**. James. **SUMNER**.}{Timothy **WALTON** Jacob **HUNTER** Richard **BOND** Everard **GARRET**. William **WALTON** C W

James **SUMNER** who was Elected by the Vestry for a Vestry man, Appeared and Took the Oathes Agreable to Law. &c. and Took his place in The Vestry.

James **BOND** a former Collector, Exhebited his Accot proved according to Law, Allowed and Ordered to be Recorded.
Ordered That the Vestry meet at **CONSTANT**s Chapel on Easter Monday Next.   William **WALTON** __ 111

[Remainder of page is blank.]

(214) [This page is written at 90° to the normal page orientation.] (214)

Saint Pauls Parish in Accompt with James **BOND** Collector of the Parish Tax   C_

To 40/. proc Bills pd Abraham **NORFLEET**	2. 0. 0.	By 1273 Taxes on ye List @ 2/.		£. 127: 6.__
To 20/ Do. pd. Moses **MEASLES** for 2 Scalps.	1. 0. 0.	By 87. Taxes Recd. & Not on ye List @ 2/.		8.14.__
To 120/. paid Ann **MC GUIRE**	6. 0. 0.			
To 10/. pd. Tobias **LASITER** for a Woolf Scalp.	0.10. 0. *Wolf*	By 1. Tax from John **GOODWIN** 2/		0. 2. 0
To 120/. pd. John **PARRISH** for keeping a poor [sic]	6. 0. 0.			£.136: 2: 0
To 40/. pd. William **UMPHLET** Reader	2. 0. 0			
To. 40/. pd Daniel **EARL**	2. 0. 0.	James **BOND** Collector of Saint		
To 20.15.10. paid Luke **SUMNER**	20.15.10.	Pauls Parish made Oath before		
To 57/6. paid Christian **WARD**	2.17. 6	me That This Accot. is Just and		
To. 100/. pd. John **WALTERS** & his wife	5. 0. 0.	True and he has Accounted		
To. 36.4.8. paid Clement **HALL**	36. 4. 8.	With This Vestry for All the		
To. 40/. pd. Jacob **HUNTER** Reader	2. 0. 0.	moneys he has Received as		
To. 6.0.0 pd. John **WILLIAMSON**	6. 0. 0	Collector. Decbr. 6th 1760.		
To 30/. pd. William **SPEIGHTS** for Wolfs scalps.	1.10. 0 *Wolf*	Timothy **WALTON**		
To. 3.7.2. pd. Elisha **HUNTER**	3. 7. 2			
To. 10/. paid William **HUNTER**	0.10. 0			
To 6/. pd. moses **LASITER**	0. 6. 0.			
To. 10/. pd. Joshua **STEVENS** for a Scalp	0.10. 0.			
To. 3/ paid James **JONES**	0. 3. 0.			
To. 5.0.0. pd. Sarah **RUTTER**	5. 0. 0.			
To. 7.1.0. paid Luke **SUMNER** for Books	7. 1. 0.			

6 December 1760

(214) (Cont.)
To. 10/. paid Richard **WALTON**	. . .	0.10. 0.
To. 46/. paid Joseph **PARKER**	. . . .	2. 6. 0.
To 40/. pd. Ann **MC. GUIRE**	. . .	2. 0. 0.
To. 5.1.4. proc and 8.11.6. pd: Jacob **HUNTER**		13.12.10.
To my Commissions	. . . . . .	6.16. 0
To 2/. pd. Wm. **WALTON** Church Warden		0. 2. 0
		£136: 2: 0

(215) At a Vestry [Remainder of line is illegible.] Monday the 27.th Day of April 1761. P_es___
Elisha **HUNTER** Timothy **WALTON** John **GORDON** James **SUMNER**.} {Luke **SUMNER** Jacob **HUNTER**. Jethro **BENTON** William **WALTON** C W.
Ordered That James **SUMNER** and Josiah **GRANBE**__ be And they are Accordingly Appointed Church Wardens. for this Insuing year.
Ordered that The Several Readers in This Par___ be Continued for this Insuing Year and that they? be Allowed at the Rate of four pounds a year for their Servis.
Ordered that the Vestry. be Adjourned to meet at The Church on The fourth Monday in July Next. James **SUMNER** C_

At a Vestry Held at the Church in Eden___ October ye 9th 1761. Present.
Elisha **HUNTER** John **GORDON** William **WALTON** Timothy **WALTON** Jacob **HUNTER**. Everard. **GARRET**. James **SUMNER** Josiah **GRANBERY**} Church Wardens
Ordered That a Tax of Three Shillings ___ ___ pence proclamation Money. be Collec___ from? Every Taxable person in This parish in order to Defray the Contingent Charges th___ of for This present year To. be Collected at the Time of Collecting Publick Taxes &c 112

(216) Ordered That James **SUMNER** Imploy a work___ To put Good Glass into The Windows of the Church at Edenton where any is broke out, and that he purchas some Tar. and have The Ruff well Tared over.
Ordered that The Church Wardens Warrant all persons as is in Arrears for their parish Taxes That have failed to List agreable to Law
Ordered that the Vestry meet }
at ye Church on ye 26th of Novr.} Josiah **GRANBERY**}
next. } James **SUMNER** } CW

At a Vestry met at the Church in Edenton on May the 12th 1762 Present
Jethro **BENTEN** Jacob **HUNTER** William **WALTON** Timothy **WALTON** Elisha **HUNTER** John **GORDEN** James **SUMNER** Abraham **HILL**{ Josiah **GRANBERY** Ch Ward
Ordered that William **WALTON** Keep Mary **FLOYED** at 6sh..11p? pr. Month Clear of the parish untill Some other Person Will keep her for Less money.
Ordered that Elisha **HUNTER** and Abraham **HILL** be and o___ Heareby appointed Church Wardens for this Present year
Ordered that the Vestry meet at the Church in Edenton On the 26th of October 1762. Elisha **HUNTER** Abraham **HILL**{ Ch. wd

(217) _762 At A Vestry held at the Church in Edento_ [Remainder of line is missing.] Present
William **WALTON** Timothy **WALTON** John **GORDEN** Jethro **BENTON**. Demsey **SUMNER** Jacob **HUNTER** Abraham **NORFLEET**{ Elisha **HU**____ Abraham **H**___ {__
William **HALSEY** Collector of the Parrish Levy for the year 17__ Produced his Acct. of his Collections and payments for the Said ____ Which is allowed. Orderd that the Said account be Regis___r_____ Vestry Book and is Stated on the Next leef
John **MC KILDO** Collector of the Parrish Levy for the yea_ Produced his acct. of his Collectios [sic] and payments for the _____ Which is allowed Orderd that the Said Acct be Regist_____ Vestry Book and is Stated on the following Leef.
Elisha **HUNTER** Produced an acct. of Twenty pounds ___ ___ Shillings and three pence for work and Disburstments ___ ___ Parrish and that he had Recd. of John **GORDEN** ___ Ninteen Pounds Two Shilling and four pence Orderd ___ the Colector pay to said **HUNTER** one pound Ten Shillin__ Eleven pence being the ballance Due on the Sd. Acct.
Orderd that a pole Tax of Three Shillings and four ____ Procl. money be Recd.. from each Taxable in this Par___ to Defray the Charges of the Said Parrish for the year And that the Sheriff Collect the Same
Elisha **HUNTER** Abraham **HILL**} C_ 113

26 October 1762

(218) [This page is written at 90° to the normal page orientation. The first line is illegible.]
___ followeth and is in these words Vizt.
William HALSEY Sherf. of Chowan to the Parish of St.. Pauls for the Rect.? of the Parish Tax 1760   Cr

Rect.. of Tythables Listed	934	1762	By Commissions on £177..3..4	
Listed	186		@ 6 pr Cent	£ 10..12. 8
	1120	Janr.. 21	By pd.. Jacob HUNTER	
Inslovents [sic]	57	27	By pd.. Mr EARL	121
	1063 at 3/4 177..3..4	Augst. 7th	By pd.. John PARISH	12
				151..12..
			Balls.. due Parish	25..10..
				177.. 3..

Edenton October the 26 1762   Edenton October 26 1762
This Day William HALSEY Sherif [sic] of Chowan Appeared in   Errors excepted William HALSEY
Open Vestry mett at the Church in Edenton and made Oath on the
Holy Evangelist of Almighty God that the above Account is just and
True Sworn before me   Demsey SUMNER

(219) [This page is written at 90° to the normal page orientation.]
Mr John MC KILDO Exhibited his Account as Collector of the Parish Tax for the year 1759 Duly pro___ Which followeth and is in these words Vizt.
Dr St.. Pauls Parish in acct.. Current with John MC KILDO Contra   C_

To proc paid the Revrd.. Mr Daniel EARL as	£	By procl. Receved for 1279 Taxables	£
part of his Salerey for the year 1759	48.. 0..0	for the year 1759 at 2/4 Each..	149..4..
To Do.. paid to Do.. by Mr Elisha HUNTER for Do	52..13..0	Errors Excepted John MC KILDO	
To procl. paid John WILLIAMSON by Do	6.. 0..0		
To Do.. paid William WALTERS by Do..	2..10..0	Edenton October 26th 1762	
To Do.. paid Jacob HUNTER by Do	5.. 1..0	Sworn to before me	
To Do paid Edward VANN by Do..	0 9..4	Demsey SUMNER	
To Do.. paid Sarah RHITTER [sic] by Do..	0 10...		
To Do paid John PARISH by Do..	3.. 0..0		
To paid Mr HUNTER for work Done on			
COSTENs Chapel	11..10..0		
To procl. paid to Jacob HUNTER	6.. 4..0		
To Commissions on 149:4:4 @ 5 pr Ct..	7.. 0..4		
To paid Mr EARL by Mr Elisha HUNTER..	1..19..0?		
	144..17..4		
Ballance Due to the Parish is	4.. 7..0		
	149.. 4..4	114	

(220) [Entire page is blank.]

(221)   (221)
                                  The Test
I do declare that I Believe that there is not any Transubstantiaton in The Sacrament of the Lords Supper; or in the Elements of Bread and Wine at or after, The Consecration thereof by any person whatsoever. The Declaration to wit:
I will not oppose The Doctrine, Discipline, and Liturgy of the Church of England, as by Law established

Timy WALTON	Jethro BENTON
Elisha HUNTER	William WALTON
Jacob HUNTO?R	Hance HOFLER
James SUMNER	William BOND
Demsey SUMNER	William HINTON
	James BOND
	Abner EASON
	Hy? BONNER
25?th. April Thos NASH.	W BOYD
1767. John BENBURY	

96

26 October 1762

(221) (Cont.)
    Sam. **SWIFT**
    Timy **WALTON**
    Jacob **HUNTOR**
    William **HINTON**
    Saml **JOHNSTON**
    Richd. **BROWNRIGG**
    Elisha **HUNTER**
    James **SUMNER**
    Demsey **SUMNER**   115

(222) _64 August 1st.}_   (222)

Be it Remembred that the Freeholders of St. Pauls Parish met the Sheriff at the Court House in Edenton on Wednesday the first Day of August 1764 and Did then and there pursuant to an act of Assembly, Choose and Elect the following persons to Serve as Vestry men for the three Ensuing ye___ Vizt. Demsey **SUMNER** Esqr. Elisha **HUNTER**, Jacob **HUNTER**, James **SUMNER**, Jethro **BENTON**, William **WALTON**, William **BOND**, Timothy **WALTON**, Hance **HOFLER**, John **GORDEN**, Luke **SUMNER**, & Josiah **GRANBERY**, Who were Summoned by the Sheriff to meet at the Church in Edenton on the 28th. Day of August At which Time and place Nine of the Said Twelve did meet and Qualify according to Law. And then proceeded to the Choice of Church Wardens for this Insuing year.

Ordered That Timothy **WALTON** and Hance **HOFLER** be and They are Accordingly appointed Church Wardens for this year.

At a Vestry This Day Held at the Church at Edenton [sic]
Present The Revd. Daniel **EARL** Elisha **HUNTER** Jacob **HUNTER** James **SUMNER** Demsey **SUMNER** Jethro **BENTON** William **WALTON** William **BOND**{ Timothy **WALTON** Hance **HOFLER**} Church Warden_

Ordered that azariah **VAUN** be appointed a Clerk and Reader and Likewise to take Care of the Church for the Insuing year, for which he is to be allowed the Sum of Six pounds proclamation mony pr year

Ordered that the former Readers be Continued and upon a Vacancy of A Reader for Mr **EARL** to appoint one

Ordered that the former Readers for their past Services be paid their Arrears

(223) S____ ls Parrish 1764} Ordered that Abraham **NORFLEET** be appoin___ Clerk of the Vestry for the Insueing year and to be allowed Forty Shillings.

Ordered that a poll Tax of five Shillings proclamation money be Levyed on Each Taxable person in this ???? parish to Defray the Charges of the parish to be Collected the Insueing year.

Ordered that Mr Hance **HOFLER** Buy a Lock and key for the Church Door.

Ordered that the Vestry meet at the Church at Edenton on the fourth Tuesday in october next. Timothy **WALTON** Hance **HOFFLER**} C. W.

At a Vestry met at the Church in Edenton Tuesday the 23d. Day of October 1764 Present
The Revd. Daniel **EARL** Mr Demsey **SUMNER** Esqr. Elisha **HUNTER**. Jacob **HUNTER**. William **HINTON**. James **SUMNER**. William **WALTON**. William **BOND**.{ Timothy **WALTON** Hance **HOFLER** } C. W.

Ordered that Daniel **MARSHAL** Be allowed Seve_ pounds proclamation for Nursing and Buryin_ Thomas **STRATTON** a poor man

Ordered that John **CHARLTON** Be allowed Two pounds fifteen Shillings proclamation for nursing and Burying John **COOPER** a poor man

Josiah **GRANBERY** who was Elected a vestry man Having Neglected to appear and Quallify as Such the Vestry proceeded to the Choice of another and 116

(224) __Pauls Parish 1764}   (2_)

Did unanimously Choose William **HINTON** who imediatly [sic] appeared and Quallifyed By Taking the oaths appointed By Law and Repeating the Declaration and Subscribing The Test and Took his place in the vestry.

The Vestry Taking into Consideration the Law for Settling the Title and Bounds of Peoples Lands By Freeholders appointed to procession the Same on oath &c. accordingly proceed to Divide the Parish into Convenient Cantons and to appoint Two freeholders in each Canton processioners to procession the Same according to Law as follows

Ordered that David **JONES** and Jacob **NORFLEET** procession all the Lands from the Head of **BENNETs** Creek

23 October 1764

(224) (Cont.) Begining at the Country Line up Chowan road to the Loosing Swamp and up the Said Swamp By the flat Branch across to **BENNET**s Creek and up the Said **BENNET**s Creek to the Country Line and aLong [sic] the Line to Chowan Road and make return Thereof to April Court next according to Law

Ordered that Isaac **HARREL** and David **RICE** Procession all the Lands from the Loosing Swamp Down Perquimons road to **SPEIGHT**s Plantation thence By the Cart road that Leads to Elisha **HUNTER**s then Down By Meherin Swamp to **BENNET**s Creek and up the Creek to the Flat Branch then By the Loosing Swamp to perquimons road and make return to april Court Next according to Law

Ordered that William **BOND** and Palatiah **WALTON** procession all the Lands included from Meherin Swamp. Begining at Jacob **HUNTER**s mill up the Said Swamp to the pipeing Branch so along the said Branch to the main road and Down the Said Road to Aaron **BLANSHARD**s old Road and along the Said old Road To **BENNET**s Creek Road up the Said road to **BENNET**s Creek Bridge and thence up **BENNET**s Creek to the Mill on Meherin Swamp and make Return to April Court Next according to Law.

(225) *St Pauls Parish 1764}* (225)

Ordered that William **FREEMAN** Junr And Jonas **HINTON** Do procession all the Lands included From **BENNET**s Creek road Begining at **BENNET**s Creek Bridge Down **BENNET**s Creek road to Catherines Creek Bridge Down Catherins Creek to the River up the River to the mouth of **BENNET**s Creek and up **BENNET**s Creek to **BENNET**s Creek Bridge and make return to April Court Next according to Law.

Ordered That Amos **TROTMAN** and Micajah **HILL** Do procession all the Lands included Begining at **SPEIGHT**s Plantation So along the Road to The Widow **SCOT**s Thence Down Catherins Creek to the road at Richard **WALTON**s Then Along **BENNET**s Creek Road to **BLANCHARD**s old Road so along The Said Road To Chowan Road and so to the piping Branch Then Down the Branch to Meherin Swamp and Down The Swamp to Elisha **HUNTER**s and from Thence By his Cart Road to **SPEIGHT**s Plantation and make Return to April Court Next according to Law.

Ordered That Charls **ROUNTRY** and John **WALLIS** do procession all the Lands included Betwen Catherines Creek The Sandy Run and perquimons Road Begining at the Widow **SCOT**s Plantation and make Return to April Court Next according to Law.

Ordered That David **WELSH** and William **COUPLAND** Do Procession all the Lands included Between the Sandy Run and Indian Town Creek Chowan River and perquimons And make Return to April Court Next according To Law.

Ordered That Peter **PARKER** and Samuel **MCGUIRE** Do Procession all the Lands included Between Indian Town Creek and Rockahock Creek Between the Main Road and Chowan River and make Return Thereof To April Court Next according To Law.

Ordered That William **WESTON** and Thomas **MCNIDER** Do procession all the Lands That are included Between Rockahock Creek and Machacoma Creek on the West Side of the main Road between the Road & Chowan River   117

(226) *St. Pauls Parish 1764}* (226)

Ordered That Thomas **BONNER** Senr And Richard **HOSKINS** do procession all the Lands that are included Between Machacoma Creek and William **HOSKINS**'s Mill Swamp to the River and And [sic] make Return Thereof to April Court Next according to Law.

Ordered that Thomas **HOSKINS** and James **BLOUNT** Do procession all the Lands that are included between William **HOSKINS**'s Mill Swamp the Sound Side and yeopim River and make Return thereof To April Court Next according to Law.

Ordered That Thomas **BACCUS** and Joseph **PARISH** Do procession all the Lands that are included Between the Main road and Sandy ridge road up to Indian Town Creek and make Return thereof To April Court Next according to Law.

Ordered that Evan **SKINNER** and William **ASHLEY** Do Procession all the Lands That are included Between Sandy Ridge Road and the perquimon line up to the Widow **ASHLEY**s Thence along the Cart road to Little **PARKER**s and make Return thereof to april Court Next according To Law.

Ordered that John **LEWIS** Junr and Josiah **SMALL** Do procession all the Lands that are included Between The Main Road perquimons Line Machacoma Creek And the Cart way from the Widow **ASHLEY**s to Little **PARKER**s and make Return thereof to April Court Next according to Law.

Ordered that the Vestry Be adjourned untill The Second Day of April Court Next   Timothy **WALTON** Hance **HOFLER}** C. W

(227) *St. Pauls Parish 1765}* (227.)

At avestry [sic] Met at the Church in Edenton on Tuesday The 23d: of April 1765 Present

Demsey **SUMNER** Esqr: Elisha **HUNTER**. William **WALTON**. William **BOND**. William **HINTON**. James **BOND}** Timothy **WALTON** Hance **HOFLER}** C Wardens

23 April 1765

(227) (Cont.) ordered That Jacob **HUNTER** and William **BOND** be and they are hereby accordingly appointed Church wardens for this present year

John **GORDEN** who was Elected a vestry man having Neglected to appear and Qualify as Such the vestry proceeded to the Choice of another and Did unanimously Choose James **BOND** Who imediately appeared and Qualifyed by taking the oathes appointed By Law and Repeating the Declaration and Subscribing the Test and took his place in the vestry.

The late Church Warden Having agreed with Susana **TROTMAN** to keep her Bastard Child from the fourth of this instant to this Day at the Rate of five pound pr. year it is ordered that She Keep it for the Ensuing year at the Same rate unless any other person will Keep it for Less it is Further ordered that The Church Wardens Bring Suit against Blount **GARROT** the Reputed father of Said Bastard and John **HOBS** and Amos **TROTMAN** his Securities to reimburse this parish

Issd for part 6:15.1: Ordered that Robert **PERKIN** be allowed at the rate of nine pound pr. year for Boarding and Clothing an orphan Child of one **EVEREDGE** of Edenton Late Deceast 118

(228) *St. Pauls Parish 1765}*   (228)

Ordered that Mary **QUIN** be allowed Six pound ten Shillings proclamation for keeping Moses **WELWOOD** three Months and five Days.

Ordered that Willis **LESTER** be allowed Two pound Sixteen Shillings for keeping Moses **WELWOOD**

Ordered that the vestry meet at the Church the fourth Munday in october Next   William **BOND**} C. W.

At a vestry met at the Church in Edenton on munday The 28th.. Day of october 1765 Present

The Revd. Daniel **EARL** Elisha **HUNTER** Esqr. Hance **HOFLER** James **BOND** Timothy **WALTON**} Jacob **HUNTER** William **BOND**} C Wardens

Luke **SUMNER** who was Elected a vestry man having Neglected to appear and Quallify as Such the vestry proceeded to the Choice of another and Did unanimously Choose Abner **EASON** who immediatly appeared and Quallifyed by taking the oaths by Law appointed and Repeating the Declaration and Subscribing the Test and took his place in the vestry.

Ordered that a poll Tax of Three Shillings and Eight pence proclamation money be Levyed on Each Taxable person in this Parish. to Defray the Charges of the Parish to be Collected the insuing year by the Sherif, which Mr Jos **BLOUNT** Sherif agrees to

Ordered that Mr Hance **HOFLER** Tile the Chancel and Glaze the windows of the Church and Repair the Doors and that he be allowed a reasonable Charge for the Same

Isd. Ordered that Samuel **BENBURY** be allowed three pound procn mony for Boarding Mary **SMITH** and her Child and Conveying them out of the parish

Ordered that the vestry meet to morrow morning at 8 oClock at the ?? Church in Edenton. Jacob **HUNTER** Wm **BOND**} C. Wardens

(229) *St. Pauls Parish 1765}*   (229)

At a vestry met at the Church in Edenton On Tuesday the 29th Day of october 1765 Present

The Revd. Daniel **EARL** Elisha **HUNTER** Esqr: James **BOND** Abner **EASON** Hance **HOFLER** Timothy **WALTON**} Jacob **HUNTER** William **BOND**} C Wardens

Ordered that Abraham **NORFLEET** be appointed Reader at **FARLEE**s Chappel in the Room of Everard **GARROT** and that he be allowed at the Rate of four? pound pr Year

Mr Abner **EASON** Produced His accompt for Serveing as Clerk of the vestry Two years at forty Shillings pr Year which is allowed

Issd. Mr Jacob **HUNTER** Produced his account for Reading at **CONSTANT**s Chapel Two years past and providing the Elements for the Sacrament £8=18=0 which is allowed

Issd. Abraham **NORFLEET** Produced his account for Serving as Clerk of the vestry for the year past at forty Shillings and Twenty Shillings for Issuing Copys of orders for the processioners which is By Law allowed   £3=0=0

Isd Ordered that John **MC KILDO** former Collector of the Parish Tax pay to the Church Wardens of this Parish the Sum of four Pounds Seven Shillings which is the Ballence Due to Sd Parish and on failure thereof that the Church Wardens Immediatly bring Suit against him for the Same.

Ordered that Mr William **HALSEY** former Collector of the Parish Tax meet the vestry at the Church in Edenton on the fourth Munday in January Next and there to Settle his account and pay the Ballence Due to the Said Parish

Elisha **HUNTER** former Church Warden Produced his accot. allowed and ordered to be recorded.   119

(230) *Dr St. Pauls Parish 1765*   (230)

29 October 1765

(230) (Cont.)
 in account with Elisha **HUNTER** former (Church Warden)   £ S D
  To procn paid Hance **HOFLER** 4£=14S Toward Sealing **FARLEE**s Chapel   4=14=0
  To procn paid to Elizabeth **HINTON** for Boarding Francis **BROWN**   4= 4=0
  To procn paid To Sarah **HUNTER** for Curing Mary **FLOYD**s foot   3= 0=0
  To procn pd To Sarah **RUTTER** for keeping her Daughter an Ideot   1=17=6
Cr St Pauls Parish in accot: with Elisha **HUNTER**   Cr   £ S D   13=15=6
  By procn Recd of William **HALSEY** Sherf   9=13=0
  By procn Recd of Timothy **WALTON**   3= 0=0
            12=13=0
Isd   Ballence Due to Elisha **HUNTER**   1= 2=6
            13=15=6

  Hance **HOFLER** Church Warden produced his accot: allowed and Ordered to be Recorded Vizt.
Dr St Pauls Parish in accot. with Hance **HOFLER** (Church Warden)   Dr   £ S D
1764 Decr-4 To 1 Day going to town to take Care of Moses **WELWOOD**   0= 5=0
  To 3 Do. to Carry him to Tyrell   0=15=0
  To 12s=8d Expences   12=8
  To 2 feriages   8=0
  To 1 Dito   5=4
  To 10/ paid to Mary **PRESSLY**   10=0
  To 1 Stock Lock for the Church   5=0
  To a Staple & puting it on the Door   1=8
Cr St Pauls Parish in accot. with Hance **HOFLER** Cr   £ S D   3= 2=8
  By procn Recd of William **HALSEY**   1=10=0
  Ballence Due to Hance **HOFLER**   1=12=8
            3= 2=8

(231) *St. Pauls Parish 1765*   (231)
  Ordered that the vestry meet at the Church in Edenton on the fourth Munday in January Next Jacob **HUNTER** William **BOND**} C Wardens

===

  At a vestry met at Edenton January 27th: 1766 Present
  The Revd. Daniel **EARL** William **WALTON** Hance **HOFLER** Timothy **WALTON** James **SUMNER** James **BOND** Abner **EASON**} Jacob **HUNTER**} Church Warden
Isd.   Major Timothy **WALTON** Produced His acct: of Three Pounds Seven Shillings & nine Pence for Sundry Goods for the Clothing of Moses **WELWOOD** a poor man which was Proved according to Law and allowed
Isd.   Ordered That William **WALTON** be allowed five Pounds fifteen Shillings for keeping Moses **WELWOOD** Nine months
  Ordered That John **PARISH** be allowed at the Rate of Eighteen pound pr. year for keeping of three orphan Children of James **GOODING** Deceast.
  Ordered that the vestry meet at the Church in Edenton on the fourth Monday in april next Jacob **HUNTER** C W 120

(232) *St. Pauls Parish 1766*   (232)
  At a vestry met at the Church in Edenton on the Eighth Day of may 1766 Present
  The Revd. Daniel **EARL** Elisha **HUNTER** James **SUMNER** William **HINTON** James **BOND** Hance **HOFLER**} Jacob **HUNTOR** William **BOND** C W.
  The Vestry proceed to Choose Church wardens for the insuing year ordered that James **BOND** and William **HINTON** be and they are Hereby appointed Church Wardens
  Ordered that Mr. Hance **HOFLER** Make Such further Repairs to the Church in Edenton as will appear to him to be Necessary Beside what He was impowered to Do by a former order and that He be allowed a Reasonable Charge for the Same
  Where as it appears that it was ordered that John **PARISH** was allowed at the Rate of Eighteen Pound pr year for keeping the three Children of James **GOODING** Decst. and it appears that William **BOND** former Church Warden Has Provided Persons to take the Said three Children
  Ordered the Present Church Wardens Provide for the Said Children on the Best Terms and that the Sum allowed **PARISH** Be Discontinued.

8 May 1766

(232) (Cont.) Ordered that the Vestry meet at the Church in Edenton on the fourth munday in october Next William **HINTON** James **BOND**} C. W.

(233) *St. Pauls Parish 1766* (233)

At a vestry Held at the Church in Edenton on the 27th Day of october 1766 according to adjournment Present

The Revd. Daniel **EARL** Elisha **HUNTER** Timothy **WALTON** William **WALTON** William **BOND** Jacob **HUNTER** Abner **EASON** Hance **HOFLER**} William **HINTON** { C. W.

Issd. Hance **HOFLER** produced his account for Work and Services Done in Repairing Edenton Church amounting to Sixty Eight pound ordered that the Same be allowed. Hance **HOFLER** produced his account for Servic__ Done By his wife in Curing __sd. Elizabeth **PARKER**s Sore Leg amounting to four pound, ordered that the Same be allowed. Phillip **MCGUIRE** Produced his account for maintaining &c. Moses **WELWOOD** for Three months, ordered That he be allowed Six Pound for the Same

Ordered that the order made for Robert **PERKIN** to maintain an orphan Child belonging to one **EVERAGE** be Discontinued.

Robert **PERKIN** Produced his account for maintaining an orphan Child belonging to one **EVERAGE** amounting to five pound fifteen Shillings ordered that the Same be allowed

Ordered that a pole Tax of Three Shillings and Eight pen__ be Levyed on Each Taxable person in this parish to Defray the Charges thereof for the insuing year

ordered that the Church wardens Commence Suit against William **HALSEY** former Collector of This parish to the Next Superior Court to be Held at Edenton, for arrears Due from Said **HALSEY** to this parish.

Ordered that the vestry meet at the Church in Edenton on the fourth Monday in January Next William **HINTON**} C. W.
121

(234) *St. Pauls Parish 1767* (234)

At a vestry met at Edenton on the 26th of January 1767 Present

The Revd. Daniel **EARL** Jacob **HUNTER** Timothy **WALTON** William **BOND** Hance **HOFLER** James **SUMNER** Demsey **SUMNER** Elisha **HUNTER**} William **HINTON** James **BOND**} C. W.

ordered that Peter **PARKER** be allowed at the Rate of Twenty Shillings pr. month for keeping Elizabeth **PARKER** a poor woman

Issd. Jacob **HUNTER** Produced his account of Reading at **COSTEN**s Chapel the years 1765 & 1766 at four pound . £8: 0:0
and for providing the Elements for the Sacrament Two Several times 0:12
ordered that the Collecter of the Parish Tax pay the Same of the present Tax. 8:12:0

Issd. Abraham **NORFLEET** produc'd His account of Reading at **FARLEE**s Chapel for the year past at four pound £4:0:0
and Likewise for Serving [sic] Clerk of the vestry for the year Past 2:0:0
Isd ordered that the Collector of the Parish Tax pay The Same of the Present Tax 6:0:0

_s_ Hance **HOFLER** produced his account of Two Pound fourteen Shillings & four pence for Sundries Toward Repairing the Church. ordered that the Same Be allowed, and paid by the Collector of the Parish Tax out of the Tax to be Collected in the year 1768.

This acct. is Stated with his other accot. page 238 Mr. Daniel **EARL** Produced his account of Three pound for Sundries for the Relief of Judith **MAINER** a poor woman and her Two Children ordered that the Same be Allowed and paid By the Collector of the Parish Tax out of the Tax to be Collected in the year 1768

Issd. ordered that Joseph **BLOUNT** Suply Judith **MAINER** with Necessaries to the amount of Twenty Shillings pr. Month untill further orders

(235) *St. Pauls Parish 1767* (235)

Whereas Mr. James **BOND** does inform the vestry that James **JONES** Taylor Doth Propose to Take Benjamin **LEW__** orphan of William **LEWIS** Deceast for the Sum of Ten Pound and Discharge this Parish from any further Charge that may arise in Consequence of Said orph__ ordered that the Same Be paid By the Collector of the Parish Tax out of the Tax to be Collected in the year 1768 provided he Comply with the above Proposal

Ordered That Mr. **EARL** agree with Some Person to act as Clerk and Take Care of the Church in Edenton at the Cheapest Rate Not Exceeding Six pound pr. Annum

Issd. Ordered That John **PARISH** be allowed four pound Ten Shillings for keeping Three orphan Children of James **GOODING** for Three months and That the Collector of the Parish Tax pay the Same of the Present Tax

Ordered That John s**IMSON** be allowed at the Rate of Twenty pound pr Annum for keeping Moses **WELWOOD** A poor man.

Ordered That the vestry meet to Morrow [sic] morning at 9 oCloc_ James **BOND** William **HINTON**} C Warden_ 122

23 May 1767

(236) ___Pauls Parish 1767 (236)

Be it Remembred that on the 27th: Day of april 1767. at the Church in Edenton Samuel **SWIFT**, Thomas **NASH**, John **BENBURY**, Timothy **WALTON**, William **WALTON** Jacob **HUNTER** and William **HINTON**, met and Took the oaths of Government, Repeated & Subscribed The Test as Vestry men

Ordered that Abraham **NORFLEET** be appointed Clerk of The Vestry for the Ensuing year.

And Likewise on the 20th: day of may 1767 at the Church in Edenton Elisha **HUNTER**, Richard **BROWNRIGG**, Samuel **JOHNSTON**, James **SUMNER**, met and Took the oaths of Government and Repeated and Subscribed the Test as Vestry men May 23d: Demsey **SUMNER** Quallified as aforesaid.

At a vestry Held at Edenton the 23d Day of May 1767. Present

The Revd Mr **EARL** Samuel **SWIFT** Thomas **NASH** Timothy **WALTON** Elisha **HUNTER** Demsey **SUMNER** Jacob **HUNTER**

Mr. Samuel **SWIFT**, and Jacob **HUNTER** are appointed Church Wardens of the Parish of Saint Paul the ensuing year

Ordered that Joseph **BLOUNT** Esqr. have Notice to Lay Before the vestry at their next meeting a State of the Parish Taxes by him Collected during his being Collector of the Same

Issd. Ordered that Robert **PERKINS** be paid By the Collector of the Parish Taxes the Sum of Six Pounds for his maintanace [sic] of Lydia **EVERADGE** orphan of Peter **EVERAGE** out of the ~~next~~ parish Taxes for 1766

(237) _____s Parish 1767 [Portions of the right side of this page are missing] (236) [sic]

Issd Ordered that Demsey **TROTMAN** be paid By _____ ~~of the Parish Taxes~~ out of the Next Collect___ of forty Shillings for his Care and Main_____ Edward **GOODIN** orphan of James **GOODIN**

ordered that Mr. **SWIFT** Send to Philidelphia for a Sufficent quantity of Glass to Glaze th_____ Edenton

ordered that Thomas **TROTMAN** be allowe_____ Rates of fifteen Pound a year for keep_____ **WELLWOOD** an aged and infirm man to be _____ of the next Parish Tax

ordered that the vestry be adjou____ till the 4th: Tuesday in July next Samuel **SWIFT** Jacob **HUNTER**} C _

At a vestry Held at the Church in Edent_____ 28th. Day of July 1767 Present.

The Revd. Mr **EARL** Samuel **JOHNSTON** John **BENBURY** Richard **BROWNRIGG** Thomas **NASH** Timothy **WALTON**} ____

James **BOND** former Church Warden Produce____ acct. proved according to Law, allowed a__ to be Recorded

Ordered that William **HALSEY** pay to James ____ Twenty Six Pound five Shillings and Eight Penc_ Ballence of his acct. Due from the Parish out of ___ money in his Hands and that he Be allowed Tw_ Pound ten Shillings & Eight Pence _____ ___Ballence? 123

(238) (237)

__enty Sixth of october 1762. and that the Ballence fifteen ___llings be allowed out of the Judgment obtain'd against ___ in the Superior Court

__dered that Jethro **BENTON** Be allowed the Sum of Six __und for keeping a Child of Elizabeth **HALL** for the Ensuing year

The Reverend Mr. **EARL** Produced his acct. which is allowed and ordered to be Recorded the Ballence of which is one Hundred & Sixty Eight Pounds four Shillings five Pence & three farthings

Ordered that Joseph **BLOUNT** Esqr. Collecter, Pay to M_ **EARL** The above one hundred & Sixty Eight Pounds four Shillings and five Pence & three farthings

_____ ordered that the Vestry be adjourned till the Second Day of october Court Sam: **SWIFT** Jacob **HUNTER** C.W.

_aint Pauls Parish in acct. With James **BOND** former Church Warden

__? 16: 1767	£ S d
To boarding Mr **WELWOOD** Three months 33/4 . .	5 0 0
To 7 yards of Chex for Do @ 3/4	1 3 4
To 3½ yards of Do for Do . . . .@ 3 . .	10 6
To making 3 Shirts for Mr **WELWOOD** @ 2/8 . . .	8 ..
To 1 pr Shoes for Do. . . . . .@ 7 . . .	7 ..
To 1 pr Hose for Do . . @ 6/8 . .	6 8
To proclamation mony paid to John **SIMSON** for keeping{ Mr **WELWOOD** Six months	{ 10 .. ..
To proclamation mony paid to John **JORDAN** for Boarding{ of? Benjamin **LEWIS** three months & a half and finding { Clothes	{ 2 17 8

(238) (Cont.)

To proclamation mony paid Shadrach BUNCH for keep- { ing Mr WELWOOD three months {	2 5 0
To Boarding of Benjamin LEWIS my Self three weeks	7 6
To finding Mr WELWOOD a bed to Ly [sic] on one year	3 ..
Chowan County	26 5 8

The above account was proved by the oath of James BOND this 28th July 1767 before me Samuel SWIFT

(239) [This page is written at 90° to the normal page orientation.] **(238)**

St Pauls Parish to Mr Daniel EARL Dr	£ S D	Pr Contra Cr	£ S D
1763. March 4th To Ballence of Last years Sallary	18	1763 Novemr.. 24th By procn mony from	
To a years Sallary	120	Wm.. HALSEY	74 13 6
April 16th. To Elements for the Sacrament	.. 4 ..	Decemr. 16th By Do.. from Do..	5 10 ..
1764 March 4th To a years Sallary	153 6 8	1764 February 11th By Do.. from Do..	10 .. ..
To Ellements for the Sacrament	.. 4 ..	April 24th. By Do.. from Saml..	
1765 March 4th: To a years Sallary	153 6 8	**JOHNSTON**	69 .. ..
To Elements for the Sacrament	.. 4 ..	1766 Novr. 25th. By Do.. from Wm.	
1766 March 4th. To a years Sallary	153 6 8	**HALSEY**	33 18 6
To Ellements for the Sacrament	.. 4 ..	Decemr. 26th: By Do.. from	
To Do..	.. 4 ..	Joseph **BLOUNT**	364 8 2¼
To Procn mony pd Joseph **BLOUNT** for Do..	.. 4 ..	1767 July 28th: By Do.. from Do	30 .. ..
1767 January 26th: To Procn mony pd archd.. **CORRIE**}		July 28th: 1767	587 10 2¼
for Sundries for Judith **MAINER** }	3 .	Errrs. Excepted pr D. **EARL**	
april 26th To Elements for the Sacrament	.. 4 ..		
March 4th: To a years Sallary	153 6 8		
	755 14 8		
	587 10 2¼		
	168 4 5¾	124	

(240) ( )

At a vestry Held at the Church in Edenton on the 27?.__ Day of october 1767. Present

The Revd Mr **EARL** Samuel **JOHNSTON** Richard **BROWNRIGG** John **BENBURY** Timothy **WALTON** William **WALTON** James **SUMNER** Samuel **SWIFT** Jacob **HUNTER**} CW

ordered that a Poll Tax of Three Shillings and four pence be Levyed on Each Taxable person in this par___ to Defray the Charges thereof for the Ensuing year

Abraham **NORFLEET** Produced his accto. [sic] of Two pound as Serving as Clerk of the vestry   £2:0__

and Likewise of four pounds for Reading at **FARLEE**'s Chapel 4 0

ordered that Mr Joseph **BLOUNT** pay the Same

ordered that Joseph **BLOUNT** pay to John **SIMSIN** the Sum of Two pound three Shillings and four pence for keeping Moses **WELLWOOD** one month and nine Days

ordered that Mr Joseph **BLOUNT** pay to Jacob **HUNTER** the Sum of three Pounds for mony advanced as Church War___

ordered that Joseph **BLOUNT** pay to John **PARISH** Senr the Sum of Three pounds for keeping an orphan Child of of [sic] James **GOODIN**s

ordered that John **PARISH** Carry John **GOODIN** orphan of James **GOODIN** to Mr. Jacob **HUNTER** Else to Receive [sic] future reward for keeping of him

The Vestry adjourned to the first Day of January Cr. [sic] next   Sam: **SWIFT** Jacob **HUNTER**

(241)   0

At a vestr_ [Remainder of page is illegible, except for random words and the following:] ordered that ___ ves--- ___ ___ ___ Tuesday in march Next Sam: **SWIFT** Jacob **HUNTER**   125

(242) __. Pauls Parish 1768   **(241)**

At a vestry met at the Church in Edenton on Saturd__ the 30th Day of April 1768 Present

The Revd. Mr **EARL** Col. Thomas **NASH** Samuel **JOHNSTON** Richard **BROWNRIGG** William **HINTON**} Sam-

30 April 1768

(242) (Cont.) uel **SWIFT** Jacob **HUNTER**} C. W.

The vestry proceed to Choose Church Wardens for the insuing year ordered that James **SUMNER** and Samuel **JOHNSTON** be and they are hereby appointed Church Wardens

Issd — ordered Mary **WOODWARD** be allowed the Sum of Ten pound This year to Support and Maintain her Six Children

Jacob **HUNTER** former Church Warden produced his accot. allowed and ordered to be Recorded the Ballence of which is four pounds Two Shillins and Six pence Due to him

ordered that Jacob **HUNTER** be paid four pound for reading at **CONSTANT**s Chapel the year 1767
ordered that William **HINTON** be paid the Sum of Six pound for keeping Elizabeth **PARKER** one year.
ordered that William **HINTON** be paid five Shillings for mending the Lock of the Church Door
ordered that Mr **KIRSHAW** be paid the Sum of Six pounds for officiating as Clerk of the Church in Edenton
ordered that the vestry be adjourned till the 22d Day of June next

(243) [This page is written at 90° to the normal page orientation.] (242)

Dr Saint Pauls Parish in Accot. With Jacob **HUNTER** Church Warden

				Cr.
June ye 5th: 1767 To 7 yds. of Chex @ 3s/2d pr yd.}			By 3 pound Recd. from Joseph **BLOUNT**	7:2:6
For Moses **WELWOOD**		1:2 2	Collector of the Parish Tax	3:0:0
Do. To [sic] yds of Ozabrigs [sic] @ 1/8 pr. yd.		8:4		4:2:6
12th Do. To making 2 Shirts @ 2/6		5:0		
March ye 30th: 1768 Do. 1 pr. of Shoes @ 6/8		6:8		
November the 12th: To 1¼ yds oznabrigs for John **GOODING**		2:0		
To Boarding of John **GOODING** 21 Days		9:0		
Do. To making 3 Shirts @ 1 Shilling		3:0		
December 21st. Do 1¾ of half thicks		6:5		
Do. To making one Coat 2/		2:0		
To 3½ yds. Irish Linin for Elizabeth **PARKER** @ 2/6		8:8		
To Boarding of Ann **HUBBORD** & 2 Children 52 Days		1:2:0		
Do. To 1 pr. of Shoes 2/		2:0		
To 1=8=3 pd. To Edward **TROTMAN** for Boarding} Moses **WELWOOD** .}		1:8:3		
To making 2 pr. of Trowzers for Moses **WELWOOD**		2:8		
To 1¾ yds. of Chex @ 2/6		4:4		
To 10/ pd. John **SIMSON** for Boarding Moses **WELWOOD**		10:0		
		7:2 6	126	

(244) *St. Pauls Parish 1768* (243)

At a vestry Held at the Church in Edenton on the 27th. Day of october 1768 Present

Mr. John **BENBURY** Mr. Samuel **SWIFT** Mr. Elisha **HUNTER** Mr Jacob **HUNTER** Mr. William **WALTON** Mr. William **HINTON** Mr. Timothy **WALTON**

ordered that a Tax of Three Shillings proclamation Mony be laid on Each Taxable person in the Said parish for this Present year

---

At a vestry met at the Church in Edenton on the 21st. Day of March 1769 Present.

The Revd. Mr **EARL** Mr Samuel **SWIFT** Mr. Timothy **WALTON** Mr. Elisha **HUNTER** Mr. Jacob **HUNTER** Mr. John **BENBURY** Mr. William **WALTON**} Mr Samuel **JOHNSTON** Mr James **SUMNER** Church Wardens

Mr. Samuel **SWIFT** former Church Warden produced his accot. allowed and ordered to be Recorded the Ballence of which is Three Shillings Due from Mr **SWIFT** which he paid to Mr. Samuel **JOHNSTON**

Issd. Abraham **NORFLEET** Produced his accot. as Clerk of **FARLEE**'s
Chapel the year Past 4:0:0
and Likewise as Clerk of the vestry the year past 2:0:0
allowed and ordered to be paid 6:0:0

(245) *St. Pauls Parish 1769* (246)

At a vestry met at the Church in Edenton on the 29th Day of April 1769 Present

Col: Demsey **SUMNER** Samuel **SWIFT** Majr: Timothy **WALTON** Capt William **WALTON** Mr: William **HINTON**}

29 April 1769

(245) (Cont.) James **SUMNER** Samuel **JOHNSTON**} C. W.

The Vestry proceed to Choose Church Wardens for for [sic] the present year, and they unanimously Chose Capt: William **WALTON** and Samuel **JOHNSTON** Esqr.

ordered that Thomas **HOSKINS** be appointed a vestry man instead of Col: Thomas **NASH** Deceasd.

Issd. To Mr SKINNER   Ordered that Capt. Thomas **BONNER** be allowed at the Rate of three pound a year for Boarding and Clothing Elizabeth **LILES**

ordered that the Church Wardens Provide a maintainance for Moses **WELWOOD** a poor man

The Vestry adjourned till the monday before September Court

At a vestry met at the Church in Edenton on? the 19th Day of Sept. 1769 Present

Elisha **HUNTER** Timothy **WALTON** Jacob **HUNTER** Demsy **SUMNER** John **BENBURY** Richard **BROWNRIGG** James **SUMNER** Thomas **HOSKINS**} Saml **JOHNSTON** Wm **WALTON** C. W.

Thomas **HOSKINS** took the Several oaths for his Quallification and Repeated and Subscribed the Test and took his place in the vestry.

ordered that the Church wardens Bring Suit against Joseph **BLOUNT** for his Collection of the Parish taxes During his Sherifalty   127

(246) *St Pauls Parish 1769*   (247)

Ordered that William **HINTON** be paid Six pounds for keeping Elizabeth **PARKER** for the year past

Issd. Ordered that Thomas **ECCLESTON** be paid the Sum of five pounds for his Trouble in Transporting Benjamin **BOWEN** to the Church warden of Berkley parish in perquimons County B_____par___Perq_____y

issd. Ordered that Mary **WOODWARD** be allowed Six pounds to assist her in maintaining her poor family for this year

Ordered that a Tax of three Shillings be laid on Each Taxable person in this Parish

Ordered that the Church Wardens Employ persons to Repair **COSTEN**s Chapel & Likewise **FARLEE**s Chapel

Ordered that John **GREGORY** be allowed at the Rate of Three pounds pr. year for keeping an orphan Child of Thomas **HOSKINS** Decst.

The vestry adjourned till the Last Satterday in October Next

1770   At a vestry met at the Church in Edenton on the 21st of March 1770 Present

The Revd. Mr. **EARL** Col Demsey **SUMNER** Timothy **WALTON** Elisha **HUNTER** Richard **BROWNRIGG** William **HINTON** Jacob **HUNTER** Thomas **HOSKINS**} Saml **JOHNSTON** Wm **WALTON** C. W.

_sd. Ordered that Samuel **GREEN** be paid one pound Three Shillings & four pence for keeping Moses **WELLWOOD** 53 days at 8£ pr Annum

Ordered that Elizabeth **RICE** be paid Two pounds Twelve Shillings & Six pence for keeping Moses **WELLWOOD**

Issd. Ordered that John **GREGORY** be paid Three pounds Ten Shillings for keeping Elizabeth **HOSKINS** one year

(247) *St Pauls Parish 1770*   (248)

Issd Ordered that Richard **HOFF** be paid Two pounds fourteen Shillings for keeping Gidion? **BRICE** Till This day

Issd. Ordered that Abraham **NORFLEET** be paid Eight pounds Eighteen Shillings & four pence for Serving as Clerk of the vestry and Reader at **FARLEE**s Chapel Till This Day.

Issd. Ordered that Mr. Elisha **HUNTER** be paid Six pounds for Repairing **COSTEN**s Chapel.

Issd. Ordered that Thomas **GARROT** be allowed Thirteen pounds nineteen Shillings & Six pence provided that he Repairs **FARLEE**s Chapel according to agreement by the Last of June next

Issd. Ordered that William **HINTON** be paid Two pounds Seven Shillings & Eight pence for Burying Elizabeth **HALL**, a poor woman

Issd. Ordered that William **HINTON** be paid Six pounds for keeping Elizabeth **PARKER** till the ninth of Februar_ Last.

Issd. Ordered that John **BLACK** be allowed Four pounds for Nursing Matthew **GARDNER** in his Sickness and Burying him.

Issd. Ordered that Jacob **HUNTER** be paid four pounds for Reading at **COSTEN**s Chapel the Last year

Issd. Ordered that Joanah **CLASA**? be allowed Thirty Shillings for Keeping Mary **FLOYD** Thirty Days   128

(248) *St Pauls Parish 1770*   (249)

Be it Remembred that the Freeholders of St. Pauls parish met the Sheriff at the Court House in Edenton on Monday the 16 of april 1770 and Did then & There pursuant to an act of assembly, Choose & Elect the following persons to Serve as vestry men for the Three Ensuing years, Vizt. Elisha **HUNTER**, Jacob **HUNTER**, Samuel **JOHNSTON**, William **WALTON**, William **HINTON**, Timothy **WALTON**, James **SUMNER**, Thomas **HUNTER**, Pallatiah **WALTON**, Richard **BROWNRIGG**, Thomas

28 April 1770

(248) (Cont.) **HOSKINS**, John Baptist **BEASLY** who were Summoned by the Sheriff to meet at the Church in Edenton on the 28th Day of April at which Time and place Ten of the Said Twelve, did meet and Quallifye according to Law and then proceeded to the Choice of Church Wardens For this Ensuing year.

    ordered that Pallatiah **WALTON**, and John Baptist **BEASLY** Be and they are accordingly appointed Church Wardens for this year

Issd.   ordered that Amos **TROTMAN** be paid Six pounds provided he procure John **GOODIN** orphan of James **GOODWIN** [sic] to be Bound an apprintice to him? [blot] at the Next Inferior Court and indemnify the parish from any further Charge on account of the Said orphan

Issd.   Ordered that John **EVANS** be allowed Three pounds nineteen Shillings & Eight pence for keeping & maintaining an orphan Child Ten months

Issd.   ordered that Charles **ROUNTREE** be allowed forty Shillings for keeping John **GOODWIN** a poor orphan Child Six-months

Issd   ordered that Daniel **MARSHAL** be allowed Twenty five Shillings for keeping Gideon **BRICE** five weeks

Issd.   ordered that Mr. Elisha **HUNTER**, be paid fifteen Shillings for work by him Done on **FARLEE**s Chapel.

(249) *St. Pauls Parish 1770*   (250)

    Mr. James **SUMNER** late Church Warden Exhibited his account on oath by which it appeared that there was a Ballence Due to the parish of five Shillings & five pence which he paid to Pelatiah **WALTON** the Present Church Warden

[This account is written in two columns, at 90° to the normal page orientation, and is partially illegible.]

Dr The Parish of St. Paul _____ James **SUMNER** C__rch Warden   [Left column]

1768
June 7th To 7 yds. Striped Holland @ 3/8? for **WELWOOD**?   _: 5: 8
    To 1 yd: & 5/8ths of Serge @ 11/ pr yd & 2 yds}
    Shalloon? @ 4/ pr yd   }   1: 5:10
    To 1½ yds Sheeting @ 1:8? pr yd. _____   3: 3
    To 1 Stick Twist & 9 hanks Thread   2: 2
Augt. To 1 pr. Shoes   6: 3
    To 2¼ yds. Linin @? 1 6 pr yd?   3: 5
    To 1½ pints High wines for him?   2
1769 To 3½ yds Linin @ 1/_ pr. yd for orphan of **GOODWIN**}   5: 3
March To 1 pr. Shoes for **WELWOOD**   6: 3
    To 3½ yards _triped holland @ 3 8 pr. Yd}
    To 6 Knots Thread   }   14: 4
    To keeping the orphan of **GOODWIN** one}
    Month @ 4£ pr year?   }   6 5?
    To 6 Shillings pd. Jacob **HUNTER** for}
    Elements for the Sacr_ment   }   6?
apl 23 To 2½ yards Linin for **GOODWIN**s orphan   4 2
    To 2 Shillings to **WELWOOD** to Get home}
    from Town   }   2
    To 8:10:8 pd Nathan **CULLENS** for keeping **WELWOOD**} 8:10: 8
    To 10/ pd Joshua **DEAL** for relief to a Sick man}   10:
    To 40/ pd. Charles **ROUNTREE** towards}
    keeping **GOODWIN**s orphan   }   2: 0: 0
                                          16:12: 1

                [Right column]   Cr..   £ S D

1769?
March 22 By £7:0:0 Recd. from Capt. Thomas **BONNER**   7: 0:0
    By 20/ from Nathan **CULLENS HARRELL**s fine   1: 0:0
May 6th By 8£ from Capt **BONNER** pr Luke **SUMNER**   8: 0:0
    By 5/ from Samuel **PERRY** Demsey **WEB**s fine. . .}   0: 5:0
    By 12:6 Tabitha **FREEMAN**s Exclusive information}   12:6
                                            16:17:6
                                          16:12:1
                Ballence Due the Parish   0: 5:5

28 April 1770

(249) (Cont.) April 28th 1770 Capt James **SUMNER** Personaly appeard. before me and proved the above acct. in Due form of Law. Sworne to before me Timothy **WALTON**   129

(250) *St. Pauls Parish 1770*   (251)

At a vestry met at the Church in Edenton the 20th Day of June 1770 Present

The Revd: Mr. **EARL**, William **WALTON** Timothy **WALTON** Richard **BROWNRIGG** James **SUMNER** Thomas **HOSKINS** Thomas **HUNTER** Elisha **HUNTER** { Pellatiah **WALTON** John Bap. **BEASLY**} C. W.

Issd: ordered that Capt: Jethro **BENTON** be paid the Sum of Twelve Pounds for keeping an orphan of Elizabeth **HALL**, till april 1769 being Two years

Capt: William **WALTON** late Church warden, produced his accot: proved and allowed, Ballence Due Him-Three pounds nine Shillings and four pence.

Issd: ordered that Capt: William **WALTON** be paid Three pounds nine Shilling and four pence, being a Ballence Due him from the parish.

ordered that William **FLURY** be allowed at the Rate Twenty Shillings pr: Month from the 8th day of May Last for keeping Gideon **BRICE**.

Issd: ordered that James **COLE** be appointed Clerk of the Church at Edenton and be allowed Six pounds for his Service the year to begin at Easter Last.

ordered that John **GREGORY** be allowed at the Rate of Three pounds Ten Shillings pr: year for keeping Elizabeth **HOSKINS** orphan of Thomas **HOSKINS** from the first of May last

ordered that William **HINTON** be allowed at the Rate of Three pounds Ten Shillings pr: year for keeping Elizabeth **PARKER** the year to begin the Twentieth of May Last

Issd: for 20 Shill Issd: for All 1771   Ordered that Katherine **HAYS** be allowed at the Rate of Eight pounds pr: year for keeping Two of Her orphan Children Mary, and Elizabeth, and that She be now paid Twenty Shillings of the Same.

(251) *St. Pauls Parish 1770*   (252)

Issd: To T HODSON Esqr. ordered that William **PARKER** be paid Three pounds Ten Shillings provided he procure Sarah **HOSKINS** orphan of Thomas **HOSKINS** Deceast to be Bound an apprentice to him at this Present Inferior Court and Endemnifie the Parish from any further Charge on acct: of said orphan

ordered that Henry **MOOR** [sic] be allowed at the Rate of five pounds pr: year for keeping Edward **STREATOR** an orphan of Thomas **STREATOR** Decst: from the first of February Last

ordered that the Revd: Daniel **EARL** provide proper Prayer Books for the Several places of Worship in this Parish

ordered that Abraham **NORFLEET** be allowed four pounds pr: year for Serving as Clerk of the Vestry the year to begin at Easter Last

Dr: The Parish of St: Paul in	£ S D	accot: wth: William **WALTON** C. W.	Cr.	£ S D
To Sundry articles Bought for the { use of persons maintained by ye parish {	2 10 10			
To making 2 Coats, & 4 Shirts . .	6			
To 2 pr: Shoes	4			
To keeping John **GOODIN**} Three months & nine Days }	1 5			
To attending at **FARLEE**s Chapel} Two Days . . . . . }	10	June 18th: 1769		
To keeping Moses **WELWOOD** 53} Days . . . . }	1 3 6	By fines recd: from Majr: **WALTON**} for the use of the Parish	- 10	
	5 19 4			
June 20th: 1770 proved before	2 10			
Richard **BROWNRIGG**	3 9 4			

The Vestry adjourned till the 2d. Day of next Inferior Court   Jno Bap **BEASLEY** Peletiah **WALTON**   130

(252) *St. Pauls Parish 1770*   (253)

At a vestry met at the Church in Edenton on the 29th Day of october 1770 Present

Elisha **HUNTER** James **SUMNER** Thomas **HOSKINS** Jacob **HUNTER** Timothy **WALTON** William **HINTON** Thomas **HUNTER**} John Bap **BEASLY** Pelatiah **WALTON** {C. W.

29 October 1770

(252) (Cont.) ordered that Mr: John Baptist BEASLY Supply Jane? JOHNSTON wife of William JOHNSTON a poor woman with Such? necessari__ as he Shall Think proper not Exceeding Three pounds

ordered that a Tax of Three Shillings and four pence Be Laid on Each Taxable Person in the Parish

ordered that Robert HUTCH be appointed Sexton of the Church in Edenton and that he keep the Church & Church yard in Good order, and that he have the Benefit of the Church yard as a pasture for his Trouble Till further orders

Issd: ___ ordered that David RICE be paid Sixteen Shillings & Eight pence for Digging a well at COSTENs Chapel

__*sd:* ordered that John ROMBOUGH be paid Twelve Shillings for making a Coffin for a poor man

Issd: ordered that John Baptist BEASLY be allowed Two pound fifteen Shillings as pr: accot:

ordered that Thomas HOSKINS be allowed his accot. of fifteen Shillings and Ten pence for Burying Sarah CHARLTON

ordered that Capt: William WALTON be allowed at the Rate of Six pounds pr: year for keeping Judith MAINER

ordered that the vestry be adjourned till Easter monday at 12 of the Clock

(253) _____Parish 1771 At a vestry met at the Church in Edento_____ of April 1771 Present

The Revd. Daniel EARL} John Bapt: BEASLEY Pellatiah WALTON} C: Wardens Elisha HUNTER William WALTON Jacob HUNTER James SUMNER William HINTON Thomas HOSKIN [sic] Thomas HUNTER

~~ordered that Collonel Thomas BONNER be app------a vestry man instead of Majr: Timothy WALTON~~

The vestry proceeded to Choose a vestry man in _____ Major Timothy WALTON Deceast and duly? _____ Collonel Thomas BONNER in his stead

The Revd: Mr: EARL, produced his account to ___ fifth of Decr: 1770 and the Ballence Due to him _____ pounds fourteen Shillings and Six pence

Issd: to Jno. GREEN ordered that John GREEN be allowed at the Rat_____ pounds pr. year for keeping Elizabeth LA-CITER ___ the year to begin on the first of January Last

__*sd. to 9th Marry?* ordered that Capt. James COLE be paid five pounds _____ Shillings & Eight pence for Boarding and Clothing Eliz_____? LILES from the 18th: May 1770 till the 18th of may 1771

Issd to Col. Thos BONNER ordered that James MEGLOCKLIN be paid the S_____ pounds Eleven Shillings and Five pence for Keeping William KERBY in his Sickness and Burying hi_

Issd. to Capt. Wm WALTON ordered that Samuel GREEN be paid ten pounds _____ Shilling & Six pence half penny for keeping Moses? WELWOOD 17 months Last past   131

(254) ordered that Henry MOOR be paid the Sum of five pounds Eighteen Shillings and nine pence for keeping and Burying Edward STREATOR orphan of Thomas STREATOR Deceast

The Vestry proceed to Chose Church Wardens for the present year and they unanimously Chose Thomas HOSKINS and Thomas HUNTER

ordered that William LISTER be allowed at the Rate of nine pounds nineteen Shillings pr: year for keeping Mary JOHNSTON a poor Woman the year to begin at Easter Last

ordered that Abraham NORFLEET be paid Eight pounds for Serving as Clerk of the Vestry, and Likewise Clerk of FARLEE's Chapel the year past.

Pelatiah WALTON former Church Warden produced his acct on oath by which it appeared that there was a Ballence of Two pounds and five pence Due to him

John Bapt: BEASLEY former Church Warden produced his accot: on oath by which it appeared there was a Ballence of one pound Twelve Shillings Due to him

ordered that Christopher JOHNSTON be paid Three pounds Eightteen Shillings for Burying Margaret RUSSEL a poor woman

Iss_____ ordered that William HINTON be paid Thirty Shillings for keeping Elizabeth PARKER from the ninth of february to the Twentieth of May 1770

__*sd.* ordered that Jacob HUNTER be paid four pounds for Serving as Clerk at COSTENs Chapel the year past

The Vestry adjourned till the Second Day of Sept: Court   Thos. HUNTER Thos. HOSKINS

(255) *St. Pauls Parish 1771*   (256)

Dr St Pauls Parish		£ S D	in accot with Pelatiah WALTON C. Warden	
To 2 Chex Shirts for }			Cr	£ S D
Moses WELWOOD}		14 6	By five Shillings &? five pence}	
To 1 pr: Shoes . . .		6 4	Recd. from James SUMNER }	5 5
To Riding to Town after}				
Judith MAINER }		5		

20 April 1771

(255) (Cont.)
To Ellements for ye Sacrament} at **COSTEN**s Chapl.}	6	
To procn: 1s: 8d to help a} poor woman out of the County . . .}	1 8	
To 4? Shirts for E. **HOSKINS**} orphan of Thos: **HOSKINS**}	7 4	
To 2½ yds: Woollen Cloth &} making . . . . .}	5	
	2 5 10	April 20th: 1771 proved before Capt. J?ames **SUMNER**
	5 5	
Ballence to P: **WALTON**	2 0 5	

Dr St Pauls Parish to John Bapt: **BEASLEY** Church Warden Cr

To procn: pd: Wm: **JOHNSTON** for Gideon} **BRIGHT** [sic] . . . .}	5	[blank]
To 1½ Gallons Mollasses Sugar} for Mary **JOHNSTON** . .}	6	
To 1 pr: Shoes for do.	6	
To 1 Blanket	15	
proved Before Capt. James **SUMNER**	1 12	132

(256) *St. Pauls Parish 1771* (257)

at a vestry met at the Church in Edenton the 18th Day of September 1771 Present

The Revd. Daniel **EARL** Mr. Elisha **HUNTER** Capt. James **SUMNER** Capt: William **WALTON** Mr: Pelatiah **WALTON** Mr. Jacob **HUNTER** Thos. **HOSKINS** Thos: **HUNTER**} CW

ordered that a Tax of Three Shillings & four pence be laid on Each Taxable person in this parish to defray the Charges thereof

ordered that John **GREGORY** be paid forty Shillings provided that he Endemnifys this parish from any further Charge concerning Elizabeth **HOSKINS** orphan of Thomas **HOSKINS** till She arrives to the age Eighteen years.

ordered that John **GREGORY** be paid Twenty Shillings for Curing Elizabeth **HOSKINS** of a Scald Head.

__sd. _rd ordered that the Revd: Mr: **EARL** be paid Sixteen pounds Eleven Shillings and Three pence for three Books for the use of this Parish.

Issd. ordered that John **GREGORY** be paid Three pounds fifteen Shillings and ten pence for keeping Elizabeth **HOSKINS** orphan of Thomas according to a former order of Vestry.

__sd. ordered that Elizabeth **HODGES** be paid Two pounds for taking Care of Sarah **WATSON**.

__sd. ordered that Christopher **JOHNSTON** be paid Twenty Shillings for Boarding Peter **BURNS** Two weeks

__sd. ordered that William **LISTER** be now paid three pound part of a greater Sum which was allowed him for keeping Mary **JOHNSTON**.

ordered that Katherine **HAYS** her allowance be Continued as formerly

ordered that the vestry be adjourned till Easter monday Next Thos.. **HUNTER** Thos **HOSKINS**

(257) *St. Pauls Parish 1772* (258)

At a vestry met at the Church in Edenton the first Day of April 1772 Present

The Revd: Daniel **EARL** Mr Elisha **HUNTER** Mr Jacob **HUNTER** Mr Pellatiah **WALTON** Mr James **SUMNER**} Thomas **HUNTER** Thomas **HOSKINS** Church Wardens

The vestry proceeded to Choose vestry men instead of Mrs: William **WALTON** and Richard **BROWNRIGG** Deceast and according [sic] Chose Mr: William **BOYD** & Capt Abner **EASON** in their Steads

At a vestry met at the Church in Edenton on the 9th? of May 1772 Present

Mr: Elisha **HUNTER** Mr: Samuel **JOHNSTON** Mr: Jacob **HUNTER** Mr: James **SUMNER** Mr: William **HINTON** Mr John Bap. **BEASLEY**} Thomas **HUNTER** Thomas **HOSKINS**} C W:

ordered that Mrs: **PETTYJOHN** be allowed Three pounds ___ Shillings for Nursing and Burying Mary **CRINDELL** a poor woman

May 1772

(257) (Cont.) *Issd.* Mr. Thomas HUNTER Church warden produced his accot: of Twenty Eight pound on oath, ordered that it be allowed

ordered that Mr: HOSKINS be allowed ten pounds Seventeen Shillings & Three pence for Glass Recd: from LOWTHER HARDY & LITTLE for the Church

ordered that Mr: Thomas HOSKINS & Mr: Thomas HUNTER Late Church Wardens be Continued another year

ordered that the Vestry be adjourn'd till the 17th Day of June next   Thos. HOSKINS Thos. HUNTER   133

(258) *St. Pauls Parish 1772*   (259)

At a vestry met at the Church in Edenton June 17th 1772 Present

The Revd: Mr: EARL Mr. Elisha HUNTER Mr. John Bap: BEASLEY Capt James SUMNER Mr. Pellatiah WALTON} Mr: Thos: HOSKINS Mr: Thos: HUNTER} C. W.

Coll: Thomas BONNER and William BOYD Esqrs: appeared and Qualified as vestry men and Took their Seats accordingly

Issd.   John Bap BEASLEY Esqr Produced his acct: of nine Shillings and Five pence which is allowed

Issd.   Abraham NORFLEET Produced his accot: of Eig__ Pound for Reading at FARLEEs Chapel and Serving as Clerk of the vestry the Year Past

Issd. to J__DEN Jacob HUNTER Esqr: Produced his acct. of five Pounds for his Reading at COSTENs Chapel finding 24 pains [sic] of Glass, and finding Elements for a Sacrament at COSTENs Chapel.

Issd.   ordered that Robert MURE be allowed Three pounds Ten Shillings for Boarding Joseph SIMPSON ten weeks

Issd.   ordered that Mr. Thomas HOSKINS Pay Katherine HAYS Six Pounds & Six Pence for Keeping her Two Children &c? To this Day and that Her allowace [sic] Be Discontinued

Issd.   Ordered that Docter DICKENSON be allowed His acct: of Thirteen Pounds Two Shillings for Sundry Services by him done to the Poor of this Parish

ordered that Elizabeth KNIGHT be allowed at the Rate Twenty five Shillings pr: month for keeping her Daughter Keziah and her Child from the 9th of may Last till Some other person will Keep them for Less

ordered that Joshua MEWBORN be allowed Eight pounds Eightteen Shillings [End of entry.]

(259) *St. Pauls Parish 1772*   (260)

Issd: orderd that Joshua MEWBORN Be allowed nine pounds four Shillings and nine pence for keeping Jacob PRIVIT 13 months till this Day and finding him one Shirt

order'd that William LISTER his allowance be Continu__ for keeping Mary JOHNSTON till further orders

Issd: ordered that the Church wardens Pay Jacob PRIVIT Two pounds Seven Shilling & Six pence Every Three mon___ to Enable him to Support him Self he being a poor old ma_

Issd: to J. G.   ordered that Samuel GREEN be paid Eight Pounds fif___ Shillings for keeping Moses WELWOOD fourteen months ___ Past

Issd: ordered that Capt: James COLE be paid Seven Pounds for Serving as Clerk of the Church for 14 months last p___ the Vestry adjourned till the 16th of Sept: next   Thos HOSKINS Thos.. HUNTER

At a vestry met at the Church in Edenton the 16th: of Se__ 1772

Present The Revd: Mr: EARL Mr: Elisha HUNTER Mr: Jacob HUNTOR Mr: Pelatiah WALTON Col: Thomas BONNER Samuel JOHNSTON Esqr: William BOYD Esqr:} Thomas HOSKINS C.W.

ordered that a Tax of three Shillings & four Pence be laid on Each Taxable Person in this Parish to be Collected the insuing year.

The Vestry adjourned till Saturday the 31st of october next Thos HUNTER Thos HOSKIN [sic]   134

(260) __int__uls__arish_772   (261)

At a vestry met at the Church in Edenton the 31st: of october: 1772 Present

The Revd: Daniel EARL Elisha HUNTER Esqr: James SUMNER Esqr: Jacob HUNTER Esqr: Coll: Thomas BONNER William BOYD Esqr: Mr: William HINTON} Thomas HUNTER Thomas HOSKINS} C. Wardens

Issd: ordered that Doctr: DICKENSON be allowed his acct: of fourteen Pounds nineteen Shillings & Six Pence till the 27th: of this instant for Phisick Administred to Sundry Poor of this Parish

Thomas BENBURY Esqr: Late Sherif laid his accots: for the years 1769 & 1770 and it appears that the Several Sums By him Paid amounts to four hundred & Eighty Two Pounds Seventeen Shillings, being the Sum Leviable By him for Said years on accot: of Said Parish and it further appears that Said Mr: BENBURY Paid off to the Several Creditors of the Said Parish Two Hundred and forty nine Pounds Two Shillings & one Penny for the year 1771.

31 October 1772

(260) (Cont.) *Issd:* ordered that William LISTER be Paid four Pounds Three Shillings for keeping Mary JOHNSTON five months and that her allowance be Discontinued

The vestry Taking into Consideration the Law for Settleing the Title and Bounds of Peoples Lands by freeholders appointed to Procession the same on oath &c. accordingly Proceed to Divide the Parish into Convenient Cantons and to appoint Two freeholders in Each Canton Processioners to Procession the Same according to Law as follows.

(261) *St: Pauls Parish 1772*   **(262)**

ordered that John DURDEN and Isaac BENTON Processio_ all the Lands from the Head of BENNETs Creek Begin___ at the Country Line up Chowan Road to the Loosing Sw___ and up the Said Swamp by the flat Branch a Cross BENNETs Creek and up the Said Creek to the Country ___ and along the Line to Chowan Road and make Return to March Court next

ordered that Thomas GRIGORY and Abraham HARREL Procession all the Lands from the Loosing Swamp Down __ Perquimon Rode [sic] to Capt: Mills RIDDICKs Plantation thence by the Cart road that Leads to Elisha HUNTERs then Down by Meherin Swamp to BENNETs Creek and up the Creek by the flat Branch then by the Loosing Sw___ to Perquimons Road and Make return to March Court ____

ordered that Maximillion MINSHEW & Frederick LACITO_ Procession all the Land Between Meherin Swamp & the Piping Branch beginning at Jacob HUNTERs Mill up ___ Said Swamp to said Piping Branch so along the Said Bra____ to the Main Road and Down the Said Road to Aaron B_AN_____ old Road along the Said Road to BENNETs Creek Road up the Said Road to BENNETs Creek Bridge and thence up BENNETs Read? Creek to the Mill on Meherin Swamp and Make Return to March Court next according to Law

ordered That James FREEMAN, & William HINTON __ Procession all the Lands included from BENNETs creek road Beginning at BENNETs Creek Bridge down Catherines Creek to the river up the River to BENNETs Creek and up ___ BENNETs Creek to BENNETs Creek Bridge and make return to March Court next according to Law.

ordered that Thomas TROTMAN, & Joseph BRINKLY processio_ all the Lands included Beginning at Mills RIDDICKs Plantation So along the road to the Widow SCOTs thence Down Catherines Creek to the Road at WALTONs then along BENNETs Creek Road to BLANCHARDs old   135

(262) __: Pauls __rish __72   **(263)**

Road so along the Said road to Chowan road and so to the Piping branch then Down the Branch to meherin Swamp then down the Swamp to Elisha HUNTERs from thence by his Cart road to RIDDICKs Plantation and make return to March Court next according to Law

Ordered that Thomas ROUNTRY Juner & George OUTLAW Procession all the Lands included Between Catherine Creek the Sandy run & Pequimons Road Begining at the widow SCOTs Plantation amd make return to march Court next according to Law

ordered that Edward WELSH and Josiah COPELAND procession all the Lands included Between the Sandy run & Indian Town creek Chowan river and pequimons and make return to March Court next according to Law.

ordered that Capt: William BOND & Abraham NORFLEET procession all the Lands included Between Indian Town Creek and Rockahock Creek Between the main road and Chowan river and make return to march Court next according to Law.

ordered that Abel MILLER and William JONES Procession all the Land included between Rockahock Creek & Machacoma Creek on the west Side of the Main road between the road and Chowan river and make return to March Court next according to law

ordered that William JONES Senr: & Henry THOMSON procession all the Lands included Between Machacoma Creek and Thomas HOSKINS Mill Swamp to the River and make Return to march Court next according to Law.

ordered that Mr: Samuel JOHNSTON & Mr: James BLOUNT Procession all the Lands Between the Sound Side & Yopim Road as far as James BLOUNTs Plantation Eastern Line along the Path out to the main road to Joseph CREESYs Plantation on Said road and make Return thereof to March Court next according to Law

ordered that Thomas WHITE & Charles BENBURY procession all the lands on the Same Side of the road as far as

(263)   **(264)**

yoppim [sic] river and make Return to march Court ne__ according to Law.

ordered that Henderson STANDING and John WILKINS Ju?__ Procession all the Lands on the North Side of the Said yoppim road to pequimons line and make return to March Court nex_

ordered that John PARISH and John BRIN Senr. Procession all ___ Lands that are included between the main road and Sandy Ridge Road up to Indian Town Creek and Make return thereof to March Court next according to Law.

ordered that William ROBERTS & William SIMPSON pr_____ all the Lands that are included Between Sandy Ridge Road and the Pequimon line up to William ASHLEYs thence along the Cart road to Little PARKERs and make return

(263) (Cont.) thereof to march Court next according to Law.

N. B. the orders for Processioners are all made out Pr. A. N.   ordered that John **COFFIELD** & Thomas **PRICE** processi__ all the Lands that are included Between the Main road Perquimons line Machacoma Creek and the Cart ro__ from William **ASHLEY**s to Little **PARKER**s and Make Return To march Court next according to Law

Issd: ordered that William **LISTER** be paid four pounds three Shillings for keeping Mary **JOHNSTON** five months and? that her allowance be Discontinued   136

(264) _____ish __73   **(265)**

Be it remember'd that the Freeholders of St. Pauls Parish met the sheriff at the Court House in Edenton On Monday the 12th. Day of April then & there persuant to an act of Assembly did Elect the following persons to serve as Vestrymen for the ??? three Insuing years Vizt Thos. **BONNER** Senr., James **SUMNER**, Jacob **HUNTER**, Wm. **HINTON**, Pallatiah **WALTON**, Thos. **HUNTER**, Thos. **BENBURY**, Natl **JONES**, Saml.. **JOHNSTON**, John B. **BEASLEY**, David **RICE**, Wm. **BOYD**,.

April 26 1773 At a Vestry met at the Church in Edenton According to Summons and Qualified according to Law, that is to say eight of the twelve, then Chose Aurt **ELBERSEN** Clark for the Insuing year to sd. Vestry at Rate of fifty shillings a year.

Present, Thos. **BONNER**, James **SUMNER**, Jacob **HUNTER** Nathl. **JONES** Wm. **HINTON**, Pallatiah **WALTON**, Thos. **HUNTER** Thos. **BENBURY** then Chose, Thomas **BENBURY** & Nathaniel **JONES** Church Wardens for said Parish.-   -

Ordered that Thos. **BENBURY** Church Warden proceed to finish the inside of the Church in Edenton in a workmanlike manner.

Issd   Ordered that David **DAVIS** be alow'd 5/4 for serving two warrents.

Ordered that Jno. **GREEN** be paid Twenty shillings for Making a Coffin and burying Voss **JACKSON**. - - - -

Issd.   Ordered that Thos. **HUNTER** late Church Warden be paid forty one pound Nine shillings & Seven pence proc. Thos: **BENBURY** Nathl **JONES**

At a Vestry met at the church in Edenton Augt. 28 1773 Present. The Revd. Danl. **EARL**

Thos: **BONNER** Thos. **HUNTER** Wm. **HINTON**} Vestry Men [Written vertically, between columns.] {Palatiah **WALTON** Thos. **BENBURY**---- Natl. **JONES**---- Church Wardens

The said Vestry made choice of Tho **HOSKINS**, Wm. **BOYD** and David **RICE** as Vestry men they Qualified according to Law.

N. B. Not? Executed __for want of Law}   Ordered that a Tax of four shillings & four pence proc be laid on Each Taxable person in this Parish to defray the charges thereof

(265) At a Vestry met at the church in Edenton Augt. 28 1773 [sic] Present

Thos: **BONNER** Thos. **HUNTER** Wm. **HINTON** Thos. **BENBURY** Nathl. **JONES**} Vestry Men [Written vertically, between columns.] {Palatiah **WALTON** Thomas **BENBURY**---- Nathaniel **JONES**---- Church Wardens

The said Vestry made choice of Thomas **HOSKINS**, Wm. **BOYD** and David **RICE**, they Qualified according to Law

Ordered that a Tax of four shillings & 4 pence proc. be laid on Each Taxable person in this Parish to defray the charges thereof

ordered that the poor quit the town if they do not they will not be alow'd any maintanance from the Parish the Underwritten Orders to be paid out of the money Levey'd this prsent year 1773

Order'd that Thos. **ECCLESTON** be alow'd twenty Six pound Seventeen [sic] & Six pence for doing the wood work of the Church agre'd upon to be finished by Next Christmas

Order'd that Thos. **HOSKINS** be alow'd forty seven pounds Six shillings & four pence

Order'd Aurt **ELBERSEN** be alow'd ten pounds

Order'd that Wm. **HOSKINS** be alow'd ten pounds nineteen shillings

Order'd that Thos. **JONES** [sic] three pounds ten shillings

Order'd that Jno. **RUMBOUGH** be alow'd twelve shillings & Six pence

Order'd that Thos. **ECCLESTON** be alow'd ten pounds Sixteen shillings

Order'd that Doctr. **DICKINGSON** be alow'd twelve pounds

Order'd that David **DAVIS** be alow'd forty nine shillings & eight pence

Order'd that Antony **DARLETT** be alow'd two pounds four shillings

Order'd that Elizabh. **GOLDSBURY** be alow'd three pounds three shilling

Order'd that Mary **WALLACE** be alow'd twenty shilling   137

(266) at a Vestry met at the Church in Edenton May 18th 1774 - - - -Present

18 May 1774

(266) (Cont.) [blank] } Vestry Men [Written vertically, between columns.] { [blank]
Be it remember'd that the Freeholders of Saint Pauls Parrish met the sheriff at the Court house in Edenton On [blank] then and there persuent to an act of assembly did Elect the followin [sic] persons to serve as Vestry Men as the Law Directs [End of entry. Remainder of page is blank.]

(267) At a Vestry met at the Church in Edenton May 18 1774 Present the Reverd. Danl. EARL
James SUMNER Jacob HUNTER Wm. BOYD Thos. HUNTER Pelatiah WALTON Thos. BENBURY} Vestry men [Written vertically, between columns.] {David RICE Wm. HINTON Aron HILL Thos. BONNER Senr. Joseph HEWES? William BOYD}Church Wardens{ David RICE
the said Vestry Chose Mr. Joseph HEWES & Mr. Aron HILL in the Room of Mr. Saml. JOHNSTON & Mr. Nathl. JONES they Qualified agreable to law
Order'd that Elizabeth PRIFVIT be alowed for Eight Months keeping Jacob PRIVIT at the Rate of Nine pounds ten shillings per year
Issd. Ordered that Abraham NORFLETT be alow'd thirteen Pounds for serving as Clerk to Chapple & Vestry
Ordered that Jacob HUNTER be alow'd Eight pounds twelve shillings & eight pence proc for Reading at CONSTANs Chapple March 1773 & 1774
Ordered that Aurt ELBERSEN be alowed three pounds three shillings & eight pence proc for serving as Clerk to the Vestry & Element [sic] for the sacrament
Issd. Ordered that Thos. WILLIAMS be alowed Eight pounds for builing [sic] the pillars of the Church out of which twelve shillings to be deducted for bricks he made use of on his own Account
Ordered that Thos. HUNTER be alowed forty poun
Thos. HUNTER agrees to finish the repair & finish the all the [sic] wooden work of the inside of the Church and the Doors in a good decent workmanlike manner to the Satisfaction of the Vestry & find all the Materials for the same for which he is to have Forty Pounds Proc. money the same work to be compleated in three months from this date?   138

(268) the Vestry to Meet the 290 Day of August at ten a Clock

St Pauls Parish 1774{ At a Vestry Held the 20 Day of August at the Church in Edenton according to ajournment
Present Joseph HEWES Thos. BONNER Jacob HUNTER Thos. BENBURY} Vestry Men [Written vertically, between columns.] } Thos. HUNTER Aaron HILL Palatiah WALTON William HINTON William BOYD {Church Wardens} David RICE
The said Vestry made Choice of Samuel JOHNSTON in the Room and place of Thomas HOSKINS
Issd Ordered that Mary WOOLARD [sic] twelve pounds eight for Maintain'g ann BARNS from the eight Day of Aug. 1773 to the 19 of Augst. 1774 @ Twenty shilling per Month
Issd: Ordered that Thos. BENBURY be alow'd twenty pounds Eleven shillings & eight pence half-penny proc that sum apearing Due by account.
Ordered that David DAVIS be alowed Ten shillings and eight pence proc for serving four Warrents on persons likely to become a Parish Charge
Thos. BENBURY laid his Accounts before the Vestry for his Colection of Taxes for the year 1771 and there apears a ballance Due to him of Twenty pounds Eleven shillings and eight pence proc he is therefore finally Discharged
Order'd that Aurt ELBERSEN be alowed ten pounds for Serving as Clerk of the church for the year 1773.

(269) __rish Ordered that [Remainder of line is missing.] do not they Shall not have any alow___ from ____ Parish
Issd.? ___ter plied Thomas ECCLESTON undertook the inside woodwork of the church to finnish in a desent manner by Christmas Day for which he is to Receive twenty Six pounds Seventeen shillings & six pence proc
Issd Ordered that Thos. HOSKINS late church warden be alowed forty seven pounds six shillings and four pence proc for Disburstments to the poor of the Parish
Issd Ordered that Aurt ELBERSEN be alowed ten pounds for being Clerk of the church, the year Expired June 17
Issd Ordered that Wm. HOSKINS be alowed ten pounds nineteen shillings proc for bricks and tile
Ordered that Thos. JONES be alowed three pounds ten shillings for a Suit in the superior court
Ordered that Jno. RUMBOUGH be alowed twelve shillings & Six pence for making a Coffin
Issd Ordered that Thos ECCLESTON be alowed ten pounds sixteen shillings glasing the windows of the Church
The underwriten orders to be paid out of the Tax when levied for the year 1773
Issd Ordered that Doct. Saml. DICKINSON be alowed twelve pounds for Medicine to the Parishaners
Issd Ordered that David DAVIS be alowed forty nine shillings & eight pence

20 August 1774

(269) (Cont.) *Issd* Ordered that Anthony **DARLET** be alowed two pounds four shillings proc for Medecine
Issd. Ordered that Wm. **CRAIG** be alowed forty shillings
Issd. Ordered that Elizth. **GOLDBURY** be alowed three pounds Three shillings
Issd. Ordered that Mary **WALLACE** be alowed one pound
Ordered that **GIBBONS** Constable be alow'd Eighteen shilling & Eight pence for serving Warents Thos: **BENBURY** CW Nat **JONES** CW   139

(270) __Pau__ Parish 1774   (267) [sic]
at a Vestry held at the Church in Edenton May 18th 177_
Present. The Revd. Danl. **EARL**.
James **SUMNER** Jacob **HUNTER** Thomas **HUNTER** Thomas **BENBURY** { Vestry men [Written vertically, between columns.] } Pelatiah **WALTON** William **HINTON** Thomas **BONNER** William **BOYD** & David **RICE** Church Wardens
The above Vestry Chose William **BOYD** and David **RICE** Chu___ Wardens for the insuing year:
the said Vestry Chose Joseph **HEWES** and Aron **HILL** in the Place of Saml. **JOHNSTON** and Nathl. **JONES** they Qualified Agreable to Law
Issd. Ordered that Elizb. **PRIVIT** be alowed for Maintaing [sic] Jacob **PRIVIT** Eight Months at the rate of nine pounds ten shillings per year
Issd. Ordered that Abraham **NORFLETT** be alow'd thirteen pounds for Serving as Clerk to the Vestry, for Orders processiong [sic] of land, and for Serving as Clerk to **FARLEE**s Chapple for two years past
Issd. Ordered that Jacob **HUNTER** be alow'd Eight pounds twelve shillings & 8d. for glazeing 20 lights of windows for Element to Sacrament and for Reading the two last years at **COSTEN**s Chapple
___sd.* Ordered that Aurt **ELBERSEN** be alow'd three pounds three shillin__ and eight pence proc for Element to the sacrament and for serving as Clerk to the Vestry for the year past
Issd. Ordered that Thos. **WILLIAMS** be alowed eight pounds proc for builing [sic] the pillors of the Church from which twelve shillings to be deduc___ for bricks made us off on his Account
Thomas **HUNTER** agrees to finish all the Inside wooden work of of [sic] the Church and the doors in a good decent workmanlike manner to the satisfaction of the Vestry & find all the materials for the Same, for which he is to have forty pounds proc money, the same work to be compleated in three months from this date
the Vestry ajourned till the 20 Day of August next to meet at ten AClock   Wm **BOYD** David **RICE**

(271) *Saint Pauls Parish 1774}*   (268)
At a Vestry Held the twentyeth Day of August one thousand seven hundred & seventy four at the Church in Edenton according to adjournment
Present Joseph **HEWES** Thomas **BONNER** Jacob **HUNTER** Thomas **BENBURY**} Vestry men [Written vertically, between columns.] {Thomas **HUNTER** Aaron **HILL** Palatiah **WALTON** William **HINTON**
William **BOYD** Church Wardens David **RICE**
The above Vestry made Choice of Mr. Samuel **JOHNSTON** in the Room and place of Mr. Thomas **HOSKINS** a__ qualified agreable to a Law in that Case made and provided
Issd. Ordered that Mary **WOOLARD** be alow'd twelve pounds Eight shillings proc for Maintaing Ann **BARNES** from the _____ of August 1773 to the 19 of Augt 1774 at twenty Shillings per? month
Thomas **BENBURY** produced his account to the Vestry __ his collection of Taxes for the year 1771 and there apears _ ballance due to him of twenty pounds Eleven shillings and eight pence proc he is therefore finaly Discharge_
Issd. Order'd that Thomas **BENBURY** be alow'd the above twenty pounds Eleven shillings and eight pence proc
Ordered that David **DAVIS** be alowed ten shillings & eight pence proc for serving four Warrents on persons likely to become a Parish charge
Issd. Ordered that Aurt **ELBERSEN** be alow'd Ten pound for serving as Clerk of the Church June? 17. 1774 for the year 1773
Ordered that a Tax of six shillings and eight pence proclamation money be collected from each & every Taxable person in this Precinct in order to defray the Contingent charges thereof to be Collected at the time when the publick Taxes is received   140

(272) *St: Pauls Parish 1774*   (269)
Ordered that Nathaniel **JONES** be alowed forty two pound Nineteen shillings and two pence proc for Maintaing Butler **HURDLE**s three children, **ARMSWORTH** and others poor of the Parish
Issd. Ordered that Thomas **HUNTER** be alowed forty one pounds for finishing the inside wooden work of the church he having done it to the sattisfaction of the Vestry

20 August 1774

(272) (Cont.) The Parish of Saint Pauls in account with Thom [sic] BENBURY late sheriff, for his Collection of the Parish Taxes due to the said Parish for the year 1771

To proclamation money paid the Vestry as per Receipt on Vestry Book	49..2.._
To money paid Jno. Bapts. BEASLEY as per Order	4..10.._
To money paid Antony DARLETT as per Order	.._..._
To 56 Insolvents alowed by Court at three shilling & four pence	9.._.._
To Commistions on 268£..16s..8d. at eight per cent	21.._.._
To money paid Agness ECCLESTON as pr. Order	10?..16.._
To moneypaid mary WALLACE as pr. Order	1..0.._
	298..15.._

Contra

By Amount of Taxes @ 3/4 on 1669 Taxables Listed for the year 1771	278..3..4
By an Order on the Collector of the Parish Tax	20..11..8
	298..15..0?

    Wm. BOYD David RICE} Church Wardens

(273) _howan County St. Pauls Parish Anno. Dom 1775   270

At a Vestry met at the Church in Edenton May 7 1775

present Thomas BENBURY Thomas BONNER Jacob HUNTER Wm. HINTON Aaron HILL} Vestry men [Written vertically, between columns.] { Pelatiah WALTON Thomas HUNTER Saml. JOHNSTON Wm BOYD David RICE

the above Vestry made choice of Mr. Wm. BOYD and Mr. David RICE late Church Wardens to serve for the insuing year

Order'd that Mr. Wm. BOYD be alowed Thre_ pounds proc for money advanc'd to Thos. WILLIAMS for laying some tile & underpining the Staircase of the church

Order'd that Chas. BONDFIELD be alow'd Thirty ___llings proc for sundry Expences nursing & finding a Coffin for Allen COURT & attendance at the Funeral

Issd. Ordered that Aurt ELBERSEN be alow'd three pound_ ten shillings & Eight pence proc for bread & win_ for the sacrament & for serving as Clark for the Vestry for one year

Ordered that Jacob HUNTER be alowed four pound proc for Reading at COSTENs Chappel for the year one thousand seven Hundred & seventy four

Order'd that John GREEN be alowed five Shillings & four pence for puting up the pulpit of the Church

Ordered that Thomas FULLINTON be alow'd twenty four shilling proc for boarding Martha HARRELL three months at eigh [sic] shillings pr. Month

Issd. Order'd that Thos. TROTMAN be alow'd Six pounds proc as pr. Account   141

(274) _____Pauls Parish A. ? D. 1775   271

Ordered that Moses WARD be alow'd twenty two shilings and ten pence proc for keeping Mary WARD three weeks

Ordered that Moses BLANCHARD be alowed fourteen shillings & eight pence proc for keeping Mary WARD two weeks

Issd Order'd that Rachel WALTON be alowed twenty nine shillings for keeping Mary WARD one Month & twenty three days

Ordered that Joshua COPELAND be alow'd fourteen shillings and four pence proc for keeping Elizabeth PARKS two Months and six days making one shift & heming a hankercf [sic]

Isued? Ordered that James NIGHT be alowed Six pounds proc for keeping a basterd Child of Keziah NIGHTs for one year and finding it Cloaths

Order'd that George WHITE be alow'd Six shilling for two bushels of Corn for Jos. DEAFNALL

_ed Ordered that Zebulon MANSFIELD be alowed fifty Shillings proc for keeping Joseph MANSFIELD four months

Order'd that Wm. JONES be alow'd nine shillings eight pence proc for keeping Elizabeth PARKS one month & twenty three days

Order'd that John HILL be alow'd three pounds eight shillings proc for keeping WAID at the rate of eight shillings pr Month

Issued Order'd that Saml. GREEN be alow'd one pound proc for keeping Mary WARD two Months

Paid? Odered that James HODGES be alowed thirty shillings proc for two pr. of shoes for Moses WELWOOD one pr. for Mary WARD & one pair for Joseph MANSFIELD

Order'd that George WHITE be alow'd thirty shillings proc for Butler HURDLEs Child Six months & finding Cloaths

do Order'd that Thomas HUNTER be alow'd two pounds Nineteen shillings & two pence proc for the Rent of a house for Jesse LASSETER and a Hundred weight of pork & one barrel of Corn

7 May 1775

(274) (Cont.)　　　Order'd that Malkiah **CHAPPLE** be alow'd fourteen shillings for keeping Elizabeth **PARKS** two months
　　　Order'd that David **RICE** be alow'd Eleven pounds ten shillings & Eleven pence proc for Jos. **GRANBURY**'s Account
　　　Order'd that Davd. [sic] **RICE** be alow'd two shillings Six pence proc **WELWOOD** [sic]
　　　Order'd that Demcy **BOND** be alow'd thirteen shillings proc for keeping Elizabeth **BURGES** and small Child two Months & thirteen days
　　　Order'd that Thos. **HUNTER** be alow'd thirteen shillings proc for tending Elizabeth **BURGES** & child thirteen days
Issd.　Order'd that Saml. **GREEN**　　　be alow'd Seven pounds proc for keeping Moses **WELWOOD** one year　David **RICE** Wm **BOND**

(275) *Saint Pauls Parish A. D. 1775*　　　　272
　　　At a Vestry met at [Remainder of this page is illegible, except for the following:]
　　　Ordered that Abraham **NORFLETT** be alow'd four pounds proc for Serving as Clark for? **FARLEE**s Chapel for the ___
　　　Ordered that Luke **SUMNER** be alow'd five pounds one shilling & eight penc_ for keeping the Vestry book for two years Six months & Sixteen days from March 11th 1758 to the year 1760
　　　Ordered that Peter **ONEAL** be alowed fifty shillings proc for Boardin_ & tending John **COPELAND** in his Sickness
　　　Order'd that Thomas **PRICE** be alowed three pounds one shilling proc for boarding a Negro Wench three months at Seventeen shillings per Month & for one blankett
Issd.　Order'd that Sarah **FORD** be alow'd thirty two shillings proc a balla___ due her for boarding Benjn. O?**RINGDELL** 142

(276)　　　　　　　　　273
　　　The Parish of Saint Pauls in Acct with Wm, **BOYD** Church Warden

Date	Description	£	s	d
1774 Februy 15	To 1 Gallon Rum 6/8 to 1 sheet for Jacob **PRIVITT** 8		2 1?	1?
July 3	To 5½ of paint 5/6 to 2 Quarts Oyl 6/8 pd. **COX** 8/	1	_	_
Augt 28	To sending a Cart for Ann **BARNS**		5	
	To Salve Precipitate Purae & Lignum Vita ___ **ORINGTON**?		15	8
	To 3½ yds. Oznabs. for Benjamin **ORINGTON**	_	_	_
Septr.. 21	To proc pd. John **LILES** for Carrying Thurtn. **HAVENS** to a spot?		8	
	to 2½ yds of sheeting & pair shoes for Ann **BARNS**		10	8
Decemr. 8?	To board of Robt. **PETE** 1 month & eighteen Days at 2½?	_	_	_
	To 2 Ounces bark 6/ to 1 puke 1/4 to 2 purges of Rubarb 4?	_	11?	_
	To 1 purge of Rhubarb for Ann **BARNS**		1	_
	To 1 pr. Shoes for Jane **PHILLIPS**		_	8
Novembr 20	To 1 [Remainder of line is illegible.]			
___	To 1 _____ for [Remainder of line is illegible.]			
Februy. 20	To 95 lb of pork @? 5 1 Bushel of Peas for ___	1	_	_
	To 1½ yard of Cottons for Elizabh. **THOMPSON** @ 2	_	_	_
	To 5½ bushels of meal & 50 lb Wt. flowr for Do. for 3 Months	1	8	
	To 2 Gallons of Molasses for Do		6?	8
	To putting Elizabh. **THOMPSON** under a Course of Physick	2	1	0
April 1	To 7 yds of Oznabs. 9/4 to 5 yds plad 11/8 for Jane **PHILLIPS**	1	1	
	To 1 Lock for **FARLEE**s Chapple		6	6
	To keeping Wm. **MILLER** one Month		1	5
Augt.? 19	To a Negro wench to nurse him		6	
	To 30 lb of bread & ten pound of flower for Sarah **SIBISON**		8	
	To 3½ yds of Checks for Wm. **SIBISON**		10	6
	To Coffin & Sheet for Wm. **MILLER**	1	0	0
	To Wm. **LILES** for Carying Wm. **HEWES** to Suffolk		10	
	To Work done by Thos. **WILLIAMS** to the Church		3	
	To proc pd. to Doctr. **CUTLER** 2 Ounces bark for **MILLER**		6	
	To proc pd. Jno. **LILES** for mending the Church gate		1	4
	To money Molasses & Flower for Benjn. **ORINGTON**		8?	
		22:	3	8

(277) _____ At a Vestry met at the Church in Edenton ____ Day of June? 1776?
　　　B_ it rememb___ that _____ of St Pauls [Next line is illegible.] on Monday the 18th? ____ [Most of the remainder of

19 June 1776

(277) (Cont.) this page is illegible, except for the following:] by the ____ And words Solemnly and Sincerely, ____ and engage under the Sanction of Virtue Honor and the Sacred Love of Liberty and Our Country to Maintain &? support all and every the Acts Resolutions & Regulations of the Said Continental & Provincial Congress to the the utmost of our power and Ability. In Testimony whereof we have hereto Set ou_ hands this 19th of June 1776

   Richd. HOSKINS David RICE Aaron HILL Pelatiah WALTON Wm HINTON Hy? BONNER Wm BOYD Tho. BENBURY Jacob HUNTOR John BEASLEY Willm BENNETT William ROBERTS 143

(278) __Pauls Parish 1776 Order'd that Wm HALSEY be appointed Clerk to ___ Vestry at the Rate of Fifty shillings per year
   Order'd that Mr Wm BENNETT and Mr William HINTON be appointed Church Wardens in the ???

issued   Order'd that Capt James COLE be allow'd ___ of One pound _____ Shillings & two pence for Burial Charg__ of the body of James HALSEY?

Issued   Order'd that Capt James COLE be allow'd Four po____ Three Shillings & Four __nce for Acting as Clerk to? ___ Church from the five months past

Issued   Order'd that Capt James COLE be appointed Cler__ sexton of the Church for the ensuing year and he? be Allow'd Ten pounds for the Same.

   Order'd that Mary CHAPPELL be Allow'd Four pounds Eight? Shillings & Eight pence for boarding Elizabeth PARKS
   Order'd that the following persons be Allow'd the Several Sums oposite their names. Vizt

John HILL for board of a boy of Job WARDs 4 months	1.._.._
Issued & Isd James KNIGHT do of a Child of Hezekiah KNIGHTs	4.._..0
Ephraim BLANSHARD do of Eliza BURGESS 5/ Woollen Cloth 9/ and a Coffin for Jesse LASSITOR 10/	1.. 4..-
David WELCH 1 Bushel Corn for Jesse LASSITOR	.. 3..4?
James FREEMAN 1 bushl do for do	.. 3..4
Robert WALTON 2 bushls Potatoes for do	.. 3..4
Palatiah WALTON for 15½ lb Bacon for do	.. 9..1
Hardy MORGAN board of a Child of Moses PHELPS 1 month	10 -
Samuel HARRELL do 2 months of do	..14 -
George OUTLAW do Sarah WALLACE 1 mo & 7 days	1.. 4..8
Hardy MORGAN do of a Child of Moses PHELPS 1 mo.	.. 7
Job PARKER for 3½ yds Linnen for Moses WELLWOOD	..11..8
Mary CHAPPELL Board & Burrying Elizabeth PARKS	2..
Josiah GRANBURY per Acct proved	7.. 4..2
Samuel GREEN board of Moses WELLWOOD 2 yrs & 1 mont_	14..11..8
do 1 bushl Corn for Jesse LASSITOR	.. 3..4
George OUTLAW board of Sarah WALLACE 1 Mo. & 20 days	1.. 6..
Thomas HUNTER for Meal & for Jesse LASSITOR per Acct.	5.. 5 1
do for Rent of a Plantn for do until next new years day	1..10..
Jacob HUNTER for Reading at COSTENs Chapple the yr 1775	4
Abraham NORFLEET do at FARLEE's do do	4
Deme?cy BOND for Board of Eliza BURGESS 1½ months	.. 8..

   By Order of the Vestry
    Will. HALSEY Cler:

(279) __Pauls Parish 1776 At a Vestry met at the Church in Edenton on Wednesday ____ 16th October 1776
   Present { Thomas BENBURY David RICE Palatiah WALTON William BENN_T William BOYD John BEASLEY Richard HOSKINS The Reverend Daniel EARL Coll Thomas BONNER William ROBERTS

   Order'd that Anthony _____ be allow'd four pounds for keeping Benjamin _____ months
   Order'd that Anthony _____ be allow'd twenty Shillings per month for keeping Geo? MOOREs child from the 1st day of July last
   Order'd that [Remainder of line is partially crossed out and illegible.]
____ William BOYD Esqr. produced his Accot against this Parish as Church Warden for the years 1774 & 1775 amounting to Twenty pound [Several words are illegible.] that the Same Allow____ ____ besides?
   Order'd that the Sum of Three Shillings current money be levied upon each and every Taxable person in this Parish to defray the Expence & Charges of the Said Parish for this present year
   Order'd that all Collectors of the Parish Tax be? pres____ __ the next meeting of the Vestry with? an acct. of their collec-

16 October 1776

(279) (Cont.) tion in order to Settle, and that the Clerk Advertise the Same

END OF VESTRY MINUTES

DECEDENT INDEX

A
ALLEYN
George 72, 81
ALPHEN
Robert 206

B
BADHAM
William 78
BEASELEY
James 34
BESSON
Stephen 13
BESTON
Stephen 12
BLACKALL
Abraham 179, 201-203
BLOUNT
John 45
Thomas 13
BROWN
Stephen 157
BROWNRIGG
Richard 257
BULLY
Henry 163

C
CAPES
Wm. 131
CHARLTON
Sarah 252
CLARK
Thomas 101
COAPS
William 115
COOPER
John 223
COURT
Allen 273
CRISP
Nichl. 47
Nicholas 57

D
DICKS
John 14

E
EVERAGE
---- 233
EVERAGE (Cont.)
Peter 236
EVEREDGE
---- 227

F
FAVOUR
Thomas 37
FERRIL
Richard 193
FLETCHER
Francis 65
FULKS
Jas. 184

G
GARDNER
Matthew 247
GEELSTONE
Mary 192
GENT
Mary 32
GOODIN
James 237, 240
GOODING
James 231, 232, 235
GOODWIN
---- 249
James 248
GOREHAM
Alexander 49
GULLIVER
F. 63

H
HACKET
Jos. 159
HALL
Clement 203, 204, 206, 212
Elizabeth 247, 250
HALSEY
James 278
HANNAH
Elizabeth 162
HARE
Eliza. 87
HART
Eliza. 87
HAVIT
Mary 185
HOSKINS
HOSKINS (Cont.)
Thomas 246, 250, 251, 256
Thos. 255
HUNTER
Isaac 191

I
None

J
JACKSON
Voss 264
JOANES
---- 91
JONES
Frederick 36
Wm. 37

K
KERBY
William 253
KIRKHAM
Ealinor 15
Elenor 14

L
LASSITOR
Jesse 278
LEWIS
William 235
LONG
Martha 150
Mathew 185

M
MACKEIL
Anthony 63
MARCUS
John 123
"Mrs." 126
MILLER
Wm. 276

N
NASH
Thomas 245
NEGROES
DUBLIN 198
NEWNAM
NEWNAM (Cont.)
---- 40, 41

O
ORINDELL
Mary 257

P
PARKER
Jean 172
Peter 200
PARKS
Elizabeth 278
PAYNE
Peter 169, 172, 179, 206
PEARCE
Isbell 201
Thomas 201
PERVINE
Rachel 150
PETER
Ann 55, 56
PETERSON
Thos. 28
PHILPS
James 161, 162
PORIGREEN
Francis 47
PRESTON
Stephen 9
PURVINE
Rachel 157, 158

Q
None

R
REED
Mary 73
REMINGTON
Ralph 190
RUSSEL
Margaret 254

S
SADLER
Wm. 49
SCOTT
Margaret 53
SKINNER
William 141
SMITH
David 68
SPIGHT
Mary 123
STRATTON
Thomas 223
STREATOR
Edward 254
Thomas 251, 254

T
TENDALL
Robert 23
TROTTER
---- 198
James 173, 179, 212

U
None

V
VANN
Mary 87

W
WALKER
Henderson 9
John 24
WALLACE
---- 26
WALTON
Timothy 253
William 257
WESTON
---- 91
WICKS
---- 88
WILLIAMS
---- 103
Danl. 79
William 62
WILSON
Robert 6
WOOD
Thomas 156
WRIGHT
Thomas 14

END

FEMALE GIVEN NAME INDEX

Agness ECCLESTON 272
Ann BARNES 271
Ann BARNS 268,276
Ann DILDE
Ann HUBBORD 243
Ann JONES 107
Ann MACKGUIRE 188
Ann MC GUIRE 212,214
Ann PETER 55,56
Anne HILL 60
Anne MANN 133,139

C. NUTEN 79
Cath. DENEVAN 50
Catharine DENEVAN 50
Ch. NEWTON 74
Chrisn. NUTEN 79
Christian NEWTON 65,66,116
Christian NUTEN 95,135
Christian NUTON 87,109,127
Christian WARD 193,214

Dinah SIMPSON 140
Dorothy MEARNS 135

E. HOSKINS 255
E. POWERS 79
Ealinor KIRCKUM 15
Elenor ADAMS 7
Elenor KIRKHAM 14
Elinor ADAMS 7
Elisa. HARRIS 35
Elisabeth HARRIS 37
Elisabeth MUNS 34,35
Elisabeth POWERS 70
Eliz. DANIELS 74
Eliz. JINN 74
Eliz. POWERS 66,79
Eliz. REED 74
Eliza BURGESS 278
Eliza. HARE 87
Eliza. HART 87
Eliza. PARKER 129
Eliza. POWERS 73
Eliza. SUMNER 129
Eliza. THOMPSON 87,91
Eliza. TOMPSON 86,95
Eliza. TUCKER 129
Elizabeth BURGES 274
Elizabeth FORD 172
Elizabeth HALL 238,247,250
Elizabeth HANMER 113
Elizabeth HANNAH 162
Elizabeth HAYS 250
Elizabeth HENTON 212
Elizabeth HINTON 172,192,203,206,230
Elizabeth HODGES 256
Elizabeth HOSKINS 246,250,256
Elizabeth JONES 107
Elizabeth KNIGHT 258
Elizabeth LACITER 253
Elizabeth LILES 245
Elizabeth MIDDLETON 185
Elizabeth MUNS 32,35
Elizabeth PARKER 233,234,242,243,246,247,250,254
Elizabeth PARKS 274,278
Elizabeth POWERS 72
Elizabeth PRIFVIT 267
Elizabeth RICE 246
Elizabeth THOMPSON 100
Elizabeth TOMPSON 107
Elizabeth TOMSON 110
Elizabeth TOM___ 89
Elizabh. GOLDSBURY 265
Elizabh. THOMPSON 276
Elizath. THOMPSON 86
Elizb. PRIVIT 270
Elizth. GOLDBURY 269
Eliz____ LILES 253

Frances THOMPSON 100
Francis FLETCHER 65
Francis PORIGREEN 47
Frans. FLETCHER 79

Hanah WALTON 79
Hanh WALTON 79
Hannah CLAY 172
Hannah WALTON 73

Isbell PEARCE 201

Jane JOHNSTON 252
Jane PARKER 185,186
Jane PHILLIPS 276
Jane TAYLOR 50
Jean EVINS 131
Jean PARKER 159,165,172
Joanah CLASA 247
Joyce BRADDY 88
Judith ____ 50
Judith MAINER 234,239,252,255
Judith SHIVE 155
Judith SLADE 50,59,60

Katherine HAYS 250,256,258
Keziah KNIGHT 258
Keziah NIGHT 274

Lydia EVERADGE 236

Margaret NOWELL 116
Margaret RUSSEL 254
Margaret SCOTT 53
Marget LEE 59
Marget RODGERSON 95
Margett RODGERSON 94,96
Margreat ASHLEY 155
Margret NOEL 127
Margret NOWAL 134
Margrett RODGERSON 87,89,92
Margt. NOEL 131
Margt. NOELL 131
Margt. ROGERS 123
Martha (MOONEY) BADHAM 78
Martha CLENNY 207
Martha HARRELL 273
Martha LONG 150
Martha MOONEY 78
Mary ANDREW 123
Mary BACCO 206
Mary BLOUNT 14,16
Mary BRADDY 88
Mary BRODY 74
Mary BUTLER 79
Mary CHAPPELL 278
Mary DAILY 107
Mary FLOYD 230,247
Mary FLOYED 216
Mary FORDICE 139
Mary FREEMAN 87,88,89
Mary GEELSTONE 192
Mary GENT 32,35
Mary GRIFFIN 155
Mary HAVIT 93,108,
Mary HAVIT (Cont.) 137,139,141,185
Mary HAYS 250
Mary HOLMS 170,180
Mary JOHNSON 48,49
Mary JOHNSTON 254-256,259,260,263
Mary JONES 60,172
Mary MACGUIRE 182
Mary ORINDELL 257
Mary PHILPS 160
Mary PRESSLY 230
Mary QUARELESS 148,150
Mary QUARLES 163,185
Mary QUIN 228
Mary REED 73
Mary RUTTER 187
Mary SMITH 228
Mary SPIGHT 123
Mary STACY 66
Mary STONE 59
Mary TALBOT 106
Mary TANNER 49
Mary TREVATHAN 180
Mary VANN 87
Mary WALLACE 265,269,272
Mary WARD 274
Mary WILLIAMS 101,123
Mary WOODWARD 242,246
Mary WOOLARD 268,271
Mildred BENTON 180
Mrs. BLOUNT 19
Mrs. BUTLER 72
Mrs. DENHAM 131
Mrs. GREGORY 117,131
Mrs. HAVIT 126,140,144
Mrs. LLOYD 50
Mrs. MARCUS 126
Mrs. PARKER 163
Mrs. PERRY 103,

Mrs. PERRY (Cont.) 113,123
Mrs. PERVINE 126, 144
Mrs. PETTYJOHN 257
Mrs. RICHARDS 100
Mrs. RUSTON 49
Mrs. SHERVIN 134
Mrs. SHERWIN 131
Mrs. THOMPSON 76,103,113,117, 126
Mrs. THOMSON 126
Mrs. WILLIAMS 62,

Nell OSHLEY 139

Olive MORGAN 74

Penelope BLACK-ALL 202
Penelope LITTLE 81
Phillis BROWN 163
Phillis DICKS 14
Precilia PERRY 100
Precilla PERRY 91, 95

R. PERVINE 131
R. PURVINE 123
Rachael PURVINE 117
Rachel ---- 134,135, 139,140,144
Rachel DOL-DRIGDE 59
Rachel DOLDRIGE 59
Rachel PERVINE 113,114,131,134, 135,150,185
Rachel PETERS 135
Rachel PURVINE 107,123,134,137, 157,158
Rachel WALTON 274
Rachell DOLDRIGE 59
Rachell PERVINE 95,96
Rachl. PERVINEY 100
Rachl. PERVINE 131,185
Rebecca HILL 60

Sarah CHARLTON 252
Sarah DEER 137
Sarah FORD 275
Sarah GILLAM 5,6
Sarah HARLOE 126
Sarah HOSKINS 251
Sarah HUNTER 172, 230
Sarah LACEY 94
Sarah MARKS 98, 100
Sarah MARKUS 107
Sarah RHITTER 219
Sarah RONDENG 87
Sarah RUTTER 170, 186,187,212,214,230
Sarah SIBISON 276
Sarah SIMPSON 39
Sarah WALLACE 278
Sarah WATSON 256
Serah RUTTER 159
Susana TROTMAN 227
Susanna AMBROSE 139

Tabitha FREEMAN 249

Widow ASHLEY 226
Widow COPELAND 42,50-52
Widow CULLEY 151
Widow DICKS 19
Widow MUNS 37
Widow PETERSON 28
Widow SCOT 225, 261,262
Widow SKINNER 144
Widow WILLIAMS 66
---- RUTTER 180
---- WILLIAMS 103

INDEX

A

AAKELL (*See also ARKEEL*)
Willim. 85
ADAMS
---- 9,126
Elenor 7
Elinor 7
Pet. 106
Peter 97,98,100, 102-107
ALDRIDGE
Eben. 27
Ebenr. 27
ALLEN
Geo. 49
ALLEY
G. 71
ALLEYN
Geo. 67,68,70,71
George 67-69,72, 81
ALLSTON
----129
ALPHEN
Robert 195,197, 200,206
Robt. 180,188,190, 196,197
Solomon 206
ALPHIN
Jo. 189
Joseph 171
Robert 171
Robt. 172,180,196
Rob___ 171
ALSTON (*See also ALSTONE, AULSTON, AULSTONE, AWLSTON*)
---- 129,130,131,134, 135,140
Jno. 128,194
John 84,86-88,123, 125,127,128,130,131, 134,135
ALSTONE
John 88,89
AMBROSE
Susanna 139
AMBROSS

AMBROSS (Cont.)
David 39
ANDERSON
---- 131,134,136, 139,141,147
J. 81
Jos. 75,80,82,84
Joseph 76,77,103, 132,133,138,142,143
ANDREW
Mary 123
ARDERN
John 9-11,13-15, 17-19
ARKEEL (*See also AAKELL*)
William 89
ARKEELE
William 88
ARKEIL
Willm. 85
ARKILL
William 103,132, 133,136,138
Willm. 84,86,119, 132
Wm. 59
ARLINE
John 57,74,79,175
ARMSWORTH
---- 272
ARNELL
Edward 176
ASHLEY
---- 226
Margreat 155
William 226,263
ASTIE
John 156,165
AULSTON (*See also ALSTON, ALSTONE*)
John 86
AULSTONE
John 85
AWLSTON
John 85

B

B.
H. 184
BACCO
Mary 206
BACCUS

BACCUS (Cont.)
Thomas 226
BADHAM
---- 48,66
Martha (MOONEY) 78
W. 81
William 40,48,49, 78
Willm. 78
Wm. 42-48,54-56
BAILEY
---- 45
BAKER
Hen. 87
Henry 67,75,80,83, 85,86,111,175,186
BALLARD
---- 43,62,63,69,87, 104
Jno. 66
BANBARY (*See also BENBERRY, BENBURY*)
John 98
BANBURY
Jno. 107
John 97,100-103, 108,110,111
Will 97
William 1-3,5,12, 15,17,101,102
Willm. 103,108
Wm. 6-11,13,18, 98,100,101,103,107
BARKER
Thomas 152,153, 155,156,171,206
BARNES
Ann 271
Joseph 140
BARNS
Ann 268,276
BATTLE
Will 84
BEASELEY (*See also BEEZLEY, BESLEY, BEZLEY*)
James 12,31,34
BEASLEY
---- 31
James 12,29,30,32
Jno. Bap. 251
Jno. Bapts. 272
John 277,279

BEASLEY (Cont.)
John B. 264
John Bap. 257,258
John Bapt. 253-255
Robert 158,162, 165,178,185
Robt. 158,186,191
BEASLY
John Bap. 250,252
John Baptist 248, 252
BEAZLEY
James 32
Robert 186
BEA____
James 27
BEEZLEY
Robt. 158
BENBERRY
Jno. 194
BENBERY
Jno. 194
BENBUARY
John 90
BENBURRY
John 120,125
Wm. 131
BENBURY (*See also BANBARY, BANBURY*)
Charles 262
J. 116,118,121,122, 125,131,136,138
Jno. 122,127,128, 144,161,165,184
John 97,104-107, 115,116,118-121,124, 127,128,131-134,136, 137-140,144,160,161, 163,169,171,172,185, 186,221,236,237,240, 244,245
Samuel 228
Tho. 277
Thom. 272
Thomas 260,264, 265,270,271,273,279
Thos. 264,265,267, 268,269
William 97,104, 105,107
Willm. 135,140
Wm. 108,131,134
_ohn 178
BENNET

BENNET (Cont.)
---- 26,43,104,112, 174,176,177,191,224, 225,261
BENNETT
---- 176
Willm. 277
Wm. 278
BENN_T
William 279
BENTEN
Jethro 216
BENTON
Iaac 180
Isaac 261
Jethro 166-168, 171,173-175,178,179, 183,187,189,195,199, 200,202,203,205,209, 210,212,215,217,221, 222,238,250
Mildred 180
Moses 180
BESLEY (*See also BEASLEY*)
Robert 161,162, 164
Robt. 165
BESSON (*See also BESTON, PRESTON*)
Stephen 13
BESTON
Stephen 12
BETTERLY
Thos. 50
BEVERIDGE
---- 26
BEZLEY
Robert 152,153, 155,156
Robt. 152
BIRD
Jno. 20,21
John 20-24
BIRTHS
---- 78,106,107,135
BLACK
John 247
BLACKALE
Abra. 87
BLACKALL
---- 113,116,131
A. 81-83
Abra. 87,117

BLACKALL (Cont.)
  Abraham 75,76,82, 84,86,87,179,201-203
  Abram. 75
  Penelope 202
BLACKHAL
  ---- 66
  A. 80
BLACKHALL
  ---- 79,190
  Abr. 86
  Abraham 77,85
BLACKNAL
  Jno. 44
  John 44
BLACKNALL
  ---- 51
BLAIR
  Jno. 9
  John 8,9
BLANCHARD
  ---- 225,261
  Aaron 43
  Moses 274
BLANSHARD
  Aaron 176,224
  Benjamin 176
  Ephraim 123,278
BLOUNT
  ---- 19
  Charles 141,173
  J. 113
  James 226,262
  Jno. 29,36,37,42
  John 1,3,7-13, 15-18,30,32,38,41,45, 84-86,97-100,103, 105,106,108,113,132, 133,135,136
  Jos. 122,148,150, 185,228
  Joseph 120,121, 127,132,142-144, 152,153,155,156, 186,191,234,236,238, 239,240,243,245
  Mary 14,16
  Thomas 1-7,11,13
BLUNT
  Jno. 86
  John 86-88,90,92, 93
BOND
  Demcy 274
  Demecy 278

BOND (Cont.)
  James 195,198,204, 206,213,214,221,227, 228,229,231,232,234, 235,237,238
  R. 189
  Richard 90,93-96, 101,102,104,110-112, 115,119,120,122-125, 127,128,166-168,171, 173-175,178,179,181, 182,183,187,189,193, 195,199,200-202,205, 207-209,211,213
  Richd. 91,94-96,98, 115,116,118,134,190
  Ric____ 195
  William 155,177, 221-224,227,228,229, 231-234,262
  Wm. 228,274
BONDFIELD
  Chas. 273
BONNER
  ---- 39,50,51,66,69, 71
  H. 81
  Hen. 56,60
  Henery 152,153, 155
  Henr. 83,85,142, 150
  Henry 10,28-30,32, 34-37,39-46,48, 52-57,61,62,65, 67-73,75-78,81-84, 104,117,120,121,142, 143,148,152-156,158, 159-162,164, 166-168,183-186, 188,210
  Henry, Jr. 75
  Hy. 221,277
  John 132,133,136
  Thomas 152,158, 159,161,162,164,177, 245,249,253,258,259, 260,270,271,273,279
  Thomas, Sr. 226
  Thos. 152,253, 264,265,268
  Thos., Sr. 264,267
  W. 150
  William 158,159, 161,162,164

BONNER (Cont.)
  Willm. 142,148
  Wm. 142,143
BONNE_
  H. 160
BOOTH
  Richard 9,12,13,23
  Richd. 19
BOWDEN
  Everard 50
BOWEN
  Benjamin 246
BOYCE
  William 153
BOYD
  ---- 66,76
  John 78
  W. 221
  William 155,156, 177,257-260,267,268, 270,271,279
  Wm. 264,265,267, 270,272,273,276,277
BRADDEY
  James 94
BRADDY
  James 175
  Joyce 88
  Mary 88
BRANCH
  ---- 37
  Francis 43
  William 35,58
  Wm. 59
BRAY
  ---- 26
  Thomas 31
BRETHELL
  William 6,7
BRICE
  Gideon 248,250
  Gidion 247
BRIGHT
  Gideon 255
BRIN
  John, Sr. 263
BRINKLY
  Joseph 261
BRODY
  Josiah 74
  Mary 74
BROWN
  Francis 192,196, 203,230
  Phillis 163

BROWN (Cont.)
  Stephen 157
BROWNRIGG
  Richard 236,237, 240,242,245,246,248, 250,251,257
  Richd. 221
BRYAN
  Mathew 35
  Matthew 37
BULLY
  Henry 163
BUNCH
  Shadrach 238
BURGES
  Elizabeth 274
BURGESS
  Eliza 278
BURKET
  Thomas 207
BURNS
  Peter 256
BUSH
  William 4
BUTLAR
  Christopher 162
BUTLER ---- 72
  Christopher 162
  J. 109,110
  Jacob 84-86,88-91, 93-95,97-108,114
  Mary 79
BUTTLER
  ---- 113
  Christ. 2
  Christopher 2,5
  Jacob 101,108, 109,113
BUT___
  Jacob 93
B_AN____
  Aaron 261

C

CALLEWAY
  Caleb 79
CAMPBELL
  ---- 163,186,190
  John 113,171
  Thomas 189
CAPES (See also **COAPS**)
  Wm. 131
CHAMPEN

CHAMPEN (Cont.)
  Jno. 74
  John 72,74
CHAMPIN
  John 79
CHAMPION
  ---- 126
  Edward 104
  Jno. 50
  John 38,56,63,104
  Jos. 126
  Olando 108
  Orland 97
  Orlando 97,100, 101,103-109,113
  Orlend 103
  Orlendo 97,103
CHAPPELL
  Mary 278
CHAPPLE
  Malkiah 274
CHARLETON
  William 45
  Wm. 18
CHARLTON
  Job 131,158,159, 161,162,164
  John 39,43,223
  Sarah 252
  William 17
  William, Jr. 39
  Wm. 13,15
  Wm., Sr. 56
CHEVIN
  Nathaniel 1,3,12,16
  Nathl. 2,5,6-13
CHRISP (See also **CRISP**)
  Nicholas 45
CITTERN
  ---- 50
CLARK
  Thomas 101
CLASA
  Joanah 247
CLAXTON
  ---- 58,59
CLAY
  Hannah 172
  Henry 137,139
CLENNEY
  Martha 207
CLERK OF COURT
  JONES
  Thos. 190

COAPS (*See also CAPES*)
William 115
COCKBURN
Adam 40-42
COFFIELD
John 263
COLE
---- 112,175,176
James 250,253,259,278
COLLINS
John 43
CONSTABLES
 GIBBONS
 ---- 269
 HARRILL
 William 180
 JONES
 James 187
CONSTAN (*See also COSTEN*)
---- 170,267
CONSTANT
---- 115,120,124,130,150,158,162,167,168,169,171,174,175,178,179,181-183,187,189,190,192,193,195,196,199,200,201,202,203,205,207-211,213,229,242
James 111
CONSTAN_
---- 173,181
CONSTA__
---- 173
CONS____
---- 195
COOPER
Fleete 92,96
John 223
COPELAND (*See also COUPLAND*)
---- 38,42,50-52
John 275
Joshua 274
Josiah 262
William 40
CORBIN
Frances 155
Francis 152,153,155,156,158,162,163,201
CORBINE

CORBINE (Cont.)
Francis 144,153
CORRIE
Archd. 239
COSTAN
James 94
COSTANT
---- 180,198
COSTEN (*See also CONSTANT*)
---- 170,219,234,246,247,252,254,255,258,270,273,278
COTTON
---- 175
COUPLAND (*See also COPELAND*)
William 177,225
COURT
Allen 273
COX
---- 276
CRAIG
Wm. 269
CRAVEN
---- 113,163
James 97-104,106-108,110-112,115,120-122,125,144,152,153,155
Jas. 116
CREESY
Joseph 262
CRISP (*See also CHRISP*)
---- 2,13,14,51
Nich. 14,28
Nichl. 11,13,18,29,31,37,40,41,43-47
Nicholas 2-10,14-17,19,23,30,32,34,57
Nich____ 10
Nickolas 1
CULL
William 60
CULLENS
Nathan 249
CULLEY
---- 151
CURTON
Richard 3
CUTLER
---- 276

D

DAILY
Mary 107
Thomas 107
DANIEL
William 112,176
DANIELS
Eliz. 74
DARLET
Anthony 269
DARLETT
Antony 265,272
DAVIS
---- 163
David 264,265,268,269,271
DAY
Wm. 49
DEAFNALL
Jos. 274
DEAL
Joshua 249
DEAR
---- 163
Jos. 131
Joseph 165
DEATHS
---- 78
DEER
Joseph 134,135
Sarah 137
DENEVAN
Cath. 50
Catharine 50
DENHAM
---- 131
DICKENSON
---- 258,260
DICKINGSON
---- 265
DICKINSON
Saml. 269
DICKS
---- 19
John 11,14
Phillis 14
DICKSON (*See also DIXON*)
John 102
DIKSON
William 164
DILDE
Ann 155
DIXON

DIXON (Cont.)
William 184
Wm. 184
DOLDRIGDE
Rachel 59
DOLDRIGE
Rachel 59
Rachell 59
DRAUGHON
Walter 82
DROUGHEN
Walter 81
DRUMMOND
---- 43
DUCKENFIELD
---- 14
William 1,2,5,6,8,13,15,17,20-22,24
Wm. 5,7-11,13,21,27,29
DURDEN
John 261

E

EACHARD
---- 26
EARL
---- 218,219,222,235-238,240,242,244,246,250,253,256,258,259
D. 239
Dan. 187,204
Daniel 187,202,204,214,219,222,223,228,229,231-234,239,251,253,256,257,260,279
Danl. 264,267,270
Da____ 208
EARLE
Daniel 208
EARLEY
William 5
EARLY
William 2,4
EASON
Abner 77,210,221,228,229,233,257
ECCLESTON
Agness 272
Thomas 246,269
Thos. 265,269
ECLESTON

ECLESTON (Cont.)
Thos. 78
EDEN
Charles 28,29
EGGORTON
James 94
ELBERSEN
Aurt 265,267-271,273
ELBERSON
Aurt 264
EURE (*See YOURE*)
EVANS (*See also EVINS*)
John 248
EVENS
Thomas 123
EVERADGE
Lydia 236
EVERAGE
---- 233
Peter 236
EVERARD
---- 50
Richard 43,48
Richd. 44-48
EVEREDGE
---- 227
EVINS (*See also EVANS*)
Jean 131
Thos. 109
EXPEDITION
Ohio, to 164,168

F

FARLAW
James 115
Jas. 116
FARLEE
---- 154,157,158,162,167,169,171,182,189,200,202,204,211,229,230,234,240,244,246-248,251,254,258,270,275,276,278
James 104,110-113,118,119,127,133
FARLOW
---- 38
James 29-32,34-37,39,40,116,118,130
Jas. 116
Jno. 31

FARLOW (Cont.)
  John 39
FAVOUR
  Thomas 37
FELTON
  Richard, Sr. 176
FERRIL
  Nicholas 206
FERRILL
  Nicholas 181
  Richard 193
FINES
  ---- 39,49,60,64,74,
  129,131,133,139,155,
  172,180,197,206
FLENCER
  John 59
FLETCHER
  Francis 65
  Frans. 79
FLOOD
  James 103
FLOYD
  Mary 230,247
FLOYED
  Mary 216
FLURY
  William 250
FOARD
  John 88,89
FORD
  Elizabeth 172
  John 185
  Sarah 275
FORDICE
  Mary 139
FORSTER
  Robt. 75,76,82
FOUNTAIN
  ---- 52
FREEMAN
  James 261,278
  Jno. 74,142,143,
  148,150
  John 63,133,142,
  152,157,158,163
  Mary 87-89
  Richard 177
  Tabitha 249
  Thomas 161
  Thoms. 159
  Thos. 162,184
  William, Jr. 225
  Willm 142,144,148
  Wm. 96,123,143,

FREEMAN (Cont.)
  Wm. (Cont.) 152
FRYER
  William 183
FULERT__
  Robt. 95
FULKS
  Jas. 184
FULLERTON
  Robert 109,116,
  135
  Robt. 87
FULLINGTON
  Robert 127
  Robt. 79
FULLINTON
  Robert 134
  Thomas 273

G

G.
  J. 259
GALE
  ---- 39,50,51,58,60,
  66,190
  Christopher 36,39,
  40,43,44,61,68
  Christor. 60
  Christr. 40,44-48,
  54-56
  Chrr. 39,47,52,53,
  55
  E. 81
  Ed. 59
  Edmd. 47,54,56,57,
  62,76,77,82,84,86
  Edmond 47,52-56,
  87
  Edmund 57,59-61,
  75,77,81,82
  Emd. 56
  Miles 141,155,156,
  169,171,172,180,190
GARDNER
  Matthew 247
GARRET
  ---- 47
  Everard 200,209,
  210,212,213,215
  Thomas 13,15,16,
  18,19,40,41,43
  Thomas, Jr. 31,32,
  40
  Thomas, Sr. 31,32,

GARRET (Cont.)
  Thomas, Sr. (Cont.)
  40
  Thos. 39,41,42,46
  Thos., Jr. 34,36-38
  Thos., Sr. 34,36,37
GARRETT
  Thos. 89,92,94,95
GARROT
  Blount 227
  Everard 229
  Thomas 247
GARZIA
  ---- 76,79
GEELSTONE
  Mary 192
GENT
  Mary 32,35
GERRARD
  ---- 12
  H. 11
  Henry 10,11
GHEAL
  ---- 134
GIBBONS
  ---- 269
GILLAM
  Sarah 5,6
  Thomas 1-4
GOLDBURY
  Elizth. 269
GOLDSBURY
  Elizabh. 265
GOLEY
  Arthur 134
GOODIN (*See also*
  GOODWIN)
  Edward 237
  James 237,240
  John 240,248,251
GOODING
  James 231,232,235
  Jams. 123
  John 243
GOODMAN
  Henry 112
GOODWIN
  ---- 249
  James 96,248
  John 214,248
GORDEN
  John 216,217,222,
  227
GORDON
  ---- 19,26

GORDON (Cont.)
  James 154
  Jno. 129
  John 169,171,173,
  174,175,178,181-183,
  187-189,193,195,196,
  199-203,205,
  207-213,215
  William 15,17,18
  Wm. 15,17
GOREHAM
  Alexander 49
GOURLEY
  Arthur 96
GRANBERY
  Josiah 166-168,
  171,173,175,178,179,
  181-183,187-190,
  193-196,199-203,
  205-211,213,215,216,
  222,223
GRANBE__
  Josiah 215
GRANBURY
  Jos. 274
  Josiah 278
GRANDIN
  ---- 111
  Daniel 111,120,134
GRANVILE
  ---- 61,66
GREEN
  Jno. 253,264
  John 253,273
  Saml. 274
  Samuel 246,253,
  259,278
GREGORY
  ---- 117,131
  John 246,250,256
GRIFFIN
  ---- 19
  Charles 17
  Mary 155
GRIGORY
  Thomas 261
GULLIVER
  F. 63
GUMBS
  Matthew 129

H

HACKET (*See also*
  HECKET)

HACKET (Cont.)
  Jos. 159,185
  Joseph 185
  Josh. 159
HACKETT
  Joseph 152
HAIR (*See also*
  HARE)
  Edward 104
  Edward, Jr. 175
  Edwd. 86,87,93,94
  Moses 162
HAIRE
  Edward 95
HALL
  ---- 121,128,139,
  153,158,163,180,182,
  191
  Clem. 173
  Clement 115,120,
  130,136,137,141,156,
  167,168,173,181,185,
  186-188,190,
  192-194,198,203,204,
  206,212,214
  Clemt. 136,142
  Clt. 151
  Elizabeth 238,247,
  250
  ____t 174
HALLSEY
  John 97,98,100-103
HALSEY (*See also*
  HOLSEY)
  ---- 131,139,151,
  163,173
  J. 121-131,136,
  138,172
  James 278
  Jno. 154,194
  John 104-112,115,
  116,118-122,125,127,
  131-133,135-137,
  139,144,148-150,154,
  160,161,169,172,180,
  185,186
  Miles 173
  Will. 278
  William 217,218,
  229,230,233,237
  Willm. 135
  Wm. 239,278
  _ohn 109
HALSY
  John 138

HANMER
Elizabeth 113
HANNAH
Elizabeth 162
HARDY
---- 29,257
John 23,27,28
HARE (*See also HAIR*)
Edward 85,89,92
Edwd. 84,85,90-92
Eliza. 87
HARLOE
Sarah 126
HARLOW
John 39
HARREL
Abraham 261
Isaac 224
HARRELL
---- 249
Martha 273
Samuel 278
HARRIL
Jethro 175
HARRILL
Samuel 176
William 180
HARRIS
---- 173
Elisa. 35
Elisabeth 37
HARRISS
George 173
HARRON (*See also HERRON*)
---- 139,151
Jos. 139,140
HART
Eliza 87
HAUCOT (*See also HOCOTT, HOWCOT*)
Ed. 59,60
Edwd. 59
HAUGHTON (*See also HOUGHTON*)
Wm. 43
HAVENS
Thurtn. 276
HAVIT
---- 126,140,144
Mary 93,108,137, 139,141,185
HAYS

HAYS (Cont.)
Elizabeth 250
Katherine 250,256, 258
Mary 250
HECKET (*See also HACKET*)
Jos. 159
Joseph 153,159
HENDERSON
---- 139
David 10,24,28
HENTER (*See also HUNTER*)
Robet. 85
HENTON (*See also HINTON*)
Elizabeth 212
HERRON (*See also HARRON*)
---- 148
Joseph 147,169, 171,172,179,185,206
HEWES
Joseph 267,268, 270,271
Wm. 276
HEWS
Elijah 49
Willm. 87
HE____
Joseph 202
HICKS
---- 54
Robert 31,35,38,39
Robt. 32,39,48, 50-52
HILL
Aaron 268,271, 273,277
Abraham 60,62, 216,217
Anne 60
Aron 267,270
Guy 177
Isac 123,172
John 274,278
Micajah 225
Moses 123
Rebecca 60
HINTON (*See also HENTON*)
---- 62,63,66,70
Elizabeth 172,192, 203,206,230

HINTON (Cont.)
Jonas 225
W. 78
Will 73
William 61,67,69, 72-74,221,223,224, 227,232-236,242, 244-248,250, 252-254,257,260,261, 268,270,271,278
Willm. 65,70
Wilm. 57
Wm. 60,65,67,264, 265,267,273,277
HOBBS
Abraham 49
Thomas 46
HOBBY
_ta_am 59
HOBS
John 227
HOCOTT (*See also HAUCOT, HOWCOT*)
Nathaniel 107,109, 177
HODGES
Elizabeth 256
James 274
HODGSON
J. 75,81-84
Jno. 84
John 76,77,103
HODSON
T. 251
HOFF
Richard 247
HOFLER
Hance 221-223, 226-234
HOLMES (*See also HOMES*)
James 190
HOLMS
James 180
Mary 170,180
HOLSEY (*See also HALSEY*)
William 43
HOMES
James 170,188,197
HORSKINS (*See also HOSKINS*)
William 173,178, 180,184-186,191

HORSKINS (Cont.)
Willm. 149-151
Wm. 184,185
HOSKIN
Thomas 253
Thos. 259
HOSKINGS
William 161
HOSKINS
---- 43,113,142, 154,257
E. 255
Elizabeth 246,250, 256
John 114
Richard 226,279
Richd. 277
Sarah 251
Tho. 264
Thomas 105,113, 226,245,246,248,250, 251,252,254,256-260, 262,265,268,271
Thos. 254-259,265, 269
W. 142,194
William 97,98, 101-104,106,110,111, 113,114,120,125,126, 147,148,158-161,163, 164,177,226
Willm. 106,107, 122,135,143,152,162
Wm. 98,100,101, 104,108-110,112,113 115,116,120,121,126, 142,148,150,151,159, 161,164,265,269
HOSK___
Wm. 126
HOUGHTON (*See also HAUGHTON*)
Richd. 131
Wm. 111,113
HOWARD
---- 131
HOWCOT (*See also HAUCOT, HOCOTT*)
Edwd. 65
HOWCOTT
E. 74
Edward 39
Nathaniel 158
Nethaniel 161
HOWKOT

HOWKOT (Cont.)
Nethaniel 159,162, 164
HOWKOTT
Nathaniel 158
HUBBORD
Ann 243
HUNTER (*See also HENTOR, HUNTOR*)
---- 76,82,130,219
Daniel 173
Elisha 166-168, 171,173-178, 181-184,186,187,189, 191-193,196, 199-203,207-217, 219,221-225, 227-230,232-234, 236,244-248,250,252, 253,256-262
Isaac 61,62,65,67, 70,72,78,80,82-86, 105,110-112,114-122, 125,127-129,132,134, 136,138,142,143,148, 150,151,162,191
Isac 129
Jacob 162,167,170, 171,173,176,180,188, 189,199-219, 222-224,227-229, 231,233,234,236-238, 240-249,252-254, 256-258,260,261,264, 267,268,270,271,273, 278
Jesse 176,178,187, 188,198
Robet. 85,86
Robt. 84
Sarah 172,230
Thomas 248,250, 252-254,257,260,270, 271-274,278
Thos. 254,256, 257-259,264,265,267, 268,274
William 107,132, 133,136,138,180,214
Wm. 129
HUNTOR
---- 73
Elisha 195,196
Isaac 68-70,73,86,

HUNTOR (Cont.)
  Isaac (Cont.)
  87-96
  Jacob 190,221,
  232,259,277
  Jesse 190,194
  Robert 88,89
  Robt. 86,87
HUNT__
  Jacob 202
HURDLE
  Butler 272,274
HUTCH
  Robert 252
HU____
  Elisha 217
HYDE
  Edward 21,22,24
  Edwd. 20
H_LL
  Clem__t 171
H__K__
  Willm. 163
H___
  Abraham 217

I

INSOLVENTS
  ---- 63,272

J

JACKSON
  Voss 264
  William 206
  Wm. 212
JAMES
  John 129
JEFFRYES
  ---- 58,59
JEFFRYS
  ---- 50
  Robert 42
  Robt. 42
JENOURE
  Joseph 64
JINN
  Eliz. 74
JOANES (See also
  JONES)
  ---- 91
  Fra. 86
  Francis 88
JOHNSON

JOHNSON (Cont.)
  Mary 48,49
JOHNSTON
  Christopher 254,
  256
  Gabriel 141
  Jane 252
  Mary 254-256,259,
  260,263
  Saml. 221,239,245,
  246,264,267,270,273
  Samuel 236,237,
  240,242,244,245,248,
  257,259,262,268,271
  William 252
  Wm. 255
JONE
  F. 79
JONES (See also
  JOANES)
  ---- 50,59
  Ann 107
  David 224
  Demsey 200,206
  Elizabeth 107
  F. 66,79
  Francis 66,68,73,
  80,82
  Frans. 74
  Fred. 31,32,34
  Frederick 16,30,36
  James 187,206,214,
  235
  Lewis 150,185
  Mary 60,172
  Nat. 269
  Nathaniel 264,265,
  272
  Nathl. 264,265,267,
  270
  Natl. 264
  Richard 107
  Thomas 64
  Thos. 190,265,269
  W. 64
  William 2,4,7,262
  William, Sr. 262
  Wm. 35,37,274
JORDAN
  ---- 35,38
  Jno. 32,36,37
  John 29,31,32,34,
  41,49,238
  John, Jr. 43
JUSTICES

JUSTICES (Cont.)
  ANDERSON
    Joseph 133
  BLOUNT
    J. 113
    Jos. 185
    Joseph 186,191
  CORBIN
    Francis 163
  HALSEY
    J. 123,124,126,
    128-131
    John 160
  LUTEN
    James 184
  PAYNE
    Peter 149,154
  SUMER
    Demsey 170
  SUMNER
    Demsey 172,188,
    190,191,196,197,206,
    212,218
    James 255
  SWIFT
    Samuel 238
  WALTON
    Thomas 160
    Timothy 214,249

K

KENSHY
  Richd. 69
KERBY
  William 253
KIMSEY
  ---- 113,126,134
  Thomas 114,117
KING
  ---- 140
  Charles 84,86,87,
  89,104
  Charls 85
  Henry 166-168,
  171,174,175,179,182,
  183,189
KINGHAM
  Robert 73
  Robt. 66,79,185
KIRCKUM
  Ealinor 15
KIRKHAM
  Elenor 14
KIRSHAW

KIRSHAW (Cont.)
  ---- 242
KITTERELL
  ---- 112
KNIGHT (See also
  NIGHT)
  Elizabeth 258
  Hezekiah 278
  James 278
  Keziah 258

L

LACEY
  Sarah 94
LACITER
  Elizabeth 253
LACITO_
  Frederick 261
LASETER
  Robert 98
LASITER
  Moses 176,214
  Robert 98,99,176
  Tobias 189,214
LASITOR
  Moses, Sr. 195
LASSETER
  Jesse 274
LASSITOR
  Jesse 278
LEDGER
  Joseph 133
LEE
  Marget 59
  Tho. 21
  Thomas 20,23,24
  Thos. 21,22,27,28
LEIGH
  Daniel 8
  Danl. 9
LESTER (See also
  LISTER)
  Willis 228
LEUTEN (See also
  LEUTON,LUTEN,
  LUTON)
  Thomas 1-3,5-7,11,
  17,18,24,29,32,43,44
  Thomas, Jr. 49,54
  Thos. 37
  Thos., Jr. 55
LEUTON
  Thomas 1
  Thos. 5,20

LEWIS
  Benjamin 238
  Jno. 142,143,150,
  190
  John 104,110-112,
  116-118,148,152,153,
  155,156,187,194,198,
  206
  John, Jr. 226
  Will. 101
  William 97,101,
  103,104,235
  Wm. 97,98,100,108
LEWISS
  John 115
  William 106,107
LEW__
  Benjamin 235
LILES
  Elizabeth 245
  Eliz____ 253
  Jno. 276
  John 276
  Williams 104
  Wm. 276
LILLEY
  Timothy 180
LINCH
  John 180
LINNINGTON
  John 10,19
LINOX
  Robt. 190
LISTER (See also
  LESTER)
  William 254,256,
  259,260,263
LITTLE
  ---- 257
  Penelope 81
  William 57,61,62
  Wm. 45,46,48,52,
  53-56,60
LLOYD
  ---- 50
LOFTEN
  Leonard 22
LOFTIN
  Leonard 24,27,29
LONG
  James 1,2,5,11,18
  Martha 150
  Mathew 185
  Pat 135
LORVICK

LORVICK (Cont.)
  John 60
  Thos. 60
LOVICK
  Jno. 47,48,52-56
  John 56,57
  Thomas 60,62,
64-66
  Thos. 61,64
LOWICK
  Thos. 57
LOWTHER
  ---- 257
LUCAS
  ---- 26
LUTEN (See also
LEUTEN, LEUTON)
  ---- 19,43,48,57,58,
60,69,131,134,140
  James 159,184,185
  Jno. 86
  John 86,105,132,
133,138,152,153,155,
156,158,159,161,168
  T. 65,70
  Thomas 9-11,13,
15,18,20-22,24,29,
31,39,40,61,62,65,
67,69,100,102,104,
114,118,131,169
  Thomas, Jr. 28,43,
54
  Thos. 22,23,27,30,
34,36,41,42,44-47,
53-57,59-61,67,68,
70,72,73,75-77,
80-82,84-86,139
  Thos., Jr. 54,56
  W. 70,72,78
  Will 73
  William 67-69,72,
73,98,99,109,118,
140,141,155,162,169,
171,173,177
  Willm. 139
  Wm. 67,70,72,76,
80
LUTON
  ---- 131
  John 90,131,166
  Thomas 17,88,124
  Thos. 86,87
  W. 71
  William 114,124
  Willm. 86,123

LUTON (Cont.)
  Wm. 124,194

M

MC CLALAND (See
also MACKCLAY-
LAND)
  Robert 186
  Robt. 190
MC CLAYLAND
  Robert 186
MC CLELAND
  Robert 159
MC CLURE
  ---- 113
  Richard 99,105,
108,113
MC GUIRE
  Ann 212,214
MC KILDO (See
also MACKILDO,
MCKILDO)
  ---- 194
  John 152,156,159,
161,165,167,168,171,
173,180,191,198,217,
219,229
MACGUIRE
  Mary 182
MCGUIRE
  ---- 190
  Phillip 233
  Samuel 225
MCKILDO
  John 207
MCNIDER
  Thomas 225
MACKCLAYLAND
  Robert 189
MACKEIL
  Anthony 63
MACKEY
  W. 79
MACKGUIRE
  Ann 188
MACKILDO
  John 174,183,191
MACKY
  William 65
MAINER
  Judith 234,239,
252,255
MANN
  Anne 133,139

MANSFIELD
  Joseph 274
  Zebulon 274
MARCUS
  ---- 126
  John 123
MARKS
  John 98-100
  Sarah 98,100
MARKUS
  Jno. 96
  Sarah 107
MARLOE
  Thomas 137
MARLOW
  Thomas 141
  Thos. 135
MARRIAGES
  ---- 78
MARSDEN
  ---- 52,59
MARSHAL
  Daniel 223,248
MARSHEL
  David 157
MARSTON
  ---- 49
MARTIN
  Geo. 66
  George 61
MARTYN
  ---- 63
  Geo. 65
  George 62,65
MATHIAS
  John 111
MATTHEWS
  ---- 37
  Thomas 35
  Thos. 45
MATTHIAS
  ---- 131
MEARNS
  ---- 163
  Dorothy 135
  William 132,135,
137
  William Skipwith
135
MEASLES
  Moses 214
MEAZLE
  Luke 9
MEGLOCKLIN
  James 253

MEWBORN
  Joshua 258,259
MIDDLETON
  Elizabeth 185
  Jno. 139
MIDLETON
  ---- 163
MILLER
  ---- 276
  Abel 262
  Wm. 276
MILLIKIN
  ---- 135
MING
  Jos. 117
  Joseph 97,98,100,
101-108
  Nathanl. 185
  Nathll. 148,150
  Thomas 189
MINISTERS
  BLACKNAL
    John 44
  BLAIR
    John 8
  EARL
    Daniel 202
  EARLE
    Daniel 208
  FOUNTAIN
    ---- 52
  GARZIA
    ---- 76,79
  GERRARD
    Henry 10
  GORDON
    William 15,17
  GRANVILE
    ---- 61
  HALL
    Clement 115
  MARSDEN
    ---- 52
  NEWNAM
    Thomas 39
  URMSTON
    John 22
  WALLACE
    ---- 26
MINSHEE
  John 175
MINSHEW
  Maximillion 261
  Richd. 43
MIRCLER

MIRCLER (Cont.)
  Lodwick 93
MITCHELL
  James 113
MITCHENER
  Jeremiah 192
MONGOMERY
  Jno. 67
MONTGOMERY
  J. 70,72,81,82,84
  Jno. 67,72
  John 68,69,75-77,
103
MOONEY
  Martha 78
MOOR
  Henry 251,254
MOORE
  Geo. 279
MORGAN
  Hardy 278
  Olive 74
MOSELEY
  ---- 14,21,22,27,31,
37,38,58,59
  E. 31,52,65,70,72
  Ed. 56,57,60,71
  Edward 13,15-20,
23,24,27-29,31,32,36,
37,39,40,42,43,46,48,
61,67,69
  Edwd. 10,23,29,31,
44,45,47,52,65,70
MOSELY
  E. 53
MOSLEY
  ---- 59
MUNNS
  Thos. 50
MUNS
  ---- 37
  Elisabeth 34,35
  Elizabeth 32,35
  Thomas 35,37,38
MURE
  Robert 258

N

N.
  A. 179,263
NASH
  Thomas 236,237,
242,245
  Thos. 221

NEGROES
  DUBLIN 173,198, 201
  Margret 165
NEWNAM
  ---- 38-41,50
  Thomas 39
NEWTON (*See also NUTEN,NUTON*)
  Ch. 74
  Christian 65,66,116
NICHOLSON
  ---- 20,24,25,27, 112
  Francis 8
NIGHT (*See also KNIGHT*)
  James 274
  Keziah 274
NOEL (*See also NOWAL,NOWELL*)
  Margret 127
  Margt. 131
NOELL
  Margt. 131
NORCOMB
  Jno. 49
NORFLEET
  Abm. 189
  Abraham 167,169, 171,180,188,214,217, 223,229,234,236,240, 244,247,251,254,258, 262,278
  Jacob 224
NORFLET
  Abraham 162,200
NORFLETT
  Abraham 267,270, 275
NOWAL (*See also NOEL,NOELL*)
  Margret 134
NOWELL
  Margaret 116
NUTEN (*See also NEWTON*)
  C. 79
  Chrisn. 79
  Christian 95,135
NUTON
  Christian 87,109, 127

O

OADHAM
  Jacob 43
ODAM
  Abraham 175
  Jacob 104,175
OLIVER
  Andrew 113
ONEAL
  Peter 275
ORINDELL
  Mary 257
ORINGDELL
  Benjn. 275
ORINGTON
  ---- 276
  Benjamin 276
  Benjn. 276
OSBURN
  Peter 50
OSHEAL
  ---- 131
OSHLEY
  Nell 139
OUTLAW
  George 262,278
  Ralph 104

P

PADGET (*See also PATCHET*)
  S. 70
  Saml. 65,67-70,72, 73
  Samuel 62,67
PADGETT
  Sam. 72
  Samll. 75,77,83
PAGET
  Saml. 72
  Samll. 43,48
PAGETT
  Samll. 67
PAGGETH
  Samll. 60
  Samuel 57
PAGGITH
  Samuel 61
PAIN
PAIN (*See also PAYN,PAYNE*)
  ---- 129,131
PAINE
  ---- 131
PARISH

PARISH (Cont.)
  Jno. 159
  John 154,161,192, 218,219,231,232,235, 240,263
  John, Sr. 240
  Joseph 226
PARK_
  Moses 175
PARKER
  ---- 117,163
  Eliza. 129
  Elizabeth 233,234, 242,243,246,247,250, 254
  J. 130
  Jane 185,186
  Jean 159,165,172
  Jno. 74
  Job 278
  John 43,59,68,73, 74,79,82,104
  Jona. 128
  Jonathan 95,96, 104,110-113,115,116, 119-121,129,130,135
  Jonathn. 127,130
  Joseph 195,200,214
  Little 226,263
  Nathan 177
  Peter 166-168, 173,174,175,179, 181-183,187,189,195, 196,199,200,202,203, 208,225,234
  Richard 60,90,92, 96
  Richard, Sr. 104
  Richd. 56,84-87, 91,92,94,95
  Thomas 195
  William 251
PARKS
  Elizabeth 274,278
PARRISH
  John 170,199,212, 214
PARRISS
  George 110
PATCHET (*See also PADGET*)
  Jno. 29
  Sam. 65
  Samll. 29,30,34,36, 37,40-42,45

PATCHET (Cont.)
  Samuel 22-24,52, 53
PAYN (*See also PAIN,PAINE*)
  Peter 98,172
PAYNE
  ---- 130
  Peter 97,99-101, 103,104,107,113,117, 149,152-156,169,179, 206
PEARCE
  Isbell 201
  Thomas 113,201
  Thos. 84
  Wm. 49
PEARSON
  ---- 26
PENRICE
  ---- 139
  Francis 140,163
PERKIN
  Robert 227,233
PERKINS
  Abraham 62
  Robert 236
PERROT
  Francis 4
PERRY
  ---- 103,113,123
  J. 65,70,72
  Jno. 65,73
  John 62,67,70
  John, Sr. 61
  Precilia 100
  Precilla 91,95
  Samuel 249
PERVINE (*See also PURVINE*)
  ---- 126,144
  R. 131
  Rachel 113,114, 131,134,135,150,185
  Rachell 95,96
  Rachl. 131,185
PERVINEY
  Rachl. 100
PETE
  Robt. 276
PETER
  Ann 55,56
PETERS
  Rachel 135
PETERSON

PETERSON (Cont.)
  ---- 28
  Tho. 21
  Thomas 20-22,24
  Thos. 20-22,27,28
PETTYJOHN
  ---- 257
PHELPS
  James 152
  Moses 278
PHILLIPS
  Jane 276
  Paul 33,34,37,38
PHILPS
  ---- 159
  James 160-162
  Jas. 160
  Mary 160
PILAND
  James 176
PLOMER
  ---- 141,144
PLOMMER
  ---- 190
POLLAK
  ---- 165
POLLOCK
  Thomas 1,2,5, 10-12,14,15,20-22,24
  Thoms. 24
  Thom__ 15
  Thos. 20-22,27
PORIGREEN
  Francis 47
PORTER
  ---- 58
  Edmd. 67
  John 3-5
POTTER
  James 73,79
POWELL
  William, Jr. 176
  William, Sr. 176
POWERS
  E. 79
  Elisabeth 70
  Eliz. 66,79
  Eliza. 73
  Elizabeth 72
PRESSLY
  Mary 230
PRESTON (*See also BESSON,BESTON*)
  Stephen 9
PRICE

PRICE (Cont.)
  Thomas 263,275
PRIFVIT
  Elizabeth 267
PRIVIT
  Elizb. 270
  Jacob 259,267,270
PRIVITT
  Jacob 276
PROCESSIONERS
  ---- 43,112,175,
176,177,224,225,226,
261,262,263
PUGH
  ---- 175
PURVINE (See also
PERVINE)
  R. 123
  Rachael 117
  Rachel 107,123,
134,137,157,158

Q

QUARELESS
  Mary 148,150
QUARLES
  Mary 163,185
QUIN
  Mary 228

R

RAINER
  Richd. 79
RAMSEY
  Thos. 113
REED
  Christian 120
  Eliz. 74
  Mary 73
REMINGTON (See
also *RIMINGTON*)
  Ralph 190
RHITTER (See also
RUTTER)
  Sarah 219
RICE
  Davd. 274
  David 224,252,264,
265,267,268,270-274,
277,279
  Elizabeth 246
  John 176
RICHARDS

RICHARDS (Cont.)
  ---- 100
  John 72,81
RICHMOND
  ---- 135,140
RIDDICK
  ---- 262
  Leml. 206
  Lemuel 206
  Mills 261
  Willis 199,200,212
RIEUSEET
  John 156
RIMINGTON (See
also *REMINGTON*)
  Ralph 183,206
ROBERSON
  Jno. 96
ROBERTS
  Charles 158,159,
161,162,164,177,184
  William 263,277,
279
ROBERTSON
  ---- 131
  John 134
  Thomas 134
ROBINS
  Francis 172
ROBINSON
  ---- 59
  Jno. 66
  JOhn 68,74,104,
105
  Thomas 163
  Thos. 135
RODGERS
  Jno. 184
  Robert 175
  Robt. 87
RODGERSON
  Marget 95
  Margett 94,96
  Margrett 87,89,92
ROGERS
  Margt. 123
  Robert 112
ROMBOUGH (See
also *RUMBERG,
RUMBOUGH*)
  John 252
RONDENG
  Sarah 87
ROSE
  Richd. 10

ROSS
  John 162
ROUNDTREE
  ---- 62-64
  Thomas 34,64,68
  Thos. 59,74
ROUNTREE
  ---- 39,46,50-52,
60,61
  Charles 248,249
  Thomas 39,40,42,
47
  Thos. 41,44,58
ROUNTRY
  Charls 225
  Thomas, Jr. 262
ROUTE
  Robert 42
RUMBERG (See
also *ROMBOUGH*)
  John 185
RUMBOUGH
  Jno. 265,269
RUSSEL
  Margaret 254
RUSTON
  ---- 49
RUTTER (See also
RHITTER)
  ---- 180
  Mary 187
  Sarah 170,186,187,
212,214,230
  Serah 159
RYAN
  Michael 50

S

S.
  L. 178
SADLER
  Richard 141
  Robert 144
  William 39
  Wm. 49,50
SAGG
  ---- 60-62,64,66
SANDERS
  Francis 175
SCOT
  ---- 225,261,262
  James 177
SCOTT
  Bat 49,50

SCOTT (Cont.)
  James 177
  Margaret 53
SHEARS
  Judah 137,141
SHELDEN
  Israel 141
SHELDIN
  ---- 140
SHELDING
  Israel 144
SHERIFFS
  ALSTON
   John 123,125,
127,130,131,134,135
  BENBURY
   John 161
   Thom. 272
   Thomas 260
  BLOUNT
   Jos. 228
   Joseph 245
  GALE
   Miles 172,190
  HALSEY
   ---- 163
   John 148,154,161
   William 218,230
  HARDY
   John 27
  HARRON
   Jos. 140
  LUTEN
   Thomas 100,102,
114,118
   William 98,99,
109,118,141
  LUTON
   Thomas 124
   William 114,123,
124
   Willm. 123
   Wm. 124
  PAYN
   Peter 172
  PAYNE
   Peter 113
  SHERVIN
   ---- 134
  SHERWIN
   ---- 131
  SHIVE
   Judith 155
  SIBISON
   Sarah 276

SIBISON (Cont.)
  Wm. 276
SIMONS (See also
SYMONS)
  John 158,159,161,
162
SIMPSON
  Dinah 140
  Joseph 258
  Sarah 39
  William 263
SIMSIN
  John 240
SIMSON
  John 235,238,243
  William 183
SIVERS
  John 32,35
SKINER
  John 156,179,180
SKINNER
  ---- 144,245
  Evan 226
  John 150,167,175
  William 88-90,93,
94,96,105,111,120,
141
  Willm. 91,92
  Wm. 91,93,96,104,
128
SLADE
  Judith 50,59,60
SLAUGHTER
  ---- 76
SMALL
  Josiah 226
SMITH
  David 68
  Mary 228
  Richd. 150
  Thos. 180
  W. 81-84
  William 75
  Wm. 76,77
SMITHWICK
  ---- 3,19
  Edd 1
  Edwad. 6
  Edward 1-11,13,
15,17,19,20,21,28
  Edwd. 18,21,29
SOMNER (See also
SUMNER)
  John 120
SPEIGHT

SPEIGHT (Cont.)
---- 224,225
Joseph 175
William 88-90,93, 94
Willm. 86,93
Wm. 91
SPEIGHTS
---- 176,177
Moses 171,188
William 183,214
SPIGHT
Joseph 152
Mary 123
Will 84
William 85
SPIGHTS
---- 177
SPRUIL
---- 9,50
Godffrey 7
Godfrey 38
Godfry 38
SPRUILL
---- 27
Godffrey 7
STACY
Mary 66
STANDING
Edward 22,51
Henderson 263
STEVENS
Joshua 189,214
STONE
Mary 59
STRATTON
Thomas 223
STREATOR
Edward 251,254
Thomas 251,254
STUART
Wm. 43
SUMER
Demsey 170
SUMNER (See also *SOMNER*)
Demcy 152
Demsey 90-96,104, 124,166-168, 170-175,178-183, 187-191,193-200, 202,203,205,206, 208-212,217,218, 221-223,227,234,236, 245,246

SUMNER (Cont.)
Demsy 245
Eliza. 129
James 117,210,213, 215,216,221-223,231, 232,234,236,240,242, 244,245,248-250,252, 253,255-258,260,264, 267,270
Jno. 67,86,88,91
John 75,80,82,84, 85-90,92-96,98,120, 125,127,134
Luke 166-168,173, 175,178,179,181-183, 186-189,192,193,195, 196-203,207-210, 214,215,222,228,249, 275
Lu__ 199
SURRENGAR
James 157
SWANN
Samuel 64
SWIFT
---- 237
Sam. 221,238,240, 241
Samuel 236-238, 240,242,244,245
SYMMONS
Nicholas 4
SYMONS (See also *SIMONS*)
Jno. 50
John 134,135

T

T.
H. 179
TALBOT
---- 126,131
Ben. 134,135
Benja. 93,116,131
Benjamin 90,105, 106,110,111,115-117, 121
Benjn. 99,100
Mary 106
TALBOTT
Benja. 93
TALBURT
Benjamin 89
TANNER

TANNER (Cont.)
Mary 49
TAYLOR
Jane 50
Thos. 123
TENDALL
Robert 23
THACH
John 201,206
THOMPSON (See also *TOMPSON, TOMSON*)
---- 75,76,103,113, 117,126
Eliza. 87,91
Elizabeth 100
Elizabh. 276
Elizath. 86
Frances 100
THOMSON
---- 126
Henry 262
TILLOTSON
---- 182,200
TITHABLES
---- 3,31,34,35,37, 39,50,51,52,58,63,65, 69,71,74,78,87,109, 113,117,128,130,134, 149,188,161,191,206, 214,218,219,272
TOMPSON
Eliza. 86,95
Elizabeth 107
TOMSON
Elizabeth 110
TOM___
Elizabeth 89
TREVATHAN
Mary 180
TROTER
---- 163
James 153
TROTMAN (See also *TROTTMAN*)
Amos 225,227,248
Demsey 237
Edward 243
Susana 227
Thomas 237,261
Thos. 273
TROTTER (See also *TROTER*)
---- 126,142,190, 198

TROTTER (Cont.)
James 68,71,142, 148,152,153,173,179, 185,212
Jas. 142,143,150
TROTTMAN
Edward 183
TUCKER
Eliza. 129
TYLER
John 3

U

UMPHLET
William 175,179, 214
Wm. 212
URMSTON
---- 20,21,25-27, 32,33,35,37,38
Jno. 21,28,36
John 22,23,29, 30-33

V

VAIL
Moseley 65,69,73, 79
VANN
Edward 219
Edward, Sr. 112
Mary 87
VANPELT
---- 66
J. 64
VAUN
Azariah 222
VEAL
---- 58

W

WAID
---- 274
WALBUTTON
John 113
WALKER
Henderson 1-3,6-9
Jno. 21
John 2,4,5,20-22, 24
WALLACE
---- 26

WALLACE (Cont.)
Mary 265,269,272
Sarah 278
WALLIS
John 225
WALSTON
William 14,15
Wm. 19
WALTEN
---- 100
WALTERS
John 180,187,212, 214
William 219
WALTON
---- 104,251,261
Hanah 79
Hanh 79
Hannah 73
John Benbury 184
P. 255
Palatiah 224,264, 265,268,271,278,279
Pallatiah 248,264
Pelatiah 249,252, 254-256,259,267,270, 273,277
Peletiah 251
Pellatiah 250,253, 257,258
Rachel 274
Richard 183,214, 225
Robert 278
T. 70
Thomas 68,69,72, 90,91,93,98,100-102, 104,110,111,116,119, 120-125,127,133,134, 138,154,158,160,172, 177,180
Thomas, Jr. 115, 132
Thomas, Sr. 67
Thoms. 115
Thos. 68,70,73,90, 91-96,115,116,118, 120,123,128,132,142, 143,148,150-152,160, 172,194
Thos., Jr. 123
Timothey 187
Timothy 166-168, 171,173,179,181-183, 187,189,191,193,196,

WALTON (Cont.)
  Timothy (Cont.)
198-200,207-209,
213-217,222,223,
226-231,233,234,236,
237,240,244-246,248,
249,250,252,253
  Timy. 221
  Will. 142
William 88,110,111,
132,136,138,166,167,
168,171,173-175,178,
179,181,182,183,187,
189,193,196,199-201,
205,207-211,213,215,
216,217,221-223,227,
231,233,236,240,244,
245,248,250-253,256,
257
  William, Sr. 151
  Wilm. 86,143,148
  Wm. 112,115,116,
118,119,142,150,214,
245,246,253
WALTO_
  Timothy 199
WAR
  late 26
WARD
  ---- 163
Christian
160,193,214
  Job 278
  Mary 274
  Michl. 79
  Moses 274
WARE
  John 163
WARNER
  ---- 48,52,53,56,58,
59
  Samll. 47
  Samuel 45
WATERS
  John 171
WATHUM
  R. 79
WATSON
  Sarah 256
WA____
  Thos. 142
WEB
  Demsey 249
WELCH (*See also*
WELSH)

WELCH (Cont.)
  David 278
WELLS
  Francis 2,4
WELLWOOD
  ---- 237
  Moses 240,246,278
WELSH (*See also*
WELCH)
  David 225
  Edward 262
WELSTEAD
  William 6
WELWOOD
  ---- 238,249,274
  Moses 228,230,
231,233,235,243,245,
251,253,255,259,274
WESSON (*See also*
WESTEN, WESTON)
  Wm. 88
WEST
  ---- 190,197
  Christopher 164,
168,182,206
  Christr. 184
  Robert 24,29
  Robt. 29
  Thomas 23,29
WESTBEESE
  Charles 73
WESTEN (*See also*
WESSON)
  William 177
WESTON
  ---- 91
  Thos. 70
  W. 79-81
  Will 73,82
  William 225
  Willm. 86
  Wm. 47,52
WHEATLY
  John 10
WHITE
  George 274
  Jno. 74
  Luke 49,50,104,
177
  Thomas 262
WICKS
  ---- 88
WIGGINS
  Thomas 197
WILBY

WILBY (Cont.)
  ---- 26
WILKINS
WILKINS (*See also*
WILLKINS)
  ---- 117,130
  Charles 55,56,59
  John 112,115-117,
119
  John, Jr. 263
  William 172
WILKINSON
  ---- 6
  William 1-3,4,6,11,
13
  Wm. 5-9,11,13
WILKISON
  ---- 4
  William 5
  Wm. 3
WILLIAMS
  ---- 59,60,62,66,
103
  Danl. 79
  George 112
  Jno. 66
  JOhn 59,64,87,123
  Mary 101,123
  Thos. 267,270,273,
276
  William 62
  Wm. 53
WILLIAMSON
  John 125,134,150,
151,170,180,188,212,
214,219
WILLKINS (*See
also WILKINS*)
  Jno. 111,115
  John 110,115
WILLSON
  ---- 6
  Robert 2
WILSON
  James 183
  Jas. 190
  Robert 6
  William 153
WOOD
  Edward 32
  Edwd. 35
  Thomas 156
WOODWARD
  Mary 242,246
WOOLARD

WOOLARD (Cont.)
  Mary 268,271
WORDAN
  James 152,153
WORDEN
  James 185
WORLEY
  John 44
WRIGHT
  Thomas 14

X

None

Y

YATES
  Thomas 35
  Thos. 37
YEALS
  Timothy 133
YEATS
  Timothy 133
YOUNG
  Peter 50
YOURE
  Jas. 129

Z

None

INCOMPLETE NAMES

_RAVEN
  Jas. 121
_RKER
  Jonathan 121
___IN
  Nathl. 10
___RY
  Wm. 10

Anthony 279
Benjamin 279
James 237
Jno. 180
John 127,171
Judith 50
Peter 171
Rachel 134,135,
139,140,144
_ohn 87

LOCATION INDEX

BRANCH
  Flat 176,224,261
  Pipeing 224
  Piping 176,177,225,261, 262
BRIDGE
  BALLARDs 43,62,63, 69,87,104
  BENNETs Creek 104, 177,224,225,261
    Caherines Creek 225
    Catherins Creek 177
  HOSKINS's 43
  Long 43,103,104
  LUTEN's 43
  Rockohock 104
  Tottering 32,34
  Tottring 112
CHAPEL
  CONSTANs 170,267
  CONSTANTs 115,120, 124,130,150,158,162,167, 168,169,171,173-175,178, 179,181-183,187,189,190, 192,193,195,196,199, 200-203,205,207-211,213, 229,242
  COSTENs 170,219,234, 246,247,252,254,255,258, 270,273,278
    Ease, of 2
    Edenton 173
  FARLEEs 154,157,158, 162,167,169,171,182,189, 200,202,204,211,229,230, 234,240,244,246-248,251, 254,258,270,275,276,278
    Indian Town 51,72,83, 86,87,94,95
    at the 42
    James BRADDEYs, at 94
    James CONSTANTs Plantation, on 111
    James COSTANs, at 94
    Knottey Pine 182
    Knotty Pine 115,120,125, 129,130,135,179,202
    Knotty Pine Swamp, on 111
    Knotty pine, at the 96
    Knoty Pine 156
    Land, part of Robt. BEEZLEYs 158
    Meherin 129

CHAPEL (Cont.)
    at 96
    Notty pine 150,189,190
    old, at Indian Town Creek 99
    standing near Sandy Run 112,118
    Sarum 141,158,162,167, 197
    upper 53,181
CHURCH
    Edenton 161,233
    at 142,153,157
    in 208,209,216-218, 222,228,229,231-233,235, 236,240,242,244-246,248, 250,252,253,256-260,264, 265,266,268,270,271,273, 277,279
    England, of 25,112,221
CITY
    Boston 6,8
    Philidelphia 247
    Williamsburgh 7
COLONY
    Virginia 8,16,25,26,104
COUNTRY
    America, English 25
    England 17,25
    great Britain 40
COUNTY
    Albemarle 20,24
    Bath 26,30
    Chowan 28,31,32,90,98, 104,109,110,113-115,118, 123,124,126,127,130,132, 138,148,149,152,153,157, 158,162-164,166-170,188, 190,191,196,197,218,238, 273
    of 97,120,121,125,136, 141
    Edgecombe 135
    Keketan (VA) 26
    Pequimons 262,263
    Perquimon 226
    Perquimons 104,177,201, 224,225,246,261,263
    Tyrell 230
    upper part, of the 97
COURT HOUSE
    ---- 42,166
    Edenton, in 68,70,84,85, 87,90,97,99,116,121,122, 132,133,136,138,141-143,

COURT HOUSE (Cont.)
  147,152,153,155,156,158, 159,161,162,164,167,199, 222,248,264,266
CREEK
  BENNETs 43,104,112, 174,176,177,191,224,225, 261
    head of 176,224,261
    mouth of 104,177,225
  BENNETTs 176
  Catharin 177
  Catharine 43
  Catharins 177
  Catherine 104,262
  Catherines 225,261
  Catherins 177
  Cathrian 90
  COLEs 112,175,176
  Garbacon 177
  Indian 43
  Indian Town 43,99,177, 225,226,262,263
  Katherine 115
  Machaccoma 103
  Machacoma 177,225,226, 262,263
  Queen Ann's 43
  Rockahock 32,177,225, 262
  Rockohock 104
  Sarum 187
  Warrick 104
DISTRICT
  Lower 37
  Upper 34
FERRY
  COTTONs 175
  Luke WHITEs 104
  Meherin 175
  Meherrin 104
HILL
  Tarripin 59,104
HOUSE
  Coll. HYDEs 20
  Fred JONES, of 31
  James FARLEE, of 127
  James FARLOW, of 116
  James FARLOWs 118
  Mary FREEMANs 88
  Sarah GILLAMs 5,6
  Thomas GILLAMs 1,2,3
  Thomas POLLOCKs 22
  Thomas WALTONs 91, 92,93,95

HOUSE (Cont.)
  Willm. ARKILLs 119
LAND
  Chapel 198
LINE
  Country 112,224,261
  County 104
  Cuntry 175,176
  Pequimons 263
  Perquimons 104,226,263
  Virginia 104
MILL
  Henry BAKERs 175
  Jacob HUNTERs 176, 224,261
  Meherin Swamp, on 224, 261
  Thomas HOSKINS 262
  William HORSKINSes 178
  William HOSKINSes 103
  William HOSKINSs 226
PARISH
  Berkley 246
  Chovan 93
  Chowan 65,72,94,105, 110,122-124,129
  Chowan, of 45,57,59,86, 87,97,98,111-114,117,120, 130,131
  Eastern 29
  Lower part 69,91,97
  No. East, of Chowan 34, 36,37,50-52,54-56,61,62,64, 66,69,74,76,78,80-84
  South West 29
  St. Thomas of pamptico 26
  upper part 69,70,79,97
  upper parts 63
PLANTATION
  James CONSTANTs 111
  James SCOTs 177
  Joseph CREESYs 262
  Mills RIDDICKs 261
  RIDDICKs 262
  SPEIGHTs 225
  SPEIGHTSes 176,177
  Widow SCOTs 225,262
POINT
  DRUMMONDs 43
PRECINCT
  Chowan 21-24,29,32,51,

135

PRECINCT (Cont.)
64,76,77
  Chowa_ 20
  Chown 1
  Currituck 19
  Pasquotanck 19
  Pequimons 10

RIDGE
  Sandy 104
  Tottring 112

RIVER
  Chowan 104,177,225,262
  Roanoke 135
  the 175-177,225,226,261
  Yawpim 87,103
  Yeopim 178,226
  Yopim 262
  Yoppim 263

ROAD
  Aaron **BLANSHARD**s Old 176,224
  Aaron **B_AN____**s old 261
  BENNETs Creek 176,177,224,225,261
  BLANCHARDs old 177,225,261
  Cart
  Elisha **HUNTER**s 177,225,262
  from William **ASHLEY**s to Little **PARKER**s 263
  that leads to Elisha **HUNTER**s 224,261,176
  to Little **PARKER**s 226,263
  Chowan 176,177,224,225,261,262
  Ferry 104
  KITTERELLs 112
  Main 176,177,224,225,226,261,263
  New 176,176
  Pequimons 262
  Perquimons 104,176,177,224,225,261
  PUGHs 175
  Richard **WALTON**s, at 225
  Sandy Ridge 104,226,263
  Sarum 175
  Saru_ 176
  Thomas **WALTON**s, at

ROAD (Cont.)
177
  WALTONs, at 261
  Yopim 262

RUN
  Sandy 112,118,177,225,262

SHORE
  North 2,22-25,28,29
  North, of Chowan 35
  So. West 2
  South 2,12,21
  West 2,22
  Western 21

SOUND
  Side 226,262
  the 24,25,28,178

SPRINGS
  Cosandy 114

STATE
  Ohio 164,168
  South Carolina 112
  Virginia 8,16,25,26,104

SWAMP
  BALLARDs Bridge 104
  Bear 104
  BENNETs Creek 104
  Gree[n]hall 126
  Honey pot 176
    head of 176
    mouth of 176
  Knotty Pine 111,112,176
  Loosing 176,224,261
  Loossing 104
  Meherin 96,129,176,177,224,225,261
  Meherrin 176
  Mill 112
  Thomas **HOSKINS** 262
  William **HORSKINS**es 178
  William **HOSKINS**s 226
  Notty Pine 104,175,176
  White Potts 112

TOWN
  Edendon 152
  Edenton 37,39-48,50,52,53-55,57,62,64,65,68-70,72,75-77,80-85,87,90,97-108,110-112,114-116,120-122,124,125,132,133,136,141,142,143,147,148,150,152,

TOWN (Cont.)
153,155,156,158,159,161,162,164,166,167,182,183,187,198,199,201,202,206,208,216-218,222,227-229,231-237,240,242,244,248,264-266,268,270,271,273,279
  Indian 30,33,34,39,40,42,47,51,72,83,86,87,94,95
  Newbern 166
  Suffolk 276

WAREHOUSE
  BENNETs Creek 191

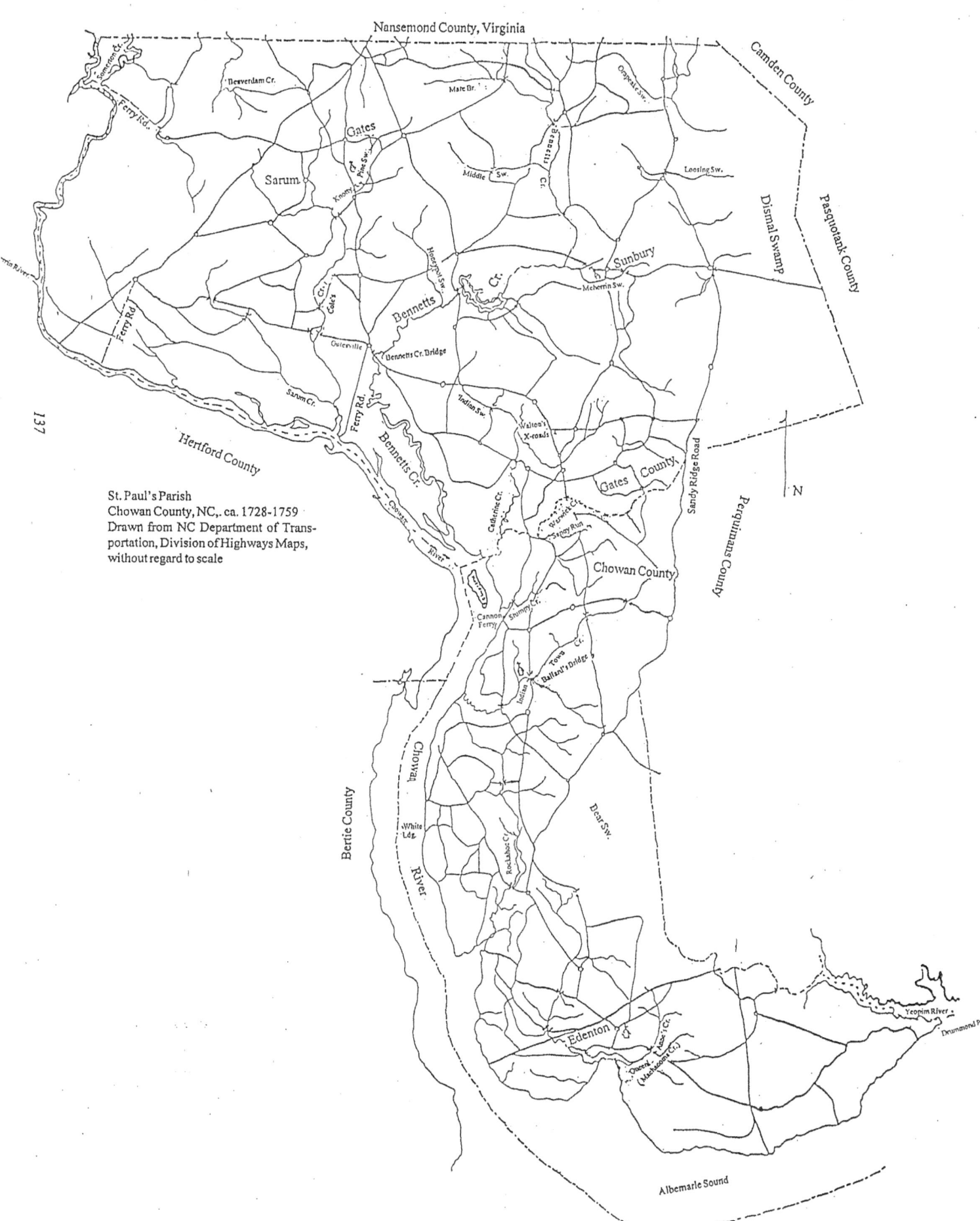